COS

# MI9

D1343318

OTHER BOOKS BY THE SAME AUTHORS INCLUDE

M. R. D. Foot
*Gladstone and Liberalism* (with J. L. Hammond)
*Men in Uniform*
*SOE in France*
ed *War and Society*
ed *The Gladstone Diaries, I–II*
ed *The Gladstone Diaries, III–IV*
*Resistance*
*Six Faces of Courage*

J. M. Langley
*Fight Another Day*

# M. R. D. FOOT
# &
# J. M. LANGLEY

# MI9

## ESCAPE AND EVASION 1939–1945

Biteback Publishing

First published in Great Britain in 1979 by
The Bodley Head Ltd

This edition published in 2011 by Biteback Publishing Ltd
Westminster Tower
3 Albert Embankment
London
SE1 7SP
Copyright © M. R. D. Foot and J. M. Langley 1979

The moral rights of M. R. D. Foot and J. M. Langley to be identified as the
authors of this work have been asserted in accordance with the Copyright,
Designs and Patents Act 1988

All rights reserved. No part of this publication may be reproduced, stored in
a retrieval system or transmitted, in any form or by any means, without the
publisher's prior permission in writing.

This book is sold subject to the condition that it shall not, by way of trade
or otherwise, be lent, resold, hired out or otherwise circulated without the
publisher's prior consent in any form of binding or cover other than that in
which it is published and without a similar condition, including this condition, being imposed on the subsequent purchaser.

ISBN 978-1-84954-131-2

10 9 8 7 6 5 4 3 2 1

A CIP catalogue record for this book is available from the British Library.

Set in Garamond by Namkwan Cho
Cover design by Namkwan Cho

Printed and bound in Great Britain by
CPI Group (UK) Ltd, Croydon, CR0 4YY

# Contents

# List of Illustrations

# Foreword

BY

FIELD-MARSHAL SIR GERALD TEMPLER, KG

Escaping and evading are ancient arts of war. In this field as in so many others modern technology has enabled new and harder edges to be put on old weapons. The story of how MI 9, the British escape service and MIS-X its later American equivalent protected and encouraged the activities of escapers and evaders has never before been told in full, nor have these secret departments' own papers hitherto been explored.

Though I was lucky enough never to be taken prisoner, perhaps I had the escape side of the business in my blood. My maternal uncle, Maurice Johnston of the Royal Artillery, was taken in Kut-el-Amara in 1915 and got away from Yozgad in Anatolia in 1918, an adventure he describes in his book *450 Miles to Freedom*; and my cousin Claude Templer of the Gloucestershire Regiment who was taken, unconscious, in December 1914 escaped successfully at his thirteenth attempt, only to be killed a few days before the Armistice.

I am proud to have been partially responsible for the setting up of MI 9, and delighted to find that the supposition I shared with others, that prisoners of war had considerable military potential, turned out correct. I am glad also to see that these secret services' successes and rare failures, and the highly efficient example they provided of Anglo-American accord, are set out by men who were involved in the struggle at the time and understand it from within.

The authors have steadfastly refused to seek sensation at the expense of truth, in contrast to far too many books of wartime adventure. Joint authorship has also helped to eliminate the personal bias that so often mars war autobiographies and the lives of individual sailors, soldiers and airmen. Moreover they have taken care, startling though many of their stories are, not to say anything that might endanger servicemen in the future.

I knew some of the early staff of MI 9, and am in no doubt that a tribute to them and to their American colleagues is long overdue.

I would also like to join the authors in recalling with pride and sorrow the prisoners who died in enemy hands, and the thousands upon thousands of men, women and children who gave their lives in enemy-occupied territory for freedom's sake. There are many heroes and heroines in this book. This is the first time that a proper tribute has been paid to that splendid soldier, Norman Crockatt, who made so many of their gallant deeds possible.

# Authors' Note

How one of us first heard of the other is best explained from War Office files:

Room 900

LONDON

7th November, 1944.

Dear Jimmy,

We have just had a visit from Brigadier Foot, who has been to Brittany to explore the possibilities of exchanging a German P/W for his son, Captain Michael Foot, who has been very helpful to us in the past and whom SAS are very anxious to recover.

Captain Foot is, as far as we know, in prison together with a Warrant Officer Hill, R.A.F., an American 2nd Lieut, and a French Dr. in some building on the East side of the Transatlantic dockyard at St. Nazaire. Captain Foot has, we understand, already made four unsuccessful attempts to escape.

Would it be possible for one of your officers to reconnoitre the position with a view to freeing these P/Ws, and possibly infiltrating some Frenchman into St. Nazaire to help them to escape?

Brigadier Foot says that Mr. Haegler, the Civil Affairs Officer at Nantes, situated in Place Louis XVI, has dealt with all the French personnel evacuated from Nantes and would be able to give first hand information as to the situation and he would probably be able to indicate one or two people who would know exactly where the P/Ws are and what the best chances are of securing their release.

Yours ever,

John Bankes

Lt. Col. J. M. Langley, M.B.E., M.C.,

I.S.9 (WEA)

G-2 S.H.A.E.F.

Nearly a fortnight later, this reply was sent to Langley's superior:

SECRET

*IS9 WEA/B/2/I1408*
*From: Lt. Col. J. M. Langley*

I.S.9 (WEA)

c/o G.S.I. (x)

H.Q. *21* Army Group

20 November, 1944

My dear Cecil,

As I am at the moment in Brussels, I have instructed Major MacCALLUM to arrange with the Americans to despatch an officer in an endeavour to rescue Captain M. R. D. FOOT.

He will keep you informed as to the progress, if any, of this operation. I am rather dubious as to the possibilities of success, and also whether we are justified in making special efforts to rescue one officer.

Yours sincerely,

Jimmy

Lt. Col. C. M. Rait, M.C.[1]

---

1    Both letters are in the Public Record Office, War Office papers (hereafter simply WO), WO 208/3422, escapers and evaders in hiding; items 116D and 55A.

On the day when this second letter was written Foot was taken to a German hospital at La Baule, unconscious after the treatment he had received from the peasant inhabitants of a farm chosen, deep in the previous night, on what he had believed to be Langley's instructions for a sound refuge during an escape, as he had picked them up at a lecture a year before.

We are glad to say that we have since got on to less distant terms. Of our personal adventures we do not propose to say much more in these pages, for, working on the real giants of secret staff work and the real heroes of clandestine escape and evasion, we know that our own careers are by comparison small beer.

This book is in no sense definitive. It simply serves to illuminate a hitherto obscure corner of the world war effort against the Axis powers, and to show various directions in which further effort, by younger and brighter historians, may illuminate a perpetually interesting subject: courage in adversity.

There are several people and authorities to whom we are glad to express our thanks. We owe a large debt of gratitude to Sir Martin Lindsay of Dowhill, whose pertinacity led him and us to the rediscovery of MI 9's main archive. Each of us had been positively assured that these files had been destroyed. In fact they had been put away so safely that their existence had been all but forgotten.

We are indebted to the Keeper of the Public Record Office for leave to quote extensively from British official files, which remain Crown copyright. A detailed note on our sources will be found at the end of the book, since references page by page are no longer feasible.

We have had a great deal of help from Gordon Lee of *The Economist*, who brought us together, sharpened our style, sorted out some of our muddles, and has been a staunch friend throughout. We are grateful also to Leslie Atkinson, Andrew Boyd, Richard Broad, Susan Broomhall, John Buist, George C. Chalou, Dick Crockatt, the late Donald Darling, Sam Derry,

Donald E. Emerson, 'Pat' Guérisse, Gerald E. Hasselwander, Mabel Howat, W. Stull Holt, Sir Ian Jacob, Joey Jackman, Charles Lamb, Jock McKee, Ron Mogg, Richard Natkiel (who drew the maps and diagrams), Airey Neave, Cecil Rait, the late Sir Leslie Ride, Grismond Davies-Scourfield, Charles Shaughnessy, Bill Kennedy Shaw, Tony Simonds, Michael Sissons, Leslie Veress, Dr A. Selby Wright and many other friends and acquaintances who have shared recollections and information with us. The staffs of the British Library, the Ministry of Defence and the Public Record Office in England, and of the National Archives and the Albert F. Simpson Historical Research Center in the United States, have gone out of their way to help us, though we owe it to all of them to emphasise that this book is in no way officially sponsored or subvented. Unattributed translations are our own. The usual caveat applies: any errors that remain are the responsibility of our two selves alone.

Our greatest debt, which we owe jointly with the rest of the free world, is almost too large to fit into print. It is owed not only to those who attempted escapes and evasions, and thus made the Axis powers' attempt to control the world more troublesome to the Axis; but also to those uncounted thousands of people, ordinary in appearance, extraordinary in courage and devotion, who made the work of the escape networks feasible. They were of many nationalities, of all ages; of both sexes, of all classes; rich and poor, learned and plain, Christian and Jew, Marxist and mystic. Without the work they did, for which a large proportion of them paid with their lives, the world today would be a meaner place; and we write this book lest they be quite forgotten.

MRDF
JML
*28 July 1978*

# Prologue

Many nations are proud of their tales of escape; none perhaps quite so proud as the English-speaking ones. Even in their heroes' lifetimes, the tales of the three men who escaped from the great camp at Sagan in Silesia through a wooden jumping horse, and the men who walked out of Colditz castle prison in Saxony under their guards' unsuspecting noses, have seeped into national legend. So has the tale of the party of Americans, each told he would be shot if any of his companions escaped, who broke away as an entire group in the Philippines, and survived. Many relatives of the fifty air force officers who were illegally shot dead by the Gestapo, on recapture after a mass escape from Sagan in March 1944, are still alive. The Sagan murders raised a justified furore; they were not unique. For instance, a naval sub-lieutenant, captured in uniform on a legitimate operation, was refused the status of prisoner of war, and spent many months in a concentration camp with his crew on forced marches to test boots for the German army. As they were led out to be shot he wrested a pistol from the guard commander and shot him dead, a few seconds before his own execution. He deserves to be remembered; as does the young man who, having slipped out of a large prisoner of war camp, travelled from Bremen to Stettin impeccably turned out as the lieutenant, RNVR, he was, bearing forged papers in the name of Lieutenant I. Bagerov of the Royal Bulgarian Navy. So does the man who got out of an air force NCOs' camp by swapping identities with a Palestinian Jewish pioneer private, and survived till autumn 1977 to run a travel agency off Piccadilly.

Though most of the cases just cited are British, of course the

British had no monopoly in escaping or in evading. The difference between these two activities must be made clear at once: an escaper is someone who, having been captured, gets away; an evader was never in enemy hands. American, British and Commonwealth sailors, soldiers and airmen often found themselves in friendly rivalry in these fields of war with Belgians, Chinamen, Czechs, Dutchmen, Frenchmen, Greeks, Malays, Norwegians, Poles, Slovaks, Yugoslavs and others. Yet the escapers and evaders from the forces of the British Empire and, later, of the United States of America had one enormous advantage over the rest: effective government help, supplied through secret channels.

Most secrets become less secret with the passage of time. Enough of the papers are now available from the two small and efficient secret departments concerned – the British MI 9 and the American MIS-X – for a connected account to be given of what they did. Their aims were to aid escapers, by tools and training, to escape; to train potential evaders to evade; to encourage secret routes along which either could travel; and to glean such intelligence as was to be found in prisoner of war camps. The directing genius of Norman Crockatt, founder of MI 9 and its head for most of the 1939–45 war, can be traced – even if only indirectly – behind almost all of the mid-century adventures this book recalls.

Crockatt and his staff felt they were innovators, as indeed on some technical points they were, but escape and evasion were by no means new; they are quite as old as war. Odysseus' flight from Calypso is a legend some three thousand years old. St Joseph – the patron saint of evaders? – organised the Flight into Egypt from Herod with his wife and the infant Jesus. The Empress Matilda did a model midwinter passage through her enemies' lines round Oxford castle in 1142, wrapped in a sheet to hide herself in the snow. A tower of the castle still stands near Oxford station, seldom noticed by tourists hurrying to the city centre. The escape of Hugo Grotius, the inventor of inter-

national law, from Loevestein castle in 1621 during the Dutch
war of independence, hidden in a box thought by his guards
to contain books, is as authentic as Matilda's, or as Charles
II's flight after defeat at Worcester in 1651 – this memorable
evasion is still commemorated in scores of English inns called
the Royal Oak. Captain O'Brien, RN, escaped from the French
in fact, and Captain Hornblower, RN, in fiction, during the
wars against Napoleon I, who himself escaped from Elba in 1815
on his way to Waterloo. The future Napoleon III escaped from
a fortress in peacetime, after six years' confinement, in 1846.
Gambetta, who proclaimed his fall in 1870, got out of invested
Paris a few weeks later by balloon: the first recorded airborne
evasion. Winston Churchill first became famous in his own
country by his escape from Pretoria in 1899.

   In the American civil war of 1861–5, the Franco-Prussian
war of 1870–1, and the world war of 1914–18, masses of prisoners were taken, and escaping and evading capture became
common, though never commonplace, activities. The English
have not forgotten Edith Cavell, shot after trial by the German
occupation forces in Brussels in 1915 for having helped some
600 British soldiers, wounded or cut off during the retreat
from Mons, to get away to Holland. A. J. Evans's *The Escaping
Club*, which inspired so many people who had read it to escape
next time round, provides the best known, but by no means
the only account of escapes from the prisoner of war camps of
those days.[2] The national museum in Dublin shows a padlock,

---

2    It was first published in 1921 and has often been reprinted. Other
     classical stories worth mentioning are M. C. C. Harrison and
     H. A. Cartwright, *Within Four Walls;* E. H. Jones, *The Road to
     En-Dor;* and H. G. Durnford, *The Tunnellers of Holzminden.*
     Sir J. C. Masterman, *On the Chariot Wheel,* 95–113, covers the
     parallel case of a civil internment camp; of interest because of
     Masterman's important secret role in the next world war, but
     really outside the subject matter of this book.

unlocked with almost miraculous ease by Eamonn de Valera when he escaped from Lincoln jail in February 1919 to take charge of the Irish revolution. Charles de Gaulle thrice escaped from German camps in 1916–17, and was thrice recaptured – experiences that helped to steel him for his skilled evasion from his Vichyste enemies at Bordeaux on 17 June 1940.

By that midsummer of 1940 the normal pattern of war, in flux for centuries, had changed yet again. One of its few constants since Charlemagne's day had been the concept that there was something dishonourable about personal surrender: capture was usually regarded as disgraceful, or nearly so, for the captive. Elaborate care was taken, for example, by the commanders of besieged cities, even in strategically hopeless cases, to put up a tactically decent defence, so that when they had to give in they could do so 'with the honours of war', and might be allowed to march out their surviving garrisons with drums beating and colours flying, the officers retaining their swords. The officer class in all European countries had long attached significance to such points; and at the close of the American civil war, a chivalrous opponent took care so to phrase the surrender that Lee could keep his sword at Appomattox. By the early 1940s these points were all but obsolete, though in Asia honour still counted for something in 1945.

Just as the use of high explosive artillery shell removed the stigma from wounds in the back, the development of air and armoured warfare transformed the fact of being captured from a personal disgrace into something more like an accident. The growth of air power was still accompanied by the myriad troubles of flight; in particular, engines might fail over enemy territory. The collapse, under the impact of armoured breakthrough and encirclement, of the fixed fortified 'front', that had dominated so much military thinking earlier in the century, ensured that capture now became a more normal incident of battle. It had lost much of its overtone of shame in 1917–18, when hundreds of thousands of men underwent it; in 1939–40 it lost more. By

1942 it was generally accepted, outside Soviet police circles and the Japanese nation, that it might happen to anyone.

Indeed it did happen in the course of the last world war to something like fifteen million people, among whom this book only deals with a tiny minority. We deal principally with the 35,000-odd members of the British, Commonwealth and American armed forces who had been taken prisoner, or had been shot down or otherwise cut off in enemy-held territory, and who yet managed to regain the Allied lines before the end of the war. The escapers among them, some 23,000, were only one in 650 – say 0.15 per cent – of the world total of prisoners of war, and the evaders were less than half as many.[3] Not many of the people of whom we write brought off their feat of escape or evasion alone; most of the escapers had had large backing among their friends in the camps they left, and most of the evaders depended to a terrifying extent on the folk who sheltered and supplied them on their way. The size of this army of helpers, many of them anonymous, cannot even be guessed at; yet without their devotion, there would be few anti-Axis travellers' tales to tell.

Even these helpers, numerous as they were, constituted a small minority among their more conformist fellows. Like escapers and evaders, they formed an elite before the word acquired its current pejorative undertone. None of the three groups was any the less interesting, or the less reputable, or the less worth historians' attention, for being out of the ordinary.

Moving from one country to another, for good, became only too common in this new dark age: an ethnic upheaval such as had hardly been seen – if at all – since the previous dark age, the *Völkerwanderung* of the fifth to the ninth centuries AD from which the basic structure of modern Europe derives. The *New Cambridge Modern History* estimates the number of Europeans resettled, evacuated, or expelled between 1944 and

---

3    Statistical summary in Appendix 1.

1952 at over 30,000,000. Such a figure – which excludes the 6,000,000 who died in transit, or as a direct result of forced migration – bears comparison with the total number killed in the 1939–45 war; again a figure not exactly known, but about 45,000,000, of whom 5,000,000 at least died in concentration camps. It is certainly much larger than the total of immigrants into the United States in the nineteenth century, which was under 20,000,000. These figures emphasise again that this book deals with a shift of people that is statistically slender, however personally agonising.

Yet personal agony was one thing that prisoners of war, at least, were supposed to be spared, under the rather oddly-named rules of war. Since the Hague conventions of 1899 and 1907, they had a distinct status in international law. This status was governed, as far as American and Western and Central European citizens were concerned, by the international convention signed at Geneva on 27 July 1929. This document, concluded in the period of euphoria that followed the universally adopted Kellogg Pact of the previous year that outlawed war, began with a statement of pious intention: that it was the duty of every belligerent to lighten the lot of prisoners of war. The essentials of the Convention can be condensed into a paragraph.[4]

Prisoners were to be treated humanely; no constraint was to be applied to those who refused to give any information beyond their own name and rank, or their service number. (The tag familiar to British and American serving men, 'Name, rank and number', was convenient to remember, and useful for administrators; it went beyond the letter of the law.) They were to keep all their clothes, including metal helmet and gas mask if carried, and private possessions, though surrendering arms, horses, equipment and service papers. They were to be placed in fixed camps away from the battle area, which were to be dry, clean,

---

4    For full text see Cmd 3941 (1931), 41 – 80, in Parliamentary Papers 1930/31, XXXVI, 471ff.

warm, and no less sanitary than the holding power's normal barracks. They had the right to correspond with their families and to practise any religion they chose. Their rations were to be no worse than those of their captors' depot troops; if insufficiently clad they were to be clothed by the holding power. Each camp was to include a hospital. Officer prisoners were to salute their equals and seniors in their enemy's forces. Pay appropriate to rank was to be provided by the holding power, and extra pay at the rate for the job to be provided for extra work – payable at the end of the war. Officers could not be required to work at all, and warrant and non-commissioned officers were only to be employed in tasks of supervision. No prisoner could be put to warlike, or unhealthy, or dangerous work, nor be made to work for excessively long hours. Inward post could include food, clothes and books. Prisoners were subject to the laws of the holding power; but might not receive corporal punishment, nor excessive penalties, nor be placed in noisome cells. The maximum disciplinary penalty any prisoner could receive, even for escaping, was thirty days' solitary confinement, though prisoners might also render themselves liable to judicial penalties, for such crimes as theft or assault. Concluding sections laid down means by which belligerents could communicate with each other about the prisoners they held, and a role for the International Red Cross; and invited any countries not among the original forty-seven signatories to notify their adhesion to the Convention by a note to the Swiss federal council.

Russia did not sign. In 1929 Russia was still an international pariah, not a member of the League of Nations and not in diplomatic relations with many countries, including the United States. The Russians' excuse for not joining was that they also had no relations with the Swiss, and were therefore debarred from doing so. In any case, so propaganda ran, soldiers of the Red Army did not surrender; so the question of protecting them was not going to arise. The Hague conventions, which arose from the last Tsar's initiative, they had repudiated already, along with all other Tsarist obligations. Australia, Canada, China, France, Germany, Great Britain, India, Ireland, Italy, Japan, New Zealand, Poland, South Africa and the United States (also not a member of the League of Nations) were all among the original signatories, though some took several years to ratify. The Germans for instance did not do so till 21 February 1934, more than a year after the Nazis came to power; the French, not till 21 August 1935. The Convention applied throughout Europe, west of the Russian frontier; but in the Far East, the Japanese never ratified at all. This series of engagements, it later became clear, was one that the imperial Japanese government had appeared to favour, since they signed it originally, but did not intend to keep; like the Washington treaty of 1922 for the limiting of naval armaments. And all the signatories held that operational necessity, an elastic phrase, might absolve them from exact compliance.

There is one further international lawyer's point that needs to be made, which is also a matter of operational necessity, differently construed. Evaders who entered neutral territory were supposed to be interned till the end of the war; while escapers were free to move on, if they could, to their own country and to continue the war. An escaper in the hands of a neutral police force, who stressed that he had escaped, was usually allowed to make touch with the relevant Allied military attaché; a process that took minutes in Switzerland, hours in Sweden, weeks or even months in Spain. An evader who gave himself up as an evader thus secured for himself a quiet billet for the rest of the war. Most evaders preferred to invent a tale of capture and escape, however sketchy; an offence against morals, but in their view a lesser offence than opting out of the war their comrades were continuing to fight.

Their special status under international law did not absolve prisoners either from respect for the law of the land in which they were held, or from the grip of the laws that bound them up to the moment of capture. All remained notionally subject to the regulations of their own service, though sensible senior officer prisoners did not insist on conventional marks of respect from their junior companions in misfortune. No one attempted to enforce those niceties of turn-out that are such a preoccupation in peacetime armed forces, and dress was usually miscellaneous and informal. Except in a few vilely-run and ill-disciplined camps, by common consent prisoners did not let their appearance degenerate to the point where it depressed their fellow-prisoners' morale. Courts martial were not held by those in captivity. Unofficial trials, and unofficial punishments, were another matter; even of these there were not many. In a large camp, prisoners who could not get on with each other could be shifted to separate messes; in a small one, the age-old remedy of sending to Coventry could apply. Collusion with the enemy, to the point of scandal or treason, was noted and reported to the proper authorities at the end of the war.

Evaders were simply fugitives. Like other fugitives, they had to eat; and, after a few days, stealing or begging were likely to be their only sources of food, unless they were taken in hand by some local inhabitant who managed to put them in touch with an organised resistance movement – best of all, with an escape line. To eat regularly in occupied territory it was virtually indispensable to have friends, or at least ration cards; preferably both. And to move about, through the innumerable police controls that proliferated in Axis dictatorships, a whole pocketful of official forms might be needed – real or forged. A few evaders managed on their own; only a few. Their most probable fate was to be discovered by the local police, or some auxiliary body. Evaders and escapers alike suffered from central European forest guards; from the painfully ubiquitous *Hitlerjugend* in Germany itself, as troublesome as boy scouts had been in the previous struggle; and from inquisitive neighbours out to curry favour with the current regime, also ubiquitous early in Hitler's war. If captured during an evasion, evaders were supposed only to have to declare their service identity to be treated as prisoners of war; and recaptured escapers could do the same.

Production of an identity disc should have been all that they needed. However, this was not the case with civilians who helped them. If detected, they could expect no mercy, and received little. They would be tried by a military court; acquittals were unknown. The sentence [in Europe] was invariably deportation to Germany, or death at once; a great many of those deported did not come back. It posed an extra problem for an escaper or evader, if he had to have help to get away: was this the sort of danger he could reasonably ask someone else's family to run?

Another difficulty for captured evaders or recaptured escapers was that they might not be believed, identity disc or no. Their frightened and excited captors, rear area troops or police or members of para-military bodies remote from direct personal contact with their enemy, could easily fancy they had caught a spy. If the man they had seized was no longer in uniform, and was carrying any coded material at all, or notes in plain language about military installations he had seen, or anything else that seemed to ignorant captors suspicious, a firing squad – with or without a summary trial first – was an imminent prospect. Hence MI 9's rule: by all means remember points of military importance noticed while on enemy soil, but on no account write them down outside the wire. Inside the wire there were surprising opportunities for passing such points on, if proper precautions were taken.

An even nastier fate than a firing squad might await airmen: a lynching from the infuriated relatives of air raid victims. This illegal yet not utterly unmerited fate befell a certain number of men – how many, it will never be possible to ascertain, because those who set out to wreak their vengeance in this way usually took care to cover their tracks; not least from their own side's security authorities, who wanted prisoners for interrogation. Equally, only the recording angel will ever know how many prisoners on all sides in the war were dispatched forthwith by their captors, who could not be bothered to keep them alive. For long periods on the eastern front SS units took no prisoners at all, by order. As a man from one of the units captured in Italy remarked, this made the fighting in North Africa seem more like a strenuous game than war.

If a shot-down airman landed far from vengeful crowds, and so avoided a lynching, he was not necessarily sure to embark on an evasion. A great many people were so unnerved by the loss of their aircraft, and by their first parachute descent, that they had not the moral stamina to try it, and docilely gave themselves up. Among prisoners, again, Mr Faintheart was as common a type as Mr Valiant. Enthusiasm for, even interest in, escape varied widely between different times, places and personalities.

The time of year naturally affected escapers' prospects. Midwinter snow showed tracks, midwinter temperatures militated against long exposure out of doors. In spring and autumn mud, especially the fearsome mud of eastern Europe, was bound to make vile the appearance of those who had to cross much of it; thus reducing escapers to the single cover of tramps, lowering their chances of finding help and raising those of police hostility. So from late spring through summer till early autumn was the main escaping season, and during this time there might be some prospect of picking up a living from raw vegetables and fruit – nuts as well, in autumn – stolen on the way: guard dogs, that escapers' and evaders' bane, permitting. The time of war mattered also. When a campaign seemed near its close, some fighting men were more ready to be taken prisoner, and less inclined to encounter the risks – never small – of evasion or escape, than they were at a period when imprisonment seemed likely to last for months or even years.

Place also necessarily hemmed in men's chances. Bomber crews shot down after a six or seven hours' outward flight from base had farther to go than fighter pilots shot down on tactical sweeps close to their own side's lines. Some types of country were far more easy to cross for those on the run than others. A city-bred airman could feel his way round western Europe much more readily than over the Carpathians or the Balkans, let alone the jungle terrain of south-east Asia.

In the Pacific the role of luck, always large, was preponderant, and usually told against the shot-down airman or ship-wrecked sailor. Air-sea rescue, heroic though its stories are, falls outside our field. Moreover, the Japanese had lately developed a loathing and contempt for prisoners of war so intense that the Asian war was different, in kind as well as in degree of ferocity, from the war in the Atlantic, on the southern coasts of the Mediterranean, or in Europe. The Gestapo slew western prisoners of war by the score, Slav ones by the thousand. The Kempeitai slew them by the thousand without regard for race, provided they were of European stock; and held most of them meanwhile in conditions in which no north-western European or North American farmer would want, or be allowed, to keep pigs.

Of the east African front we have found nothing to record. North Africa will play some part; and western and southern Europe will be more prominent than eastern, for quite different reasons. It must never be forgotten that for four years, from June 1941 to May 1945, the bulk of the German army was concentrated on the eastern front, at grips with the army of the USSR; and that the fate of the free world hinged on the titanic contest between the German and the Russian dictatorships. But as the Russians had never signed the Geneva Convention, the millions of prisoners they lost suffered abominable fates; which no one in the West has the data to describe, though everyone can join in lamenting. Out of some six-and-a-quarter million prisoners taken from the Red Army and the Soviet air force, nearly five million were slaughtered at once, or died later in enemy hands: a sombre debt, not quickly forgotten. This book deals with what the available British and American archives cover: the services set up to provide such help as was possible for escapers and evaders, and to glean intelligence from prisoners still held in camps.

Everyone in the Allied forces was taught that it was his duty to escape, if captured, and that the Germans' favourite parrot-cry to every new prisoner, 'For you the war is over', was false; that if all else failed, prisoners could hope to divert a percepti-ble proportion of enemy manpower into guarding themselves. Duty apart, there is a simple point worth making early: people from free societies can hardly bear to be cooped up. Men from the Australian outback, or Texas, or Alberta – men who would not hesitate to drive 200 miles to have a drink with a friend – were seldom prepared to put up indefinitely with a regime that confined them to a compound 200 yards square. Even towns-men from industrial England or Wales, used to an ugly and a narrow round, could find the meanness of a prison camp more than they meant to endure.

Nevertheless, reluctance to re-engage in the war could, and often did, apply quite as much to those already made prisoner as to those who had failed to seize a chance, however slender, to evade: prisoners were by no means all enthusiasts for escape. Docile obedience, their captors' first demand, was rendered willingly enough by the timid and by the weary. It was also the counsel of prudence. Some prison camp commandants readily adopted the terrorist tone of their regime. Luckily for the great bulk of prisoners of war in German hands, most of the worst German sadists had gravitated down to the concentration camp guards of the SS; and nearly all prisoners of war were kept out of these inner circles of hell. In Italy, and still more in Japan, real brutes were to be found in charge of prisoners of war; and the Germans retained a few as well, mixed in with the courteous elderly officers called out of retirement, who were usually in the commandant's chair.

How were brutes going to react to escapes? The Geneva Convention implied the legality of escaping, but brutes do not care much for law, and the Japanese cared nothing in practice for the Convention. An important, though hitherto little recognised, achievement by Norman Crockatt and the staffs who worked with him arose from the careful watch they kept on enemy reactions to escape work of all kinds. There were not many precedents to follow. In the 1914–18 war, German and Austro-Hungarian authorities who discovered escape kit, whether in transit or during camp searches, or on the persons of recaptured escapers, had simply confiscated it. In 1939–45 the Germans did the same again: possession of such kit was not as a rule regarded as being an offence in itself.

Crockatt foresaw trouble about the bulk dispatch of aids from government sources, and rightly appreciated that wherever this was tried, it would probably soon be discovered. He expected that when evaders were caught in plain clothes, carrying aids to evasion which were clearly not home-made, they would be treated as spies; tried if they were lucky; and probably shot. To his equal surprise and delight, here he was proved wrong. The fate of those who helped evaders, and were caught, was as bad as anything that had been foreseen, but as a rule the evaders themselves survived.

Their moral struggles were not quite over when they became prisoners of war. Problems in ethics as well as tactics beset those who wanted to escape. Ought one, for example, to try to escape from a prison hospital? The Germans held that, once your enemy has spared your life in accepting your surrender – 'giving quarter', in the phrase of the old wars – you have no right to make any attempt to fight again; and that you compound your offence if you make your attempt from a hospital, where your enemy has had the courtesy to put you for your health's sake. Crockatt, like Holt of MIS-X, had a firm reply to all this: a fighting man remains a fighting man, whether in enemy hands or not, and his duty to continue fighting overrides everything else.

A gloss needed to be put on this doctrine at once, where techniques of escape were concerned. Killing, maiming, or even

striking a sentry, an official, even a civilian who stood in the
way of an escape, was a crime, against the civil law as well as
the laws of war; and special stress was laid, in lectures on escape,
on warning potential prisoners against any such action, which
was liable to bring reprisals as well as individual penalties.

A less dangerous but more complex difficulty arose over
parole. German and Italian captors often invited Allied prisoners to give their parole – their promise that they would not
attempt to escape. Stringent orders reminded the Allied forces
that they were not entitled to give their parole at all, unless for
some limited time and specific useful purpose – a visit, say, to
a dentist or a bath-house. If a prisoner gave his parole for the
purpose of being taken for a country walk near his camp, and
used the walk to reconnoitre routes for possible escapes, was
he behaving honourably or rightly? Most prisoners interested
in escaping took the robust view that their legs were on parole
not to run away, while their eyes and their minds remained free.

One other relevant point needs mention here. Crockatt set
his face like flint against ever inserting escape aids in Red Cross
parcels, or in medical supplies. His object was to ensure that
the Axis high commands had no excuse for confiscating food or
medical parcels, or for refusing to accept and distribute them.
This policy undoubtedly saved a great many prisoners' lives;
they would otherwise have perished of malnutrition, as so many
prisoners from the Red Army did.

In general, the work of MI 9 and MIS-X sought to avoid,
or at all events to deprecate, any action which so incensed the
enemy that it imperilled the lives or damaged the health of prisoners of war. In the Far East conditions were, as a rule, a great
deal worse than in Europe and there was not much captives
there could do but endure.

A particular frame of mind was needed to make men abandon the ignoble safety of captivity for the changes and chances
of life on the run. Men who were contrary, enterprising, adventurous, quick-witted by nature usually did better than plodders,

though they almost always needed plodders to help them in the meticulous tasks of fabricating disguises, forging passes and copying maps.

Once a man had made up his mind to escape, and had help enough from less adventurous spirits if he needed it, what other characteristics did he require? Bodily strength would seem an obvious need, and yet Douglas Bader got out of a German prison hospital – as he had managed to pilot a fighter aircraft – when he had two artificial legs; and one of the present writers got from Dunkirk to England, by way of Marseilles, just after he had lost an arm. Bodily strength, in fact, was useful, but health was far more so, and strength of mind was more vital still. A paradoxical, and not perfectly common, combination of qualities was called for. Foresight was needed, but not too much of it. The best fighters are those who have most carefully, but not over-carefully, foreseen the emergencies that may arise in combat, and have retained the capacity to improvise. Time spent meditating about possible difficulties might result in spotting ways round or through them. On the other hand, the meticulous planner might be so appalled at the size of the task ahead that he gave up. As A. J. Evans put it in *The Escaping Club*, 'Anyone who lets his mind dwell too much on what may happen will never escape from any prison in Germany'.

Acting ability was a help, to substantiate whatever false personality the escaper or evader took on, such as German NCO, housewife or electrician, Norwegian commercial traveller or French forced labourer. Language provided a comparatively slight obstacle, so long as one did not pretend to be an enemy among enemies. The Third Reich – the Third and Last, as prisoners liked to call it – was so full of foreign labourers and other sorts of displaced persons that tram conductors and booking-office clerks no longer much noticed rough accents or an imperfect command of German grammar and vocabulary, unless there happened to be an escape scare in force in the neighbourhood. Deep in the countryside, a foreign accent or appearance might attract attention, as anything foreign – that is, from more than a few miles away – always does there; a reason why prisoners sought, when they could, the anonymity of crowded towns. One rapidly got used to the sight, shocking at first, of people in German uniform riding in trams, or going into shops; it was harder to get rid of the idea that every stranger, and particularly every official, was staring at one and regarded one's appearance as odd. The more one could adopt an actor's insouciance in the presence of strangers, the better.

Courage, and plenty of it, was needed far more than acting skill; and courage of a cold-blooded and lonely rather than a hot-blooded sort. The courage that moved an escaper or evader, and the courage that moved the helpers of either, may have been the same in kind, but certainly differed in degree. Of the two groups, the helpers ran much the graver risks; they needed therefore to be even braver. Those who were brave, original, adaptable and nimble – both in body and in mind – and could display all these qualities at once, did best: if they were decisive. Promptness was really vital: indecision could be quite as fatal during an escape as during a traffic accident.

One other attribute needs to be mentioned, next to the power of quick decision and hardly less important: luck. Unlucky escapers never got out of camps, unlucky evaders fell at the first fence of a chance control from a passer-by in a country lane, or even at the ticket-office of a railway station. Lucky ones soared through difficulties that ought to have kept them pent: the sentry was asleep, or simply looking the other way; the wire fence had been inefficiently put up; the train control never reached their carriage; the people to whom they appealed for help knew how to keep their mouths shut. Men and women involved in clandestine work could, and often did, push their luck too far. The feeling 'If I can get away with that, I can get away with anything', could too easily visit them when they had a lucky break; unless they remembered constantly to be suspicious, unless they took unremitting care, rashness resulting from good luck might readily lead to bad. This was not quite the case with escapers and evaders. They had less need to be obsessed with security, and might be floated clear through to safety on one huge wave of luck, if they were buoyant enough to trust themselves to it.

Luck helped, in any case, with the significant business of keeping up one's own morale in the course of an escape or an evasion. Much meticulous planning might have to go into an actual escape, and much into providing clothes and documents adequate to sustain a disguise; almost all evasions were necessarily conducted on the spur of the moment, and many escapes had to be run likewise, whenever anything unforeseen happened – as it might at any moment, and usually did.

One of the feelings uppermost in an escaper's mind, at that instant of keen elation when he passed the wire and was again, for however short a time, his own master, was the sense that he had regained the initiative from his captors. As Cyril Rofe the future travel agent put it in *Against the Wind* of an early breakfast in some Bohemian bushes after his first escape, 'As we lay there watching the sun rise, our cocoa tasted like nectar. We might have been gods on Olympus, only we felt happier... No other day was ever like it.' The fact that one had actually got *out* was an enormous stimulant to morale; it did not always last through to the end of an escaper's journey.

Moreover, the closing stage of an escape or an evasion – traversing the battle front, or crossing into neutral territory, or hiding in a neutral ship – was often as difficult as the original break out of a camp, or abrupt dissociation from a wrecked ship or aircraft; and this final stage, when physical and emotional exhaustion were at their most intense, was a real test both of endurance and of fieldcraft. Many, too many, attempts foundered just when success was in sight. This above all was the moment when a prisoner needed a sense of humour and a sense of proportion; needed not to take himself and his fate too tragically;

and to be able, if he was hardheaded enough, to observe what errors he had made and how he might do better next time.

A number of escapers believed, with Kipling, that 'he travels the fastest who travels alone'; though they were advised to travel in pairs, to keep each other's spirits up. The combination of a plodder with a man of more mercurial temper was sometimes a help, but it was far more important that the pair should know, like, and rely on each other thoroughly. The old Anglo-Indian phrase about 'a good man to go tiger shooting with' was acutely in point; the risks of an escape were hardly worth running with a stranger, who might let one down in a crisis.

Yet if escapers or evaders were going to make any serious progress across occupied territory, outside the lands of the Axis proper – Germany or Italy or Japan – in all of which till September 1943, and in Germany and Japan thereafter as well, the hostility of the locals was to be taken for granted – did they not have to trust themselves to total strangers, whose reliability out tiger-shooting must be largely a matter of guesswork? It was part of the function of MI 9 and MIS-X, the secret services with which this book deals, to cope precisely with this risk.

There was another function that they fulfilled, if it is not attributed to them by what the Germans call *Hineininterpretierung* – interpretation backwards from the present to the past, not the same as hindsight. The present writers believe that Crockatt, the head of MI 9, had insight into the state of mind of prisoners of war, an insight based on reading, reflection and discussion with many people qualified to know. He did not only appreciate that forlorn feeling of being fed up and far from home that visited almost everyone in the first few days of captivity. He appreciated also that frenzy, amounting almost to mania, which could set in later – years later – when it seemed as if imprisonment was going to last for years more yet, perhaps forever and a day. 'Stir-crazy' is the modern convicts' term for the affliction. In the wars of 1939–45, some people suffered from stir-craziness in Italy, Burma or Java, many in Germany and Japan. Crockatt thought it might lessen the sharpness of their pain if they were aware that a distant staff cared intensely about their plight, and was hard at work to relieve them.

Problems of security made it impossible for the men most in need of assurances on this point, the wildest and least disciplined of prisoners of war, to be told much if anything even of the existence of MI 9 and MIS-X; but a great many others found the dreariness and the monotony of life in a prisoner of war camp made at least a shade more bearable by the knowledge that a reasonably competent body of men, some very ingenious and some very brave, was busy trying to get in touch with them and to bring them safely out of enemy hands. This psychological safety net could calm the nerves of those at work on the high trapeze of tunnelling, pass forging, or escape planning.

In the violence and muddle of war, common sense often has to go out of the window. It is the task of the commander of insight, and of the staff officer of real capacity, to mitigate that effect: to bring some sense of purpose, and some hope, into the chaos of fighting and of waiting about – much more waiting about than fighting – of which war consists. One of the main functions of the escape services was to provide hope and a sense of purpose for those to whom the war might otherwise become quite pointless: those fastened in the greyness of a prisoner of war camp where nothing seemed worthwhile any more.

# Approach March

To enable the reader to make proper sense of the rest of the book, a brief sketch is needed of the staff network in which the escape services worked.

Thanks to the age-old tradition that capture meant disgrace, no official encouragement or support for escape was provided by any general staff until well on in the 1914–18 war. By 1917 British intelligence chiefs had realised that prisoners of war, both friend and foe, constituted valuable sources for them, hitherto untapped. In that year a small new sub-branch of the War Office intelligence directorate was set up, called MI IA, to look into this and, in particular, to secure from German prisoners in camps in the United Kingdom specialised knowledge which they had not revealed at their primary interrogation in France. MI IA was to handle also anything that could be secured from British prisoners in Germany. It set about organising secret communication with officer camps by coded letter. No startling results were obtained, but enough was done to suggest that the still rudimentary system might be worth following up, should 'the war to end wars' turn out to have failed in that object.

For most of the 1920s, few British or American civilians thought another great war at all likely. Even in the service departments in Whitehall, up to 1933 none was expected for ten years at least; and the subject of prisoners of war slumbered. On the continent of Europe there was slightly more interest. The French instituted in 1926 a retrospective award, an escapers' medal for successful, or even well attempted, escapes from Germany. One French general, P. G. Dupont, a corps commander at Verdun, had had an enterprising idea. He had trained his men to be ready, if they fell into enemy hands, not only to seize any chance they could to escape, but also to look out for every possible opportunity to commit sabotage, notably when out on work-ing parties in farms or factories. General von Brauchitsch, later German commander-in-chief in the West, lectured on Dupont's idea at Munich in 1937, when the Germans were getting ready for the next round. His lecture text reached England, and was studied with interest at the War Office.

By the autumn of the following year, war was visibly nearer. In November 1938, a few weeks after the Munich agreement, two staff officers in separate branches of the War Office began to work – quite independently, and unknown to each other – towards the same end, the re-creating of some such body as the old MI 1a, modernised to suit the current forms and phases of war. One of them had served in the original branch; the other, from a less conventional career, had secured a more influential post.

A. R. Rawlinson, the father of a future Tory solicitor-general, had been a young intelligence officer (IO) in MI 1a in 1917–18 and therefore had some experience in the problems of reinter-rogating prisoners and of promoting escape and evasion. As a reserve officer, he had been called up for a few months' service after the Munich crisis, and was remobilised in August 1939 into a revived MI 1a, as a captain, a GSO 3 on the War Office's establishment.[5] The other was J. C. F. Holland, the lonely origi-nator of the commandos as well as the deception services and the special operations executive (SOE). He was an unusually modest and self-effacing member of a traditionally self-effacing caste, a regular officer from the Celtic fringe with Indian civil service, clerical, and academic forebears. Too ill to take up a regimental command in the Royal Engineers when at last due

---

5    This book has to be crammed with ranks; in a military history, it
     is necessary to show who was senior to whom. Readers in a less
     rank-sodden age need not count this a fault.

for one late in 1938, he was posted as a major to GS (R), a tiny research branch of the War Office – the only other member of it was his typist – and told to research on any subject he chose. His predecessor had worked on army education. Holland, having won a DFC as a pilot and worked with Lawrence in Arabia, chose irregular warfare, a subject on which his mind had preyed continuously since 1917; all the more keenly, after he had fought in the British army on the losing side, and been badly wounded, in the Troubles of 1919–21 in Ireland. According to his friend and colleague Joan Bright Astley, 'He had an independent mind, an acute brain, a loving and poetic heart; he was quick, imaginative, and of a fiery temper.'

During the winter of 1938–9 irregular warfare became a subject topical enough to engage the interest of the chiefs of staff. Holland's branch was renamed MI R, and he brought in a friend to join him – Major, later Major-General Sir Colin, Gubbins who became a leading personality in the SOE. Gubbins was a gunner; he and Holland had been officer cadets together. Holland's lively mind continued to play over the possibilities of work on and over the borders of normal fighting, while Gubbins prepared a series of pamphlets destined to be widely distributed during the impending world war, on sabotage, ambush and other guerrilla activity.

Holland and Gubbins were each the son of a don who had served in the East and been a protégé of Lord Curzon's. Both were original thinkers, who yet kept their originality within the bounds of common sense and practicability. Both foresaw that there might be hundreds of thousands of prisoners in the next war, each of whom might be turned into a small thorn in the enemy's side; and that there might well be hundreds or even thousands of evaders as well, loose in the enemy's rear areas and in need of guidance. Who was to be their guide?

Rawlinson's superior in MI 1a, then a brevet lieutenant-colonel, a future DMI, later Field-Marshal Sir Gerald Templer, was posted to the Expeditionary Force in France at the beginning of the war, before Rawlinson had had time to do more than formulate some outline plans and while Holland had much else besides escaping on his mind. Templer's initiative – possibly stemming in turn from a hint from Holland, with whom and Gubbins he had discussed the subject already – brought it to the point of decision.

On 28 September 1939, with the full agreement of Major-General (Sir) Noel Mason-Macfarlane, his superior in France, Templer wrote to Major-General Beaumont-Nesbitt, the director of military intelligence, to propose prearrangement of code communications with German camps. About the very day on which he received Templer's letter, Beaumont-Nesbitt was called on by M. C. C. Harrison, one of the authors of *Within Four Walls*. Harrison followed up his call with a long letter on the value of an interservice department to help prisoners of war to escape by providing them secretly with maps, compasses and money. Holland was called in to advise, and on 13 October put up a substantial paper on the 'very thorough organisation' that was going to be needed. Among the advantages he foresaw was the siphoning off of enemy manpower into non-productive channels. He observed that the Admiralty and the Air Ministry would also of course be involved; and his paper was accordingly referred to the Joint Intelligence Committee.

That committee's papers are still unavailable to public inspection, but it undoubtedly approved Holland's paper in principle. A short, sharp exchange of letters followed between Beaumont-Nesbitt and his opposite number at the Air Ministry, Air Commodore K. C. Buss, about which of the three services should form and control the new organisation. Beaumont-Nesbitt was prepared to accept responsibility for army and navy prisoners, but thought that the RAF, with its superior knowledge of navigation, would need different training and treatment. Buss felt strongly that the interests of all three services would best be served by a single organisation under the War Office, with liaison officers from the navy and the air force. He was thinking solely in terms of the previous great war, in which army prisoners had far outnumbered air force ones, and did not foresee the problems that would soon be posed by evaders. Buss won the day, a victory which the Air Ministry later came to regret and made a strenuous effort to reverse.

The JIC seems to have recommended that the new body should come under an escaper from the previous world war, and Holland put up several names. He argued nevertheless that any former escaper was bound to be too much prejudiced by his own experiences. He was sure that a strong man without bias was needed who could display the energy and drive of a leader as he controlled and coordinated the team of experts working under him. He had the right man ready at his elbow in MI R, and proposed him to Beaumont-Nesbitt on 30 November: Major N. R. Crockatt, whom he had known for nearly thirty years.

Norman Crockatt had just turned forty-five. He had been a regular infantry officer with an excellent fighting record in the war of 1914–18. He had earned a DSO as well as an MC in the front line in France, where he had been severely wounded. He was transferred to the staff, and served as brigade major – the most arduous and most exposed of staff posts – both in France and in Palestine, where he was again wounded. He had become bored with peacetime soldiering, and left the army abruptly in 1927 – daring to walk out in the middle of his staff college course – to become a stockbroker. Holland, impressed with his personality from boyhood, had secured him early for MIR and recognised in him the man for whom the new venture called. Crockatt's natural grace of bearing, set off by a tall well-proportioned figure and piercing greenish eyes, made him a noticeable man in any company; in an age of drab clothes and battledress he wore at every opportunity the colourful gear of his regiment, the Royal Scots. Moreover, as a former front-line combatant who had also served on the other side of the divide, he could understand and appreciate the antagonism that

combatants were likely to feel for the staff, could make allow-
ances for it, and could do his best to reduce it.

He was also clear-headed, quick-witted, a good organiser,
a good judge of men, and no respecter of red tape: excellent
qualities for his early struggles in the War Office. That august
yet cumbrous department moved so slowly that no one in it had
so far brought Rawlinson into the discussions. The discovery
that an entirely new section was to replace MI IA came as a
complete surprise to him. However, he at once made himself
known to Crockatt. Both were too much soldiers and too little
bureaucrats for there to be any confusion or dismay about who
was displacing whom. It says much for both their characters
that Rawlinson worked cheerfully under Crockatt's immediate command for the rest of the war. It took little more than
three weeks – quite brisk going, by the peacetime standards
from which the War Office was trying to shake itself free – for
Holland's proposal to be executed. A minute of 23 December
from Beaumont-Nesbitt's assistant to a strictly limited circle
– MI 5, MI 6, the director of naval intelligence, Buss, Mason-
Macfarlane, and the DMI's two existing deputies, one for
operations and one for intelligence – created MI 9 officially, put
Crockatt in charge, and located it in room 424 of the Metropole
Hotel in Northumberland Avenue, a couple of furlongs away
from the War Office main building.[6]

Crockatt defined his objectives thus, in a retrospective
survey of his work at the close of the war:

a. To facilitate escapes of British prisoners of war, thereby
   getting back service personnel and containing additional
   enemy manpower on guard duties.
b. To facilitate the return to the United Kingdom of those
   who succeeded in evading capture in enemy occupied
   territory.

---

6    Text in WO 208/3242, historical record of MI 9, 15.

   c. To collect and distribute information.

   d. To assist in the denial of information to the enemy.

   e. To maintain morale of British prisoners of war in enemy
      prison camps.

He remarked at the same time that although his department came under the military intelligence directorate, its tasks were in fact a mixture of operations, intelligence, transport and supply.

It fell into two main halves, one covering the affairs of British and Commonwealth prisoners, escapers and evaders, and the other dealing with captured enemies. It was important to make sure that each half worked in harmony with the other. Holland and Crockatt had divined this already, and Crockatt determined to keep the halves properly coordinated. His capacity as a commander held them steady all through the war. He put Rawlinson, promoted to major, in charge of the enemy prisoners' side, with which MI 1a had been mainly concerned, and of the Combined Services Detailed Interrogation Centre (CSDIC). This part of the organisation was at first called MI 9a, while MI 9b handled escapes, evasions and intelligence from prisoners in enemy hands. In December 1941 MI 9a became a separate department, MI 19, still under Rawlinson, who continued to look to Crockatt for any guidance he needed. Crockatt, promoted to colonel, became deputy director of military intelligence (prisoners of war) – DDMI (P/W) – and commanded both MI 19 and MI 9. The revised MI 9 was divided into five sub-sections: b for liaison with other branches and services and interrogation of returned escapers and evaders, d for training, x for planning and organisation of escapes, y for codes, and z for tools. Later in the war, in September 1943, when the success of MI 9's work was at last beginning to impress the high command, the whole organisation was expanded, and Crockatt became a brigadier.

Under MI 9d a school was set up in Highgate in north London, to which intelligence officers from all three services could go to be briefed on the intricacies of evasion and escape, and to learn how to pass them on to their units. Its title was non-committal – Intelligence School 9. The symbol IS 9 thus became widely known among fighting services and staffs, and as we shall see provided a convenient cover for MI 9's field units later in the war.

The six earliest officers to join Crockatt in what one of them, Clayton Hutton, called the 'vast barn-like office' of room 424 had, like himself, all seen active service in the previous world war, and five of them could be relied on to do nothing rash that would compromise MI 9, and alert the Germans to the vigorous official support that escaping and prisoners' intelligence was now to receive from Britain. In the earliest and most precarious stages, when they were starting from scratch with the knowledge that initial blunders would be the hardest to put right, they worked closely together as a team. They had strong individualities, but Crockatt managed to correlate their efforts.

Rawlinson we have met already. The chief of staff was V. R. Isham, a regular captain in the Suffolk Regiment, known as 'Tiger' though in appearance and demeanour more like a hungry wolf; Clayton Hutton called him 'as tall as a lamp-post and nearly as thin'. He had an intimate understanding of the service bureaucratic maze; unhappily his health gave out after three more years of threading through its intricacies, and he was invalided out in 1942. K. R. Stirling Wylie of the Royal Scots who replaced him for a few months was a sound administrator, but not one gifted with the sparkle Crockatt preferred in his companions. Stirling Wylie's successor was the ideal man for the post, C. M. Rait.

Cecil Rait of the Artists' Rifles, very much a fighting soldier, who had spent the Great War in Highland regiments, and played a part second only to Crockatt's in MI 9, though his strength and importance have seldom been appreciated. A friend said of him that, 'born one war too early, he should have been a commando officer'. Between the wars he had worked in a City issuing house and learned that 'all that glisters is not gold', a fact which Crockatt in his enthusiasm for some new scheme occasionally forgot. He was loyal to his chief, and wholly uninterested in self-promotion; indeed he joined MI 9 in the rank of major, which he had earned in battle in his early twenties, with a decoration for gallantry, to serve in the captain's appointment of GSO3 under Isham, who was technically his junior. Later he had a spell under Rawlinson as a GSO2, thus deepening his understanding of how the whole branch worked, before he came to stand at Crockatt's elbow as a lieutenant-colonel (GSO1).

The original team was completed by three IOs, de Bruyne, Winterbottom and Clayton Hutton. De Bruyne joined as a second lieutenant, Royal Horse Artillery, and rose in the branch to be a lieutenant-colonel; he liked to be called 'Bruno', but as he had run the family sheep farm in southern Chile before the war his colleagues preferred to call him 'Bo-Peep'. He was a smallish, dapper man with a lively air and a toothbrush moustache, an efficient liaison officer and a particularly skilled interrogator of returned escapers and evaders. Leslie Winterbottom had a complementary personality. In many years as personal assistant to Gordon Selfridge, the Oxford Street store tycoon, he had learned tact and perseverance. His quiet, unassuming, yet determined manner made him an ideal choice for the task of liaison with British prisoners' families. He was in charge of coding, and secured the co-operation of parents, wives and girl-friends which was vital for success.

The third IO, the most wayward and original of them all, the joker in the pack, was Christopher Clayton Hutton, universally known as 'Clutty'. His task was to invent, design and adapt aids to evasion and escape, the gadgets that were MI 9's best known product. His enthusiasm was as unlimited as his ingenuity, or his capacity for getting into trouble with the staid authorities of service and civilian officialdom. At one time or another he was in difficulties with senior officers of all three services, with MI 5, MI 6, Scotland Yard, the Customs authorities, the Bank of

England, the ministries of food and of production, and several local police forces. He prefixes to his lively war autobiography this extract from a letter sent by Crockatt to an army provost marshal: 'This officer is eccentric. He cannot be expected to comply with ordinary service discipline, but he is far too valuable for his services to be lost to this Department.'

There were also two liaison officers appointed early: the jovial Commander P. W. Rhodes, RN, who had spent over two years in German camps after Jutland – always known in the section as 'The Admiral' – and 'Johnny' Evans, the author of *The Escaping Club*. Evans was reduced for the moment to the rank of pilot officer, though he soon became a squadron leader; he was often opinionated, but his opinions on escape could not fail to command respect. He and Rhodes could both offer useful advice on methods of smuggling gadgets into camps, as well as giving lectures that held their listeners' attention, and representing, when there was need to do so, the special needs of their own services to soldiers in MI 9. Rhodes moved on from naval liaison to be the commandant of the Highgate intelligence school, where Evans was one of his star performers; through it passed several hundred British and American intelligence officers.

What gained Crockatt's team their eventual successes was a combination of two characteristics: high quality and small size. Size preoccupied Crockatt almost as much as quality and he was determined to fight against the bureaucrats' tendency to let new developments proliferate. He believed that small is efficient. After the war he must have read 'Popski's' anecdote of the unimportant GSO3 in a very large headquarters, who so impressed his visiting commander-in-chief that he was promoted to major, and within eight months became a brigadier, still doing work of minimal weight; he may have smiled wryly, he would not have approved. He carried with him from the Stock Exchange a distrust of mere size, as well as a nose for the bogus prospectus; and he knew that claims for manpower, office space, even furniture or telephones – let alone the odder and more esoteric goods for which Clayton

Hutton would soon be in the market – only attracted administrative enemies. To keep what is now called 'a low profile' seemed a counsel of prudence, and if promotion suffered, work did not. By the time he did require to expand, in the winter of 1943–4, he had given the war establishment authorities so little trouble that they made no difficulties for him.

In the course of this book, MI 9's relations with the service departments will become clear, and only a few prefatory lines are needed. It turned out to have a triple value for the Air Ministry. It alleviated the aircrew shortage, by recovering missing airmen who could be reinserted into fighting or at least into training squadrons; it provided a lot of technical data about how and why aircraft had been shot down; and it played a significant role in finding targets for air attack, as well as in assessing bomb damage. For the Admiralty there was comparatively little that it could do, though it provided a few precious items of naval intelligence, particularly on the submarine war that was vital for the British. For the army, it recovered a number of senior officers, General O'Connor not the least of them, and played some part also in the accumulating of data about the enemy. But MI 9, unlike most of the other MI departments, did not ostensibly contribute to the routine distribution of news about the enemy's doings. One startling example of this comes from well on in the war.

Early in 1943, combined operations headquarters was toying with operation 'Cornet', a plan to destroy the Moehne dam, a source of the Ruhr's water supply, with a team of thirty parachutists. Derek Verschoyle, once the devastating literary editor of *The Spectator,* consulted de Bruyne for some routine information, on such obvious points as whether the neighbouring anti-aircraft post was live or dummy. De Bruyne had to reply that, 'Although information of this nature does come our way, it would be improper for us to assume the role of purveyors.'[7]

---

7    25 February 1943, in WO 208/3262. A minute earlier in the same
     file records that, on the only maps suitable for briefing the party

'Cornet' was dropped; the dam was conclusively breached in May, in a raid of tragic gallantry by bomber command of the RAF. The raid's significance for the general theme of this book was that thereafter lynching became a perceptible risk for aircrew shot down over Germany, as it was already in Japan. But we must return to Whitehall, and MI 9's relations with the various ministries.

Treasury approval for MI 9's existence had been signified as early as 21 December 1939. Crockatt at first drew on the DMI for funds, which were never stinted to him; he took care not to demand unreasonable sums. In the summer of 1940 he was allowed to draw up to £5,000 in foreign currency, most of which was spent in providing aircrew with purses containing about twelve pounds a man among their other escape aids. More was provided when it was needed. There were occasional shortages of particular currencies, such as Norwegian kroner, but no financial crises. Nor, the Treasury made sure, was there ever any need to contemplate forgery.

Clayton Hutton got into hot water from time to time with the ministries of Labour and of Supply, and with the Board of Trade, but never into water so hot that MI 9 was imperilled.

One other government department was important to it; the Foreign Office. The war years were not that office's grandest, nor do Halifax and Eden stand at the top of any list of foreign secretaries in order of merit, and MI 9 might have stood in some danger of being regarded as yet another disturbing and unwelcome newcomer. The hostility with which Eden and some of his permanent staff regarded SOE boded ill for another more or less secret body that might move athwart lines the Foreign

---

on how to escape into the Low Countries, 'the German-Belgian frontier is marked in the wrong place.' Indeed, 'the exact line is not known for the whole length of the frontier': a vivid instance of the depth of the gulf that divided wartime London from the Continent. (Bankes to de Bruyne, 8 February 1943, ibid.)

Office laid down, or simply make more work. On the other hand, diplomats had a clear and visible duty to approach the protecting power – Switzerland – whenever formal complaints were needed about the treatment of British prisoners of war in Axis territory, and this duty the Foreign Office's staff carried out with assiduous skill. A whole branch of it was given up to the affairs of prisoners of war. It was in constant touch with the relevant administrators in the three services and with the International Red Cross, and in occasional touch with Crockatt.

Forward on the edge of occupied territory, looking after escapers or evaders who got into neutral ground was the responsibility of the service attachés in the nearest British embassy or legation. One of these deserves early mention: Harrison's co-author Cartwright, who had been recalled to government service in 1938 as an observer in the Sudetenland. A brilliant stroke by the military secretary next posted him to Berne as military attaché; he spent the war there, rising to the local rank of brigadier. (This meant that he outranked by one star any possible Swiss opposite number: only the commanding general in the Swiss army ranks above colonel.) As a former escaper, Cartwright was excellently qualified to draw information out of arrivals in Switzerland from Axis-held territory. He was also able to detect the occasional impostors whom the Germans tried to feed, through him, on to the lines they suspected the British ran across southern France. And his record and character gave him weight enough to impress young men, unused to freedom, who were living it up in the nightclubs of Berne or Zurich while waiting for a passage home, and might become indiscreet in their cups.

Discretion brings us to Crockatt's major preoccupation at home. He early perceived that secret and semi-secret services like to work in a dense fog of security, in which the germs of inter-secret-service jealousy breed fast. The relations between MI 9 and the several other British secret services deserve a few words.

With the most secret and most important of them, Colonel Bevan's London Controlling Section (LCS), the tiny body that directed strategic deception and sought to mislead the Nazi high command about the future course of the war, dealings were very few and wholly amicable. The LCS knew enough about its own business to be sure that it had no need of MI 9's activities. Bevan had been a friend of Crockatt's for years, and knew what MI 9 was for. He knew also that the long and unpredictable delays in prisoner of war post were bound to militate against its effective use for his purposes. In the whole of R. F. Hesketh's long report on the LCS's masterpiece, operation 'Fortitude' – the cover plan for 'Overlord', the Normandy invasion – MI 9 is not mentioned at all. Before the LCS was set up, about halfway through the war, there were no troubles with its predecessor, NID 17M, for Ewen Montagu was as well informed and as cautious as Bevan.

Of MI 5, the security service, not much can yet be said. Its own archives have never ever 'gone public', and those of MI 9's papers that bear on individual cases of treachery, real or suspected, while in enemy hands are all closed to research till 2010 at least. Crockatt must have had frequent consultations with MI 5 when he helped to set up the Wandsworth interrogation centre for refugees from Europe at the Royal Victorian Patriotic Schools, where security was soon taken out of his hands altogether by MI 5. There has never been any sign that MI 9 behaved in any way that MI 5 disapproved, and the older department gave the younger every possible help in checking the bona fides of occasional suspects.

SOE was not formed till July 1940. Like MI 9 it was a descendant of MI R. Crockatt already knew, liked and had worked with Gubbins, who was SOE's mainspring, before ever MI 9 was founded. Their mutual respect and confidence seeped through to their subordinates, and as a rule SOE and MI 9 co-operated fruitfully; as a rule, but not always. For one of SOE's other predecessors, section D of MI 6, had not always seen eye to eye with MIR, and in parts of SOE, as in most of MI 6, the germs of jealousy to which reference was made just now were endemic.

Before we reach them we must deal in passing with SOE's third predecessor, Electra House, the propaganda branch of the Foreign Office. After a year's unseemly bureaucratic wrangle, this was separated from SOE again to become the political warfare executive (PWE) under Bruce Lockhart. Among the many crosses PWE had to bear, MI 9 was not one. Certainly PWE never undertook to direct propaganda towards British or American prisoners of war. Both MI 9 and MI 19 must have been among PWE's sources of data on the state of enemy and enemy-occupied territory, but just what information Crockatt passed to Bruce Lockhart, the available files do not show.

Let us turn now to the oldest and grandest of the secret services, to which MI 9 was closely bound, not quite in Cinderella's servitude to her elder sisters, but sometimes too close for comfort. There was one powerful reason, from the still keenly remembered past war through which its senior men had served, why MI 6 was likely to be suspicious of any other secret service operating on the confines of its own work, particularly if that service employed women agents. As Crockatt put it, in his end-of-war summary of MI 9's achievement, 'The oft repeated statement that Nurse Edith Cavell, who apparently worked for S.I.S. the secret intelligence service, or MI 6 during the last war, had been discovered through assisting a prisoner of war seemed to dictate the whole attitude of S.I.S. towards the Section [i.e. MI 9]. They were determined to prevent evaders and escapers from involving them in any way. This attitude may have been correct from their own security aspect, but it was a terrific handicap to those trying to build up an organisation.'

The principal sound reason for many SIS staff officers' hatred of SOE was that SOE sought to promote just those states of civic turmoil that would make life for an SIS agent in the same area awkward, and render his work – particularly the transmission of his results – all but impossible. For all MI 6 knew – and they did not pause to think the problem through – the same might be true of escape agents; it was certainly likely to be true of escapers, whom escape agents might be expected to assemble near themselves. Any Allied personnel at all, existing – let alone operating – in the neighbourhood of an MI 6 agent, unless they had been soused in MI 6's concepts of the clandestine life and how it should be lived, were anathema to MI 6 officers of the old school. Several of these old hands were by now eminent in the organisation, and one or two deserve a word of comment.

Admiral 'Quex' Sinclair, head of MI 6 when the war began, died in early November 1939, a few days before catastrophe engulfed some of his subordinates at Venlo on the Dutch-German border. His successor, (Sir) Stewart Menzies, had been in the intelligence business for many years, knew everybody who was anybody, and supplemented a regular cavalryman's brain with dexterous polish. He was much misapprehended outside his own service and much respected within it. The man who was most feared within and without it was his assistant chief, (Sir) Claude Dansey.

Colonel Dansey's spry and impatient manner complemented Menzies' grace and Life Guards charm. He was the older man – sixty-three already when the war began and an acute foreign observer, Colonel Paillole, meeting him for the first time in 1942, noticed that Menzies deferred to him. Dansey was in fact one of those powerful men who prefer to keep their power hidden; an *éminence grise* rather than a ruling monarch, but a highly influential personage for all that. What Dansey wanted done was done, and what he wanted undone was undone. He could have broken Crockatt, or anyone else in MI 9, as easily as he blew his own nose; and Crockatt knew it. What official hold did MI 6, and Dansey as Menzies' deputy for operations, have over the work of MI 9?

When disaster struck in the Low Countries and France in May and June 1940 MI 9's world, like everyone else's, was turned upside down. Not much had been done to prepare the British Expeditionary Force for escape and evasion work; yet about a tenth of it had been taken prisoner, and several thousand evaders were left behind as well when its main body withdrew through Dunkirk. RAF aircraft shot down over the newly occupied continent kept adding to these evaders' numbers. Most headed for Vichy France, as did most of the earliest escapers; and there the authorities concentrated as many of them as it could lay hands on in fortress internment at Marseilles. On 6 August 1940 Menzies, no doubt with Dansey's approval, saw Crockatt and made him a proposition. MI 6 offered to set up an escape line to run from Marseilles into Spain.

It is unlikely that Crockatt had the remotest idea of the motive that prompted this offer. He had no direct contact with the War Cabinet; Menzies had. The high command of MI 6 knew already what the rest of that service soon knew and soon resented: that a Cabinet decision of 22 July had created a new subversive organisation, SOE, which was independent of MI 6's control. MI 6's longheld monopoly of undercover work in enemy-held territory was thus broken. Its chiefs were determined to prevent the arrival of any more competitors, liable – as far as they could see – to hinder and disrupt their work of obtaining intelligence, as they supposed SOE would do. Even if Crockatt had been aware of all this, he had no alternative but to accept Menzies' offer. It contained a practical proposal for solving his immediate problem.

Dansey fixed the details. A young man called Donald Darling had agreed to go to Spain to restore overland secret communication with France. He was instructed to set up also an escape line to run from Marseilles to Barcelona, and thence to Gibraltar or Lisbon. Darling was an excellent choice, since he had lived both in France and in Spain, spoke both languages fluently, and knew the eastern Pyrenees well. He reached Lisbon in mid-July, made friends with Sir Walford Selby, the ambassador, and moved on to reconnoitre Catalonia. Thence he was peremptorily recalled by Sir Samuel Hoare, the newly-appointed ambassador in Madrid, who felt himself unable at that delicate moment in Anglo-Spanish relations to countenance any activity to which Franco's government might take exception. So Darling had to settle at Lisbon, some two hundred miles farther from Marseilles than London is, and tackle his task from there.

His cover was that of vice-consul in charge of refugees, and he picked the code name of 'Sunday'. His affairs in London were first handled by an elusive character called 4Z. When 4Z finally faded out, his successor was led to believe that he had never reported at all, on mobilisation at the beginning of the war: a typical fragment of secret service mystification. This successor, J. M. Langley, was not appointed till after his successful escape from France in the spring of 1941.

Langley – one of the authors of this book – was in fact the point of junction between MI 6 and MI 9. He was nominally on Crockatt's staff, but was paid and commanded by MI 6. In practice, his task turned out to be the encouragement of escape and evasion lines in north-west Europe, and he was able to serve his two masters without the difficulty foreseen in the Sermon on the Mount. In Denmark, the Low Countries, France and Iberia in fact MI 6 had a say in what MI 9 was doing, and some degree of operational control over lines which in several cases preferred to run themselves. In the rest of the world MI 9 had an entirely free hand till the American MIS-X came to join it, subject of course to the agreement of force commanders on the spot.

Staffs of several British services found, when the United States entered the world war in December 1941, that the Americans with whom they had to deal were determined to do things their own way, did not require advice, and proceeded to make most of the early mistakes the British had made. Words of warning, even if uttered in the friendliest spirit, were unwelcome, and the American armed forces were tough enough to endure the results. MI 9's experience was quite different. Escape and evasion provided a body of common predicaments for British and American fighting men, and the Americans, finding a British set-up in working order that was already producing results, were delighted to join in. Post escape and evasion training, interservice already on the British side, became inter-Allied as well. Field operations in support of evaders and escapers, notably in Italy and Yugoslavia, were carried out by mixed teams of American and British soldiers, sailors and airmen, who worked together in friendly rivalry to do their best for their passengers.

A few words are needed on the American control of escapes and evasions, though this is no place to explore the politics of the wartime Pentagon. (The Pentagon was not in fact completed till 1943, and the many buildings in which the service departments were scattered round Washington till then presented a real, if minor, staff difficulty.) The military intelligence department there (MID), dating back to the middle 1880s, had been a main division of the general staff since 1918 but was still quite small when the war began, as this table shows:

Strength of American
Military Intelligence Department[1]

| | Year | Officers | Civilian Aides |
|---|---|---|---|
| | 1938 | 20 | 48 |
| | 1940 | 28 | 167 |
| December | 1941 | 200 | 656 |
| | 1942 | 400[2] | 1,106[3] |
| | 1944 | 581[3] | 1,000[2] |
| | 1945 | 575 | 931 |

1 Extacted from 'A History of the Military Intelligence Devision', 3, a long typescript: United States National Archives historical MS 2–22/AA/C$_2$ (undated, not earlier than 1950).

2 [Estimate.]

3 [Maximum for 1938–45.]

During the war, the department kept changing both its composition and its functions; sometimes to fit in with major reshuffles, always to keep abreast with the aim it was set. This aim was 'the prompt production of accurate timely intelligence'. One result of these frequent chops and changes was that it was not till late in 1944 that the staff machine was fully effective. Correspondingly, the parts of the MID that dealt with prisoners of war also developed piecemeal, though 'close liaison' between British and American intelligence organisations had been ordered from the spring of 1941. Within MID, a military intelligence service (MIS) was established in 1942, and remained the active operating agency in it for the rest of the war. MIS included a prisoner of war interrogation section (PWIS), begun in April 1942 to deal with captured enemy prisoners. The initiative for this came from the United States naval intelligence staff, and derived from the great advantages the Royal Navy had already secured from MI 9a. It was not till 6 October 1942 that – on a proposal from Stimson, the Secretary of War, to the chiefs of staff – another, more secret, section was set up to deal with escape and evasion work by United States forces. This section, only tenuously connected to the rest of MID, was MIS-X. To conform with British precedent, both sections dealing with prisoners were brought under a single head, called the Captured Personnel and Materiel branch (CPM), which was created on 22 October 1942. In practice the branch never dealt with captured material – it all went direct to the technical branches of MID; and CPM's influence on MIS-X was seldom much more than notional.

MIS-X's sub-sections covered interviews with returning prisoners and evaders, correspondence in code with those still behind barbed wire, the location of camps, training and briefing, and the securing and distribution of escape kits and purses. On every point, there was close, constant and cordial co-operation with MI 9, down nearly to the end of the war.

The reasons for this were as much personal as institutional.

It was manifestly for the benefit of the Anglo-American alliance that the intelligence branches of both allies should work together against their common enemies, Germany and Japan. In particular, United States and British Commonwealth aircrew in Europe and in North Africa were attacking the same targets, turn and turn about. Those of them who became prisoners mostly passed through the same camp, Dulag Luft at Oberursel, and all of them underwent interrogation by the same Luftwaffe intelligence staffs; all were in danger, beyond that, from the same Abwehr and Sicherheitsdienst (SD). So co-operation was sensible; and the personalities set to make it work made it agreeable as well.

Few secrets were kept from 'Wild Bill' Donovan, the future chief of OSS, and the air force general 'Tooey' Spaatz when they paid their fateful visits to London in the summer of 1940, as Roosevelt's special emissaries sent to check the gloomy reports from his ambassador, Joseph P. Kennedy. Having much else on their minds, they probably made no inquiries about MI 9; there is certainly no record in the war diary that either visited the wide open spaces of Room 424. However, Donovan was aware of MI 9 when he visited England in the spring of 1941. And when Spaatz returned early in 1942 as commander of the AEAF, he lost little time in getting in touch with Crockatt, and less in finding an American officer to work alongside MI 9, who was to do what he could to duplicate its work for the benefit of the Eighth Air Force, then the principal American offensive weapon in the theatre of war.

He chose W. Stull Holt, an academic historian from Johns Hopkins University, who had fought in the American air force in the previous world war, of which he retained unsordid memories. Holt, from the very first, got on excellently with Crockatt, de Bruyne, and everyone else he needed to meet. Long afterwards, one of Crockatt's closest subordinates recalled indeed that the DDMI (P/W) seemed to exert almost a magnetic influence on Holt, who was his warm admirer, and anxious to learn from him in every possible way.

Holt was in England from June, making informal inquiries; and drafted a sensible card of orders on how to behave in enemy hands, issued on Spaatz's authority on 21 July 1942. Three days later, Holt received a formal briefing from Spaatz, in the presence of two senior staff officers. He was to act as liaison officer with DDMI (P/W); to receive escape kits, maps and purses from the British, and to distribute them to all three USAF commands in the United Kingdom – bomber, fighter and ground attack; and to supervise the relevant training of operational aircrew. Moreover:

- You will collect information by correspondence with American P/W in enemy camps.
- You will send instructions and requests for information to Americans in enemy camps.
- You will advise on counter-escape measures for enemy P/W in American prison camps.
- Once this command becomes mobile you will be responsible for the interrogation and collection of information from enemy P/W in American control.

On top of all this, Holt was to co-operate with 'one appropriate unit established in the War Department' – MIS-X was not created till over ten weeks later – and moreover, to 'observe the strictest secrecy and exercise extreme caution in disclosing some aspects of the work even to senior officers.' Spaatz's initiative, and Holt's energy and common sense, thus gave escape and evasion work a flying start in the European theatre of American operations, in a staff branch simply called P/W & X.

Major-General G. V. Strong, the head of MID in 1942–3 – on no account to be confused with his English namesake, Major-General K. W. D. Strong, who was for a time General Eisenhower's chief of intelligence – warmly supported the work of MIS-X, which was created while he was chairman of the American Joint Intelligence Committee. He chose to head the CPM branch Colonel Catesby ap C. Jones, an efficient and imperturbable general staff officer, who also did all he could to further the aims of MIS-X; which, with interrogation of enemy prisoners, comprised the whole of his bureaucratic empire. Jones was a Southern gentleman, descended from the Catesby ap R. Jones to whom command of the *Merrimac* fell in the first action ever fought between ironclad warships, in 1862. It was his task, as it was Crockatt's in London, to make sure that the enemy-prisoner and own-forces'-prisoner halves of the machine never counteracted each other, so he necessarily took a good deal of interest in detail; but he interfered as little as he could.

The effective head of MIS-X from its inception was Lieutenant-Colonel J. Edward Johnston. Ed Johnston, a very wealthy man – heir to the Lucky Strike tobacco fortune – had good looks, an even Southern temper and a beautiful wife as well. He had plenty of the calm that a good secret service staff officer needs, and coupled to it the drive and competence of a good business man; MIS-X had no more troubles at its summit than MI 9 did.

A little needs to be said about how MIS-X got on with the rest of the American war machine. Army-Navy rivalry was not of great importance to it; even the US Navy was prepared to admit that an army department might be of some use to it in teaching sailors and naval airmen how to behave on land. Nor were there serious troubles about money. Johnston told Crockatt, teasingly, on 30 June 1943 that 'MIS-X has been given some confidential sums – not any such huge sums as you are able to obtain'; this was a reflection of the British secret service's legendary reputation. Most of the financial papers are still withheld, in America as in Britain, but one fragment of interest has slipped through: Johnston's confidential annual budget prepared in late September 1944 was for $160,735.04 (excluding pay), of which $40,000 was to go on escape kits, $20,000 on pocket radio equipment, $40,000 on special rewards for escape assistance, and $8,000 on foreign currency. These figures are so tiny, compared to the colossal sums the USA were then spending daily, that they may only have been put forward as cover for something larger.

The Americans did not have as many secret services as the British; this simplified life for MIS-X. No trace has been found of difficulties with the FBI. Some details will emerge below of relations with OSS. Where those relations mattered most, in the field in Yugoslavia, they were friendly enough. There are some indications that OSS harboured imperialist designs on MIS-X; perhaps one day someone in the know will explain what they were.

In sum, the organising of escape and evasion was one aspect of the world war in which the Americans and the British could and did co-operate with little of the friction that marked their relations on, say, Asian strategy. There were of course quarrels on minor and trumpery points; some choosy American aircrew, for example, disliked British escape kits and did not hesitate to say so, though others found them wonderful. But by and large, all went smoothly. Relations were often indeed, as Churchill said in another context, 'an absolute brotherhood'.

Crockatt's own impressive personality counted for much in this. Not only did he stimulate Holt; he made a tremendous hit in Washington (and, in passing, in New York) when they both visited America from 28 January to 15 March 1943. His bonnet and tartan trews and the panache with which he wore them enhanced the originality, almost the eccentricity, of his approach to war; people felt in him the practical daring of a young Lochinvar.

The Americans went even beyond the concepts he had adopted, and spread through their armed forces a new idea. This was that a man who was shot down or cut off on enemy territory, or who became a prisoner of war in any other way, was to regard himself not as a limp plaything of the nearest visible authority, but as a combatant posted to a new unit. He remained wholly in the service of the Crown or of the

President. The new unit, whether of potential escapers or of actual evaders, was as a rule much more loosely organised than the battalion, regiment, ship or squadron from which he had come; that it was organised at all seemed almost incredible to a newly-arrived prisoner, observing the stench, smoke and din of a large barrack hut, or to a recently shot-down evader, confronted with a railway rush-hour crowd or a big provincial cafe. Yet organised, in its unobtrusive way, it was. If an evader found himself in touch with an escape line he must obey every order from it, as promptly and as explicitly as he had obeyed orders from his previous commanding officer. And every prisoner of war, nominally – legally even – under the control of the enemy camp commandant, was really subordinate to the camp's senior British or American officer, the SBO or SAO. In the camps where British and American prisoners were mixed, the SAO and the SBO decided between themselves which was the senior. Each junior might perhaps tacitly reserve the right to command his own nationals in an emergency, on a vital difference of opinion with his colleague; one or two such cases arose in Germany in the closing stages, in April 1945. If ever a camp commandant and an SAO or SBO issued contra-dictory orders – which, again, hardly ever happened – prisoners knew where their duty lay.

This then was the system. How in practice did it work?

# First Encounters: 1940

MI 9's original vast single room in the Metropole Hotel was hardly suitable for the sort of business its staff had to transact, and they had to work in it long before the open-plan office became fashionable. At least they worked fast, in the breathing-space afforded by the lull in actual fighting.

On 5 January 1940 Evans, not even yet formally a member of the department delivered a model lecture to half-a-dozen colleagues, some of whom in turn were lecturing to army and air force audiences in France before the spring was out. Evans was never much of a man for being told what to do, instead of deciding for himself, and he soon gave up air force liaison altogether in order to devote himself to the business of collecting a strong team of lecturers from among the escapers of the previous war. He assembled ten others who, like himself, had succeeded in getting back from behind the enemy's lines, including – before he went east – M. C. C. Harrison. All were happy to lecture on the difficulties of being a prisoner of war, on the attitude prisoners should take to each other and to their captors, and on the problems and methods of escape.

Notes for a specimen lecture, drawn from later in the war and bearing the unmistakeable stamp that Crockatt set on all MI 9 teaching, though with none of his distinction of style, will be found in Appendix 2 below. All these lectures had in common insistence on the secrecy of the subject, and on the importance of resolute and imaginative action taken firmly but not too fast. It was always stressed that the best chances of escape were to be found in the first few days or hours, even in the first few minutes after capture. This applied particularly to soldiers, for front-line troops might well be too busy with their current battle to bother to pursue a prisoner who simply ran off, and to airmen, for they might first fall into the hands of gamekeepers or other rural authorities who had never themselves before had the task of guarding an alert, robust adult. An evader had to begin by getting very promptly clear of the wreck of his aircraft, if he was near it; but a careful survey of the country round him, to establish if he could exactly where he was, came next on his list of priorities in Europe, and was even more advisable in Asia.

Such calls for prompt and steady action were similar enough to the aggressive doctrines already familiar in well-trained combatant units, to get MI 9's and MIS-X's lecturers a ready hearing from an appreciative audience. A constant difficulty with combat aircrew was to persuade them that 'capture was not merely a remote possibility but a daily fact.' One difficulty beset them all the same: the reluctance of old-fashioned commanders to admit that their men might ever surrender. As late as 1943 a few units, including one famous fighting formation – the British 7th Armoured Division – could be found in which no escape training had ever been given at all. General Patton's views on the subject were transformed when his son-in-law became a prisoner; thereafter his troops got the full MIS-X treatment. Admirals were particularly stubborn in refusing to allow their crews' time to be wasted, as they saw it, in a piece of training hardly likely to be relevant to a sea career. They were to this extent justified, that among subjects of the Crown who eventually escaped or evaded capture only one per cent came from the navy. No United States Navy escapers or evaders were recorded at all by MI 9. MIS-X knew better; but they were indeed few, all from the Pacific. Those who were eventually rescued after their ships had been sunk by enemy action – the future President Kennedy and the future Earl Mountbatten provide two famous examples, among many thousands – are not included in those MI 9 figures, for they had never been in enemy-held ships or territory; nor are the celebrated prisoners recaptured from the

*Altmark* in Norwegian waters in February 1940, for they were merchant seamen.

In naval actions in winter on the high seas, the prospects of surviving to be taken prisoner were indeed slight. For sailors whose work was going to take them close inshore in light craft, the outlook was different. A few enterprising commanders, notably Mountbatten, early appreciated the need for escape training of such people as Royal Marine commandos, beach-masters, beach pilotage parties, midget submarine crews, and the crews of light coastal forces; a number of interesting escapes and evasions resulted.

For the air force, as for the army, the prospect of capture was less remote than for the crew of a great warship, and encouragement, mild at first, for MI 9's lectures was given by high commanders. The audiences to whom they spoke were not the dullards of a peacetime regular army of the early 1900s. They were most of them young, eager men, under-informed about war, anxious to learn; angry at the political trap that had snapped round them, making them fight Nazism instead of pursuing some more peaceable career; and brought up on a different set of unspoken assumptions from those that governed the minds of their elderly commanders. Many of them had read such books as *The Escaping Club*, and the concept of escape as a quasi-romantic adventure was one that they could readily seize. One of the lecturers' first and vital tasks was to be as unromantic and as matter-of-fact as could be. They had to stress the need for a would-be escaper to be severely practical: what was he going to wear, what was he going to eat, how would he carry his food, where was he going to go, how would he find his way, who was he going to be? All these were essential questions, and unless a man knew the answers to them already he had no occasion to ask the basic one, how was he going to get away from his immediate prison?

One of Crockatt's principal aims at this early stage in the war was to inculcate and foster in the armed services the quality to which he had to give the cumbrous name of escape-mindedness: the constant readiness, if caught in enemy hands, to work for and to seize on every conceivable chance of getting out of them. His lecturers preached escape-mindedness all over the BEF, the AEAF, home forces, bomber command, fighter command, the fleet, anyone who would hear, and preached it with success. To such an extent indeed did they succeed that the phrase, 'It is an officer's duty to escape', has now become more or less proverbial; and the duty to escape applied to all ranks, not only to commissioned officers. Crockatt stressed perpetually that on this point of duty there was no differentiation between ranks at all.

He knew that training was important, but believed his intelligence role to be more important still. Winterbottom, Evans and Rhodes all had a busy spring working out a satisfactory code which could be hidden in an apparently perfectly innocent letter sent by or to a prisoner of war. (Evans had plenty of energy for code work as well as lecturing.) Many officers and a few other ranks had already made private arrangements with their wives for some sort of coded interchange. Few married readers will have any trouble in reconstructing for themselves the sort of simple system that a couple could set up which nothing but a brilliant flash of intuition could ever break – provided it was well thought out and carefully used. Such systems were known in MI 9 as 'dotty codes', not so much because they were unprofessional efforts and therefore out of the normal run, as because they quite often used a row of dots in the heading or the text of the letter to show where the message began and ended.

With the help of a Foreign Office expert called Hooker, Winterbottom and his colleagues developed a code called HK through which several people were communicating with London from Germany by November 1940. One of them, John Parker, who had been caught in a raid on Guernsey, had much trouble in getting the Germans to grant him prisoner of war status instead of shooting him as a spy. He made up for the failure of his raid by extra industry in passing on his code. Like several codes developed later, HK was at once fairly simple to use, and in skilled hands unusually hard to detect. All the user had to do was to indicate by the fashion in which he wrote the date that the letter contained a message, show by his opening words which part of the code he was using, and then write an apparently normal chatty letter, from which an inner meaning could be unravelled with the code's help. Full details of exactly how this could be done, with real examples, were published in 1971 in a book by a Scottish Jew who was dental officer in, among other camps, Colditz.[8]

The incoming messages when decoded were passed to Crockatt, who made up his mind what distribution they needed. Some could go straight to service technical departments such as MI 14; the Air Ministry in particular would be interested in anything bearing on the performance of Allied or of enemy aircraft, the navy's operational intelligence centre was always hungry for movements of ships and submarines. More political matters Crockatt would probably pass to Dansey who would give them what further distribution he chose. It was a considerable intellectual burden for a man to carry alone, yet Crockatt was a man who enjoyed responsibility. He preserved his good looks and debonair ways all through the war and beyond; to act as the focal point through which so many reports passed seemed positively to refresh him.

As well as his main duty as head of a section in the intelligence directorate, he had the unruly Clayton Hutton to supervise on top of all the routine administration. 'Clutty' had as busy and as productive a spring as anyone. He got the British Museum to collect for him from second-hand bookshops in Bloomsbury

---

8    J. M. Green, *From Colditz in Code*, 161–86. A single example had appeared nearly twenty years earlier in Richard Pape's best-selling *Boldness be my Friend* at 155, with an indication of the system's range and value. See the specimen code in Appendix 3.

about fifty true escape stories of the 1914–18 war; had them summarised by the sixth form of Crockatt's old school, Rugby; realised from the summaries the indispensability of maps; flew to Edinburgh, saw the managing director of Bartholomew's, and secured all the maps he wanted. Still proceeding on 'not what you know but whom you know' lines, he secured some silk from a friend in the textile world and struggled with a jobbing printer to transfer the maps to silk. Adding pectin, a natural gelatin, to the printer's ink turned out to be the way to get a perfect impression. Funds ran to buying plenty of white silk, and soon most operational aircrew carried at least a silk map of Germany, about eighteen inches square, stored somewhere about their flying kit. A friend at his club put him in the way of some Japanese pulp convertible into thin non-rustling paper; more and more specialised maps resulted, some of them hidden between the front and the back of playing cards. (Some cards are on show at the RAF museum at Hendon.)

Clayton Hutton's next preoccupation was with compasses. He found a firm of instrument-makers, Blunt's in the Old Kent Road, run by two elderly brothers with imagination, enterprise, and a highly skilled staff. He conjured up a thousand feet of steel strip for them. Within a week they had five thousand magnetised bars, nearly an inch long, ready for him and he and they went on to design numerous other types of miniature compass. Tiny brass cylinders, a quarter of an inch across, with a luminous compass needle balanced within them, could be hidden in a pipe or a fountain pen, or in the back of a service button or cap badge. Ones twice as large, painted over, formed sound bases for collar studs, which were still then commonly worn by men of all classes and would arouse no kind of suspicion; an escaper or evader could scrape the paint off with a fingernail when he needed to use the compass. As many as 2,358,853 compasses of various designs, including 1,301,937 half-inch brass ones and 91,591 studs, were made and distributed by MI 9 during the war. Five hundred of the half-inch ones were specially hand sewn into shirt collars and belts for the British First Airborne Division just before the attack on Arnhem.

Clayton Hutton turned his mind next to other normally carried, unsuspicious objects which might be magnetisable. People often, in those days before the Biro, carried a lead pencil attached to a breast or inside pocket by a sliding metal clip, usually made of tin. It was easy to make the clip of steel, magnetise it, and punch a tiny dent beneath it at its point of balance so that it would swing on its own pencil's tip. Simpler still, though a shade less secure: in an age when almost everybody who shaved at all shaved with a safety razor, Clayton Hutton eventually arranged for all razor blades sold through forces' canteens to be magnetised, with the north end of the magnet at the same end as the start of the maker's name printed on the blade. So thereafter, anyone taken prisoner with his kit who was allowed to keep his razor – which was by no means always the case – had at least one compass with him, if he could find a piece of thread on which to swing it.

Saws came next. MI 9 produced several formidable hacksaws. One, used successfully by one of the authors to cut his way out of an improvised cell and still in his possession, measures 4 ½" x ½" is edged on one long side only, and has a hole at one end so that it can be hidden by being dropped down a trouserleg or some convenient crevice on a bit of thread or string. One was used at Arnhem, in a battlefield emergency, as a surgical saw. Some had a rudimentary grip. A species that was fitting flints into antlers to make picks in palaeolithic times did not really need a grip provided by authority, as people could usually work out their own from an odd bit of wood. The strong-wristed could use their bare hands, perhaps with a handkerchief as baffle. And a hacksaw of course could be magnetised, and swung on a thread, as easily as a razor blade.

Clayton Hutton also secured some surgical saws – Gigli saws was their technical name – which were in fact pieces of very strong wire with a serrated edge; readily enough concealed – in a textile cover – as bootlaces. These led him on to his most extraordinary invention: the escape boot. It looked like an ordinary fleece-lined flying boot with a strip of webbing round the ankle. Hidden in a cloth loop at the top of the boot was a small knife. If the wearer cut the webbing with the knife, he separated the leggings from a pair of respectable black walking shoes; if he slit up the seams of the leggings, he had the two halves of a fleece-lined waistcoat, waiting to be sewn together, as well.

This was a trifle too good to be true. The boot was popular with aircrew at first, because ordinary flying boots were conspicuous, and could easily draw attention towards evaders to whom all unfriendly attentions were unwelcome. Yet when converted into a shoe it still suffered from a vice of flying boots – in wet weather it got waterlogged and made running difficult; even walking in it could be tiring. Worse, if one flew at any height, it was not warm enough. Chill air seeped in through the ankle webbing, and made the wearer's feet bitterly cold at great heights. This fault turned out incurable, and the boot was abandoned.

Several instances from the 1914–18 war led Clayton Hutton to consider convertible uniforms – that is, RAF or other service uniforms which might, by a few deft touches, be made to resemble those of the Luftwaffe or the German army. A still more ingenious device was the setting into a blanket – an obvious present for a prisoner from a doting, if fictitious, aunt – of the cutting-out pattern by which the blanket could be converted into a civilian overcoat; the pattern showed up when the blanket was washed, even in cold water. But this was later on in the war, in 1944; we must come back to Clayton Hutton's most inventive six months in the first half of 1940.

His most widespread aid, for which thousands of people who had never heard his name were grateful, was the escape box: a pair of flat transparent acetate plastic boxes, one fitting closely inside the other, filled with malted milk tablets, boiled sweets, a bar or two of plain chocolate, matches, a few benzedrine tablets for energy and a few halazone tablets for purifying water, a rubber waterbottle to hold about a pint, a razor (with magnet-ised blade, of course, as well as soap), a needle and thread, and a fishing hook and line. Few if any fish were caught, but the line was invaluable if one's braces (suspenders) broke, or if one's arm needed a sling. The original model for the box was the flat tin of fifty cigarettes, which became harder to get in the spring of 1940 because Clayton Hutton had just bought 10,000 of them from W.D. and H.O. Wills; this proved not quite large enough. The end product would fit comfortably in the outer front map pocket of battledress trousers or in the lower side pocket of a service dress tunic; more comfortably still, after an ingenious American pointed out in 1942 that it needed to be slightly curved to fit the human frame, and that rounded corners would damage uniforms less. In a final refinement Halex Limited, the manufacturers, produced a single plastic box with a watertight screw-neck top, including a compass built into it, so that the user could find his way without having to unpack any of his intricately assembled set of goodies. This did not turn out well; too many of these boxes leaked. After the war, surviving boxes made admirable sewing- or button-boxes for airmen's or commandos' wives.

These boxes were automatically distributed to aircrew going on operations, one per man, as soon as station IOs had grasped the system and enough had been manufactured; that is, more or less universally in the RAF from the autumn of 1940 and in the USAAF from the middle of 1942. Fleet Air Arm pilots in aircraft carriers were supplied at their admirals' and captains' whim. In theory, a box would keep a man going for forty-eight hours, while the hunt for him flared up and then died down, and he lay hidden.

With the boxes, those going on flights overland received also a coloured purse containing currency for any country that was to be flown over, and a small brass compass, and the relevant silk map, and a hacksaw file. Purses were of course accountable, as they contained money, and were supposed to be collected by the

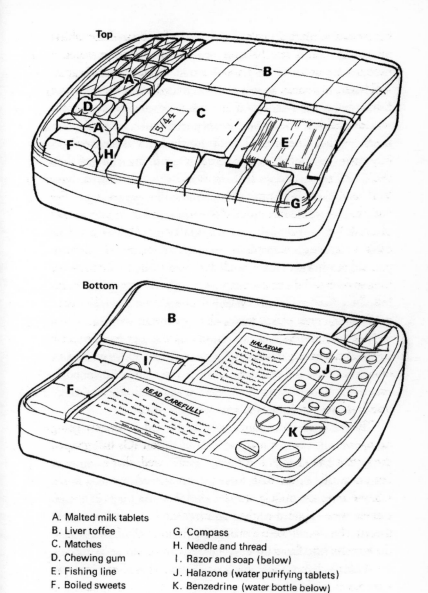

**Top**

**Bottom**

A. Malted milk tablets
B. Liver toffee
C. Matches
D. Chewing gum
E. Fishing line
F. Boiled sweets
G. Compass
H. Needle and thread
I. Razor and soap (below)
J. Halazone (water purifying tablets)
K. Benzedrine (water bottle below)

IO – automatically, again – at the debriefing at the end of each flight. The whole process soon became one to which everybody got used, and in which people trusted warmly. There is even a tale that once, when by one of those muddles familiar to anybody who has been any sort of junior manager the escape kits failed to turn up at a newly-opened airfield in Tunisia, USAAF aircrew there refused duty until they did: they were not delayed long.

There was also a Polish squadron IO who, when his squadron's tour of duty was over, persuaded a foolish bank clerk to change all the money in its purses for sterling, and gave a stupendous party on the proceeds. When Crockatt remonstrated, his excuse was, 'Well, sir, I thought you would like us to celebrate the fact that none of us had to use the money'. Crockatt took no further action; but he delighted to tell the story to visiting potentates.

This too lay some years in the future in the early months of 1940 when Russia was supporting Germany, France was still unbeaten, and America, Italy and Japan – to speak of no smaller powers – were all still neutral. Crockatt and all his staff had to begin by operating in a void, and it is a tribute to the soundness of their judgement that hardly any of the decisions they took in this opening, theoretical phase needed to be reversed.

Premises were an obvious problem. As the country gradually adapted from peace to war, many large private houses and hotels that could no longer be privately staffed were requisitioned and many hutted camps were built. MI 9's immediate need was for interrogation centres. Rawlinson's MI 9a had a hutted camp at Cockfosters in north London for any German airmen who might be shot down over Great Britain, and MI 9b secured a floor of the Great Central Hotel at Marylebone station. An eyewitness account from two years later by Airey Neave is too good to leave unquoted:

> Before the war, the Great Central Hotel held a strong attrac-
> tion for me. Not that there was any romantic experience to

record – a drink or two, a hilarious bath at four o'clock in the
morning before taking a milk train from Marylebone in white
tie and tails.

I was drawn to the magnificent dullness and solidity of
the hotel. I liked the brass bedsteads, the marble figures on the
stairs and the massive afternoon tea. Outside this refuge my
young world was threatened by Hitler. Inside, I could pretend
that I belonged to a safer age.

We were directed to the reception desk where two years
before a splendid blonde in black had been on guard.

Now there was a sergeant at the desk.

'What is this place, sergeant?'

'The London Transit Camp, sir.' He studied me politely.
'Where are you from, sir?'

'Germany.'

He did not bat an eyelid.

'Quite so, sir. Then it will be MI 9 you want. They are on
the second floor.'

I climbed the wide stairs, with my cheap suitcase, still feeling I was a prisoner arriving at a new camp. The corridors
were stripped and bleak. Everywhere I could hear the sound of
typewriters and the bustle of troops in transit.

I entered what had been a large double-bedroom, which
now served as an office for the interrogation of returned
escapers by MI 9. In place of the brass bedsteads were trestle
tables and wire baskets. For half an hour, I gloomily watched
the rain falling in Marylebone Road, and the mist obscuring the
distant barrage balloons.

The senior staff at the centre – one or two of them living in
what was left of London society, with a varied body of acquaintances – were well placed to check escapers' bona fides and
impressed on all of them the absolute indispensability of silence
about their helpers. There was a rule, imposed by Churchill
himself, that nobody could be held at the centre for longer than

forty-eight hours before being allowed to rejoin his relatives in the British Isles if he wished to do so, unless there were grave reasons for suspecting him of some crime. If there were such reasons he had to be charged and placed under arrest.

Cockfosters and Marylebone were both virtually empty at first, but as soon as fighting began in earnest in northern and Western Europe they justified themselves. 'Much useful information', the war diary reported, was secured at Cockfosters about the organisation and tactics of the Luftwaffe from prisoners taken in the Norwegian campaign. There was a curious scare there in June 1940; for the coders of MI 9, keeping an eye on prisoners' mail into Cockfosters from Germany, discovered and broke a series of code messages which seemed to indicate a German plan to release the prisoners there by a heavily armed parachute landing in the neighbourhood. This was probably only an ingenious propaganda move by Goebbels, intended to terrify the British about the insecurity of their own capital's suburbs. Peter Fleming at any rate concluded in retrospect that the Germans never had any real intention of using airborne troops outside the projected invasion area on the south-east coast. The Cockfosters incident, a skirmish in the war of nerves, no doubt had some bearing on the dispatch of over 500 prisoners to Canada before the end of the month.

The Marylebone centre also rapidly proved its worth. The Norwegian campaign provided a small quota of escapers and evaders, but it was not till 10 August 1940 that the bulk of them were got back to London from Sweden, to which nearly all of them had made their way. Their experiences had been dictated by the severe terrain of Scandinavia and by other purely local aspects of the war. Much more of general use and importance was to be got from a score or two of officers and men, who passed briefly through German hands in May and early June 1940 – or narrowly escaped doing so – during the great *Blitzkrieg* in the west, and came to the Great Central Hotel when they reached England. MI 9 reacted remarkably promptly; though

its war diary complained also that the distribution of returning troops was so higgledy-piggledy that there was virtually
no way of making sure that returned escapers passed through
its mesh.

About once a month the army issued a short confidential
white paper called an army training memorandum. (The word
'confidential' was not used; the front cover was marked 'NOT
TO BE TAKEN INTO FRONT LINE TRENCHES', a phrase
from the previous great war.) The thirty-fourth issue, on 31
July 1940 – the text must have been ready some time earlier –
included a two-page appendix on escape training in the light of
these recent lessons learned. A copy went to every single officer
in the army, so no regimental officer needed any longer to feel
ignorant of the outlines of the subject, or unable to explain it
to his men.

Much stress was laid on the importance of escaping quickly
while still in the hands of fighting troops, and on seizing chances
promptly when they were offered. It was also clear that to possess
or to secure civilian clothes was of cardinal importance, since an
escaper could fade into the crowd inside them in a way that was
not open to a uniformed man. A warning was dropped, all the
same, that 'a civilian helps an escaped prisoner at the risk of his
own life'. One paragraph is worth quoting in full:

The following points as noted by an escaper from France in
civilian clothes illustrate the importance of conforming to the
habits of a country from which a prisoner is attempting to
break out:

Do not march in a military fashion, but adopt a tired slouch.

Try and 'collect' a bicycle. They proved invaluable to
several escapers.

Do not wear a wrist watch. Carry it in your pocket.

Sling your haversack: French peasants commonly carry one
in this way, but never as a pack on their backs.

Do not use a cane or walking-stick: it is a British custom.

> Get rid of army boots and adopt a pair of rope-soled shoes as worn by peasants, if procurable.
>
> French peasants are generally clean-shaven, though a slight growth of beard is not uncommon.
>
> A beret is a very effective disguise.
>
> Village priests are likely to be helpful. Care should be exercised in approaching them and one should avoid being seen talking to them.[9]

A further paragraph stressed that 'Many escapers brought back valuable military information. Escapers should notice everything they can of military importance both before and after escape.' This was a presage of what Crockatt had always foreseen as a vital role for MI 9, the furnishing of a series of up-to-date pictures of what was going on in the enemy's camp. The return of an officer and two cadets in a small boat from Dunkirk, guided by one of Clayton Hutton's miniature compasses, was a striking minor feat of navigation and a small feather in the section's cap; Crockatt was aware that there were more important things to be done when the dust of battle had settled.

When the *Blitzkrieg* swept over the Low Countries and northern France in May and June 1940, nearly two million French soldiers and airmen became prisoners of war. So did about 50,000 people in British uniform, almost all of them from the army, and only three of them as it happened equipped with an MI 9 code.[10] In addition, about 2,000 British wounded for whom there was no room in the ships were left behind

---

9    Army training memorandum 34 (1940), 18.
10   WO 208/3242, 300. An earlier estimate – MI 9 war diary for 31 August 1940 – put the total of British prisoners at 34,000 (WO 165/39). The war diary mentioned on 31 May 1940 that a Squadron Leader Turner, who knew the code, was a prisoner. So did another RAF officer and a naval officer, both captured a few days later.

in hospitals in Flanders, Artois and Picardy when the main Expeditionary Force withdrew from Dunkirk. So rapid and so chaotic had been the course of battle that at least another 2,000 British were left wandering about the countryside, either because they had lost their units in the confusion, or because they had deliberately absconded, sooner than obey an order to surrender. Perhaps a thousand of these fugitive evaders eventually found their way back in time to be of use in the war. One or two deserve special mention.

As the seventh Earl of Cardigan gathered up his reins to lead out the Light Brigade on its fatal charge at Balaclava, he was heard to murmur, 'Ah well, here goes the last of the Brudenells'. He was wrong; another Earl of Cardigan fought in France in 1940 as a subaltern in the Royal Army Service Corps, was captured at Boulogne, jumped off a lorry, walked out alone southwards into Spain, and has published an account of his adventure, *I Walked Alone*, which is a model for anyone stuck in a similar fix. One of his recurring themes is the readiness of ordinary peasants to help him, by providing food, drink, clothes and shelter, in spite of the danger they knew they ran in doing so.

Such help was available for many other wanderers, but most of them were picked up by the local Belgian or French police and handed over to the Germans, who dispatched them to prisoner of war camps. A very few managed to go to ground, and were absorbed into peasant communities; of no more use to the war effort, but at least out of enemy hands. Of these again a few quietly stayed on after the war was over, instead of risking a trial for desertion if they returned whence they came. One trio of privates who took refuge in a French peasant's cottage even found they were being held virtual prisoners, in the confident belief that the British secret service would one day pay a large ransom for them.

Those who were captured and then marched right into Germany, without being able to get away *en route*, did not all reach their prisoner of war camps in a mood favourable to the

French or the Belgians. Many of them felt let down by their neighbours; they did not appreciate the extent to which earlier the British had let their neighbours down by failing to stand up sooner and more firmly to the Nazi menace; and they did not want to contemplate a journey back across Belgian and French territory. If escape-minded at all, they aimed for Switzerland or Sweden or south-east Europe.

However, the earliest escapers all got away on French or Belgian soil, and their plain course lay west or south. One couple walked through to Finisterre, got away from Camaret near Brest by boat, and were in England for Christmas. Hardly any others who tried to get away through Brittany succeeded this early in the war.

One lucky pair of officers, one in the army and one in the navy, did not have to walk so far. They slipped away from the column while being marched into Germany and found a small yacht on the Norman coast. With the leave of its owner – a French professor – they sailed it away, crossed the Channel, were ignored by two British destroyers on anti-invasion patrols in spite of their frantic efforts to attract attention, and sailed right up the Beaulieu River to land. The soldier, Major (later Colonel) Leslie Hulls of the Highland Division, had escaped from the Turks in 1918 and claims the unique distinction of having escaped successfully in two world wars. Two privates in the same division, called Campbell and Oliver – Campbell had never left South Uist in his life till he went to join the army at the age of nineteen in 1939 – also got out by sea, a harder way; they stole a boat near St Valéry and rowed across to Sussex.

Everyone else who got away had to turn south in the wake of the mass Franco-Belgian civilian exodus and cross as best they could the demarcation line set up between German-occupied and unoccupied France. Personal experience leads us to another instance, the case of Jimmy Langley. As a young subaltern in the Coldstream Guards, badly wounded in the arm and head, he was left behind on the beach at Dunkirk because the stretcher on which he lay took up space in a boat that four men could fill. He was made prisoner, still prone, and had his shattered left arm amputated. With other wounded officers he was moved to a hospital in Lille, whence, withdrawing the parole imposed on him by senior British army doctors, he escaped on 10 October 1940 by the simple expedient of getting a corporal to give him a leg up through an unguarded lodge window. The stump of his arm was still suppurating. He had hopes of an address a mile away, where the family responded marvellously, giving him plain clothes and a night's shelter. He had money enough for fares; and after some weeks' scarifying odyssey, turned up in Marseilles.

Other escapers and evaders found almost uniformly, with Cardigan and Langley, every sort of readiness to help them among the poorer sorts of people and every sort of reserve among most of the rich. Once they got over the demarcation line they were still liable to arrest by the local police, but were no longer at all likely to be handed over to the enemy. The Vichy government's policy was to concentrate them successively at Marseilles, where they were lodged in Fort St Jean; from January 1941, at St Hippolyte du Fort at Nimes; or at La Turbie, just outside Monte Carlo; not quite prisoners, not quite free. In Marseilles, officers were only required to report for a Monday morning roll call at which rations were issued; most of them promptly sold their rations on the black market and lived in lodgings on the proceeds. Fort St Jean, at the entrance to the Vieux Port, had been a collecting point for the Foreign Legion. It bore Lyautey's motto over the gate: 'You have asked for death, I will give it you', hardly the warmest of welcomes for a recent ally. In principle, the fort was where British and Commonwealth serving men who reached Marseilles were supposed to go; but there were other and less official parts of the city where they could try to settle. Moreover, as usually happens when many people gather after a disaster, a few of them with natural gifts for leadership emerged and began to take control.

One was a simple Presbyterian pastor, with no idea of controlling anybody but himself, yet with equal faith and strength of character. Donald Caskie, the minister of the Scots Kirk in Paris, had never made any secret of what he thought of the Nazis. He preached against them often; his favourite text was Hosea's 'they have sown the wind, and they shall reap the whirlwind'. He therefore thought it prudent to leave Paris before the Germans reached it, and managed to get as far as Marseilles. There he took charge of the seamen's mission. This soon became known in the Marseilles underworld, and beyond, as a comparatively safe spot to which British soldiers and airmen, as well as seamen, could be directed. Caskie performed a series of small miracles sheltering and feeding them, and was helped and encouraged to do so by an eminent evader from the Highland Division's stand at St Valéry-en-Caux on the north Normandy coast, I. P. Garrow.

Ian Garrow, a tall, dark-haired captain in the Seaforth Highlanders in his early twenties, who spoke school French with a noticeable Scots accent, had shown considerable enterprise and resource in getting across France from coast to coast under his own steam. He made it his business to look after the other ranks of his own division who also reached Marseilles, enlisted Caskie's help and was ready to assist outsiders as well. The sense that 'Auld Scotland counts for something still' was strong in them both. The local police soon became aware of Garrow's and Caskie's activities; as each was so obviously a Scot they took for granted that both of them were acting as a front for some hidden manipulator from the legendary Intelligence Service. The two were in fact entirely on their own. Caskie was inclined to trust that the Lord would provide. Garrow, a shade more sceptical, made contact with the American consul and with various rich expatriates. He also made Home splendid local friends, notably Louis and Renee Nouveau and a fearless New Zealander, Nancy Fiocca, better known from Russell Braddon's life of her as Nancy Wake, and later one of the stars of Maurice Buckmaster's 'independent French' section of SOE.

They were able to prepare a few makeshift escapes with the help of friends and the friends of friends and by the end of the year had laid the groundwork of an organisation that was to become famous. Langley was among their helpers, though not on a large scale. He registered at Fort St Jean, but was allowed as usual to live out and soon met Garrow who employed him – a one-armed man excites sympathy rather than suspicion – as a courier to secure money from a rich source on the Riviera. The money was deftly fitted, by a trick – without consulting Langley or Garrow – into the pockets of the gang who had arranged the Blue Train robbery, that criminal sensation of the summer of 1939. Langley went before a medical board of which Dr Rodocanachi, a strong resister, was a member, and was at once repatriated, only to get recruited in March 1941 on a cursory inspection by Dansey to replace the shadowy 4Z as P15.

The fine summer of 1940, and the several million refugees who had taken part in the exodus of May/June and were trying to struggle home, produced a brief evaders' paradise and made life more simple also for those who escaped on the line of march into Germany. There were so many thousands of people crowding every large railway station, so many hundreds trudging across damaged main road bridges, such a flood of homeless waifs that a few more could slip into the stream without remark. Richard Broad for example, a subaltern in the Highland Division at St Valéry, was ordered by his battalion commander – just before the division surrendered – to take seven privates with him back to Scotland by any means he could find; the compass bearing of Paris was the only information he was offered to help him. 'Snow White and the Seven Dwarfs', as the party inevitably became known, were carried through in the end by Broad's simple courage and unwavering resource; a feat of enterprise and stolid endurance that included a spell in a nunnery at Honfleur, clean contrary to the relevant order's rules, for which the Mother Superior was given papal absolution after the war.

Evaders were far more numerous at this stage from the army than from the air force, but some air force ones made more stir. The most energetic of them, Wing Commander (Sir) Basil Embry, who later rose to be an air chief marshal, had a splendid record: captured after a parachute descent over Flanders, he escaped, was twice recaptured, and twice escaped again – leaving the odd dead sentry behind him – saw Hitler enter Paris, and turned up in England a few weeks later, wearing clothes – a top hat included – he had lifted off a scarecrow in a Belgian field. His was a personality so vigorous and so forceful that people listened to him and remembered what he said, much more than was the case with duller or shyer men. His example and his energy did much to fix evasion firmly in the heads both of MI 9's staff and of the Air Ministry's, as one of the modes of war to which they would thereafter need to pay full heed.

MI 9 recognised in fact that it had been a mistake to lecture so far almost exclusively about escaping and about resisting interrogation if caught. These subjects remained of course in their lecture syllabus and such films as *Name, Rank and Number* – of which Rawlinson had supervised the making in April 1940 – hammered home some of their lessons all over the armed forces. But from the autumn of 1940, lectures to airborne commando and RAF units all stressed evasion as well as escape.

This is an instance of how ready Crockatt was to change his mind, when there was clear evidence that he had made a mistake. Flexibility of this kind was not a leading characteristic among most of his army contemporaries, yet from it much of MI 9's effectiveness arose.

Another basic point about which Crockatt changed his mind was where he was going to work. In Northumberland Avenue, only a block or two away from the main War Office building, his staffs were too much hemmed in by the massed bureaucrats of Whitehall. Anything unorthodox was not only frowned on but commented on; too many people outside his section were aware of his staff's movements and visitors. He had already decided to move if he could when on 13 September 1940, as the Battle of Britain approached its climax, a German bomb grazed a corner of the Metropole Hotel and started a fire. The actual damage was slight but the confusion and disorganisation in the building, not to speak of the smoke and the mess, were considerable. Crockatt decided to move into the country, and three weeks later did so. His whole section took over Wilton Park, a country house on the eastern edge of Beaconsfield in the Chilterns, just north of the London-Oxford road. In those days it was fairly well into the country, though within twenty-three miles of Charing Cross.

Camp 20, Beaconsfield, was the name by which Wilton Park came officially to be known. A sizeable hutted camp grew up between the house and the lodge gates, as the original early Georgian manor turned out not to be large enough to hold everyone on Crockatt's staff. The air was clean, there were views over beech woods, there were plenty of comfortable small houses in Beaconsfield in which married officers could live out; Crockatt's own home at Ashley Green lay eleven miles to the north. It was a good quiet place from which to press on with secret work.

Even Clayton Hutton was content: he had 'office accommodation that would have satisfied even Cecil B. de Mille'. Moreover, he found a private hide-out not far away on the edge of a disused graveyard, where he supposed – correctly – that none of the locals would care to come, and find out what he was experimenting with late at night; though later in the war an American colleague tracked him to it without difficulty. He pursued there various hobbies of his own, designing anti-tank grenades and a modern version of the lethal jungle blowpipe, as well as improving the escape kits he provided for MI 9.

All the staff found the move from London an advantage. In calm, quiet country air work went faster and more smoothly, and they were still only an hour or so away from the capital if needed for a conference. Crockatt continued a habit he had long found useful: any conversation that threatened to be awkward took place, if he had any hand in it, at Rules restaurant in Maiden Lane, off the Strand. 'A soft answer turneth away wrath' always seemed a good text to him; hospitality and Rules' cook helped him out of several awkward corners and encouraged his subordinates to work with him more cheerfully than ever.

From the lawn at Wilton Park they could only too easily see the glow of the second great fire of London reddening the sky on the night of 29/30 December 1940.[11]

---

11   Wilton Park's post-war history deserves a footnote. (Sir) Heinz Koppler took it on as a government-sponsored Anglo-German discussion centre, intended to introduce young German prisoners of war brought up under Goebbels to the ideas of a freer world. He carried the name with him down to Wiston House in Sussex, where the Wilton Park conference centre continues to provide a forum for intelligent analysis of current affairs by international audiences, particularly Germans and Americans, and a European discussion centre now runs in parallel with it for the benefit of the EEC.

# Building the Lines: Evasions 1940–42

The earliest evaders to return to the British lines were coming in even before the Dunkirk evacuation was completed in the first week of June 1940. Pilots shot down among friendly French or Belgians were mixed in with the stream of army stragglers. A flight lieutenant in bomber command called Parkinson, for example, survived the famous attack on the Meuse bridges on 14 May, though his aircraft did not; only thirty-two out of sixty-seven Fairey Battles returned. He got as far as the French battle-line, but was then mistaken for a German, and shot up. Langley met him in Marseilles, severely wounded, in January 1941. He found his way back to England, and became a Halifax pilot in a squadron which was engaged in drops to resistance; on one of these operations he was killed.

Quite possibly there was a light dusting of German agents in the evaders' mixture as well. Langley's battalion commander, the future Lord Skelmersdale, observed in the beach-head on 2 June that:

> About midday a strange figure in French peasant clothes, and speaking English, was brought in under escort to Divisional Headquarters. He said he was a pilot who had been shot down some ten days before near Abbeville. He had bailed out, and a French farmer had given him some clothes. He had made his way across country to Dunkirk. He said that the Germans were not making any attempt to break into the perimeter, that on the road by which he had come into Dunkirk they had only the equivalent of a platoon position; all their columns were pushing on to the south and towards Paris. I believed his story

and for the first time I felt that we should be allowed to get
away from Dunkirk.

First Division may have swallowed this tale; in retrospect,
scepticism is indicated. Had the pilot known anything at all
about the land battle, and about his own whereabouts when
shot down, he would have moved south from Abbeville, crossing the Somme somehow; stealing a boat, or swimming, if he
could find no unguarded bridge. Then he could have joined the
French. Instead, he implied he had travelled eighty miles, across
several rivers and canals – all with their bridges broken or under
German guard – through territory held by the newly victorious Wehrmacht. His tactical information moreover was clean
contrary to the truth: on 2 June a severe German attack was
made on the Dunkirk rearguard, repelled by Admiral Abrial's
French troops. He was brave and resourceful; whether he was
a genuine evader, or a German speaking excellent English
and reconnoitring the English segment of the beachhead,
remains unclear.

Conditions that summer were fine for evaders. Not only
was the weather set fair, but the Germans were almost as
surprised by the suddenness and completeness of their victory
as the French and Belgians were staggered by the extent of their
defeat. The best German intelligence officers were busy reaping
the harvest of Venlo and The Hague, cleaning up MI 6's prearranged networks; no one had yet done much about organising
those controls over movements that are so detestable a feature
of any dictatorship.

Moreover, there was tremendous readiness to help the Allied
cause in that originally small but uncommonly tough segment
of the newly conquered populations which refused to accept
the fact of conquest. People like Madame Fraser at Arras or
Langley's helper the Veuve Samiez at Lille were rare and splendid enough, but neither was unique. Every large town had a
few, almost every village might have one at least. The Poles, the

Belgians and the Dutch, with memories of centuries of occupation behind them, had more than the French or the Norwegians, but they might crop up anywhere. Many were priests; many were women; all were brave, far beyond the ordinary. The more successful of them were prudent as well, and so survived. (Of the two people just named, Madame Fraser lived to receive a George Medal; Madame Samiez disappeared altogether.)

A word is perhaps needed here to explain why this book has so far been written so largely in the masculine gender. The truth is that hardly any women in Allied uniform were taken prisoner; the world of prisoner of war camps was an almost exclusively male one. Indeed one of the major social horrors of being a prisoner of war, almost as bad as – some ardent spirits would say, even worse than – being deprived of one's liberty to move outside the wire, was that officer prisoners, who seldom left their camps, often had to go for months on end without setting eyes on a woman at all. On the other hand, evaders often found that they had to trust themselves entirely to women; and without the courage and devotion of its couriers and safe-house keepers, nearly all of them women, no evasion line could keep going at all. Several lines – we shall come to one in a moment – had women as their leaders. Evasion, like other forms of resistance, was one of the spheres of action in which women proved themselves again and again to be at least as effective as men, and earned the equality that the other sex has at last begun to re-acknowledge.

What in fact was MI 9 doing about helping to set lines up?

Darling found his cover of vice-consul in charge of repatriation at Lisbon useful. It gave him opportunities for meeting people who were travelling to or from Marseilles, and through some American acquaintances he began to exchange letters with Garrow, and to send money in to him. He was helped by various Americans, and by Madge Hoist, the English-born wife of a Norwegian Quaker shipbroker who had an office in Marseilles. Her husband, perhaps without Darling's knowledge, was working with SOE, which was in process of setting up the earliest of its own extra-secret evasion lines for moving agents in and out of France. These lines have been described in detail elsewhere. They were run by Leslie Humphreys, a friend of Langley's; and there was a good deal more interchange between them and MI 9's lines than the senior staffs of SOE or SIS were ever told of.

Indeed it was from an accidental and unintended by-product of a seaborne operation for SOE that one of the best and biggest evasion lines developed. Very early on Anzac Day, 25 April 1941, a Pole and a Maltese working for SOE were put ashore on a beach near the Etang de Canet, a few miles north of the eastern end of the Pyrenees. Modern tourism has turned the beach into a crowded bathing resort; at the time it was almost empty. They were landed by a skiff from HMS *Fidelity*, a 1,500-ton heavily armed merchantman of Marseillais origin and obscure purpose, lost with almost all hands not long afterwards. Later that night, the skiff overturned in a squall, before it could regain its parent ship; one man from it swam ashore.

He told the gendarme who shortly arrested him that he was Patrick Albert O'Leary, an evading Canadian airman. He was sent to St Hippolyte du Fort near Nimes, to join the British prisoners who had been moved there from Fort St Jean in Marseilles. Garrow got to hear of his arrival and of his personality, and managed to meet him. Each took instantly to the other, and was ready to trust him; even though Garrow could spot at once that O'Leary was not born an English speaker, and did not use the language in an accent that bore out his French Canadian cover. His name in fact was, and is, Albert-Marie Guérisse, and his nationality Belgian. He had served as a doctor with a Belgian cavalry regiment, during their eighteen days' campaign in May 1940; had got away to England; had not cared for what he saw of his compatriots' early efforts at setting up a government in exile; and had taken up with the crew of the *Rhin*, a formerly French Q ship of which the name was changed to *Fidelity*. In the shadow of the tremendous personality of the *Rhin's* captain,

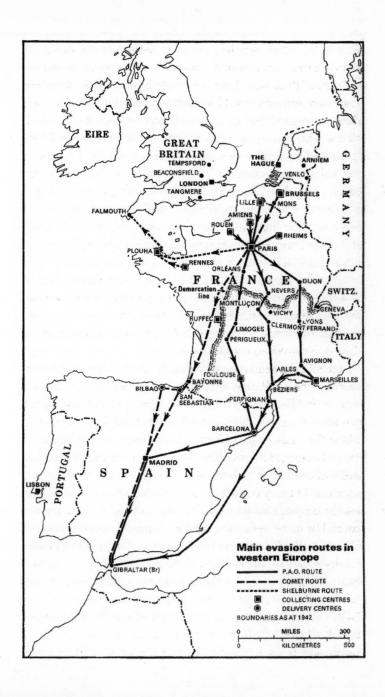

**Main evasion routes in western Europe**

Peri, who changed his own name to Langlais, Guérisse secured a British naval commission as a lieutenant-commander. At first he told no one but Langlais that he was a doctor, for he did not relish the prospect of spending the rest of the war tending wounded. He preferred adventure; thanks to that squall, he found it. By midsummer, MI 9 and P15 knew that Garrow wanted to employ Pat O'Leary.

P15, after checking O'Leary's real identity in the files, mentioned it to Dansey, who at once blew up, and threatened the direst penalties for anyone who mentioned the name Guérisse again during the war. He took an even dimmer view than Guérisse did of all the colonies of exiles in London; probably he thought nobody perfectly secure but himself and the King of England. However, he was prepared to let Garrow recruit the Belgian, and from Garrow's and Guérisse's work together, great results followed.

When in October 1941 Garrow was at last arrested by the French police, and interned at Mauzac in the Dordogne, Gurisse took over command of the line they had set up. It was known thence forward officially as PAO, after the cover initials of its head. His own friends in it called him Pat, and it is as 'Pat' that the line is generally remembered today. All told, about six hundred people moved to safety down it in a year under his charge: airmen, soldiers, and volunteers for the free French and Belgian forces.

Its great strength came from the fact that the people, who formed its guiding core all knew, liked and trusted each other. They understood each other quickly, without long explanations; they were all well aware of the risks they ran, individually and in common. The enormous advantages of this inner cohesion were offset by a countervailing, catastrophic snag: one of them was no good. His companions, being the sort of straightforward people that they were, did not take this in till he had handed fifty helpers over to the Gestapo.

London was not able to do much for the line in Garrow's

day, because communications were so weak; this in turn was because the value of evasion had not yet been appreciated, either in the upper reaches of the Air Ministry or anywhere else in the services' high command. SIS and SOE, like everybody else, were busy trying to fit themselves out for war in circumstances nobody had foreseen, and took care to keep any French-speakers capable of operating a secret wireless set to themselves. (Up to March 1942, SOE's wireless affairs were handled for it by SIS, a further cause of friction between the two bodies.)

Darling sent money in to Garrow when he could. Through the elephantine personality of Nubar Gulbenkian ('Carnation', so called because he wore one out foxhunting), who had been recruited into secret service while out with the Old Berkeley Hunt and was too rich to attract suspicion, a garage was secured at Perpignan where Michel Pareyre ('Parker') could collect parties before they set out to tackle the nearby Pyrenees. Pareyre was to be paid £40 an officer and £20 a man, figures previously cleared with the Treasury. Gulbenkian's valet managed to drop an iron on Brauchitsch's exquisitely polished toecap at Vichy, but otherwise his mission attracted no adverse notice. Pareyre, on the other hand, found himself so closely watched by the local *gendarmerie* and by the Vichy *milice* that he could do little himself. Garrow nevertheless, with encouragement from him, opened up some useful friendships with the local smugglers. Smugglers, and other guides, quite regularly took parties of people round or over the mountains, in either direction. Darling, badly as he had got on with the ambassador in Madrid, got on hardly better with (Sir) Harold Farquhar, the British consul in Barcelona, but the consulate was at first more effective than the embassy in fugitives' interests. It may be suspected indeed that Farquhar spent a good deal of his own money on these people, before the embassy's policy altered and it began to help.

Any fugitives who could not claim to be subjects of the British Crown might easily be deflected, as many British subjects also were, into one or other of the Franco regime's concentration camps. The huge one at Miranda de Ebro, forty miles south of Bilbao, was perhaps the worst. Thence they could only be extracted after prolonged negotiations, in Madrid and on the spot, by some embassy or legation attaché.

One of the attachés at the British embassy, (Sir) Michael Creswell – codenamed. 'Monday' – proved himself a tower of strength. He undertook a great deal of the delicate and difficult work of ferrying British escapers and evaders round Spain. Sometimes, when the lines and Barcelona had provided a large enough party, he could put together a whole coach-load of ostensible students, and send them down to Gibraltar. More often he or his colleague Henry Hankey – son of the former secretary to the Cabinet – had to use their own motor cars, and people whose journeys needed specially to be kept from prying eyes had to learn to travel in the boot, at least for the frontier crossing into Gibraltar. Sir Samuel Hoare, the ambassador in Madrid, was prepared to drop his initial hostility and look the other way.

Obviously what Guérisse needed was a clandestine wireless operator, so that he could communicate promptly with London or Gibraltar or both; none was to be had. Langley eventually found a Frenchman called Ferière, who struggled through the indispensable course of training during the winter of 1941–2.

On 5 January 1942 Darling moved his base from Lisbon to Gibraltar, where he stayed till late in 1943, nominally as a civil liaison officer – a deliberately meaningless phrase: the civil population had already been evacuated. He ran a one-man interrogation office which was invaluable for the work of MI 9. He took every newcomer from the Continent through every move of his escape or evasion, and having a retentive and orderly memory built up in his own head a complete picture of the means of moving about north-western Europe. This enabled him to spot at once anybody who was trying to feed himself onto an MI 9 line while in fact working for an Axis agency: a valuable safeguard.

He had already in the autumn of 1941 begun to have doubts about one of the 'Pat' line's most ardent helpers in the north of France: an evader from the BEF who called himself Captain Harold Cole, and was known as 'Paul' in his underground work. A glance at the army list showed Darling that there was no officer in it of that rank and name, and he alerted London. An inquiry at Scotland Yard threw up Harold Cole as the name of a con-man and housebreaker, a petty criminal quite well known to the police; and a Sergeant Harold Cole had absconded from the BEF in the spring of 1940, with his sergeants' mess funds. Langley flew out to Gibraltar in March 1942 with Ferière, by now at the end of his wireless training; Guérisse came out down his own line, ending the journey in the boot of 'Monday's' car, for a conference with Langley and Darling.

They persuaded Guérisse that Cole would not do; as he had already begun to suspect himself. He had summoned Cole to Marseilles in the previous autumn, charged him with spending the line's money on loose-living, and knocked him down; Cole got away, and went back to Lille. There, it was later discovered, he had been arrested by the Abwehr in early December 1941, and changed sides. On 8 December, the morning after Pearl Harbour, he helped two Germans at Abbeville disguised as RAF evaders to arrest the Abbé Carpentier, a devoted priest who had been using his private printing press to keep the line supplied with bogus identity cards and passes to cross the demarcation border. Long afterwards, it emerged that the Abwehr office in Brussels were using Cole extensively, under several aliases – Delobel, Joseph Deram, Richard Godfrey – to penetrate Garrow's line.

Guérisse was persuaded at Gibraltar that Cole must now be shot on sight, and that all addresses known to the evident traitor were to be changed. As it turned out, Cole was arrested by the Vichy French police in May 1942, and given a heavy sentence; this put him out of the way, but not for long.

Ferière went back into France with Guérisse, but proved a broken reed: his only desire was to rejoin his own wife.

Langley sent in instead, by Lysander, Jean Nitelet, a Belgian airman who had lost an eye in action; but Nitelet was arrested a few weeks later by the French while clearing up after a small parachute drop of stores. It was not till October 1942 that the 'Pat' line at last got a full-time wireless operator: the young Australian Tom Groome, who from his French-born mother had learned excellent French. It says much for Guérisse's ingenuity, and for the silent courage and devotion of his helpers, that several large seaborne operations were laid on during 1942, using a British-owned armed trawler, the *Tarana*, to evacuate several score evaders and a few escapers as well. Two parties left from a deserted villa near the solitary hotel, the little Hotel du Tennis, at Canet-plage; their comfort not increased by the blocking-up of both the villa's lavatories during a wait prolonged over several days.

Guérisse was never the sort of man to let formal obstacles stand in his way, and one thing he did appalled Darling, who did not dare report it to the irascible Dansey. As imprudently as improperly, Guérisse used as an extempore courier a Swede called Gosta Wedeborg, master of the Red Cross ship *Vega* which plied between Gibraltar and Marseilles. Wedeborg was perfectly safe, but the use of a Red Cross channel to assist MI 9's business in any way went clean against Crockatt's orders as well as international law, as Darling took prompt pains to make clear.

Several of the helpers in the 'Pat' line had distinguished careers in F section of SOE later in the war: notably Nancy Wake, terror of the Germans in the Auvergne; Tony Brooks, who ran a small and highly efficient railway sabotage circuit that did much to bring rail traffic in southern France to a standstill in the summer of 1944; and Andrée Borrel, the silent heroine of the big SOE 'Prosper' circuit's disaster in Paris in 1943. She died in German hands, as did Madeleine Damerment, who was dropped straight to a Gestapo reception. None of these four could have been assured long life if they had stayed in the escaping business, for all work in that was dangerous as well; yet Langley did sometimes reproach himself that he had not tried harder to keep some at least of these young, promising and already distinguished people, before Buckmaster's able recruiter Jepson snapped them up for SOE.

At the same time as the 'Pat' line grew, flourished, and fell into difficulties, another line originated in Belgium, spread across France into Spain, and had comparable successes and failures; but in quite different ways.

One day in August 1941 four strangers, three men and a girl, called at the British consulate in Bilbao. The girl, who spoke for them all, though the frailest of the four, turned out to be their leader. One was a private soldier called Colin Cupar, an evader from St Valéry who spoke not a word of French; the other two were Belgian officers who wanted to join the Allies. The consul happened to be away that day. The vice-consul, Arthur Dean, was not wholly inexperienced: it had been his task to shepherd the Duke and Duchess of Windsor out of France fourteen months before. A few words apart with Cupar convinced him that he at least was genuine: who on earth were the others? The girl was invited to talk while Cupar and the officers waited in the next room.

She was thoroughly forthcoming. She explained that she was a Brussels schoolmaster's daughter named Andrée de Jongh, aged twenty-five, a commercial artist by profession but with some training as a nurse, brought up to revere the memory of Edith Cavell. (She was of course unaware of Nurse Cavell's secret parallel career as an intelligence agent.) She had, with some Belgian friends' help, organised a chain of safe houses between Brussels and the western Pyrenees, every detail of which she was ready to give; might she come back another time with some more British evaders? It would be, she indicated, safer for the people who were currently housing them to be relieved of the honour of doing so; and perhaps such young men as Cupar could be of some help in the war? Was there, Dean asked, anything she wanted? Well, she replied, it would save her from some embarrassment if she might have Cupar's fare, which she had had to borrow from a relative.

Would she care to wait? She waited for nearly a fortnight, hiding up in a small hotel, while the wires hummed with cipher traffic between Bilbao, Madrid and London. Dansey denounced her as an obvious plant. Bilbao, with patience and skill, replied that in the judgement of those who had met her, she was a girl of radiant integrity, as well as something of a beauty, and physically hard as nails – otherwise she could never have managed the mountain crossings, and it was established she had not been smuggled in by the geographically easy way, by Irun or Fuenterrabia from Hendaye. To Bilbao's assurances that she was straight Dansey gave in the end a grumbling assent; letting women run anything was against all his principles, though at this moment he was dealing with another exceptionally capable woman, who was head of an intelligence network in France.

So began a saga of secret warfare that has few parallels, alike for the courage of those concerned and for their skill in surmounting barriers, both physical and police. At first called 'Postman', the line was soon named 'Comet'. Its tale has been told repeatedly; we only need here to inquire what London could do to help.

London's front man was Creswell ('Monday'), who was captivated by Andrée de Jongh's intense and forceful personality the moment he met her. Her advance post on the French side of the border, manned by Madame Elvire de Greef ('Tante Go') at Anglet near Biarritz, usually had warning of when she was going to come south, and passed a code message on to Creswell; he then drove up to Bilbao, or San Sebastian, and took with him anything he thought Andrée might need. Money he was able to supply for her in plenty; most other things she did her best to refuse. She ran the line with her friends and contemporaries – it was very much a young people's affair, though her father, to whom she had said nothing, divined what must be going on and insisted on helping her, a course eventually fatal to himself. They were all absolutely insistent on keeping the running of the line entirely, finance apart, in their own hands; and long refused to accept a wireless operator, because they felt that to have one would insidiously lead them somehow under London's control. Only very slowly was 'Monday' able to convince Mademoiselle de Jongh that he and London were not trying to control anybody except the Nazis; they only wanted to get on with the war.

On one point he did soon manage to convince her, through his ability to descry the strength of her anti-Nazi feelings. He explained to her how severe the Allied shortage of trained aircrew was, and what an enormous advantage it would be to the RAF and to the other Allied air forces to get back shot-down airmen who happened not to have fallen into captivity. So thoroughly did Andrée ('Dédée') de Jongh and her friends appreciate this point that they came to specialise in evading aircrew, as soon as they had worked off a backlog of evaders from Dunkirk whose whereabouts they happened to know. Their promptest effort was to return all seven of the crew of an RAF heavy bomber, shot down near the Dutch-Belgian frontier late in 1942, to Gibraltar in a week. Only a run of lucky accidents gave them the chance to handle that party quite so fast, but the incident naturally enough did both the line and its London sponsors a great deal of good.

Gestapo pressure on it was constant, and led to numerous arrests, but most of the people arrested kept silent; and the essential figures – Andrée de Jongh herself, her father, 'Tante Go' near Biarritz, and Florentino Goicoechea the Basque mountain guide – kept out of the Gestapo's way. Andrée's father had the good luck to be out when the Germans called at his flat in February 1942 and arrested his other daughter, who subsequently died of what she had undergone at German hands. He fled to Paris, where he and Andrée lived in a succession of flats, paid for by MI 9's money. At the Brussels end, the line was run thereafter by Baron Jean Greindl ('Nemo'), whose ostensible task was to run a small Red Cross organisation that relied on Swedish funds to assist refugees. He was able to improve and extend the de Jonghs' range of sure acquaintances, so that before long every place in Belgium of any size had somebody reliable in it, who could collect evaders for the line. In July to October, 1942, the line brought out fifty-four people, most of them aircrew; this was about its average rate of traffic, except in midwinter.

Gradually, as evader after evader returned safely to Allied territory, it became clear in London that there was a large – indeed a growing – body of potential helpers on the Continent. Readiness to help increased as Axis occupation dragged on, and the occupied came to understand in practical detail what Nazism was like. Helpers were never to be found universally; there were always people who were too timid or too uninterested or too fond of leaving things exactly as they were. Yet every day the Germans stayed in Bohemia, Moravia, Poland, Norway, Denmark, Holland, Luxembourg, Belgium, France, Yugoslavia, Greece, a few more hearts turned against them; till even those who had at first welcomed them – *mieux Hitler que Staline* – wanted them to go.

MI 9 saw first that this body of helpers existed, and Crockatt made it his business to spread the word. MI 6 became convinced rather more slowly, for most of its senior staff shared George V's distrust of foreigners; and MI 6 in any case was geared to the distribution of single items of highly secret information, rather than to the dissemination of so broad and vague a concept. It was perhaps a weakness in the British organisation of the war that few if any general politico-military surveys of the state of opinion in Europe were – so far as is known – prepared officially, and made available outside Foreign Office and PWE circles.

The next body after MI 9 to take in the unexpectedly wide range of available help was the Air Ministry. Aircrew training, pilot training especially, was one of the air force's principal headaches, and any relief for it, however slight, was welcome. The rapid rate of technical change of the 1940s meant in any case that aircrew were in constant need of training and retraining in the more and more complicated skills of their craft; aircrew returned from an escape, or better still from a prompt evasion, could be fed with little trouble onto existing courses, before going back onto operations, and at least would not need retraining in the basic skills of airmanship.

Moreover, it gave a splendid lift to the morale of operational squadrons if people who had gone missing in action reappeared a few weeks later. In such a case, an ounce of practice was worth a pound of principle: people could see for themselves that the escape-and-evasion lectures were worth attention, because they produced visible results.

Yet, tremendously encouraging though it was to squadrons to get their lost friends back after all, there was one obvious catch: security. Anybody reappearing in an RAF or USAF mess after a brief recent spell in occupied territory was bound to be deluged with questions: what was it like, where did he go, what did he do, whom did he meet; above all, how did he get away? Few of these were questions that could be answered with any safety to the helpers working on the Continent, whom it was MI 9's task to protect, and successful evaders or escapers were universally ordered to clam up and say nothing. The timid at least among these helpers deserve sympathy: the risks involved were not light. Anybody found helping evaders could hope for a concentration camp at best, both for him or herself and for everyone else living in the same house, irrespective of sex or age; while all the evader had to do was to produce his service identity discs, thus ensuring his own transfer to a prisoner of war camp. Evaders were often threatened with worse, but like all European threats to non-Soviet prisoners of war these threats were empty. It is worth noting that the same offence of harbouring an enemy national on the run, if committed in England at the time, carried a maximum penalty if proved in court of two years' imprisonment plus a £500 fine. British and American staffs were painfully aware of the dangers of reprisal that hung over potential helpers, and did nothing willingly to make them worse. Crockatt guided them as usual to take a robust and practical view.

Experience soon showed that there were plenty of anti-Nazis and anti-Fascists all over Axis-occupied Europe – a phrase that excludes the Axis powers' home territories – who were anxious, who demanded even as a right, to be allowed to court these dangers.

For them, this was a way of atoning for the ease with which their homelands had been overrun; and the right was one the British four were ready enough to grant. They did not grant it in any spirit of readiness to fight to the last foreigner. Great pains were taken to ensure that all successful evaders and escapers were properly warned about the indispensability of keeping their mouths shut on their helpers' identity, location, even existence; and the same point was stressed repeatedly in all training lectures on escape and evasion.

Unfortunately, as every sergeant knows, orders given are not always orders carried out. There were a few tragedies of helpers betrayed: some unavoidable, because re-arrested airmen were put under Gestapo pressures they were quite unable to bear; others not. As Rawlinson once put it in wartime talk with Langley, 'loquacity will always triumph over security'. One case in particular has stuck in Langley's memory, and needs record. An early RAF evader got ample and friendly help from a farmer and his wife near Amiens. Strictly against the orders he was given at his interrogation on return to England, he passed on their name and address to his closest friend; who wrote them down on a slip of paper, tucked it in the back of his wallet, and forgot about it. More than a year later, the friend was shot down over the western desert, and the Germans found the slip of paper, still in his wallet. The farmer and his wife were arrested, confronted with it, and shot. A French gendarme who took part in the arrest and had seen the slip of paper passed word out through an evasion line. Crockatt after long deliberation decided not to press for a court martial, but the story – with all the names and places left out – was a powerful one for use in lectures.

The security problem arose in a particularly sharp form when it came to briefing participants in the raids mounted by combined operations headquarters into enemy-occupied Europe. On the whole MI 9's policy remained fixed: all help short of addresses, but nothing that would run the least risk of compromising any helper. Commandos, parachutists, landing craft crews were given careful training in how to evade, as well as in how to resist interrogation if they had the misfortune to be captured, but were not told of particular people or places they could approach.

While 'Biting', the successful parachute raid on the Bruneval radar station on the night of 27/28 February 1942, was being prepared, MI 9 got ready a lot of addresses of people in north Normandy, who were known to have given reliable help to evaders in the summer of 1940, and passed it under top secret cover to the planning staff at COHQ; one of whom, in all good faith, passed one of the addresses on to Wing Commander Pickard, who was to pilot the leading aircraft. Pickard memorised it; and mentioned the fact some two years later to Langley, whose best man he was, at Langley's wedding. It is an interesting illustration of how easily security can be breached. This address turned out to be of no use to Pickard, who was shot down and killed on the still mysterious operation 'Jericho' on Amiens prison in March 1944.

Dansey, who had an even lower opinion than Crockatt of the security-mindedness of junior officers and of other ranks, closed a long debate on preparations for 'Biting' by laying down that no addresses were to be given out to the force, on the grounds that the raid would certainly alarm the neighbourhood, and that the chance of a successful evasion from the beach was too small to justify the risk. The precedent, once set, was normally followed. A few distinguished evasions after raids did take place, but they were due to the evaders' own enterprise and initiative, sparked off by their MI 9 training. Corporal Wheeler of 2 Commando sent back a valuable military report on the St Nazaire raid through the military attaché in Madrid, and added that 'the propaganda value of the raid was enormous.' Three other men deserve mention, French Canadians from Dieppe who were picked up by the 'Pat' line after making their own flying starts: Dumais, Labrosse and Vanier. All went back to Europe later and did outstanding work for escapers and evaders.

For a single party, a special exception was made: 'Blondie' Hasler's marine commandos, the 'Cockleshell heroes' of operation 'Frankton'. Particular care was taken to provide them with advice, including cover stories. They were launched in five two-man canoes from a submarine off the mouth of the Gironde, early in December 1942. Two canoes got as far as Bordeaux harbour, where they attached some limpet mines to several large ships. Hasler himself and his companion Corporal Sparks were the only two to get away after the attack. They made – as ordered – for the small town of Ruffec, north of Angouleme, which lay on the demarcation line between the two halves of France. (The line was kept in being, as an obstacle to movement, although for a month past both halves of France had been in German occupation.) There they managed – by good fortune as much as anything else – to make contact with the 'Marie-Claire' line.

'Marie-Claire', born Mary Lindell in Surrey in 1895, impeccably English in upbringing and manner, had lived for many years in France, and as the Comtesse de Milleville had a position in Parisian society; in 1942 she had three children in their teens. As a nurse in the previous world war she had been decorated for gallantry under fire, and the late summer of 1940 had found her hard at work in Red Cross uniform – with her English medal ribbons worn in front of her French and Russian ones, so that no one in the least skilled in medal reading could doubt her nationality. She smuggled British officer-evaders over the demarcation line towards Caskie V mission at Marseilles. Tact was never her longest suit; courage she possessed abundantly. She went straight to the German commander in Paris, General von Stülpnagel, with a tale of babies that needed to be reunited with their parents on the Riviera. Stülpnagel introduced her to Count von Bismarck, a great-grandson of the founder of the Second Reich, who gave her permits for herself, a baby, a nurse, and a mechanic; and plenty of petrol coupons. The rest was, comparatively, easy.

She fell foul eventually of the Paris Gestapo; not before she had transported several officers to safety, and inspired scores of French people of many callings to stiffen their own nerves against the occupation. After a spell in Fresnes prison she came out through Spain in the disguise of an elderly governess, and met Farquhar in Barcelona. He equipped her with a note that got her promptly into touch with P15 when she reached London in July 1942.

P15's staff had by now doubled: it consisted of both Langley and Airey Neave, who had been posted to it as 'Saturday' on making the home run from Colditz. They interviewed in a flat above Overton's restaurant, at the bottom of St James's Street, where they had a series of wrangles with the Countess, a lady used to having her own way. She pronounced herself unable to work with Tom Groome, the only wireless operator they could offer her; they were unable to train in time the substitute she suggested. They had trouble enough convincing Dansey that she could be allowed to go back to France at all, for anybody who had once been in the hands of the Gestapo was automatically suspect.

In the end, she went back without a wireless operator, and was landed near Limoges from a Lysander in the small hours of Trafalgar Day, 21 October 1942. She rapidly picked up the threads of her organisation, of which a demarcation line crossing point near Ruffec was a prominent feature. But security and the lack of an operator alike prevented her from knowing of 'Frankton', the Bordeaux raid, in advance; and the lack of an operator kept London from knowing that at the moment 'Frankton' took place she was in hospital with five broken ribs after a bad road accident. Her elder son Maurice, who was nineteen, took Hasler and Sparks in charge, and hid them in a safe house at Lyons; whence in the end they returned in safety. She met them there at the end of the year; characteristically, her first action was to hand Hasler her nail-scissors and order him to remove his magnificent blond moustache.

MI 9 and P15 drew the same lesson: wireless contact with any line was all but indispensable.

So far this account has dealt primarily with north-western Europe, but Crockatt never forgot that MI 9's range of responsibilities was worldwide.

For the first nine months of the war, the Near East – confusingly called the Middle East by the British military authorities, who placed a large headquarters in Cairo – was no more than a staging area and training ground. The Italians had reached a peak if preparedness in 1935–6, and were not yet ready for another war; they hung back from their Axis obligation till they saw the French crippled in the battles of May – June 1940. Greed then overcame judgement, and on 10 June Italy hastened to join the winning side. The French held them off locally, but had to cede them occupation rights in Corsica and in a few border departments of south-east France. From their colony of Libya, their army marched with some flourish of propaganda trumpets sixty miles across the desert into Egypt, and then sat down in the sand.

The British commander in Cairo, Sir Archibald (later Earl) Wavell, one of the most intelligent soldiers the British army has ever bred, realised that at that moment the British had little to live on but their wits, and determined to use his wits to the full. He sent for Colonel Dudley Clarke, who had served under him in Palestine before the war, and was currently engaged in Great Britain in organising another of Holland's inventions, the earliest commandos; they had been given a trial run in Norway under Gubbins. Wavell put Clarke, whose code name was 'Galveston', in charge of a body with a perfectly neutral and unobtrusive name: A Force. A Force's task was to manufacture strength out of weakness: to organise by every available means the deception of the enemy high command.

It was also, as a cover for its still more secret work on deception, to undertake the training of fighting men in evasion and escape, and to organise any help they were likely to need. Harrison was sent out from England in August 1940 to set up N section of A Force, as that body's escape side was known. Unhappily neither the climate nor the staff manners of Cairo suited him, and he felt at a loss between the pomposities of GHQ on one side and the facade of irregularity put up by the humorous – but deadly efficient – Dudley Clarke on the other. A Force's head office – according to David Mure, who was in a position to know – was in a disreputable house 'in the Kasr-el-Nil near Groppi's. At the time, this building was used as a brothel. Galveston, a man of exquisite courtesy, was reluctant to inconvenience the ladies and permitted them to continue their activities in those parts of the house which he did not actually require for his.'

Cairo organised one operation that did not do well. An agent was sent into Vichy France, with no co-ordination of what he was doing with London, or with Darling's advanced post in Lisbon. The agent, the subsequently celebrated A. D. Wintle, was no more tactful than Mme de Milleville; had indeed boisterous habits, not suited to the French circles in which he sought to move; and lacked her quiet, steely capacity for getting her own way. He went to Marseilles, where his task was to set up a line that would run by sea to Beirut in one or other of the Vichy ships that still plied the Mediterranean; but he was soon in Toulon jail, whence he escaped over the border into Spain. Farquhar got him sent through to London; where Dansey made sure he also saw the inside of a British jail, to teach him better manners. (He had already had a short spell in the Tower, for being rude to an air commodore. For most of the rest of the war he was in SOE.) He can serve as an example of the eccentrics, the social oddities who got attracted to irregular and clandestine units. Crockatt tried to employ as few of them as he could. But we must go back to Cairo.

MI 9's – that is, N section's – survival, and even success, in the maelstrom of Cairene secret service politics derived partly from the body's manifest usefulness, partly from its small size compared to its rivals, and partly from some fortunate postings. Its head there, from 21 September 1941 to the end of the war, was a regular soldier with a flair for intelligence work, Lieutenant-Colonel A. C. Simonds. Before the war he had worked in Palestine with Wingate under the watchful eye of Wavell; he and Wingate worked together again, also under Wavell, on a quasi-clandestine expedition into Ethiopia early in 1941. He was then called on to form SOE's Greek country section; and was summoned thence by Dudley Clarke to take charge of escapes and evasions.

The fact that Tony Simonds had been in SOE helped MI 9 in several ways. His having left it endeared him to MI 6, and to PWE. His having been in it gave him invaluable insights, even beyond what he had picked up from Wingate and the Jewish special night squads, into methods of irregular activity; and provided him with an understanding of the SOE system, and some acquaintances among the more permanent of SOE's often transitory staff. On several occasions this led to close and valuable co-operation in the field between SOE and MI 9. He recorded himself that MI 6 had been even more valuable to his work, particularly in providing wireless sets and channels.

Cairo was in many ways a miniature version of London; and just as SOE had to duplicate several of SIS's facilities, which in a

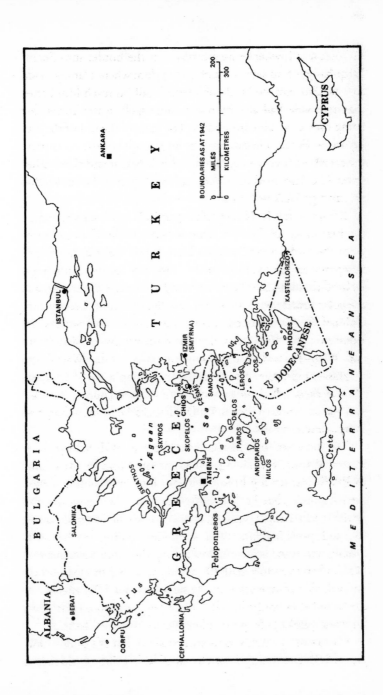

more perfect world might have been shared between them, MI 9's and MI 6's offices in Cairo included separate forgery squads, 6's very small, 9's consisting of a single man. Professional pride made it hard for them even to acknowledge each other's existence, but at a real pinch they could be made to work together by their seniors.

At first there was only a hairline cleavage between N section and the rest of A Force; and though the gap widened with time, N section had many reasons to be grateful to Dudley Clarke, who did a great deal of the heaviest initial work himself.

It was he for example who took the initiative for creating a magnificent set of evasion lines across the Aegean, which Simonds inherited from Victor Jones and Ogilvie-Grant, the original heads of Clarke's Greek N section detachment. The key to these lines lay on the west coast of Turkey, and was turned by two naval officers who had become consuls: Commander Wolfson in Istanbul (Constantinople) and Lieutenant-Commander Noel Rees in Izmir (Smyrna). Wolfson had both Jewish and Russian ancestry, and he was resolutely anti-German. Rees, whose mother was Greek, came from one of those Anglo-Levantine families that dominated so much of Near Eastern trade; he was proud to remember that when Nelson's fleet had called at Smyrna, the Rees of the day had victualled it at his own expense. Noel Rees had been vice-consul in Chios, and knew the Dodecanese well. He continued the family's traditional largesse in the public interest by paying out of his own pocket for the initial arrangements he made, through friends in the local fishermen's communities. He built up a clandestine naval base near Çeşme, opposite Chios on the peninsula west of Izmir. From it N section's caïques could operate, as well as odder craft on odder duties. He even persuaded the local Turks to declare the peninsula a prohibited area, thus preserving the base from too much risk of German counter-attack.

These arrangements carried a distinct flavour of old-fashioned secret service work; as is only suitable in such a context, there is nothing left on paper about method, and precious little about personalities. What can be found, though, are some notes about results; which are striking.

As early as 5 May 1941, Major P. A. Cohen was in charge of a party of 120 Australian evaders from Greece by caïque; he landed them that day in Crete. They could hardly know that they had stepped out of the frying-pan into the fire: by the end of May, Crete too had become the scene of a British defeat. Five thousand troops were left behind there. Wavell gave them discretion to surrender. Many did; many others were picked up; and nearly a thousand managed to evade instead. Most of these evaders were brought away in the late summer and autumn of 1941; a trickle went on for the next three years, as one Cretan village after another ceased to be a safe refuge.

Rees set up a caïque route through the Northern Sporades, via Skiathos, Skopelos and Skyros; there was also a hidden advance caïque base farther south, at Antiparos, supplied by submarine. Before the routes were properly at work, a party of thirty-one Anzacs bought themselves a boat in Skyros, and sailed through to Port Said, where they arrived on 25 May. A wry Cairene air force joke put it that any aircrew known to be at large in Greece for as long as a month ought to be posted absent without leave.

Scanty extempore and incomplete records made in Cairo suggested the rough figures for evaders, some of whom might for a short time have been prisoners, and might therefore technically be categorised as escapers, shown in the below table.[12]

Two submarines, *Thrasher* and *Torbay*, once brought nearly two hundred people away from Crete between them in a single voyage each in the midsummer of 1941. Their sister ship, *Triumph*, was lost in January 1942 at Antiparos, where the Italians caught a party of twenty-two evaders in the charge of an MI 9 guide called G. D. Atkinson who was recaptured with

---

12    WO 208/3253, appx D, 6; E, 4.

them. He had himself escaped from Greece, by caïque from Athens to Alexandria, in the previous year. He showed the usual readiness of those fighting men who had just got away from enemy territory to go back into imminent danger. N section favoured this, and used as many escapers as it could to take part in forays into Axis-held areas; for the fact of being an earlier escaper from an enemy prison camp could provide a cast-iron cover to account for one's presence at large in enemy territory. It was only necessary to have devoted time and thought to a watertight explanation of where one had been and what one had been doing since the escape.

Evaders in Eastern Mediterranean 1941

| Month | Greece | Crete |
|---|---|---|
| May | 302 | — |
| June | 24 | 195 |
| July | 6 | 79 |
| August | 59 | 129 |
| September | 35 | 11 |
| October | ? | ? |
| November | 20 | 107 |
| December | — | 14 |
| Minimum totals: | 446 | 535 |
| Minimum grand total: | | 981 |

Greece is one of the countries for which a full account of the clandestine war remains to be written, in spite of the admirable summaries from the SOE and the political sides that some participants have already prepared. When it appears, some of the brightest pages in it will deal with these early caïque operations, as they threaded their way through the sun-drenched Aegean islands under a hostile sky.

Now and again beauty, danger and courage were outmatched by farce. One mainland and two inland incidents may confirm this. Flying Officer Marting, shot down over Derna on 30 October 1942, got promptly away from the captors who had flown him to Athens, walked boldly up to each Greek he met, and asked 'Say, d'you work for A Force?' The thirteenth one did, and he reached Cairo via Smyrna in December. A muddle between a censor and a war correspondent let out the news, in a BBC broadcast, that as many as 400 evaders had assembled on Melos; they were whisked away to prison in Italian fast craft before N section's more leisurely caïques could arrive to collect them.

An Australian private, seeking the south coast of Crete during an evasion that had started well – he was already in plain clothes, of a ramshackle sort – found that he had to cross a main road under constant German watch. He had no time to wait for dark. The only hope of cover seemed to be as a shepherd. He came upon a dozen sheep in the charge of a shaggy biped bundle of rags, before whose face he crackled his only inducement, a white five pound note. The bundle at first said nothing, but repeatedly lifted his head sharply, in the Greek sign for 'No'. When an hour's attempts to chaffer had produced no more result, the bundle remarked in broad Glasgow Scotch 'Gae and find yer own bluidy sheep. I've spent half a day getting this damn lot.'

These Greek adventures necessarily took up much of the time and attention of N section's Cairo staff, some of whom managed to participate in them directly. Ogilvie-Grant for instance parachuted into the Peloponnese, on the night that Simonds joined A Force, to try to organise a large group of evaders, believed to be over 700 strong, who had assembled in the Taiyetos range west of Sparta. He was soon taken prisoner, and so were most of those he was trying to rescue.

N section needed to look westward into the desert, as well as northward across the sea.

Climate and terrain, as usual, dominated what could be

done and what had to be left undone. Most of the doctrines of desert survival that it was the section's duty to preach ought to have been fixed belief already in properly trained units, in which battalion, company and platoon commanders who were up to their job would already have made it their business to discover the essentials. Among these the will to evade came first; then water, with which to keep alive; then a compass, to know which way to go, and stout boots, to make the stony ways walkable. Though a great deal of the desert is sand, a great deal more is sharp rock, not readily passable by barefoot Europeans. But care of his men's feet was all but instinctive in an infantry officer, and was hardly a point on which an N section lecturer needed to dwell.

Clayton Hutton's silk maps were available, for what maps were worth in those wide open spaces; travelling in the African desert was in every way remote from travel in Europe, but it was conceivable, even in small parties on foot, even alone. N section's lecturers did their best to persuade people to try it, if the sudden twists and quirks of manoeuvre in open warfare left them cut off from their friends. Those unsure of themselves could head north, till they met the one coast road, though on that it was more than likely that they would find themselves made prisoners of war; or even press on to the coast itself, on the remote off-chance that they might be able to signal to some naval craft on the right side. The more adventurous course was to head south, then east for a good while, then north again, and hope to make contact with Allied forces.

One lecturer deserves special notice, both for who he was and for what he did: Jasper Maskelyne, of the famous conjuring family whose sleight of hand had delighted thousands of people in the Britain of the 1920s and 1930s. He did important work in camouflage and deception in Britain in the summer crises of 1940, had some dealings with Clayton Hutton, could not get on with that still more wayward genius, and at Wavell's request went to try his hand at battle magic in Egypt, the home of so much magic more ancient than his own. Simonds found him in the summer of 1942, apparently in charge of an engineer dump on the Suez Canal – his cover was admirably dense – and annexed as much of his time as he could. Maskelyne was a highly skilled as well as an entertaining lecturer, and during the next two and a half years he instructed over 200,000 men – most of them aircrew, British and American – in the arts of escape and evasion. He travelled 135,000 miles, through a dozen Mediterranean countries, to do so, and earned congratulatory letters from General Twining, Commander-in-Chief, Fifteenth USAAF downwards; besides exciting the interest, even the enthusiasm, of the audiences he addressed. He turned his inventive mind also to the problem of parachute packaging, and devised an entirely satisfactory method of dropping W/T equipment safely. All this activity, secret as it was, provided admirable cover for what Maskelyne regarded as his really important work: the erection and removal of dummy ships, tanks, lorries and aircraft to suit the current ingenuities of Clarke's Thirty Committee.

In one way evading was simpler in North Africa than in Europe or Asia; there was hardly any local population about whom the evader needed to worry. Thirty years of Italian colonial occupation had sickened most Libyan Arabs of the occupiers, and for an evader who had the good luck to run into an Arab encampment his troubles were probably over – if he had the manners to keep away from the women. In Bill Kennedy Shaw's words, 'it was the Arabs' hatred of the Italians far more than their love of the unknown British that put them so wholeheartedly on our side.'

Advance A Force, as N section was known in the desert, was able to go farther, with the help of some distinguished desert navigators who operated, in uniform, on the fringe of the Allied forces in north-east Africa. Bagnold and Prendergast, the unit's two successive commanders, and Kennedy Shaw, its intelligence officer, made the Long Range Desert Group (LRDG) a body of unusual hardihood and capacity. All three had explored the desert in some detail before the war, as had the Belgian Vladimir Peniakoff ('Popski') who worked with them for a time before establishing his own private army (PPA) late in 1942. The best of their patrol crews were New Zealanders; Rhodesians, yeomanry and guardsmen provided most of the rest. Their numbers were always small – the two forces together hardly mustered 400 strong – but their influence on the war was disproportionately large.

Their toughness is attested enough by their Sergeant Moore's march – 210 miles, over sand, in ten days, wounded in the foot, with no food and little water, after his truck had been burned out by joint air and ground attack – or by another party who made a similar march, after a similar disaster, and emerged with a look in their eyes that Shaw remembered from a photograph of Cherry-Garrard when he got back from 'The worst journey in the world'.

Shaw's book provides a good example of the sort of thing they could do to help evaders:

> One day in August [1941] an Arab brought word to Siwa that a wounded British pilot was hiding near Bir Bidihi, a desert well a hundred miles inside enemy territory. A patrol went off to bring him in, but at the place described there was no sign of any pilot. After searching for a time they found the mouth of a rock-cut cistern, dry after the long summer. As a last chance they shouted down this and to their surprise out scrambled an Arab, very frightened and denying all knowledge of British pilots. The patrol's hopes fell again, when suddenly from the cistern mouth appeared a bald, pink head followed by the smiling face of the missing airman. 'Why did you say he wasn't here?' demanded the patrol. 'Oh,' said the Arab, 'only yesterday he was telling me that the English soldiers never had beards, so I thought you must be Germans.'

Peniakoff had tales to tell of returned evaders also; some of them were waifs, such as the driver attached to the 7th Armoured

Division who neither knew nor cared whether the sun rose in the east or the west. Once it was clear in Cairo that LRDG was a reliable travel agent, a few advance A Force parties were carried out into the desert by it as well, with the double object of looking after evaders, and of setting up dumps of stores and water at which escapers – if later there were any – could refresh and equip themselves for a long eastward walk. Peter Grandguillot was in charge of one of these parties in the early summer of 1942, and is credited with a remark to Peniakoff that sums up crudely the fighting soldiers' view of the staff: "*Ce sont des cons*" – referring to our masters in Cairo – "*mon vieux Popski, mats nous allons être plus malins qu'eux.*" He assembled an adequate network of friendly Arabs all along the Gebel Akhdar, who did useful work collecting shot-down pilots and occasional army evaders; including the odd survivor from SAS or LRDG raids that had not gone quite smoothly. All were in the end returned back to the Delta, via Kufra or Siwa oasis, in LRDG trucks. One of A Force's more far-flung representatives, discovered a shade dishevelled in some dunes near Tripoli by an advancing Eighth Army armoured car subaltern, when asked what on earth he was doing there, replied with quiet dignity, 'I live here'.

Yet the last word on this system must be left with Shaw: 'A good many men in the Eighth Army must owe their lives to L.R.D.G., but for every lost man found by us how many are still in the desert, now only a skeleton with a few rags of clothing round it and an empty water-bottle beside and, maybe, with its teeth fastened in the dry stem of some desert shrub?'

# 'First in, First out': Escapes 1940–42

The faster the getaway the better, as MI 9's lecturers never tired of repeating. One instance of the application of this doctrine by the enemy is too striking to leave unquoted.

Freiherr von Werra, shot down over England during the summer battle in 1940, made no secret to his fellow-prisoners in Derbyshire of his intention to escape; got out, with several friends, through a tunnel; and presented himself next morning in flying kit at the nearest airfield. His story was that he was a Dutch pilot who had crash-landed in the hills on his way back from a flight over Germany; his base was supposed to be near Aberdeen. He guessed, rightly, that a telephone call to Aberdeenshire to check his bona fides would take hours. By the time it came through, he was already strapped into a Hurricane, studying the controls; these turned out not to include a self-starter. When the station IO caught up with him, he was gesticulating for a starter trolley. He went cheerfully back to a prison camp, and was soon packed off to Canada. A letter was supposed to precede him, to warn the Canadians that he needed special attention. He arrived before the letter; jumped off the train between port and camp; walked south for at least a night and a day, an astounding feat in a Canadian winter, crossed the frozen St Lawrence, and reached the still neutral United States. He returned to Germany for a hero's welcome, and was sighted by some British prisoners while advising on the security of Colditz. His fellow officers in England had found him rather a braggart, but at least he had the nerve to try to put his boasts into practice; and the world was left a little poorer when he crashed again, this time fatally, into the North Sea in October 1941.[13]

His idea, that a pilot could find his way home much faster and more neatly than any other kind of escaper, was naturally well thought of by MI 9 and MIS-X, and regularly mentioned in lectures to aircrew. Several ingenious pilots attempted it, hardly any succeeded: the odds against finding an unguarded startable aircraft that already had enough petrol in it for the intended journey – let alone troubles over maps, takeoff, enemy fighters, Allied antiaircraft – were too high. There were, though, some memorable near misses.

Sam Kydd, a rifleman captured at Calais, found himself one of a team of two hundred labourers clearing the snow off an airfield runway near Thorn (now Toruń in Poland) in March 1942. Most of his companions knew that two among them were RAF officers, who had swapped identities with a pair of men sent into their fort at Thorn – part of the vast Stalag XXA – on fatigue. (A German camp's number depended on the *Wehrkreis* – military district – in which the camp lay.) On a horribly cold day the two pilots sidled away from their working party, ostensibly to shelter in the lee of the airport buildings about 150 yards away; actually, to reconnoitre three Messerschmidt fighters that stood in front of them. Suddenly they ran to one of the aircraft, scrambled on board and started the engine. It was too cold: it failed to run properly and the noise attracted attention. Kydd 'looked up to see a squad of Jerry Luftwaffe blokes rushing down the airport building steps and belting over to the plane, brandishing their revolvers. The two officers climbed out reluctantly and were marched into the airport buildings.'

---

13    There is a biography of him, *The One That Got Away*, by K. Burt and J. Leasor, which disposes of the legend that he was killed in air action in Russia. The suggestion that he had several score followers, who also walked out of Canada and were collected by U-boats off the New England coast, must be dismissed as fiction.

Douglas Bader, the legless fighter pilot, made his escape by climbing down a sheet rope from a prison hospital in northern France, a few hours after he had been shot down in 1941; he was shortly recaptured. Finding himself in a camp near a German airfield equipped with Messerschmidt 110 twin-engined fighters, he asked MI 9 through the usual channels for that aircraft's starting instructions; and got them, by some device of Clayton Hutton's. But by then he had been moved on to another camp, and before long he was tucked away in the supposedly secure fortress of Colditz with no chance to use them.

Maskelyne recounts another escape attempt by air which actually succeeded, in circumstances as uncannily odd as that author's name would suggest. In the late summer of 1942 an RAF pilot and his observer crash-landed in a Sicilian lake, swam ashore and were taken prisoner. They were promptly put into a Savoia bomber and flown off towards the mainland for interrogation. One of them spoke Italian and fell into a technical argument with the Savoia's crew. To settle a detail in dispute, he stepped up to the pilot's seat, and then suddenly seized the pilot by the throat with the threat that he would crash the aircraft and kill them all unless the pilot flew to Malta. The pilot complied, the other British airman found a course and hung his vest out of the window as an extempore white flag, the intercepting fighters and the AA gunners held their fire, and the ruse succeeded.

The fierce mood of these escapers can be guessed at: an example of the strong reaction that men can make against the sudden indignity of capture, unusually lucky in its moment. More often, capture acted as a depressant. The fact of being a prisoner was gloomy enough in itself, and many prisoners of war began by looking for a scapegoat as well; probably finding one in some other service.

Inter-service rivalries, endemic in all armed forces, were still keen among British prisoners early in the war. Naval men felt with unconscious arrogance that they came from the senior service, on which the nation's security would continue to depend. Soldiers, only too often, felt resentful against airmen for lack of support; they did not take in that the air force, like the army, was doing its best with such paltry resources as the country had made available in the despairing 1930s. Nor did many of them understand that the RAF had nevertheless put up a substantial air effort at the time of Dunkirk, an effort none the less real for having been invisible from those desolate beaches. Though the RAF was much the newest, it was the most aggressive of the three British uniformed services, and its members took more than their proportional share in escape and evasion. American airmen heavily outnumbered American ground army escapers and evaders, though of course outside the Philippines comparatively few American soldiers were captured. American prisoners were not quite so much troubled by inter-service rivalries as British ones and their inter-regimental rivalries were much less keen.

Anybody who queries the comparatively small number of ordinary seamen, private soldiers, aircraftmen, in this narrative about fighting forces that were mainly composed of them can soon perceive the reasons. In the lowest rank one did not as a rule fly; except for privates in airborne units, who certainly held their own among escapers and evaders: they took part by scores for example in evasions after Arnhem. Moreover, the qualities of enterprise and initiative that helped to make a man into a successful escaper or evader were just those qualities that were likely to have raised anyone who had them to the rank of corporal, at least, before he had been long enough in uniform to run much risk of capture.

Rank still held some importance for prisoners; not only because they were still paid by it. Officers and other ranks were promptly separated from each other by the Germans and Italians; before this was done, many officers – particularly if they had heard an MI 9 lecture or absorbed their training memorandum thirty-four – urged on their own men the common duty to escape. Within officers' camps, seniority laid down automatically who was to be SBO or HAO. Other ranks' camps were more democratically organised: a camp leader was elected. Some large Stalags had both a camp leader and a 'man of confidence' – also elected – who was junior to him and handled any day-to-day negotiations with the Germans that were necessary, about such matters as camp routine, work schedules and diet. Thoroughly escape-minded Stalags might also elect an escape committee, if one was not appointed by the camp leader. In Oflags, the senior officer knew (or should have known) that his duties included appointing an escape committee chairman – usually known as X – and consulting with him about who should belong to the committee. He also needed to appoint a camp IO, who would probably belong to the escape committee but would have much on his mind besides escaping. In case he forgot or had never been told of his duty, he was likely to be reminded by the first person under his command who was aware of an MI 9 letter code; for the coding instruction included an order to make sure that the SBO knew that through the code he could communicate with home, and that one of the code's purposes was to make escapes more easy.

Before a senior officer or a camp leader could expect his escape committee to achieve anything, the first necessity was to impose a reasonable degree of discipline on his fellow prisoners. Discipline and morale in armed forces, even while forcibly unarmed, are as interdependent as the two sides of a coin. Groups of men with too little discipline, or too much, get disgruntled; well and flexibly organised groups stay cheerful and remain devoted to their cause.

Simple devotion of an old-fashioned kind inspired many escapers, including some of the bravest and the earliest. Indeed it is no longer possible – if it ever was – to discriminate between the people who embarked on an escape on the strength of an MI 9 lecture, and those who did it on principles they had learned at their father's or their grandfather's knee, or were inspired by the novels of Henty they had read as boys, by the doctrines of

John Buchan absorbed in adolescence, or by such real adventure stories as Johnnie Evans's book. The Newbolt-Henty-'Sapper' strain of patriotism that bordered on chauvinism was undoubtedly prominent among wide swathes of the British officer class in the 1920s and still had influence as recently as 1940. Yet by then even the most foolhardy of patriots had to admit that warfare had become more technical since Wolseley had marched to Coomassie. From some advances in technique MI 9 could manufacture opportunities. Its best chances came, needless to say, among those groups of prisoners whose self-assurance and confidence in their real superiority over their captors was at its highest.

This self-assurance, that has made the English so much and so justly disliked abroad, could take exuberant forms. Douglas Bader was one of the outstanding players at the interesting and dangerous sport which prisoners called goon-baiting. It had affinities with the abominable town children's game called Last Across, of which the winner is the last to scamper across a street in front of a motor car. The ideal goon-baiter baited his goon – German camp guard or official – up to the moment at which the infuriated victim unbuttoned his holster or unslung his rifle; at which point the baiter stopped teasing him, and became all affability and conformism. It called for steady nerves and careful judgement; mistakes were easy and fatal.

Men whose morale was high enough to go in for goon-baiting were the sort of men with whom Crockatt wanted to work. Manifestly he could only do so if they could communicate; this was where Winterbottom's work on coding paid its dividends.

As early as November 1940, MI 9 could claim that it had 'succeeded in corresponding effectively in code with various Ps/W in Germany and this activity is developing'. It then took about five weeks for a letter to pass in either direction. The first batch of mail to arrive from Germany at all, on 27 August, had been a bulky one – thirty bags, containing all told about

120,000 letters and cards – reactions at the British end must have been reasonably brisk.

A large proportion of the original contacts with prisoners in Germany were made by way of what Winterbottom's sub-section, it may be remembered, called 'dotty' codes, privately prearranged with relatives. One of the earliest of these private code users, Captain (Sir) Rupert Barry of the Oxfordshire and Buckinghamshire Light Infantry, asked his wife to pass on a message to the War Office. It reached MI 9; through his private code he was instructed to wash half-a-dozen handkerchiefs in his next parcel. These bore on them details of how to use the HK code which he wielded thereafter with equal skill and efficiency; he was for four years the coding officer in Oflag IVC at Colditz castle in Saxony. This was a punishment camp, set up under Article 48 of the Geneva Convention to house officers who had made, from the German point of view, tiresome attempts at escape already. The concentration of many exceptionally keen and skilled escapers in a single stone courtyard did not have the sort of results the Germans had foreseen, and Colditz has now become a popular by-word for Teutonic inefficiency. That this was so was as much due to Barry's supervision of the link with MI 9 as to anything else.

The basic system was simple. Prisoners asked, in coded letters home, for particular items that would help them to escape: maps, money, and clothes above all. A coded reply forewarned them what markings would be on the parcel that contained what they required. A moment's sleight of hand in the parcels office might be all that was then needed. Failing that, the German or Italian parcels clerk could be bribed; or the parcels office could be burgled. At Colditz, parcels used to arrive in quite large batches by an evening train. They were then locked up overnight in an office in the prisoners' courtyard and an armed sentry was placed on the door – relieved every couple of hours – till morning. The prisoners simply waited till they knew a bribable sentry was on guard; persuaded him to mount guard round the corner for a couple of minutes; unlocked the office with their own key, removed the interesting parcels, paid the sentry and called it a night. The Germans had fitted an alarm system inside the office; which, unknown to them, a French prisoner had bypassed. Crowds in the parcel office could probably manage a snatch next morning if by bad luck there had been no bribable sentry on watch the night before.

Camp commandants were usually elderly men, and most of their guards were low-quality troops, unfit for battlefield service. They had pitted against them some of the best, as well as some of the worst, of the Allied forces: not only the army skrimshankers, who had let themselves get captured for the sake of a quiet war, but also the exceptionally daring men, commandos and parachutists who had volunteered for all-but-hopeless missions, aircrew who had gone back for a second or even a third time to a thoroughly awakened target in order to make quite sure they bombed the right spot. It was about as easy to keep some young airmen in as it is to pick up a blob of quicksilver. Against such first-class material, a second class commandant backed by third-class troops could not rely on making a respectable showing. It was fortunate indeed for British, Commonwealth and American prisoners in Germany that they were almost always guarded by the Wehrmacht, and not by Himmler's SS. The corruptibility of the ordinary low-grade German or Italian guard, proved over and over again, was a weak link in the defences of Nazism and Fascism, wholly unsuspected in the staff stratosphere that advised the dictators; but foreseen by Norman Crockatt, who broke through it. His main weapon was tobacco, provided in large quantities for every prisoner of war camp. Tobacco parcels were hardly ever searched and were available in quantity; the enemy never seemed to take in the use that some prisoners made of them. Elderly survivors who can remember how hard tobacco was to come by during the war and how frightful service issue cigarettes sometimes tasted, can conjecture the impact on a gullible central European private of large packets of Player's or Wills's cigarettes or tobacco. (It was a purely accidental benefit for Ed Johnston's personal fortune that Lucky Strike was among the brands used in the second half of the war to supply United States prisoners' tobacco parcels.) Coffee, otherwise all but unobtainable in Germany, even on the black market, after 1941, contains quite as powerful a drug as tobacco, and was a big bribe in prisoners' hands.

This was another point at which discipline in camps was important. On the ideal system that MI 9 and MIS-X approved, the SBO and SAO – or SBNCO and SANCO – controlled the whole business of trading with the enemy; wading in insidiously from the shallow end, by getting guards to accept the occasional tip of a few first-class cigarettes in return for trifling turnings of a blind eye, till men were caught in deeper than they had bargained for and were accepting large gifts of tobacco, coffee or food in exchange for substantial returns: clothes, tools, even passes or maps or wireless valves. In the real world greed often overcame drill. In large other ranks' (enlisted men's) camps especially, the more commercially minded and greedier prisoners rapidly started up deals with anyone they could find to treat with them, and bought with such barter- able goods as they had to offer whatever was going to suit their personal comfort best. Not many camp leaders had the gifts of command and persuasion combined that enabled people like Warrant Officer J. A. G. Deans, RAF, to impose his personality on several hundred airmen and persuade them to carry out the whole of their trading through channels directed by himself, so that the whole camp, and above all the potential escapers in it, would benefit.

No misuse of Red Cross facilities was involved in all this. As Crockatt put it at a secret press conference in 1944, 'Never since the war began and never till the war ends will we ever utilise a Red Cross parcel for any work of this nature. They are to us completely and absolutely sacrosanct.' He and Ed Johnston were far too concerned about the value of Red Cross parcels for sustaining their men's health, and even in crises their lives, to be able to contemplate any sort of avoidable risk to their safe arrival. The International Red Cross Committee (IRCC) moreover gave an undertaking, mistrusted by the Germans, that they would never enclose escape equipment in their parcels.

A few former prisoners may say to themselves at this moment, 'But surely I remember getting a parcel with maps or money or hacksaws or compasses hidden in it, that had a Red Cross label?' Not quite: odd parcels, travelling post free as all prisoner of war mail did, might easily have a label bearing a red cross affixed to them by the carrier, but the IRCC was acting in such cases purely as a postal agent. It took no more responsibility for the contents than any other postal authority would take for a betting slip, or an unbirthday present, or a parcel bomb. Private, or apparently private, parcels transmitted by the IRCC were quite distinct from the Red Cross parcels for which the IRCC's donors subscribed, and on which in times of famine prisoners of war depended largely for survival. By the winter of 1944-5, their rations might be down to a few hundred calories a day and only Red Cross food would keep them alive in a state to work.

There was another feature of Red Cross parcels, provided quite unawares through the IRCC, which was important to escapers: the boxes in which they came. These were sometimes made of stout cardboard, sometimes of plywood. The plywood sides of Canadian Red Cross boxes in particular were invaluable as tunnel linings, and in great demand by active escape committees. This provided Crockatt with another opportunity for taking a robust and practical view of how people ought to behave.

In addition it provided prisoners with a good opportunity for seeing who was on whose side. The boxes also made admirable bedside tables, clothes lockers, book bins, in hutted camps all but devoid of furniture except for beds. A prisoner devoted to his own comfort would accumulate as many boxes as he could. One ready to work with the escape committee would willingly put up with the inconvenience of having no lockers, or only one, if the committee needed the timber.

In some particularly escape-minded camps, notably Oflag IVC at Colditz and Stalag Luft III at Sagan, the tunnellers were able to levy timber from everybody's bed boards. Prisoners slept in rough wooden bunks, containing anything up to ten short crosswise timber planks; it was soon proved that people could sleep quite soundly on three, and the tunnellers took the rest. The original beds at Colditz were metal; replaced in mid-war by the Germans when they discovered that their prisoners were turning inessential parts of their beds into tools.

Tools were an incessant preoccupation for prisoners, who stole them whenever they could. They held that the eighth and tenth commandments applied to prisoners' property, but not to the enemy's. Theft was probably their main source; next to it came supplies from MI 9. Clayton Hutton and Maskelyne devised numerous hiding places for tools, some of them quite heavy. A screwdriver could travel in the handle of a baseball bat or the blade of a cricket bat; a hacksaw could be hidden in an object as small as a comb or a toothbrush. Coded warnings of how to find the tool preceded the parcel.

Clayton Hutton's masterpiece in this field was the escape knife, based on the ordinary boy's pocket-knife, but elaborated: besides a strong blade and a screwdriver it included three saws, a lock- forcing tool, and a small but efficient wire-cutter. It was big to hide and heavy to conceal, but anybody who did manage to smuggle one through a search had a formidable weapon to hand with which to get himself out of prison.

The Germans soon thought of putting all parcels through an X-ray machine. London was promptly informed. Two responses were available; both were used. One was to insert maps, money or any other thin flexible objects to be sent between the outer and the inner skin of a specially constructed tin, usually filled with powdered or condensed milk. (Ordinary tins of this type, with the brand name Klim, were popular with prisoners as cooking utensils, and were indispensable for the ventilation systems of many tunnels.) The tin showed up as a black cylindrical blob on the X-ray. If pierced by a suspicious investigator it was pierced through the top or the bottom, never through the side, so the cache remained undiscovered. The second, simpler response was to abstract the particular parcel before it reached the X-ray machine; we have just seen how effectively this was done at Colditz.

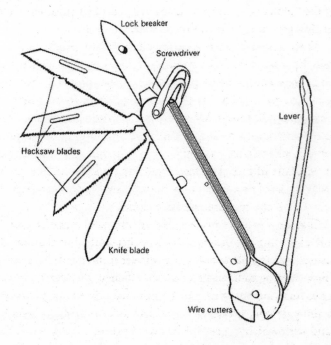

All told, MI 9 dispatched 1,642 parcels discreetly described as 'special' in 1941–2, and 5,173 ordinary parcels as well, many of the latter full of tobacco. The proportion safely received is not recorded; we might guess at two-thirds. The straight parcels helped to provide cover for the bent ones, by getting the German handlers used to the appearance of such innocent-seeming labels as the Licensed Victuallers Sports Association, the Prisoners' Leisure Hours Fund, or the Welsh Provident Society; these were among the three dozen notional bodies invented in MI 9 to sponsor their traffic. Elaborate care was taken to make sure that authentic postmarks were used, and that newspaper which formed part of the wrapping material was printed near the parcel's ostensible place of origin.

Parcels offices were normally staffed by prisoners under a German corporal's supervision: why should the Wehrmacht waste manpower on a job that prisoners could perfectly well do for themselves? Many parcels clerks became as dexterous as a conjuror at abstracting items from a pile, slipping extras into sacks, or any other feats of legerdemain that were required, and some developed a sort of sixth sense for the one item the enemy must not be allowed to inspect in a heap of innocuous parcels. At Oflag VIB for example at Warburg the parcels staff were on decently friendly terms with their captors, and never had the least difficulty in spotting and abstracting parcels that contained escape stores. The packing staff in MI 9z was tiny, and presumably each packer had too distinctively personal a style; it was lucky that no one in the OVRA or the Gestapo noticed.

MI 9y, the coding sub-section, invented a great many notional characters as well as notional firms: fictitious aunts, uncles, girlfriends, old school chums, who wrote to selected prisoners out of the blue, sometimes in thoroughly familiar terms, always with the catch-date at the top to warn the prisoner that the letter was in code. This multiplied the channels through which information could pass back and forth between London, and later Washington, and the camps, but it had disadvantages. One was that the staff of MI 9 was not enormous, and it would hardly do for the same handwriting to be used for letters to unrelated prisoners in the same camp, bearing quite different home addresses and signatures. This elementary mistake was sometimes made, all the same. Quite a number of outsiders must have devoted part of their spare time to copying out texts provided for them, without understanding why: a mild security danger.

From the prisoners' end there was less danger on this security front. Code users were picked by MI 9 lecturers – about one per cent of the army and navy, most fighter pilots, and six per cent of other aircrew – from those who seemed to be the soberest and most level-headed of their audiences, and would be unlikely to make indiscreet remarks on getting an affectionate letter from a girl of whom they had never previously heard. The original instructions they got while they were being taught the code – a simple enough business, picked up by a bright pupil well inside an hour – included an extra warning, beyond the warning they had had in their previous escape and evasion lectures, that this was a subject on no account to be mentioned in mess, or when off duty: 'No discussion on the Code must take place between yourselves or anyone else. Be on your guard at all times against talking of these matters and, in the interests of everyone, report to this branch any breach of security which comes to your notice.'

Security became second nature for code users; indeed it had to be, for all camp Xs, for tunnellers, for everyone engaged in preparing an escape at all. Security is more than a word; it concerns people, and their feelings, as well as public events. Code users' feelings were liable to get trampled on. Like any other prisoners, they were separated from their families; correspondence, like almost everything else, was rationed; and it was an extra hardship to have to give up some of the few letters that one was allowed to send, for the sake of what was really service business, however deftly it might be concealed as gossip or chat about golf. Winter- bottom's tact was here in conflict with his sense of duty. He came to be good at detecting when code users were running restive, and spelled them off when he could. On the whole, this extra burden was cheerfully shouldered in the camps. He had a number of awkward cases to handle in Great

Britain, when wives discovered from indiscretions by their husbands that their men were deep in correspondence with one of his notional girl-friends.

Of course there were a few slips. For example, when a more elaborate code than Hooker's or the one that Green used had been devised – in this, the message itself was coded on a pattern set by a group of five random letters – one forgetful fictitious aunt wrote to 'Dear Bimbo', when bimbo was the code group in question.

At the enemy end, there were no slips at all. Several camps reported after the war that German security officers suspected that there was some sort of code for correspondence between prisoners and the Allied high command, but in no case were the Germans able to discover how the code worked. Once a prisoner in hospital in Italy was found to have been rash enough to carry on him at that precise moment the complete workings of the second five-letter code, 'Bob'. Though the document could not be got away from his clothes before they were searched, the fact at least was known and promptly reported; that particular code was not used again.

A worse upset occurred in Stockholm, whence an over-zealous British attaché, discovering that he could initiate the dispatch of parcels to prisoners of war direct from Sweden, started cramming them with goodies, tools, and code instructions as well. Winterbottom had the awkward task of getting to Stockholm, overawing his senior, explaining to him what he had done wrong, and winding up that code also. The worst trouble came late in 1942, in the only serious tiff that marred Anglo-American amity on the escape and evasion front.

The origins of the American correspondence section, MI 9's opposite numbers, may be traced back to 9 February 1942, when an intelligence analysis unit at the headquarters of the USAF's combat command at Boiling Field, Washington, D.C. pinpointed the need for codes to be developed and taught to 'members of our Air Forces in case of capture'. The unit had perceived the need in course of conversation with a visiting RAF wing commander. Exactly what steps followed remains unclear, but the need for the correspondence section was obvious enough; it must have been crystal clear to Johnston when he did three weeks' attachment at Beaconsfield at midsummer. After a word with him, Crockatt sent out the following order to every camp he could reach: 'Until Americans in all-American camps all code work to be under orders of British code organiser who will decide users to employ and country to address letters stop London Washington in close touch exchanging information stop for your information if necessary'. Holt and Johnston were immediately given the run of MI 9's code number two, and any other help they needed.

Sadly, some of their most intelligent RAF companions found as time went on that 'the mentality of the average American P/W did not make them suitable operators for coding'; the codes some of them got from Washington were thought to be dangerously easy to break;[14] and worse was to follow. In midwinter 1942-3 Crockatt became convinced that his entire system of code communication with camps was endangered by the misuse, in his view, that the Americans were making of the parallel systems they were trying to set up. Without these communications a large part of MI 9's work would be rendered futile: neither could escape aids be passed safely into camps, nor – much more important – could a great deal of valuable intelligence be smuggled out. He therefore put up a particularly strongly worded paper to the DMI, in which he explained the elements of the whole business of coding – the need to choose only a few people to do it, and those both bright and reliable;

---

14   Compare the occasion in the previous war, when within three hours an American of genius read a message in the field code about to be adopted by the American and British armies in France: it said 'This message is absolutely indecipherable' (Ronald W. Clark, *The Man Who Broke 'Purple'*, 36-8).

the incessant need for secrecy, within the Allied camp as well as in the face of the enemy; and the indispensability of using codes that were not too easily broken. He concluded, modestly but firmly, that unless action was taken to enforce these points he could no longer shoulder the responsibility of commanding MI 9. Davidson the DMI sent the paper across the Atlantic to Strong; an immediate improvement resulted.

In fact the tiff proved a blessing in disguise. From it there resulted visits to America early in 1943 by Crockatt, Winterbottom and Simonds, which did a great deal to improve liaison between MI 9 and MIS-X and sharpened up the work of both.

The principal defect of code letters was that they took so long to travel. Seven weeks for question and answer exchanged between Germany and England was reckoned fast; in Italy it was often more like seven months, sometimes nearer twelve. Could nothing be done by wireless?

From the start, prisoners were on the look-out for chances to beg, borrow or steal wireless receivers; Goebbels's propaganda broadcasts provided odious fare for people brought up in a more truthful and less opinionated society than his. An RAMC officer from the 51st Highland Division indeed succeeded in smuggling his portable receiver into Oflag IXA, Spangenberg, by the simple but none the less brilliantly conceived expedient of placing the small suitcase in which it was concealed behind a radiator in the corridor leading to the room in which all officers were searched before entering the camp. After the search he merely picked up the suitcase and walked into the camp. Later when he was transferred to another camp it travelled hidden in a medicine ball, which was deftly substituted for another one that had been cleared by the German security staff as containing no forbidden contraband. Several other camps bought sets, or constructed them out of bought or stolen parts. Many shot-down airmen, and some army prisoners, were wireless technicians and were glad to keep their hand in by trying to manufacture sets out of odd scraps of metal. Clayton Hutton meanwhile was busy discovering the smallest receivers he could find in Great Britain and devising hiding-places for smuggling them into camps by post.

In late 1940 and in 1941 MI 9 prepared newsletters about the course of the war and distributed them to prisoner of war camps by ordinary post, partly to sustain prisoners' morale, partly it was hoped to lower the morale of enemy censors. Early in 1942 the scheme was dropped; most of the newsletters were well out of date before they arrived, and by then MI 9 were aware that many – indeed most – Oflags and many Stalags had secured a wireless receiver.

Through coded post Crockatt and Winterbottom informed these camps of a code which MI 9 might use to them and of the times and wavelengths at which coded broadcasts would be made. It is always dangerous to indicate one code through another,[15] but the risk in this case seems to have been well judged: there are no indications that the Germans read the messages, or were even aware of them. The system, Crockatt knew, was by no means 100 per cent reliable; a Gestapo search might always discover a receiver, any sort of accident might prevent the operator from having secure access to his set at the critical moment. Still, it seems to have been of some value – how else for instance could MI 9 communicate quickly in the summer of 1943 with so many camps in Italy? – and more will no doubt be known about it when the whole of the section's archives become available for research.

In reserve, Crockatt had access if he needed it to the tremendous engine of the BBC. Powerful transmitters could reach anywhere in the world easily, and he resolved that in some grave emergency – such as an order by Hitler that all prisoners of war in Germany were to be disposed of – he would use BBC channels

---

15    Cp. M. R. D. Foot, *War and Society*, 63, for a startling example from Ireland during the Trouble.

to issue orders. Meanwhile he did occasionally use a source so popular and so austere that it was above suspicion.

This was the weekly Wednesday evening broadcast in the Forces programme by the Radio Padre, whose audience was once estimated by the director of religious broadcasting to number seven million. These talks, as much a wartime institution as Tommy Handley's 'It's That Man Again', were given by the Very Reverend Dr R. Selby Wright, a future moderator of the Church of Scotland. He was in frequent correspondence with Winterbottom; and if he began his talk with the phrase 'Good evening, Forces', this meant that a code message was concealed in it. (He was aware of the fact, but not of the message.) The whole talk was thereupon taken down in shorthand – accidents allowing – in several prisoner of war camps, and the text was puzzled out afterwards. This wireless traffic was in one direction only. Several camps built transmitters; MI 9 smuggled some materials from which this could be done, others were improvised out of what could be obtained on the spot. But Crockatt ordered that they were never to be used, unless in dire emergency, and no such crisis ever arose.

The authority of Professor R. V. Jones has been lent to a statement to the contrary. Howard Cundall, one of his civilian assistants, was in an aircraft shot down over Brittany early on 4 November 1942. The second pilot evaded successfully into Spain. The rest of the crew were captured, Cundall from a small boat in which he was trying to sail home from the Baie de Mont St Michel on 8 November. The Germans thought they had a full crew and did not suspect that Cundall was a passenger, nor did they discover how much he knew about radar. His main difficulty was in passing himself off as a genuine flight lieutenant (as which he was dressed) among his fellow prisoners.

He clearly knew a lot about wireless, eventually became the secret wireless maintenance officer in Stalag Luft III at Sagan, and built a transmitter, or rather collected the parts for it; but the camp history states categorically that 'The transmitter was never assembled for use'. Cundall's friends feel that he must have transmitted, and a short war biography of him states that he did; it is even claimed that he managed to maintain a daily schedule with London during the camp's long march westwards in the spring of 1945. This we frankly cannot believe. Dansey would have been quite within his rights to use Cundall as an MI 6 agent, even without telling Jones, who sat between himself and Cundall on MI 6's staff tree; had he done so, would Cundall have remained at large for a fortnight after being shot down? Undoubtedly Jones received important information from Cundall about German night fighter radar while Cundall was a prisoner of war. It seems most likely that Cundall sent his messages in code letters, and allowed the romantic legend that he sent them over the air to accumulate, as legends do. He was drowned in a yachting accident in 1974.

But we have run ahead of our subject, the actual escapes of 1941–2: it is time to survey what was happening in the field.

First we need to look at two neutral countries. One was the Irish republic, where some RAF Sunderland flying-boat pilots found a chance to apply a standard MI 9 doctrine: seize a holiday or at least a week-end to escape on if you can. They were interned at the Curragh, on a bare plain in Co. Kildare some twenty-five miles westward of Dublin. It is a relief for once to handle Irish history without having to go back to 1169, but one historical reference does impose itself for this place: it was the scene of the notorious episode in the spring of 1914 that unsettled the relations between the British government and army. By 1940 it included two triple-wired enclosures, side by side, one for interned Germans, the other for British. Those held in either were allowed out on parole one day a week, on the understanding that they avoided certain bars reserved for their enemies, and that they did nothing while at large to facilitate an escape.

It happened that one of Crockatt's senior officers, who had better remain unnamed, had a home near Dublin, and was able to set up some safe houses nearby. Moreover, one of the RAF pilots knew an MI 9 code, so it was easy to fix up in advance a time when they could come out. A party of nine of them decided to break out through the main gate at dusk on 25 June 1941, the evening after the Irish Derby had been run on the racecourse nearby. They guessed that their guards, unlike Bavarian or Italian ones, would fire to miss – first round, anyway – instead of firing to kill. None of them had been out of camp that day; but a confederate, who had, managed to divert the gate guard's attention by feigning drunkenness and being sick close by the gate. While the guard concentrated on him, the nine slipped away.

The alarm was raised unexpectedly fast, and two were soon recaptured at an Irish army road block before any of them could reach MI 9's getaway cars. Four of them threw themselves on the mercy of a private friend whom they had met while out on parole; the friend rose to the unexpected occasion; all seven were soon provided with false papers from an MI 9 source and took the train to Northern Ireland. Meanwhile there was a newspaper storm, centred on the untrue allegation that the escapers had broken their parole by settling the final details on the racecourse during the Derby meeting. One of them, Hugh Verity – subsequently commander of the Lysander flight of 161 Squadron which did so much for resistance – had the pleasure of hearing, in the dining car of the train going north, a British officer on leave in plain clothes say to his companion, 'I see from the paper that they have not yet caught all those RAF fellows. I wonder where they are now.'

The Irish government put in a protest so sharp that MI 9 refrained from organising any more escapes, though they continued to send in escape equipment if anyone in the Curragh asked for it. When Verity many years later revisited the scene of this adventure with his wife, he found that some of her relatives who lived nearby still looked on the work of MI 9's helpers in 1941 as treasonable.

There is no trace in the available MI 9 records of any liaison with the French authorities in the first six months of the section's existence; for security's sake, it is to be hoped that none took place. In the aftermath of the armistice of 22 June and the tragic affray at Mers-el-Kebir on 3 July 1940, some Vichy French officials were savagely anti-British; the Dakar affair in early September did not make them any milder. British evaders from Dunkirk who got as far as Marseilles, and pushed on to French North Africa in the hope of being repatriated via Tangier and Gibraltar, were quickly disillusioned. About three score of them were interned in the village of Aumale, known since the Algerian revolution as Sour el Ghozlane, sixty miles south-east of Algiers, in part of a building which served as a lunatic asylum for Arab women. Later evaders, and sailors and airmen cast up on French North African shores, kept adding to their numbers; the appalling conditions in which they had to live kept reducing them. None of them at first knew an MI 9 code; but one of the airmen was a devotee of *The Road to En-Dor* and *The Escaping Club*, and wrote such odd letters to his wife that she referred them to the Air Ministry, and was put in touch with Winterbottom. MI 9 sent, hidden in a pack of playing cards, a plan for taking the whole party off by boat from a small deserted beach east of Algiers, to which they would have to find their own way, got the scheme acknowledged, and fixed a date in October 1941. Almost at the last moment a cable in clear arrived from Aumale which caused the whole scheme to be cancelled. All the ninety prisoners – to call them internees would understate the degree of constraint under which they lived – were moved to a specially built fort at Laghouat, 200 miles south of Algiers and deep in the desert; the nearest railhead was 100 miles away. They were well wired in and guarded by active and hostile Arabs. A recent arrival among them had a code: Charles Lamb, a Swordfish pilot in the Fleet Air Arm. He also had enterprise and an eye for country, and had a little experience in clandestine air landings; he had recently carried out one with success, and been captured on the second

when sent to land his Swordfish on a salt lake that turned out
more lake than salt.

Some of his more conventionally-minded companions
discovered a small unused cellar beneath their stone-paved
room and embarked on a tunnel from it; storing the spoil from
the tunnel in the cellar. It was 190 feet to the outside of the
enceinte wall which lay beyond the main wire.[16] Everybody
took part, and on the night of 6/7 June 1942 twenty-nine officers and men went through it. Dick Cooper of SOE was at large
for three days; everyone else was recaptured before him. After
the failure of the tunnel project, Lamb used his code to draw
MI 9's attention to the suitability of the surrounding desert as
a landing strip (there is now an airport near the site), and to
request that aircraft from Malta fly in to rescue them. The Air
Ministry would have turned the proposal down flat, but the
Malta-Fleet Air Arm angle of approach had an originality that
appealed to Norman Crockatt. He was bitterly disappointed
when Lamb had to cable to cancel the operation: conditions in
Laghouat were so bad and brutal that he could no longer rely
on enough of his colleagues to carry the escape through. The
survivors were liberated when 'Torch' freed north-west Africa in
November 1942, and the camp housed Axis prisoners thereafter.

Guarding prisoners in the western desert was a task which the
Germans left as a rule to the Italians, who performed it efficiently. It was one of the aspects of war – like midget submarine
work, but not so dangerous – at which they were accomplished.
Not much good indeed was done to future Anglo-Italian relations by the ferocity they applied to those put in their charge.
In principle, prisoners were not held in camps in the desert

16   Details and diagrams in a note by Squadron Leader R. G. Brickell,
     RAFVR, the consulting engineer to the project, in *Journal of the
     Institution of Civil Engineers*, xx, 108–12 (April 1943). We owe this
     reference to Dick Cooper, one of the leading spirits.

for long. They were far more easily administered in mainland Italy; the Axis forces had trouble enough feeding and watering themselves without burdening their supply system with extra mouths that were only a military liability – not to speak of the temptation an isolated prisoner of war camp might hold out to the Special Air Service or the Long Range Desert Group.

'Ultra' signals, deciphered German accounts of aircraft and ship loads, were presumably used to protect prisoners in transit from Africa to Italy from air or sea attack. The protection was not perfect; one ship at least, loaded with some 500 prisoners, was sunk by torpedo. Her crew abandoned both her and her human load, who were locked in the hold; about half of the prisoners managed to get out into the sea, and were rescued. A Japanese crew, on a similar occasion, tossed some grenades down the hold before they battened it down and took to the boats; whence they fired on prisoners swimming in the water. Just, in fact, as Africa was mild compared to Russia, even Russia could be mild compared to the Pacific. But Africa is our present concern.

Reports are scarce, and no archives bearing on Axis camps in Cyrenaica have surfaced at all; there are no doubt many good tales to be told of people who escaped from them, with and without MI 9's help, though only two have come our way: both from 'Popski'. The first is barely credible. He was lurking in the Gebel Akhdar in July 1942, when

> one morning a little South African was brought in. He had escaped from a prison camp near Benghazi ninety-two days previously and for over two and a half months he had wandered by himself in the inhospitable southern desert where in the dry season no Arabs go. He had lived on a little water he found now and then in the radiators of abandoned vehicles and scraps of food left in opened tins, making his way slowly eastwards through the endless desert. At times his mind had wandered and he had been unconscious for several days. Yet such was the greatness

of heart of this little clerk who had spent his life in an office in
Johannesburg that, after he had been only a day with us he asked
to be allowed to remain in the desert and help us with our work,
rather than being evacuated to Egypt by the next convoy.

'Popski' himself, whose own heart was not small, then reconnoitred the port of Derna, on foot and in khaki drill uniform;
everybody wore such ramshackle clothes in the desert that
the Italians all took him for a German, and the Germans for
an Italian, and he made sure he had to do no talking. He spotted gaps through which men could get out of both the transit
POW camps there, each filled with prisoners from lately fallen
Tobruk; and 'made for home with a light heart'. He believed that
'The apprehension of personal danger can be easily mastered
once the lesson has been learned that nothing worse than death
can be expected – and the prospect of death, though it can be a
bother, is not particularly terrifying to most of us.'

Through his Arab friends he sent word in to the prisoners
about routes out and provided guides; fifty men had joined
him by mid-August and he sent them back to Cairo on LRDG
lorries. Meanwhile he pitched in a letter to Piatti, the Italian
general who was base commander at Barce, to inform him that
official note had been taken of the 'cowardly and barbarous'
executions of Senussi Arabs who had, 'following the dictates of
humanity', succoured unarmed Allied escapers, and he threatened sharp reprisals: the letter was never acknowledged, but the
torture and execution of Arabs stopped.

Simonds complained, when he took over his escape work in Cairo,
that 'there was no underground organisation in Greece or Crete
with whom we were in direct contact', and a man in a position to
know dates the beginning of effective resistance in Greece as late
as October 1942. By that time there were few prisoners of war left
in Greece, and most of them were too badly wounded to move.
Normal Axis policy, as in any other occupied country, was to hold

prisoners in transit camps till they could be sent by the trainload to a permanent camp in the home country. MI 9 and MIS-X lectures included a few words on how to escape from a train; preferably from its right-hand side and as it went round a left-hand bend, to make it more difficult for the guards to shoot. They would certainly shoot to kill; for if the whole train stopped any number of other prisoners might seize a chance to break away as well.

There were two main transit camps in Greece; one in Athens, and one in Salonika which was closed down on 5 October 1941. A British sergeant-major at the latter made a vividly bad impression on many men who passed through the camp, because he seemed to go so far out of his way to co-operate with the enemy; no doubt he had to answer for this at some court martial when the war was over. Even from close to his brooding presence, escapes were not impossible; and one from a near-by prison hospital is too odd to go unmentioned.

Squadron Leader Edward Howell, a regular fighter pilot taken prisoner seriously wounded in Crete, found God nine months later as he lay despairing in his hospital bed. This kind of illuminating clarity came to a number of prisoners; several have testified to the feeling that some kind of providence kept a definite eye on them during their escapes. Howell's exit from Salonika was certainly providential. He still could not use his wounded right arm; his left shoulder was not quite healed. He clambered onto a brightly lit wall at the edge of his hospital, about twenty degrees off a sentry's line of sight, and walked noisily along it; the sentry did not stir. Within spitting distance of a party of German soldiers playing cards, he climbed noisily over another wall. They did not stir either. He walked out of Salonika, was succoured by friendly Greeks, and eventually got away to Turkey with a party of Greek army officers.

'Sandy' Thomas, whom Howell met when he got back to Cairo, had also been captured wounded in Crete, and had had a still more adventurous time. He was a young New Zealander – he ended the war as one of Freyberg's crack battalion commanders

– who had, at the fourth attempt, cut his way out of the main Salonika camp, and had hidden for several months with the monks of Mount Athos. Noel Rees finally rescued Thomas, and the five companions he brought with him by small borrowed boat from Greece, by collecting them from a village some seventy miles north of Smyrna in two magnificent Rolls-Royces.

With neither of these escapes can MI 9 claim that it had much to do. Their interest for our present purpose is that they show the sort of atmosphere in which MI 9 and MIS-X had to work in the Balkans, and give a faint idea as well of the quality of some of the people involved.

The weariness, the fever and the fret of life in the big camps in Italy has most of it gone unrecorded. At the end of the war responsible officers and senior NCOs were found to prepare camp histories of a score of the main German camps; some of them bulky. Nothing of the kind seems to have been done for Italy; no doubt because, at the moment of the Italian change of sides in 1943, no one had time to organise it, and by 1945 the business of tracking down former SBOs in Italy and getting them to put pen to paper was too complicated for anyone to undertake it. Two years' instead of two or three weeks' passage of time would in any case have blunted their memories. Few camps tried to keep records; fewer still, to smuggle records through two more years of captivity in another country.

The best account we have of life as a prisoner of the Italians is, nominally, in fiction: autobiographical novels by Dan Billany, a Yorkshire schoolteacher who was captured in the desert and wrote two books while on the run in the Apennines in the winter of 1943–4. He was killed in action in obscure circumstances before he could revise either. *The Cage*[17] depicts life in Campo 49, an orphanage on the Lombard plain near Parma.

---

17   Revised for him by David Dowie. The last thirty pages of his still more powerful *The Trap* describe his first few months as a prisoner.

Escapers in Italy were faced with their profession's worst difficulty in an acute form. Getting out of one's camp was never more than half the battle, sometimes much the more easy half. Getting out of occupied territory afterwards was never easy; as a rule it was insuperably difficult. The difficulties in Italy were aggravated by the Italians' insatiable curiosity. The phrase 'mind your own business' is unthinkable in Italian. Anyone was liable to be exposed to a torrent of questions about his identity, his relatives, his past, his future, the state of his health, his boots, his soul. Using public transport meant subjecting oneself to public scrutiny and interrogation. If one walked instead, it was seldom possible – least of all in midwinter with the mountains deep in snow – to avoid all villages, and in villages by day children would start questioning; if they got no useful answers they would go to fetch grown-ups. By night there were dogs to raise the alarm and Fascist policemen to see who had woken them.

It is therefore not surprising that hardly anybody got out of Mussolini's Italy, against his will, before his fall. One among the very few who did is Anthony Deane-Drummond. He was fond of the extremes in warfare; claimed to have joined L detachment, from which SAS sprang, even before David Stirling; and was captured in February 1941 in south central Italy after the raid on the Tragino viaduct. He describes vividly in *Return Ticket* how impossible he and his fellow parachutists found it to march or to fight through crowds of women and children; how they had tamely to surrender, to avert civilian casualties; and how he tricked his way out of a military hospital in northern Italy and managed by luck and fieldcraft combined the difficult and mountainous frontier crossing into Switzerland. Another subaltern, M. E. Stewart of the Intelligence Corps, escaped from another prison hospital in central Italy in the same month, and also reached Switzerland safely. MI 9 can claim some credit for both these escapes, as both officers had been carefully trained in the principles of escaping and evading techniques; though no amount of training can foresee every conceivable emergency, and a lot has to be left to the courage and enterprise of the individual on the spot.

Next we must survey the main escape arena: Germany. MI 9 got off to a flying start: it had established code communication with every Oflag there within seven months of Dunkirk, promptly received numerous requests for escape materials, and as promptly dispatched them.

Successful escapes began as early as the spring of 1941. The very first person to get out of a permanent prisoner of war camp and on to neutral ground was a private in the Army Dental Corps called L. A. Coe, who was in Switzerland before the end of March. So was the first Indian officer to escape, Jemadar Jehan Dad of the Royal Indian Army Service Corps. Unfortunately, no further details about either are known.

So many people, officers in particular, had escaped already and been recaptured, that the Germans had set up two *Sonderlagern* special punishment camps, one at Posen (now Poznań) in western Poland, the other and more famous at Colditz castle in Saxony. Tunnellers were busy in several camps, including even the air transit camp, Dulag Luft at Oberursel near Frankfurt-am-Main. Eighteen prisoners escaped from it early in June 1941 through a tunnel that began in the room of the SBO, a regular RAF wing commander who had already several times been denounced as too friendly with the Germans, by people who did not understand that he was buttering the Germans up in order to deceive them more thoroughly. They had fallen into such friendly ways with him that they not only took him out to dinner, thus enabling him to look over the surroundings of the camp, but – unprompted – provided the prisoners with a wireless receiver. This was Day, the future hero of Sagan: he had a useful colleague both at Dulag Luft and at Sagan, Roger Bushell.

None of this party were at large for more than a few days; foresters caught most of them in the fir and beech glades of the nearby Taunus range. But they felt they had had an interesting run for their money; and they soon reported their adventures home by coded letter. Future relevant MI 9 lectures included a stronger warning about forest guards. There were no more significant escapes from Oberursel; Day ceased to be SBO, and went off to inspire escapes elsewhere.

The technical difficulties of escape from a permanent camp are not all that severe, as a rule. There were some places, like Spangenberg castle which housed Oflag IX, which presented almost insuperable physical difficulties. Even in this fortress people were prepared to try escapes with home-made rope and grapnel, none of them successful. In the village below, prisoners in Oflag IX A/H, called Haina Kloster, suffered from an alternative difficulty. Two hundred officers were confined in a space only seventy-five yards square, surrounded by a barbed wire fence nine feet high and nine feet thick, overlooked by armed sentries equipped with machine guns and floodlights. So they had no privacy from each other or from their captors, and thus could get none of the preliminary tailoring, pass-forging, map-studying done, without which an escape stood no chance of success. Camp floodlights were always turned off during air raids; frequent, unpredictable patrols replaced them.

There were a few really original escapes, in spite of the similarity of the problem in all camps. What prisoners generally called 'the Warburg wire job' may be singled out; it took place from Oflag VIB. The camp was set up in October 1941 for 2,500 officers and 450 orderlies, all British, in huts on a high desolate plateau three miles from Warburg station. Fleas, mice and rats abounded at first – it took four months to get the camp clean – and food was short. A strong escape committee brought off one remarkable coup in which ninety-four people took part: forty-one got out of the camp, while the others set up massive diversions to distract the sentries. The method of exit was sublimely simple: ladders and duckboards made from stolen roofbeams, to take the escaping party up, across, and down beyond the wire. The party left, all forty-one within three minutes, at the end of August 1942, just before the camp was disbanded. Three of them, marching steadily west-north-west on an MI 9 compass course by night and lying up by day, were across the frontier in Holland by mid-September, paused for nine days in a friendly farmer's barn, and were then taken over by the 'Comet' line which brought them out of danger. They were the first three over the wire: Major A. S. B. Arkwright of the Royal Scots Fusiliers, Captain A. H. S. Coombe-Tennant, Welsh Guards (now a priest at Downside Abbey), and Captain R. J. Fuller of the Royal Sussex Regiment, who brought off the difficult feat of pretending to be insane when the party ran into a temporary hitch at Lille.

Again, it was the first two out who got right away when a party left Oflag VB at Biberach on 13/14 September 1941. Two dozen people had the use of a tunnel which had taken three months to build. Justly enough, its two main inspirers were the first to leave through it and the only ones to get the full benefit of it: Michael Duncan of the OBLI, and Barry O'Sullivan of the Royal Armoured Corps. MI 9's hand in this escape, though not revealed by Duncan in his book, can reasonably be inferred from it. He and O'Sullivan had met and teamed up in the Straflager at Posen. They travelled together for part of their way westward across Bavaria and then separated; each knew, from smuggled large-scale maps, exactly where he wanted to go. They crossed into Switzerland in the Schaffhausen salient and were clearly aware of every twist and angle of it at the points they chose to cross; information that must have reached them from maps prepared under Crockatt's guidance and sent in by Clayton Hutton's ingenuity.

Once they had made themselves known to Cartwright, he sent them back to England down the 'Pat' line, on which they had to travel at a particularly awkward moment; their hosts would say nothing but 'There has been a bit of an accident' – Carpentier's arrest, though they did not say so – and thought that their passengers safety overrode everything else.

From Colditz itself escapes had already begun by this time. Peter Allan of the Cameron Highlanders, an excellent German speaker, was smuggled out of the fortress in a pail-lasse, and got clear away from the neighbourhood; his German was indeed good enough for him to accept a lift from an SS officer, who drove him a hundred miles towards Vienna. There Allan's money ran out, and so did his luck. He appealed to the United States consul; but was unable to persuade that cautious diplomat that he was a genuine British escaper, not a Gestapo provocateur fishing for an excuse to close the consulate down. He fell asleep on a park bench, broke down under interrogation from a passing policeman, and was back at Colditz doing his month's solitary a fortnight after he left.

Reid and Barry meanwhile were deep in their second attempt to get out of Colditz by tunnel. On 29/30 May 1941 they, six other British officers – including Colonel German, the SBO – and four Poles slipped into a tunnel that began in the prisoners' canteen. The Germans had just locked the canteen, with a new type of lock they thought insurmountable. Reid had no trouble dismounting it, and thought moreover he had bribed a sentry near the tunnel's exit: he had paid over 100 Reichsmarks, and another 400 were to follow after he had gone. Unhappily for the escapers, the sentry told his superiors, and they were arrested one by one as they crawled out onto the lawn. The sentry got a fortnight's leave, but the remaining 400 Reichsmarks of MI 9's money remained available for other attempts.

Several of the Colditz escapers are justly famous, and the whole camp would have agreed with the opinion of one of them, that 'imprisonment was a spur to new achievement', and that 'The real escaper is more than a man equipped with compass, maps, papers, disguise and a plan. He has an inner confidence, a serenity of spirit which make him a Pilgrim'. When it was Neave's turn to go to Colditz, after an eastabout escape from Thorn had petered out too soon, he found that 'It was stimulating to live in this hive of industry', for 'success can

only be achieved by a minute mastery of detail and a study of
the mind and methods of the enemy.'

Two old Wykehamists, gifted to an unusual degree with that
intelligent pertinacity which is one of the school's hallmarks,
who were in the same regiment – the King's Royal Rifle Corps –
escaped together from Stalag XXD at Posen on 28 May 1941, by
hiding successfully in the rubbish dump: two subalterns, A. M.
I Sinclair[18] and E. G. B. Davies-Scourfield,[19] who got out with
their major, R. B. Littledale. Though the Nazis had annexed
western Poland, its Germanisation was still far from complete,
and these escapers got a great deal of help from the Poles: one
of the joys of escaping in Poland was that the population was so
strongly anti-German. They were passed on to Warsaw, where
they spent several months in an Englishwoman's flat, frequently
being entertained to more or less formal dinners by a succession
of hosts, and engaged in incessant discussions about when it
would be safe to move on and in what direction. Eventually, in
January 1942, they cast up in Sofia, where the Bulgarian police
promised them asylum and then promptly sold them to the
Gestapo. Littledale and Michael Sinclair escaped again on 17
January, from a train near Vienna; Sinclair was almost at once
recaptured, but Littledale was at large for nearly six months
more, in Bohemia. They all met again eventually in Colditz.

In that castle-full of professional escapers, a hard core of
escape-minded characters was provided by threescore Dutch
colonial officers, cheerful strong seasoned men whose military
bearing put the British to some shame. As a mild form of goon-
baiting, the British tended to straggle onto parade, hatless and
dishevelled, while the Dutch were always punctual and immaculate. The two nationalities agreed to pool their resources for

---

18   Portrait as frontispiece of J. E. R. Wood, *Detour.*

19   A curious concatenation: Davies-Scourfield, Garrow and Foot all
     once sat together in a German class taught by W. R. P. Ridgway, who
     will figure in ch xi. And see R. Eggers, *Colditz Recaptured,* 72–83.

escaping. Most of the Dutch spoke fluent German, which few Englishmen there but Michael Sinclair could manage; hence the idea of pairing a Dutch and a British officer for an escape. By 1942 the escape committee 'was well provided with keys and could gain access to any part of the castle', even the French, even the Poles had agreed to co-ordinate their escape attempts with the rest, and some serious work could begin.

Pat Reid, a captain in the RASG, was in charge of escape planning from January 1941, and had Airey Neave as his deputy from August. He organised a regular, permanent, twenty-four-hour watch on the enemy, in which all the British prisoners were glad enough to join. This did not only mean that a cry of 'Goons up' heralded every German guard's entrance to the prisoners' courtyard, or to a particular staircase in it; it meant that every sentry's beat, every arc light's timetable, the entire routine of the garrison were studied as intensely as any young lover ever watched the movements of the beloved: the enemy's methods received such painstaking attention that no chink in his restraining armour could go unspotted.

The Poles took the lead in lock-forcing; the British learned from them fast. Squadron Leader Brian Paddon became particularly expert. Reid, who was an engineer in civil life, had an eye for how buildings are put together, which led him to discover a disused passageway that ended in an attic over the Germans' guardhouse. This part of the castle included their officers' mess. Through this passage he sent out, on 5 January 1942, Neave and a Dutch officer Tony Luteyn, dressed in home-made German officers' uniforms. Their cardboard leggings would not have looked well after a rainstorm, but they passed after dark. Neave, with Etonian self-assurance, returned the salute of the sentry outside the guardroom door, and they strolled away down a side path towards the married quarters. By the time Reid had finished closing up their exit behind them, his watchers were able to tell him that the getaway had at least started well. In fact they got clear away; survived a check at Ulm by walking out of a government office by a back door and another at Singen close to the Swiss frontier by bluff; and in little more than forty-eight hours were safely on Swiss soil.[20]

Their absence was covered at the frequent Colditz *Appels* – roll calls, at which the guards painstakingly counted and recounted an often shifting mob of prisoners – by a couple of Reid's 'ghosts', officers whom the Germans wrongly believed to have left the camp (two devoted men, Flight Lieutenant J. W. Best and Lieutenant M. E. Harvey, RN, 'ghosted' in Colditz for eleven months on end[21]). Next night another pair left by the same route: J. Hyde-Thompson of the Durham Light Infantry and another Dutchman, Lieutenant Donkers. They came unstuck at Ulm main line station. The girl ticket clerk, suspicious already of two vaguely odd-looking Dutch electricians who had booked to Singen on the previous evening, jibbed at being asked for tickets to the same station by a similar pair, and called for the station police, to whom the escapers soon confessed their true identity. Reid had not tried to cover up for four: Colditz was already aware. He decided that 'From now on, no more than two escapers at a time would travel the same route:' a sensible precaution.

There was a constant coming and going through those castle gates, officially; and of course all these sorties provided opportunities for prisoners to try unofficial exits as well. Michael Sinclair had bad sinus trouble; the commandant, a stickler for convention, saw that he was sent out for treatment by a specialist in Leipzig. There, on 2 June 1942, Sinclair eluded his escort. Reid had provided him with a forged *Ausweise* (permit) that enabled him to travel by train, and enough of MI 9's money for his fare to France. He turned his tunic inside out and discarded

---

20    Details in Appendix 4.

21    WO 208/3288, 5–6. R. Eggers, *Colditz: the German story*, 114–15, 154–9, gives an entertaining account of how utterly this system baffled the Germans.

his cap, so with his thorough command of German he could easily pass as a civilian. He had got as far as Cologne before he was detected at an extra strict control of papers, following on an air raid the night before.

Paddon, whom no lock could hold, decided in his own words that 'he travels best who travels alone' when caught with a Polish fellow escaper on Leipzig station, while both were posing as Belgian forced labourers. They had skipped from a military hospital near Dresden, to which they had been sent from Colditz for treatment. On 11 June 1942 he left Colditz officially again, to face a court martial at Thorn for the crime of insulting a German NCO. Colditz sent one of its sharpest sergeants to keep an eye on him, and he was seen into a cell at Thorn. By morning the bird had flown. Some RAF sergeants, including a friend of Paddon's, had a route to Stettin ready, his need was greater than theirs, they put him on it and he was in Sweden in a week. Paddon's nickname, 'Never-a-dull-moment', was well earned. He had a force and gaiety of manner that was all but irresistible, except to camp guards, and used it with effect on the crew of the first Swedish ship he found. Not everybody was so fortunate. Flight Lieutenant H. H. Vivian for example walked out of Stalag Luft III at Sagan at the end of September 1942 disguised as a medical orderly. He hunted in vain for a ship successively at Danzig, Stettin, Stralsund and Sassnitz. Discouraged, he decided to abandon the attempt to cross the Baltic and to try his luck westabout instead. He had a set of false papers that was invalid outside north Germany, so he destroyed them; went to Berlin by train; and had the bad luck to fall at once into a police control he could not pass with no papers at all.

Another half-successful walk out from Sagan had been made a few days earlier by Flight Lieutenant A. van Rood, dressed as a *Hundeführer,* a guard-dog's keeper. He got right down to the Swiss frontier, but was arrested before he could cross it; re-escaped in Leipzig on the way back; and was almost immediately recaptured. Such walks out were dreamed of at

Colditz, but seldom secured. Reid himself escaped thence on 14 October 1942 with Hank Wardle of the Canadian air force, who had long been his closest helper, Ronnie Littledale, and one of Colditz's rare naval officers, Billie Stephens, a survivor of the great raid on St Nazaire. This interservice and international team climbed out through a barred window – cutting the bars with an MI 9 saw – and managed to slip across various brilliantly lighted pathways while sentries' backs were turned. They then succeeded in climbing down the moat, and with infinite difficulty scrambled out through a cellar flue. All four were in Switzerland within a week. (Littledale did not survive the war; he went back to his regiment, and was killed in action in Italy.)

Besides courage, clothes, food, money and luck, an escaper across a dictatorship had, as Vivian's example has just shown, to have papers. Forging papers was an essential war sub-industry throughout resistance, and prisoners of war worked hard in it. Their main product in Germany was *Ausweise,* work permits and travel permits for foreign labourers. In Colditz, they created a home-made camera out of the lenses of a dismantled pair of field glasses and some cigar boxes; MI 9 sent in both film and developing chemicals. With this, the photographs for identity documents could easily be made. Miniature cameras – Clayton Hutton invented one which could pass as a large cigarette-lighter – were among the most important of the stores smuggled into Germany and Italy by him. Yet the photograph was only part of the problem.

It was possible to fake print by drawing by hand in Indian ink, but only if infinite, meticulous care was taken. A few people, architects or draughtsmen before they joined up, had the patience and skill to devote themselves to this thankless but indispensable task. Without their painstaking efforts, a great many of the escapes that succeeded would have failed. One of the most competent of them was John Mansel, a territorial company commander in the Queen's Regiment who was taken prisoner near the Somme in May 1940, almost as soon as he came under fire. He too was a Wykehamist, trained to hold fast. His diary, published soon after he died recently, provides an unforgettable picture of the daily life of an officer prisoner. He took care to put nothing in it that would get him into trouble with the Germans if it was found in a search, and took even greater trouble to make sure that they never saw any of his products inopportunely. It took him an average of eight seconds to conceal any clandestine work he was doing and to reestablish himself as an innocent draughtsman.

Could the required papers be sent in, through the usual channels, by MI 9 or MIS-X? Writing in the aftermath of the war, an assertive ex-prisoner from Sagan held that this should have been done. He would have liked 'printed reproductions of all identity documents, travel permits, etc. used by the Detaining Power, with full particulars of the exact circumstances in which each is used', some with signatures ready forged. This was crying for the moon.

MI 9's staff did make various attempts to send in *Ausweise* and other useful documents, but were not really well placed to do so. By the time an escaper had made the home run to London, and described the kind of document minutely enough, and produced a specimen stamp, and MI 9 (or more probably MI 6) had copied it, and the copy had been sent back in to a camp from which it might be usable, the rules had probably been changed, so that the document had become obsolete. This presented a problem as insoluble as Mr Gladstone's struggles depicted by Sellar and Yeatman in 'trying to guess the answer to the Irish Question; unfortunately, whenever he was getting warm, the Irish secretly changed the Question'.

Stamps could be forged easily enough with stubs of linoleum, or even potato, and every underground apprentice knows how easy it is to forge a signature with the help of a newly hard-boiled egg. One of the main objects of camp 'traders' was to secure the loan of documents, so that stamps and lettering could be copied. The bent way for camps to keep abreast of the

ever-shifting German regulations was by full and careful interrogation of returned escapers, all soon as they were accessible.
One early escaper, for instance, had carried in lieu of an *Ausweis*
a letter typed on a stolen typewriter that purported to be signed
by the head police official at Koblenz. He heard the policemen who recaptured him – who did not know that he spoke
some German – laughing their heads off because the letter had
been signed by the *Polizeikotntnissar,* not the *Polizei-präsident*:
a mistake not made again. If this interrogation was carefully,
even exhaustively carried out by someone who knew his business, large advantages might follow. It could be an important
solace for a recaptured escaper to know that his comrades would
benefit from his mistakes; with any luck he could benefit from
them himself.

Although all the best-known escapes from German camps were
made by officers, a great many more were made by other ranks.
Officer prisoners were forbidden to work at all; though many of
them did in fact work hard at academic subjects or at amateur
theatricals, or very hard indeed at the emotionally engrossing
profession of escape. Private soldiers, on the other hand, were
required to work, and NCOs often asked that they might work
as well; this much diminished the time and the energy they had
to spare for preparing escapes, though it might improve their
physical fitness for the long journey home. A great many of
them nevertheless at least tried to escape; over four thousand
got into Switzerland, by no means all of them from Italy. Most
other ranks (enlisted men) were put into *Arbeitskommandos,*
labour camps, where conditions varied enormously. Some were
vast, harsh hutment areas, with poor food, sadistic guards, stern
taskmasters and nasty work. Some were mines – coal, lignite,
salt particularly; some were forest camps, mild enough in
summer or with a weak supervisor, harsh in winter or with a
sour one. Seven-day working weeks were common, for example at Stalag IVA in the lignite-mining area. Any particular

prisoner's chances of escape hinged much more on the luck of what camp he was in than on any preparations he or MI 9 or MIS-X could make to rescue him.

For instance, those who had the misfortune to be imprisoned at Lord Man's Town – Stalag IVF, of which the administrative headquarters lay at Hartmannsdorf in Saxony, four-fifths of the way from Leipzig to Chemnitz (currently named Karl-Marx-Stadt) – might be put in any of ninety-five *Arbeitskommandos,* working at a score of trades. Between four and five thousand British troops, and a few hundred from the Dominions, were held here for most of the War. But there were hardly any officers, there was no escape committee, there is no sign that any material was received from MI 9; and so nothing useful at all, on the escape front, got done. A few people ran away out of mere boredom, but with preparations so Inadequate that they were soon and easily retaken. Others were better organised, better led, or simply luckier. People who were filing to be good at escape needed the ingrained toughness of a Richard Pape; they needed also the single-mindedness dinned into Pape by Douglas Bader, when both happened to be passing through Dulag Luft at Oberursel at the same time.

An instance is provided by A. E. Hawtin, a sergeant-major in the Oxfordshire and Buckinghamshire Light Infantry, the same regiment as Rupert Barry. With that sense of exact timing for which sergeant-majors are famous the world over, Hawtin observed a space of a few seconds during which neither of the sentries marching and counter-marching across the gate of his camp near Thorn could actually see it, pounced on his opportunity, and within a week was on board a ship that took him safely to Sweden.

A collective, rather than an individual instance comes from Stalag Luft IIIE, in the four brick huts of a former Saxon youth hostel at Dobrilugk-Kirchhain. The whole camp was only some 150 yards square; a hundred guards bottled up nearly 200 NCO prisoners from the British, Australian, Canadian, and New

Zealand air forces and from the Fleet Air Arm; a couple of RAMC medical orderlies and a solitary paratroop private made up the total. (The paratrooper was there because the German airborne forces were part of the Luftwaffe; of which the administration did not care to notice that British airborne forces were part of the army.) Under the inspiration of W/O R. J. Alexander, the elected camp leader, an escape committee was formed in autumn 1941. Morale was high; 'The whole Camp was united in any scheme designed to damage the German morale, or to further escape plans'. There was little contact with MI 9; there was no wireless, and only a single code user, and no trick parcels were received. But the concentration of so many high-spirited men in so small a space produced its own effervescence.

A dozen of them got out, through a hole in a hut wall into the neighbouring rifle range, in October 1941 while all the Abwehl staff were attending a camp concert. One was caught in the middle of the same night for being fool enough to whistle an English song as he walked through a village; the others were soon rearrested also. The trouble was that searches in the camp were so frequent, and the place so small, that there was no opportunity for forgery so no one had false papers to see him through the controls that proliferated whenever there was a local alarm.

On the other hand, there were several ex-miners in the camp, and they settled down to make a tunnel: a somewhat tricky task, as they struck water eight feet below ground. In the end, it was 227 feet long, shored up by bed boards, and ventilated by two-inch-diameter air holes; besides a brick covering one of which a restless German general stood for some minutes during a prolonged search by fifty men. He happened not to kick the brick; the searchers found nothing of importance – the tunnel spoil was all hidden beneath the huts – and in early May 1942 there was a mass escape: fifty-two people got out. All were recaptured within ten days, and did fourteen days' cells; the camp was then closed down, and its inhabitants went to reinforce the escaping teams at Sagan.

Contrast a large camp with a small.

D. D. W. Nabarro, a sergeant in the RAF, was shot down over Kiel in a Whitley in January 1941. He was one of many thousand prisoners of several nationalities at Bad Suiza in Thuringia. On 25 November 1941 he and a Belgian friend talked their way past the guard on the gate at half-past six in the morning with a story that they had been detailed to clean the commandant's office. They took a train westwards, were recaptured, and re-escaped at once. They went on walking westwards till they had left the Reich altogether, and in Luxembourg 'realised that we had got out of Germany by the fact that people looked so much more cheerful'; a wry comment on the delights of dictatorship. They got right through.

Five days earlier, J. A. McCairns, a fighter command sergeant pilot shot down over Gravelines in July 1941, had escaped from the same camp with three friends. They hoped to seize an aircraft somewhere near Weimar and fly it home, but were unlucky: they were soon back behind bars. In January 1942 McCairns got out again, this time with success; he crossed south Germany, France and Spain, was commissioned when he got to England, and began a distinguished new flying career in the clandestine Lysander flight of 161 Squadron.

From another huge work camp, at Steglitz in the south-western suburbs of Berlin, Nabarro's early-bird device had been anticipated. Driver W. C. Bach, RASC, one of the camp interpreters, whom the sentries knew quite well by sight, slipped out through the main gate at twenty past six in the morning on 31 October 1941, as if on his way to the German officers' barracks; changed into plain clothes in a toolshed, out of the sentries' sight; took a through train to Stuttgart, on which only soldiers' papers were checked, and another to Lorrach; walked to the Swiss border, on which he had exact information; lay up for a night in a dug-out; and was at his Swiss uncle's house near Winterthür just after midnight on 2/3 November, after walking round both sides' frontier police on the border.

An interesting escape was made from the same camp late on Anzac day, 25 April 1942, by Sergeant J. Prendergast of the Welch Regiment. He had come to Berlin from Salonika in a party of 190 men of supposedly Irish origin, whom the Germans wrongly believed to be ready to change sides. He befriended Sergeant John Bryan, RAF, and they escaped together with ease, opening their hut's shutters from inside and cutting some unlit wire. From a suburban station, they picked up a goods wagon labelled for Antwerp; faking the seal on the door. They reached Antwerp at dusk next evening. Prendergast's prose is too vivid to summarise:

> I got out through the window to make for an air raid shelter about 30 yards away, where I was to wait for Bryan. On my way to the shelter a German guard saw me and called, 'Hallo, hallo' after me. I took no notice and walked quietly on to the shelter. I stood near the door. The guard followed me and came into the shelter. I was standing in one of the blast protection slipways, close against the wall. The guard had a torch in one hand and a revolver in the other. I waited till he got level with me and hit him under the chin, knocking him out. I put him in the far corner of the shelter. I waited some time for Bryan, but he did not come.

No one can blame Bryan for staying in his truck, but it was Prendergast who got home the sooner. He walked along by-roads, clean away from Antwerp, past Brussels, across the battlefields of Waterloo and Mons, into France, and on to Château-Thierry. There some friendly French people took him in care, saw him down to Nimes, and handed him over to 'an organisation', probably the 'Pat' line.

One more escape from Bad Sulza gives an example of the ordinary soldierly virtues in action, heightened by the sort of enterprise that Crockatt inculcated. Two privates in the Argyll and Sutherland Highlanders, named Macfarlane and Goldie, prisoners since St Valery, broke out of their Thuringian barrack hut late on 20 March 1942 with a jemmy. Over their battledress they wore the blue overalls in which they worked. These were boldly marked KG – *Kriegsgefangener,* prisoner of war – on the back, in red. They each wore, and took care never to take off in public, a forty-pound rucksack which completely covered the marking. 'We attracted a certain amount of attention on the road because of our large packs but we made a point of keeping ourselves cleaned and shaven and also cleaned our boots regularly. No one stopped us on the way.' They had the luck their courage deserved, endured a week in a railway wagon of salt bound for Belgium, and were picked up by 'an organisation', probably 'Comet', when they got there. They were back in Scotland by midsummer.

# Counter-attack

The German and Italian armed forces got on badly with their countries' secret police; this is normal practice in dictatorships. They did not always manage to keep their antagonism hidden from their prisoners either. In some large camps in both countries a secret police officer was attached to the permanent staff, to keep an eye both on the prisoners and on their guards. One in Biberach was nicknamed 'Snow White' by the prisoners, on account of his white hair and moustache 'and the line of henchmen which followed him everywhere in single file'. The German army adjutant at Biberach 'disliked running a prison camp but, far more, he disliked Snow White, the Gestapo Security Officer, who always appeared with him on parade.' The two were so near an open quarrel that it was easy for the prisoners to fudge the count at any *Appel;* one absentee was concealed from the Germans till he had got away to Switzerland – Chandos Blair, of the Seaforth Highlanders, the first British officer to escape from Germany, who walked out on 30 June 1941. 'The Adjutant's reaction to this was to whisper to a British officer: "Don't tell anyone, but I'm very pleased" – it was a "smack in the eye" for Snow White.'

This was all very well, but prisoners could never rely on such good fortune. There is a general tendency in dictatorships for more and more power to accrue to the secret police, who come to dominate the whole state. This was particularly noticeable in Germany. There, the armed forces' security service, the Abwehr, was eventually taken over altogether by the party service, the SD: not to the advantage of any prisoner of war. The Italian OVRA was never as strong as its German counterpart, but it could be sharp and nasty enough; in Mussolini's rump republic of Salo in the last eighteen months of the war, working hand in iron glove with Himmler's SD, it could be very nasty indeed, and it has left odious memories behind, both in the French Alps and in Yugoslavia.

The Abwehr, the SD and the OVRA used ordinary police methods, little changed since Fouché's and Metternich's day, but used them more intensely; and they added to them several technical refinements that had not been available before. The horrors of the electrified torture chamber were usually reserved for worse enemies of Fascist regimes than escaping prisoners of war, or evaders. The telephone provided trouble enough; it was easy to ask a suspect to wait for a few minutes, while a telephone call verified his identity. Whether the call went through promptly was another matter; by and large, the longer the war went on the more Continental telephone communications suffered from bombing and sabotage.

The main attack on escape lines was mounted on their messengers and wireless operators. As one of the least fragrant of the Gestapo's collaborators once put it, 'my object was always to break up the liaisons, even more than arresting the chaps; what could they do without communications?' This routine standard procedure applied with rather less force to escape lines than to other kinds of clandestine circuit, since it was undesirable from an Axis point of view to have members of the Allied forces wandering about on Axis territory out of control; still, in remote areas what harm could they do?

In many districts of eastern and south-eastern Europe, in parts of Italy, in parts even of France, people could hang about for months without ever seeing a German uniform, almost without being aware that they were in an occupied country. If they had the manners and the linguistic skill, they could settle down among peasant friends, but the price of this friendship was to accept a peasant's way of life: a life bitterly poor and of unremitting toil, mitigated by occasional drunken feasts. The

Germans believed that if they controlled the nodal points of communication, particularly the main line railway junctions, they could more or less control the movement of undesirables; thus leaving people who fell in with peasants stuck in a single district. The forgery equipment needed to pass even a routine provincial railway junction control did not exist in the remote hills. This stolid and unimaginative practical clincher did not appeal to some of the livelier Gestapo heads in occupied provinces. In particular, active counter-attacks were put in against MI 9's two best and biggest lines across Belgium and France.

We left the 'Pat' line in difficulties, not yet insurmountable, at the end of 1942. The German operation 'Attila', the occupation of the hitherto 'free' zone of Vichy France, multiplied police controls; unrestricted movement became harder than ever.

Over the border in Monaco, nominally an independent and a neutral state, the Gestapo's writ was supposed not to run, nor was that of Vichy. All the same, Monte Carlo was too small and too weak to provide any kind of safe or lasting refuge. A few British people hung on there, and of these a few in turn remembered where their loyalty and indeed their duty lay. Miss Eva Trenchard – her surname alone should have made any Axis security officer jump – kept, with her sister, a small Scotch tea shop, which did little enough business, but provided shelter at one time or another for two dozen airmen on the run. Her flow of customers to be hidden stopped when the Germans broke up the 'Pat' line, from which most of them had been sent. The flow of senior French and German policemen who came to amuse themselves at the casino grew larger after 'Attila', and Monte Carlo ceased to be safe at all.

How did the Germans come to unravel 'Pat'?

Garrow was arrested by the Vichy police in October 1941 and sentenced – by now they had plenty of evidence against him – to ten years' detention, which he began to serve in a concentration camp at Mauzac, scene of a sensational escape exploit by some SOE agents in the previous July. Guérisse was now able to repay Garrow's help in getting him out of St Hippolyte du Fort. He got a Jewish tailor in Toulouse called Paul Ulmann and his wife, working against the clock, to fabricate a guard's uniform; bought a guard with Nancy Fiocca's help; smuggled the uniform in; and, hiding pistol in hand behind a bush fifty yards away, watched Garrow's painfully recognisable walk as the Scotsman left the camp with the shift coming off night duty at dawn on 6 December. (Vichy police were much less thorough than German POW camp guards: there was no bother about passes.) This *coup* undoubtedly saved Garrow from a much worse concentration camp in Germany. London insisted that he return to England.

As they parted a few days later in the Pyrenees, Guérisse's last words to Garrow were 'Can this go on much longer?' Garrow soon repeated them in London to Langley and Neave, who were haunted by them. For Neave had travelled down the 'Pat' line himself in April 1942 with Hugh Woolatt, another successful escaper from Germany, and knew many of 'Pat's' *passeurs*: such as Louis Simon, formerly of the Ritz in London, or Francis Blanchain the guide, or Louis and Renée Nouveau in whose flat he had stayed and been photographed in Marseilles. It is a mark of the 'Pat' line's confidence, and of its amateurishness, that so dangerous a document was ever created or kept. Guérisse was drawing in his horns. He sent out down his line to London Mme Nouveau who then took up work with the Gaullists, and also Blanchain, who married in England a young German girl called Paula Spriewald who had been one of the line's most gallant couriers. Tom Groome he hid at Montauban north of Toulouse, with a family called Cheramy (Madame Cheramy was English), and Louis Nouveau he sent to the post of honour and danger in Paris.

Groome was caught at his set early in January 1943 by a routine direction-finding team: he had no routine look-out, a howler. He, the Cheramys, and his young courier Edith Redde were all arrested and driven to Toulouse. During his interrogation, he suddenly leapt onto the table and dived through the window. He fell thirty feet, but could still run, and did. He hid in a doorway. 'Tragically [in Neave's words], he was given away to the pursuing Gestapo by a craven bystander.' His courier had the level-headedness to tiptoe away in the confusion and reported to Guérisse as much as she knew of what had happened.

She did not know that Groome, with a revolver in his back, had managed to signal to London – by omitting a security check – that he was in enemy hands. The omission was at once spotted. When next Groome's set came up on the air, with an anodyne message and no security checks at all, Dansey directed the reply. Groome was to go to Ventimiglia on the Riviera, and get in touch with the chief of police in Genoa, who had several Allied escapers in hiding. These escapers were notional, but Dansey had a genuine grudge, dating from before the war, against the Genoese policeman, who fell into serious trouble as a result of Dansey's ruse; which was designed to make trouble between the German and Italian police forces.

Still, the shadows were closing in round the 'Pat' line. Its members all felt that when the Gestapo got round to cross-questioning Harold Cole, there would be bad trouble.

The final blow came in fact from an unsuspected quarter. Louis Nouveau was approached in Paris, in that same January of Tom Groome's arrest, by a man who called himself Roger Le Neveu, who offered his services as a guide. As there was now no wireless contact with London – London, at that stage, would anyhow probably have had nothing to say – Nouveau was out on his own. He gave Le Neveu odd jobs to do; they were done well. Then he let him take a party of airmen south; they were safely delivered; so was a second party. With the third party, of five airmen, Nouveau travelled as well as Le Neveu; all seven were suddenly arrested when changing from an express to a local train at St Pierre des Corps, a suburb of Tours.

Le Neveu turned up in Toulouse on 2 March, and made a rendezvous in a cafe, through Ulmann, with Guérisse, who asked him whether he knew who had been giving people away in Paris? Yes, said Le Neveu, and Guérisse was arrested on the spot.

London knew within three weeks. Guérisse wanted to take all the responsibility on himself, and thus prevent further damage. Fabien de Cortes, a young member of the line arrested with his leader, was helped by him to jump from the train on the way to Paris, and got to Geneva, where he told 'Victor' what Guérisse had told him about Roger Le Neveu, alias Roger Le Legionnaire, perhaps an associate of Cole's. De Cortes went back to France and was soon rearrested, but the essential news had got through. He, Nouveau and Groome, it may be added, all survived their concentration camps; he and Nouveau died recently; Groome is still alive.

The 'Pat' line was dead; but it refused to lie down. There was an untameable grey-haired and grey-eyed woman of sixty or so, Franyoise Dissart, who lived near the Gestapo headquarters in Toulouse, and detested the Germans. 'She had a cat, well known in the French underground, called Mifouf', who, 'seated beside her, seemed to understand her moods.' It was on her shoulder that Groome's courier went to weep on the day of his arrest. She and Mifouf, who lived to be eighteen, were almost the sole survivors in the field of the 'Pat' line. She continued, according to Neave, 'to send escapers to Spain until the Liberation, escorting some from the Swiss borders herself, after Marseille had become too dangerous, with great ingenuity and indomitable spirit.'

Even before they had, as they believed, disposed of 'Pat' and cleared the eastern Pyrenees, the Germans turned on 'Comet' at the western end. They had never been far away from it; its earliest stages had been marred by arrests, its leader had already lost her sister to captivity and had her father on the run. On the other hand, the need for it grew steadily, as the RAF's bomber command developed its techniques for raiding Germany by night, and the tremendous engine of the Eighth USAAF began to threaten German industries by day. 'Comet' had so extensive a network of watchers in south Holland and north-eastern France, as well as all over its Belgian land of origin, that it had become an important cog in the war machine: without the panache of 'Pat' and without Guérisse's command of the sort of language soldiers understand,[22] but with tremendous courage and integrity. It was daily becoming more of a target for Gestapo action, both at the Pyrenean and at the initiating end.

In Paris, over Christmas 1942, Andrée de Jongh at last persuaded; her father that the work had become too dangerous for him to continue any longer, and next time she travelled towards Spain she took him with her. They stayed with 'Tante Go' at Anglet near Bayonne, but a storm of even more than the usual winter's ferocity was raging: a mountain crossing on foot for a man in his middle fifties was out of the question. Andrée and three young pilots set off all the same and paused for an evening meal, as had become her custom, at a farm above the village of Urrugne. The storm was still so frightful that even Florentino Goicoechea the huge Basque guide agreed that there could be no crossing that night, and stumped off home to his wife in Ciboure.

Next morning, 15 January 1943, the weather was a little less vile. A police party pounced on the farm, on a tip from a local wastrel (who managed to disappear altogether). One of the pilots talked.

So Andrée de Jongh could not pretend to be innocent; but the Germans were for weeks reluctant to believe her straightforward admission, that she had organised the line herself. She did not say, as she might have done, that in sixteen double journeys over the mountains she had escorted 118 people. 'Tante Go's' husband Fernand de Greef worked as an interpreter in the

---

22　Cp. Neave, *Saturday at MI 9*, 107–8.

German *Kommandantur* at Anglet, an admirable cover for stealing passes and stamps, and found out such fragments of news
about her as he could. The de Greefs and their local friends tried
to discover some way of spiriting Andrée out of the local gaol,
but as usually happens the cutting-out plans did not work fast
enough, and she was sent off to Paris for further inquiries.

In the first week of February the Brussels Gestapo office,
acting quite separately, struck at 'Comet' hard. They arrested
about a hundred people, including Elvire Morelle, a close friend
of Andrée's who was her current courier between Brussels and
Paris. Jean Greindl ('Nemo') the local head of the line was safe
for the moment and seized the opportunity to make the main
surviving guides – the twenty-year-old Peggy van Lier and the
d'Oultremont cousins, Georges and Edouard, who were not
much older – move away to Paris. There they met Frédéric de
Jongh, who had returned to duty, made more stubbornly anti-
German than ever by his second daughter's arrest. He insisted
that they move on southward; they could not shift him. Donald
Darling never forgot Peggy van Lier's arrival at Gibraltar a week
or two later, after a rough two days in the bilges of an orange-
boat; nor how radiant she looked after she had had several baths
and washed her red-gold hair. Langley met her when she reached
England by air and before long found himself much impressed
by her; they were married in 1944, and have five children.

Greindl was taken, at the Swedish canteen in Brussels, on
7 February; and was horrified to meet his own wife, who had
lately had their second baby, when he was first interrogated by
the Gestapo. She pressed his hand, and held out her rosary; they
had no chance to talk. He was kept after trial and condemnation
to death in a barracks, where by a strange irony he was killed
by an Allied bomb in an air raid on 7 September. A party of his
companions were shot at the Tir National on 20 October, against
the grass bank where Edith Cavell had been executed in 1915.

Frédéric de Jongh died before them. All through the spring
of 1943 he had guided parties travelling on the line across Paris

from the Gare du Nord to the Gare d'Austerlitz. He had lately engaged a new courier, a small fair-haired man with prominent blue eyes who called himself Jean Masson. Masson warned him that a large party would arrive on 7 June; and walked up to de Jongh, smiling broadly, with five English airmen and an American. As they shook hands, a dozen German policemen appeared and arrested them.

'Masson', whose real name was Jacques Desoubrie, was a Gestapo double agent, another and a prouder Roger Le Neveu. In the Gestapo office in the Rue de Saussaies he spat on the floor at his captives' feet, and sneered at them; one of them hit him. But Frédéric de Jongh was taken away to Mont Valérien and shot.

All these casualties had fearful repercussions in London as well as in the field. They came at about the time of the major 'Prosper' disaster to SOE's independent French section in Paris, of the catastrophe of de Gaulle's delegate's arrest, and of some major earthquakes in the intelligence world as well. As usually happens at such moments, senior staff officers started to blame one another.

This was an occasion when Crockatt's greatness displayed itself. He went in for no idle recriminations, and he defeated every attempt by disappointed rivals to blame P15, or to clip that minute sub-department's wings till it was wholly earth-bound. Dansey did not join those who said that the troubles in 'Comet' showed that P15 had no proper control over its agents, allowed too many nubile young women to go swanning round western Europe, had no sense of security, and was imperilling the really important agents; of MI 6. The Air Ministry's intelligence branch made a serious bid to take MI 9 over. But Crockatt fought back, and was able to get the same ministry's manpower and training branches to testify w the value of the existing arrangements. Dansey, rather grumblingly remembered the proverb about the devil you know, and took Crockatt's side; then it was the air intelligence staff's turn to grumble.

And 'Comet' still carried on. Almost incredibly, the group of young people that Andrée de Jongh had mobilised two and three years before turned out to be self-perpetuating. Never has there been a clearer example of the principle laid down (from the comfort, be it said, of an English armchair) by the Gaullist author of the '*Chant des Partisans*':

> *Ami, si tu tombes*
> *un ami sort de l'ombre*
> *Te remplacer.*

When Greindl was caught, Baron Jean-Francois de Nothomb, aged twenty-three, took over the work. He had taken a leading part in the efforts to rescue Andrée de Jongh at Anglet; he had several times crossed the Pyrenees both ways himself; he had presence, enterprise, energy, faith. Nothomb came out to Gibraltar in the boot of 'Monday's' car, for a consultation with Rait and Neave in late October 1943; got their assurance that they were trying to help him, not to control him; and went back to work. (Some more political department than P15, reading the telegrams with limited understanding, caused a minor secret uproar in Whitehall over this, for Nothomb's pseudonym was 'Franco'. After several more successful journeys in and out of Spain, he was arrested in Paris on 18 January 1944; also betrayed by Jacques Desoubrie, whom his line had been too devout to kill. (Desoubrie lived to stand his trial and be executed at Lille at the end of the war.)

Madame de Greef – 'Tante Go' – was arrested, but talked herself out of trouble promptly: she knew too much about the Germans' dealings in the local black market, and threatened to Tell All. That shut her captors up. They let her go. She refused to stop work; she carried the line on for a further six months, till the Allied armies reappeared in France.

Both Andrée de Jongh and Nothomb disappeared entirely, as Guérisse and Groome had done, behind the screen of Himmler's *Nacht und Nebel* system: night and fog shrouded them entirely. The light inside each of them continued to burn, and they all survived the war.

As the air threat to Germany increased, and as it became clear even to quite obtuse Gestapo men that the flame of resistance was not easily – perhaps was never – going to be stamped out, a more sophisticated approach to escape lines was tried. Virtually nothing is known about this; no papers bearing on it have turned up. If as seems possible it was a young Luftwaffe intelligence staff officer's idea, and if he survives today, it is much to be hoped that the originator will now come forward.

Briefly, the scheme was to find a working escape line for aircrew, and to insert a loop in it. Along the loop would be placed, in a down-town terrace house, a tough and knowledgeable interrogator. He would pump all the passengers for every scrap of order-of- battle and technical information he could get, and then pass them back to the line; not forgetting to issue a dire warning that they must never ever tell anybody about the conversation that had just taken place. His cover for demanding the information would be, 'Look, here we all are, risking our lives for the sake of your miserable skin – you only have to show a copper your identity disc, we get crucified, see? Now, just to make quite sure you're not a Gestapo nark, sent here to play tricks on us, tell me' – and so on. Rumour places this device sometimes in Brussels, sometimes in Antwerp. That something like it existed, is indicated by a remark let drop by Giskes, the Abwehr man whose 'North Pole' operation emasculated SOE's work in the Netherlands, about 'the principle that intelligence is more valuable than elimination'.

Had German intelligence about the RAF and the USAF been more complete, they might have appreciated how acute the shortage of trained aircrew was all through the Allied air forces; and might have revised their calculations about the comparative value of gaining intelligence and of passing trained men back to re-start operations.

Certainly there were numerous attempts to feed double agents onto such underground railways as the Allies had in operation. We have dwelt rather on the cases of 'Pat' and 'Comet' because much is known about them, and because we cannot help admiring their leaders' superlative courage; yet, though pre-eminent, they were not alone. In many other areas than the regular Brussels-Paris-Bayonne or Paris-Lyons-Marseilles-Perpignan runs, there were locals trying to help, and Germans trying to hinder.

In Alsace for example, secret clubs, mainly of older and experienced people, some French and some Polish, had been formed locally to help clandestine travellers to cross the Vosges, but by the spring of 1943 they were having trouble, brought on by double agents who had penetrated them. Similar troubles were experienced there by a couple of groups of boys in their late teens.

Alsace was by no means the only area to meet this trouble; as witness a disagreeable run of incidents in Crete. Some months after the Allied withdrawal, in midwinter 1941/2, there were still over one hundred evaders – perhaps as many as 300, counting in the Cypriots and the regular Greek soldiers who wanted to get away – at large on the island. The Germans sent out into the hill villages quite a lot of agents who spoke Greek fluently, and tried to pass themselves off as British evaders in search of help. Cretan peasants needed all their proverbial cunning and parsimony to avoid getting caught in this carefully baited trap.

Similar pretences were attempted, with more or less successful results, in every area from the Peloponnese to the North Cape in which resistance was started up spontaneously by the local population. It was the Abwehr's duty to seek out double agents and encourage such attempts; and as usual the party security service, the SD, tried everywhere to be a little in front of the Abwehr rather than behind it. MI 9's and MIS-X's job, like that of all the other Allied secret services, was – among other things – to be aware of its danger and to be a little farther in front of the enemy still.

Counter-attacks on MI 9's activities went on of course in POW camps, as well as in occupied countries; against prisoners trying to escape, as well as against lines that dealt mainly in evaders.

The fate of British prisoners of war in Italy may be contrasted with the fate of Italian prisoners of war in Britain. So far as the meagre sources reveal, the British prisoners in Italy had a depressed and disagreeable life, felt themselves unfairly bullied, and despised their captors. There was one telling occasion, near the Brenner pass, when some Italians tossed packets of cigarettes to a gloomy-looking group of guarded British prisoners waiting for a train. The prisoners with one accord turned their backs and left the cigarettes lying on the ground, sooner than accept a courtesy from their detested foes. In southern England on the other hand small unguarded parties of Italian prisoners of war in chocolate-coloured battledress were a familiar sight by the winter of 1942–3, all over the countryside. Farmers were delighted to have the labour, many country girls liked the Italians' manners, and quite a few of the Italians liked England enough to want to settle in it after the war. Nothing comparable happened in Germany. The trouble there, as it had been on a world-famous occasion in 1914, was that it was not always quite clear who was in charge.

A weakness in the *Kriegsgefangenenwesen*, the German system for holding prisoners of war, arose from the bureaucratic vice of over-organisation. So many authorities had their finger in the prisoners' pie that the chain of command was not always clear; and officers unsure of their responsibilities did not always know to whom they should apply for advice. From the prisoners' point of view this had advantages. Ludicrously enough there was no one body which effectively kept all camps briefed on methods used for escapes, or for the smuggling of escape equipment. Was smuggling a matter for the frontier or customs police, or for the armed forces' security branch, or for the party's main security office – for the *Grenzpolizei*, the *Abwehr*, or the *Reichssicherheitshauptamt*; or even for the *Kripo*, the ordinary criminal police? This question was never properly answered, nor even posed. The Abwehr put out a monthly bulletin, but did not assert its authority over its rivals.

Consequently, a few of Clayton Hutton's tricks became known early – gramophone records, glass-topped games, and bookbindings all soon became suspect, and in many camps books regularly underwent the indignity of having their covers wrenched off in the parcels office before being handed over the counter. But no systematic effort was made to disseminate lists of the many cover organisations invented by MI 9 to hide parcels of escaping gadgets; one camp – Querum – reported of those in charge of parcel censorship that they 'had little idea of what to look for and where', and was not the only camp so lucky.

In some camps there was perpetual goon-baiting and constant activity, preparing for and executing escapes; in others, prisoners and guards alike seemed torpid, and dull acceptance of things as they were was the dominant mood. Personalities on both sides counted for a good deal. A few self-important guards and security officers enjoyed throwing their weight about. Becoming a prisoner is usually fatal to self-importance, but a few prisoners managed to retain some, and even to impose on gullible guards.

Two handfuls of prisoners were regarded by their captors as people worth special consideration. About a dozen general officers, captured during the ebb and flow of fighting in the western desert, were segregated in Italy: first at the Villa Orsini outside Sulmona, east of Rome; then at the Castello di Vincigliati above Florence. The two senior generals at Florence, Neame and Carton de Wiart, had both won the Victoria Cross in the previous war, and Sir Richard O'Connor was the victor of the astonishing armoured thrust that had culminated at Beda Fomm: clearly these were men worth watching. The Italians never knew that O'Connor had one of Winterbottom's codes; that the generals were therefore in steady, if slow, touch with Crockatt; or that they spent a great deal of their time tunnelling. Late on 29 March 1943 O'Connor, de Wiart, and four brigadiers escaped, and two of the brigadiers, both New Zealanders, Hargest and Miles, got into Switzerland: almost the most senior British officers to escape in either war.[23]

The other small party was housed in much grimmer conditions in Colditz, and there named the *Prominente*. It consisted of relatives of the famous: Churchill's nephew Giles Romilly, captured in Norway as a war correspondent for the *Daily Express*; the second Earl Haig, son of the field-marshal who had beaten the Germans in 1918; the Earl of Hopetoun, whose father Lord Linlithgow was Wavell's predecessor as Viceroy of India; and field-Marshal Alexander's nephew Michael, who was captured in rather odd circumstances in the desert. They gave no kind of trouble, but were an incessant worry to the Colditz staff, who knew they would answer with their own heads if a single *Prominent* escaped. Douglas Bader, who also cast up in Colditz, gave the Germans as much trouble as all the *Prominente* put together: his own prominence was medical, not social. Not many people have flown an aircraft, let alone led a fighter wing in combat or done a rope escape, with two artificial legs.

At a much less exalted level, ordinary German detectives in uniform did a lot to make escape preparations difficult, if not plumb impossible. There was one in Colditz so persistent that the French called him *la fouine*, the weasel; and the British and Americans generally adopted the name of 'ferret' for this type of diligent interrupter. At Sagan, as a rueful report put it at the end of the war, 'They crawled under huts looking for tunnels, dug spikes into the ground to uncover sand, peered through windows, eavesdropped, and entered rooms.' Perpetual ferreting was probably from the Germans' point of view as valuable a precaution as any that they took. If a prisoner knew he was likely to be inspected at any hour without warning he could not make himself maps or clothes or passes for an escape.

---

23    Miles, having reached Spain safely, killed himself.

The prisoners' counter was what was known in air force camps as the duty pilot system. A man, or a pair of men – Sagan East compound had two on at a time, for an hour's spell, on a fortnightly roster; it involved almost the whole local prisoner population – would sit or stand as unobtrusively as possible in sight of the gate, and would keep a log of all German entries and exits. The duty pilot could in theory say off-hand how many Germans were present in the compound, and which way they had gone. One exasperated German *Feldwebel* (sergeant-major), who thought his own men were slacking, once asked if he could borrow the duty pilots' log to make a check. In the most escape-minded camps – such as Sagan, Colditz, Eichstätt, Heydekrug – the duty pilot system lasted for twenty-four hours out of twenty-four; the current duty pilot kept a sharp eye on the gate even during an *Appel*. At Colditz the prisoners, who knew more about electricity than the Germans did, had no trouble in tapping the direct current supply when the guards turned it off every evening, and had a warning system that operated with coloured lights – stolen from a German attic full of Christmas decorations.

As the prisoners there were kept – so their guards hoped – separate by nationalities, Anglo-Saxon, French, Poles and Dutch, they ran separate duty pilot systems for each national staircase. Even the almost impeccable Dutch had two disagreeable accidents, when their warning system broke down and the Germans discovered what they were not supposed to know; and the British nearly had one. Whenever this happened, as it did now and again in less high-powered establishments, the SBO or SAO meted out an official punishment, and the delinquent duty pilot had to endure the contempt of his fellow-prisoners as well. It did not happen very often; aircrew after all had been trained to concentrate on what they were doing, because their own lives depended on it in the air.

Eavesdropping, mentioned a moment ago among the ferrets' functions, might of course be supplemented in permanent camps by microphones hidden in the walls. MI 9 lectures regularly included a warning against this, and no sensible prisoner ever said anything indoors that he would mind if the enemy heard. It was at first difficult to remember that one could never relax one's guard indoors, even with an old friend; one soon got used to the precaution of carrying on all discussions of security interest while out for a walk. Even there, it was necessary to be sure that a ferret did not creep up into earshot. Security in fact, in the view of one who had learned the hard way, came *well above all other considerations* in the course of escape planning.

An incessant ferrets' and prisoners' preoccupation was tunnel spoil. At Colditz, the first indication the Germans got that a tunnel was being built anywhere was the discovery of a pile of rubble in an attic that had been empty when last inspected. At Sagan, the whole camp had been built on purpose on soil that was largely sand, which showed up wherever it was put: an extra awkwardness for the numerous bodies of tunnellers there. Oliver Philpot, acting as an auxiliary for one of these teams, gave a sketch in his war autobiography of the general war news in the summer of 1943.

> And in this scene of titanic struggle – what was I doing? Perched on a beam in the roof of a hut in a Silesian forest – waiting to receive twelve bags of sand through a roof-hatch, to take them along the rafters in the gloom without snagging them against the innumerable nails, then to drop them down another hatch. An operation of war? Or a childish game?

Besides ferreting, the Germans could adopt several other, obvious precautions: guard dogs, for example, to patrol inside and outside prisoners' compounds at night; electrified fences, a dwindling German asset towards the end of the war when power supplies were so often cut; and ground microphones, introduced after the Biberach and other early tunnels had broken, to give the Germans warning of similar work in progress. Round the east compound at Sagan, for instance, microphones were sunk nine feet deep in the ground at thirty-three-foot intervals, outside the wire; and a seven-foot-deep anti-tunnelling trench was dug all round the compound inside it. The prisoners amused themselves calculating the amount of German labour dissipated in this trench-digging task; as its purpose was military, it was not one that the Geneva Convention allowed prisoners of war to dig for themselves.

No wonder that Aidan Crawley calculated, on good evidence, that only through one in every thirty-five of all the tunnels ever started in Germany did any prisoner succeed in getting outside his camp.[24] The brilliance of the escape for which Philpot had been working, and in which he eventually took part, lay mainly in how it baffled the ground microphones. The story, almost too well known to need reference, is to be found in Eric Williams's *The Wooden Horse.* While he, Conder and Philpot worked away in the tunnel below the wooden horse, a body of their accomplices kept running up to it and jumping over it: thus making so much *brouhaha* that the microphones missed the tunnellers' scrapings in the thud, thud, thud of running feet.

The Geneva Convention forbade in its Article 46, 'collective penalties for individual acts'. It was therefore within the Convention's letter, if not its spirit, for the administration of a large Stalag, IX C, to lay down the rule that all boots and trousers were to be handed to the guard every night: an effective stopper on escapes, especially in winter. Needless to say, the rule was too cumbrous for guards on remote labour detachments to bother about it, and from those it was comparatively easy to abscond.

When a party of thirty-five miners all broke out from a louse-ridden *Arbeitskommando* from the same camp, and were

---

24 Aidan Crawley, *Escape from Germany,* 33, a book based on a great deal of work its author did at the end of the war, at the Air Ministry's request, going through the reports of former RAF prisoners; among whom he had been eminent in his work on escape.

all re- caught, they were sentenced to two hours' trench-digging daily for a month after an eight-hour shift down the mine. This, again, might be held by a sea-lawyer just to be within the law; it certainly left the victims too weary to escape again for some time. When the big break came from Dobrilugk, in May 1942, two collective punishments were imposed both on the escapers and on their fellow prisoners: compulsory clogs and a rapid forced march round and round the parade ground. There was some rough justice in this: in so small a camp, everybody was bound to have been involved in preparing for a mass escape, whether as an actual participant or no. The bare-foot escaper who was shot dead, because his re-captor misun-derstood a gesture meant simply to indicate 'Can I put my boots on now?' was simply a victim of bad luck, and of a tendency noticed over and over again in German prison guards by more placid British observers, to over-excitability. But it is dangerous to postulate national vices. Collective punishments at Colditz, which were quite frequent, were probably justifiable on similar grounds of collective guilt; no case ever went before a court.

An American private, Harold J. Farrell of the 26th Infantry Regiment, who was wounded and captured at the battle of the Kasserine pass in Tunisia on 18 February 1943, observed when he was repatriated sixteen months later: 'On some kommandos, Ps/W work fourteen to fifteen hours a day seven days a week. When they mention Geneva Convention to guard, he taps his rifle and says 'Here is my Geneva Convention'.'

One collective punishment was notorious: the manacling of Canadian prisoners, in reprisal for unhappy incidents during the raids on Dieppe and on Sark. In both cases a German pris-oner's dead body was found by his own side, with his hands tied behind his back. The beach at Dieppe was a shambles; anything may have happened there. The commander of the Sark raid 'did not see what else, in the time-trouble induced by strong tides, could have been done to force a reluctant prisoner through the moonlit gorse but tie him up, and held it excusable that he was stabbed quickly when sudden tumult broke out round him.'[25]

Hitler was furious, and ordered the handcuffing of several thousand Canadians; he also seized the occasion to issue his notorious *Kommandobefehl*, which condemned commandos, saboteurs and parachutists on legitimate operations of war to summary execution, if captured, or to the lingering mercilessness of the SD. It will be necessary to refer to the *Kommandobefehl* later; our immediate concern is with the handcuffs. For a few days the Canadians had a thin time. Prompt reprisals in kind in camps in Canada, and the threat of more, soon had effect on German policy at the summit; at the operating level, the German common soldiers who had to do the manacling did not like or enjoy the task. Before long, handcuffs were to be affixed for an hour a day only; and soon, in decent camps, an NCO would bring them into a hut, lay them on the table, salute, and depart. At Colditz none were used lest the prisoners add to their store of metal for tool making.

This would not have pleased Hitler, had he known of it; like much else, it was a detail that was kept from him. He was a man who loved to meddle, but from a distance; and just as he never visited a concentration camp, he never during the 1939–45 war visited a camp for prisoners of war. In February 1919, before he had attracted any notice outside his regiment, he had been a guard on a camp of French and Russian prisoners awaiting repatriation; probably not an experience he wanted to remember. He had been a prisoner himself for a year in considerable comfort at Landsberg-am-Lech while he wrote *Mein Kampf*, the foundation of his private as of his public fortune. He originated the manacling order to feed his parvenu's insatiable passion for exercising authority in odd and striking ways, but did not bother to follow through.

---

25   Conversation with J. G. Appleyard, 1942, quoted in Foot, *SOE in France*, 187.

His malign influence can be sensed in the background of Nazi German policy towards prisoners of war. It was evident at the time to those whose duty it was to look, that there were few kinds of atrocity from which a system led by Hitler was certain to shrink back; and no amount of propaganda, then or since, about how sweet-tempered Hitler could be and how delightful he was with children – so was Lenin – should blind us to that brute fact. Himmler could make trouble enough on his own account, and had gathered round him in the SS men like himself, who had forgotten mercy and loving-kindness. Littledale had the ill luck to be hiding in Prague at the time of Heydrich's death early in June 1942 at the hands of Czech assassins from England. The SS who rampaged through Prague in search of suspects seemed to him 'almost insane, and were very brutal', and his report made a particular impression on Crockatt when he was able to study it in the spring of 1943.

There was a real possibility that, as the war went worse and worse for Germany, the Nazis would use their prisoners as a bargaining counter; and that sheer massacre was the fate that might be meted out to the camps was a nightmare never far from Crockatt's mind. MI 9 did not only have to take care, in general, that none of its activities made things worse instead of better for prisoners of war. It had to take particular care that it never gave the Nazis the slightest excuse for a massacre. This was a significant brake on the section's activities.

There were a few Allied prisoners in German hands for whom not even MI 9 was able to do anything, because they were kept hidden away from all communication with the outside world: no prisoner in the Lubianka, or the Bastille, or the darkest dungeon of a robber baron in the dark ages was more firmly shut in. All of them had had training in what to do if they fell into enemy hands, but the training had not envisaged that there were some categories of fighting men to whom, after the *Kommandobefehl* of October 1942, the Germans refused the status of prisoner of war.

One such party included John Godwin, an Englishman brought up in Argentina who became a sub-lieutenant in the RNVR and took a commando sergeant, two petty officers and three seamen on a shipping raid near Haugesund, in a fjord north of Stavanger. They operated with limpet mines in canoes from a coble, a broad-beamed small boat, hidden on a bushy island; a Norwegian motor torpedo-boat had brought them across from the Shetlands on 29/30 April 1943. They sank a few ships; but had disappeared by the time MTBs came to collect them in mid- and late May.

Having sunk one minor German warship, they had tackled another which was too big for them, and had been captured. They were held to fall within the scope of the commando order. After a spell in close confinement at Grini prison near Oslo they were sent via another concentration camp to Sachsenhausen. John Godwin was an officer, though a very junior one, in the oldest continuing organised fighting service in the world, and knew what was expected of him:[26] leadership and courage. He gave both in plenty.

He and his party – less one called Mayer, who was presumed Jewish and disposed of separately – spent fifteen months in Sachsenhausen, officer and men together, living on turnip gruel and a little bread, and marching thirty miles a day, seven days a week, round a closed cobbled track to test boots for the German army. Their spirits remained unquenchably high. They cracked jokes with each other, despised their gloomy guards, knew their own side was going to win the war, and did not brood about their own fate.

This came late on 2 February 1945, after their day's march. They were summoned, with others, to execution. As they passed through one of the camp's many gateways, there was a scuffle. Godwin drew the firing party commander's pistol from his belt and shot him dead, before being mown down himself. As no

---

26  Cp. Beesley, *Very Special Intelligence*, 108n.

one senior to him was present at his death, the best the decorations system could do for Godwin was a posthumous mention in dispatches. As Boethius remarked, splendid men often go unnoticed because there is no one to tell their tale.

# Italian Imbroglio

In the Rome-Berlin axis, Mussolini had always been the weaker partner. He had put so much effort into the Ethiopian and Spanish wars that his army was in no state to fight an equal in 1939. He only entered the European war in June 1940 when it looked as if Germany had already won it. His air force's sole intervention in the Battle of Britain led to a ludicrous though minor defeat. His navy fared ignominiously at Taranto and Matapan. His army did well, momentarily, in Somaliland, but by the end of 1941 had lost that and the empire of Ethiopia as well. Stiffened by the Afrika Korps, it held out in Libya till the end of 1942, but failed to hold Tunisia the following spring; and operation 'Husky', the invasion of Sicily in July 1943, proved that his system was rotten. He was quietly arrested on 25 July, and within seven weeks his country had changed sides.

The Allies' attack on Italy had long been foreseen by their chiefs of staff, though as the campaign in Tunisia drew to its close in the late spring of 1943 the Germans remained in doubt about the next Anglo-American objective. Their doubts were kept alive by a series of deft deceptions, one of them long famous: they were led, in the teeth of the evidence, to believe that operations impended against Sardinia and the Peloponnese. The combined chiefs of staff never in fact hesitated; they settled on Sicily, followed by the Italian mainland.

Montgomery was to be the British force commander, and attended closely to the details. Among them, he laid down a doctrine for Allied prisoners of war. He always liked neatness and order, and abhorred the slovenly; he was not much attached to irregular operations of any kind. He therefore insisted that directions were to be sent to Allied prisoners on Italian soil that they were to stay in their camps until the advancing armies overran them. He expected the campaign to be brief, a matter of weeks. A moment's hindsight reminds us all that the dogged and prolonged Italian campaign was not like that in the least: nearly twenty months of close combat ensued, more similar to the trench warfare of 1914–18 than any other part of the century's second world war, and only in the last week or two did the battle open up. Montgomery had intended something altogether different.

He probably gave his directive on this point – the document has not survived, or at all events has not surfaced in late May or early June 1943, when nominally on leave in London, resting after the rigours of the Tunisian campaign. There may well have been, on a matter then so secret, no document, but an order transmitted by word of mouth. At any rate Crockatt received and transmitted the direction that, in the event of an invasion of mainland Italy, prisoners of war were to stay put, to await release; not to attempt to break out of camp, or to assist the Anglo-American air forces in their attacks on the enemy's communications. It is a tribute to the efficiency his organisation had attained that almost every camp's SBO received the message in time. The Americans, through Holt and Washington's correspondence section, were happy to conform.

Crockatt was still enough of a practical fighting man to take in the military worth of groups fresh out of a prisoner of war camp: it was bound to be low. Individually many of them might be capable of some single astonishing, even heroic feat; and collectively, in tunnelling squads, some of them had acquired a strong sense of team unity. But in his judgement they were bound to lack that disciplined cohesion, born of months of training together and years of regimental tradition, by which a sound infantry unit imposes its will in battle. Besides, however willing, about half of them, airmen or gunners or tank crew or men from service units, had had little or no infantry training, and only the sappers among them knew the first thing about demolitions; and they were unarmed. Montgomery did not relish the idea of having his future supply lines hampered by unauthorised bridge demolitions, and Crockatt did not relish the idea of sending Clarke and Simonds to badger the air and Q (G-4) staffs at Allied Force Headquarters (AFHQ) about arms supply. So he was happy at what was being done. He decided to send orders to the German as well as the Italian camps to discourage mass break-outs, for he feared that these would only lead to mass reprisals. The odious excesses of Himmler's concentration camp guards in the Third Reich were by now becoming known to a limited circle, to which Crockatt belonged; two years later of course they had become a world sensation, of a horror matched only by the first uses of nuclear weapons in anger, and by the much later revelation that concentration camps were rife in the Soviet Union as well. Crockatt had the foresight to envisage that if his prisoners overreached themselves, they might all find themselves packed into cattle trucks and sent off to extermination, Geneva Convention or no. The Italians' record was much milder, but he had an uneasy feeling that they too might, if pressed too hard, display the ferocity of a cornered rat.

He told Washington in mid-June that his current policy in Europe had three main lines: to deprecate mass break-outs, both for fear of reprisals and because ex-prisoners would be such inefficient troops; to order prisoners to stay put at the end of the war; and to encourage escapers to carry information in their heads. The Americans concurred.

The end result in Italy was less happy than Crockatt or anyone else had foreseen, for reasons over which neither MI 9 nor MIS-X had any control at all. It can be put brutally briefly: well over half the prisoners, who stayed put as ordered, were quietly scooped up by the Germans and taken by train into Germany. Only the more rebellious and more enterprising ones got out, and by no means all of these got clean away. The most probable reason for this seems to have been a catastrophic staff muddle, at a level so senior that no one has quite cared to clear it up.

According to Simonds' vivid recollection, he was hurriedly summoned to AFHQ in Algiers early in September 1943, and urged by several senior officers to exert himself to the utmost to rescue Allied prisoners of war in Italy. Instructions to this effect had come, he understood, from the Prime Minister himself. The Italian surrender, be it remembered, was announced on the September 8, Montgomery's army had disembarked near Reggio on the September 3, and operation 'Avalanche', the Salerno landing, began on the September 9. Every facility was to be placed at Simonds' disposal; except that he was not to endanger any naval craft, and could only request aircraft sortie by sortie, taking his turn with other bodies – such as SOE, OSS, or SAS – which might need aircraft also. He got to Taranto hard on the heels of the British 1st Airborne Division, and assembled a few teams of uniformed helpers; he intended to send them forward, in front of the advancing Allied armies, to find escaped prisoners and guide them back within the Allied lines.

A few surviving files indicate the sort of troubles with which he and his colleagues had to wrestle. Few British officers had fluent Italian, so it was necessary to recruit local helpers immediately, and guides and interpreters. Almost all the Italians who proffered themselves blenched at the very thought of parachuting, let alone the act; and as so often happens, some of the loudest talkers were the least anxious to run into actual danger.[27] Field escape section number three was set up by an operation instruction from Simonds to Captain F. P. Falvey on 7 September with the vague aim to 'organise where necessary the rescue of all escapers and evaders in your territory as is possible under existing conditions'. Falvey had some money and an Italian-speaking sergeant called Pittarelli, but he had

---

27   Cp. Kipling, 'M.I.', verse 9.

BOUNDARIES AS AT 1942

| | MILES | |
|---|---|---|
| 0 | | 300 |
| 0 | KILOMETRES | 500 |

neither wireless nor transport. He begged a lift to Taranto with the ships that carried the airborne division, and liberated eight prisoners there on the 10 September, the day after he arrived; on 11 September he was reduced to touring the city in a horse and buggy. 'The city is full of former rabid fascists', he reported; and 'I believe that it is generally felt by the Italians that the war is over for them.'

Captain Christopher Soames, subsequently a son-in-law of Churchill, a commissioner of the European community in Brussels, and a recent recruit to the House of Lords, commanded field escape section number two, with the Eighth Army. He was to 'utilise all known available means to produce a network of helpers behind the enemy lines and make local plans for the early rescue of ground troops and air crews at large within enemy territory'. Simonds' assistant, Major J. V. Fillingham, who gave this order to Soames, believed at the moment the Italian surrender became public that 'Steps have been taken by Italian authorities to release Allied prisoners immediately'. All that happened was that the guards at prisoner of war camps were withdrawn; they marched off to the nearest barracks, leaving the gates open.

In every camp, the SBO called a parade and announced the order to stand fast. Crockatt's name was not used; it was certainly unknown to most of them. The order came with the full and distant authority of 'the War Office' or 'the Air Ministry'. Simonds himself had been telling Fillingham, a few days before, that 'NO ATTEMPTS MUST BE MADE TO INDUCE OR PROVOKE MASS BREAKOUTS', and nothing outrageous happened. A few British camp commanders, particularly quick-witted and well informed, foresaw the possibility that the Germans would come to collect them, and encouraged those who wanted to do so to take to the hills; most, having received an order, stuck to it.

As far back as the early spring of 1941, during some staff discussions about interrogating German prisoners in the event of an invasion of England, Crockatt had noted in a minute the 'DUTY OF AN OFFICER TO ACCEPT RESPONSIBILITY AND ACT ON HIS OWN INITIATIVE'. This was the doctrine to which everyone paid lip-service; only the best put it into practice. To disobey a War Office or Air Ministry order was always a serious offence, but sometimes it had to be done. The army's official *Field Service Regulations* indeed laid down that an order ought to be disobeyed, if 'some fact which could not be known to the officer who issued the order' made disobedience necessary, to comply with the known intentions of the superior who had given it. The handbook went on to say, with a foretaste of *Catch-22*, that 'If a subordinate neglects to depart from the letter of his orders when such departure ... is clearly demanded, he will be held responsible for any failure that may ensue.'

Yet was this the case foreseen, in which unexpected developments would justify men on the spot in doing what they had been told not to do? Most camps had hidden wirelesses, but neither the BBC nor the Italian broadcasting services were privy to the German high command's intention, and the fog of war lay densely over Italy. Churchill, ordering Alexander to do all that he could to rescue prisoners, forgot to let Crockatt know that he had done so. Even had he sent word to Crockatt, the latter would hardly have had any means at his disposal for passing instructions on to all the many camps quickly enough. MI 9's secret broadcasting system suffered from an unfortunate defect, apart from all the security troubles that attended on reception at the camp end: transmission was often too fast for out-of-practice operators to take it in.

Several people were found to complain, then and later, of the chance that was missed. Larry Allen for example, an Associated Press correspondent captured from HMS *Sikh* off Tobruk on 14 September 1942 and treated as a prisoner of war – he was offered an immediate exchange in return for naval information, to which he simply replied 'Don't be silly' – protested when eventually he got back into United States hands that Colonel

Marshall, the British senior officer in the huge camp PG 21 at
Chieti, had been too strict; and that the War Office's orders had
been too inflexible.

The stand-fast order had reached the other ranks' camps as
well as the officers'. In Italy, as in Germany, MI 9's codes had
been spread round a select few with no trouble. A number of air
force warrant and non-commissioned officers were code users;
and in big camps for army other ranks, codes could be carried
in and quickly taught by medical officers or chaplains.

Most prisoners of war were simply caught napping by
the Italian armistice and change of sides. Those who had not
devoted much, if any, thought to escape had neither food nor
clothes available with which to sustain themselves on a walk
towards the Allied lines, which turned out to be stuck hundreds
of miles away. Many prisoners absconded for a few hours, for
the pleasure of walking where they wanted for a change instead
of being pinned to the track round the inside of the camp's
perimeter wire; and then came back, because they had neither
bed to sleep in nor money to live on, (Though most non-
Soviet prisoners of war were paid, holding powers took care
to pay them in special currencies that were worthless outside
their camps.)

Some, afflicted by the disease that in Germany was called
*gefangenitis* – much like that legionaries' *cafard* which readers
of P. C. Wren will remember, a state of depression bordering
on accidie – were distressed at their guards' disappearance, and
found life unguarded uncomfortable. Others found it only too
comfortable, particularly if they had secured some money by
selling some possession unlooted by their original captors, or
if they had tumbled upon some complaisant girl-friend. One
of Simonds' most enterprising escape organisers, Jock McKee,
pushed forward as far as Sulmona, and found there an incho-
ate mass of more than a thousand ex-prisoners of war: not by
any means anxious to leave the district, which they knew, for
whatever perils this forceful young captain was determined they

should rejoin. Twenty-three people accompanied him when he left. The Germans scooped up most of the rest, though not all.

Some hundreds were left at large, drifting south-eastwards along the Apennine foothills, in effect begging food from the peasantry; lending a hand with the wine harvest, or any other odd job about the farm, by way of payment, or on the remoter slopes helping to keep an eye on the sheep. As late as 7 November Soames was reporting that his constant trouble had been to keep parties of escapers on the move. They had an exasperating tendency to linger wherever they found a beautiful valley or a beautiful girl; and were crassly ungrateful to their guides, whose dangerous work they took for granted.

Others were more resolute, and found helpers of their own if they did not come across N section's. There was a marked and sudden contrast between the Italy of midsummer 1943, when those officious busybodies who pullulate in every dictatorship were inciting mobs to outrage against parachuted aircrew, and the Italy of early autumn, after Mussolini's fall and Badoglio's surrender, when newly arrived aircrew and newly self-liberated escapers alike found four peasants out of every five at least ready to advise, and often ready to aid.

Altogether, Simonds reckoned in retrospect, about 900 prisoners came through to southern Italy before the end of the year. Soames at the time put the figure at about 2,000. Several exciting books have resulted from some of their adventures, such as Tony Davies's *When the Moon Rises* about his march down the spine of Italy with Michael Gilbert the novelist and Toby Graham the future ski champion and professor of history. And many prisoners – certainly several hundred, perhaps over a thousand – decided that they had had enough of military inactivity, and would plunge at once into whatever work of active fighting they could find locally.

For in Italy the concept cherished in MI R before the war got under way, of escapers as innumerable small but sharp thorns in the enemy's side, had some splendid developments. The OVRA had kept the Italians as firmly bottled up as the KGB oppresses the peoples of the USSR today, but the fall of Mussolini and the armistice provided hope, that essential food for resisters; and against the republic of Salo people were ready to run risks and carry arms to an extent that had been unthinkable under the Fascist monarchy.

Many escapers made touch with nascent partisan bands – 'patriot forces', as they were called by British and American staff, a shade patronisingly – and much enhanced their military worth through their own experience and skill. There were several cases of privates and one of an ordinary seaman who were elected to command battalions, and two Australians in Piedmont each commanded a brigade two thousand strong.

MI 9's actual staff in 1943 can claim no credit for any of this, nor can MIS-X. From the previous summer onwards a frequent question at the secret lectures for airmen on escape and evasion had been, 'Can't we go and join the resistance, and wait until the ground battle catches up with us?' The standard reply was No. Aircrew had been expensively trained, and were needed back urgently to get on with the air war. Their plain duty was to return to their own lines, if they could, instead of embarking on an entirely different kind of combat. Much the same applied to sailors. Soldiers were not quite on the same footing as the others, unless they belonged to technical corps and were trained in the use of material unavailable to resistance – surveyors, tank drivers, electrical engineers: their place also was clearly back with their own corps. For infantry and commanders there might well be a role in resistance, but they were not encouraged to look for it. The language difficulty was real, though not insuperable. A less tangible, but more important obstacle was lack of training in how to behave as an underground worker.[28]

---

28  See George Millar, *Horned Pigeon*, 258–9, for his sub-Alpine conversation on this point with the celebrated 'Xavier', Richard Heslop.

This hardly mattered in the closing stage of a campaign, when two or three weeks' all-out effort would see the enemy's backs – the stage that most people quite wrongly thought the war had reached in Italy in mid-September 1943; but it counted for a great deal in town and country alike till that closing stage arrived. Uniformed men were seldom good at adapting briskly to the exigencies of clandestine warfare in plain clothes.

If they did try to do so a legal point arose, which escape lecturers felt bound to make. As one of them put it bluntly, 'Never carry arms in civilian clothes. If caught you stand an excellent chance of being shot.'

For this particular set of tasks in Italy, N section of A Force came under the G-3 (operations) branch of AFHQ, and not as usual under G-2 (intelligence). Simonds minuted to Dudley Clarke on 9 September that 'We should never have got such support under G-2,' and added at once that the backing G-3 gave to N section was due to the high regard the operations staff had already developed for A Force, the parent body. He spent two months in the heel of Italy, in charge of a force called Simcol of which the aim was to recover as many former prisoners of war as possible. It slowly dawned on everyone that the high hopes with which the force was founded had been dashed. The advance that was to have swept up the peninsula like a knife through butter had got stuck. For technical reasons, not much use was made of sea power to outflank the Germans' fixed defensive line; there were not enough landing craft, and staffs were unused to the finicky, intricate details involved in setting up a large landing. Simonds had much wider responsibilities than Italy on his mind, and had to go back to Cairo to look after them.

Before he left, he glanced round his mess table late in October 1943 and saw that he had lunching with him another regular soldier, a steeplechase jockey, a Harvard and an Oxford don, an American ex-sergeant of the Foreign Legion, a French Communist who had fought in Spain and an Englishman who had fought against him, a Cambridge undergraduate, a Polish embassy counsellor on half pay, a tea taster, a stockbroker, a police detective, three Italians – a prince, a priest and an intelligence officer – a Cockney, a South African lieutenant-colonel, an American from the Bowery, a merchant marine skipper and a Fleet Street fashion artist. It was a pity that so little could be found for such a galaxy of talent to do.

Out of the wreck of many hopes there emerged one shining example of the British genius for making the best of a bad job: the Rome escape organisation.

This was run, *à l'improviste*, by Major S. I. Derry, a territorial gunner battery commander who had been captured in the desert in January 1942, escaped at once and was recaptured by the same formation – the IO recognised and named him – next July. He had unexpectedly been made head of the escape committee at Chieti, when all the other members had been betrayed by an informer and packed off to another camp. The whole Chieti camp was moved by the Germans to Sulmona, and thence unceremoniously bundled into trains for Germany. The guards 'all seemed to fire at once when one of the group made a bolt for it at Sulmona station. Captain Jock Short covered only twenty yards in his suicide bid for freedom, before he crumpled and fell, riddled with bullets. He would not have been more efficiently shot if he had stood before a firing-squad.'

Derry's resolve to escape was strengthened, not weakened, by Short's death; after a sleepless night, he jumped off the back of the train next morning, while it was going fast. In doing so he permanently injured his leg, but he survived; and found that he was within twenty miles of Rome. He made friends, in pidgin Italian, with local peasants, who fed him, and introduced him to a dozen British escapers who were hanging about in some near-by caves. Their numbers swiftly grew to fifty; they all looked to Derry, the only officer, for a lead. With a village priest's help, he smuggled a message in to the British legation in the Vatican, and got in reply successively a little money, and a request to come to Rome. He entered the city hidden in a pile of cabbages going to market, was conducted by tram to the Tiber, and handed over in St Peter's Square to Monsignor Hugh O'Flaherty, an Irish priest who had little reason to love the British but still less to love the Nazis.

O'Flaherty took him to a safe house – ironically, to the German College: it was extra-territorial papal territory, and the nuns who lived there were Christians, not Nazis. He borrowed one of O'Flaherty's soutanes – luckily they were much of a height, about six feet three each – and thus disguised he entered the Vatican City proper by a side door. There he met the British minister, Sir D'Arcy Osborne, a descendant of the great Duke of Marlborough and of that Earl of Danby who had taken a leading part in inviting William of Orange to invade England in 1688.

Osborne had already been inundated with requests for help from ex-prisoners whose Italian guards had vanished and who had seized the opportunity to make themselves scarce before the Germans closed in. He invited Derry to take over the business of organising housing and feeding these people, and any more who turned up; Derry accepted. He had had no clandestine training whatever, but he had plenty of energy and common sense, and a mass of willing helpers. His own admirable *The Rome Escape Line* explains vividly what he did, which can only be summarised here.

A few British officers who had got into the Vatican before Rome's military authorities closed the frontier, and had been interned there, provided him with some office help. An international group of volunteers, mostly British, but including Irish, Dutch, Poles, Frenchmen, Greeks and Yugoslavs as well, several of them in orders, acted as couriers. Hundreds of Italian families put themselves at risk. The Germans appreciated that several thousand prisoners of war had slipped through their fingers, and introduced their usual remedy: the death penalty for those found harbouring them. As is so often the case in occupied countries, some people came forward to denounce their neighbours; treachery was an ever-pressing danger, and so was the probability that the Germans would try to feed people into Derry's system and break it up from within.

Pressures soon got so intense that he had to give up working from the German College, and retired within the legation's apartments inside the Vatican, where his presence was inadmissible. So he lived as ghost-like an existence as Best's or Harvey's in Colditz, though not for quite so long. By a stroke of good fortune, John Furman and Bill Simpson, gunner subalterns whom he had known well and liked much in Chieti, turned up in Rome in early December, in the company of a Cypriot private of Czech origins called Joe Pollak who spoke perfect Italian. Derry had suspected Pollak of being the traitor who shopped the Chieti escape committee and greeted him coolly; but was soon persuaded of his mistake. The three became his principal helpers; all were arrested at different times, and all got away again. Derry himself was carefully enough hidden never to fall into German hands; as English was his only effective language this was as well.

Their main object was to keep escapers from congregating in Rome. To do this they had to have numerous addresses of farms and other safe houses in the surrounding countryside, to which they could guide them, and money for fares, and subsistence money for the escapers' hosts, and masses of black market food, which had to be found, paid for and safely transported. Money, security and communications were their three nightmares.

One officer much Derry's senior was brought into Rome: Major-General M. D. Gambier-Parry, one of the armoured commanders in the desert war. Derry naturally offered to hand over control to him, but the major-general preferred to stay strictly out of sight and to leave the struggle in the hands of those who already knew the ropes.

As for money, Sir d'Arcy Osborne sent to London (via Lisbon, with the help of his Portugese colleague) a telegram so piteous that even the Treasury, even the trading-with-the-enemy department maintained by the Foreign Office jointly with the Board of Trade, relented enough to let him purchase lire for his 'crying and urgent demands'; even though these lire had to reach him in devious ways.

Less tortuously, but not less dangerously, some lucky officers in Rome were able to find anti-Fascist aristocrats who would cash cheques on London banks for them, and trust to time, honour and the course of the war for repayment. Derry himself engaged in a few transactions on the grey, if not the black market in currency which he felt to be dubious at the time and was not astonished when the British field cashiers he met after Rome's liberation on 4 June 1944 flatly refused him £154 in sterling to honour a debt of 100,000 lire. By then he knew his way so thoroughly round the economic by-ways of Rome that he was able to raise the sum and clear the debt through the jet-black market himself, within the five days from liberation he had promised.

The oddest feature of these transactions was that Osborne could produce neither receipts nor accounts for public money that he expended. He was so obviously straight, and the needs of the men he looked after were so obviously pressing, that all the usual rules were waived; though in late September 1944 the southern department of the Foreign Office reminded his chancery that some sort of receipt might as well be submitted while memories were still fresh. In retrospect, there are some entertaining passages on file about the propriety of changing official sterling on an enemy black market – 'You should not present appearance of exploiting difficulties of lenders you have in view, but at the same time we are not entitled to help them out at the expense of public funds.' One thousand pounds of the money Osborne had secured he had paid for by a cheque to his butler's mother for a Catholic mission in the Fulham Road. In his annual report for 1944 he praised the 'invaluable work' of Derry and all the helpers, and certified that he had 'strictly restricted expenditure and relief to the charitable purpose of saving lives, to the exclusion of any military objective.'

He paid just tribute also to 'the generosity and kindness displayed at great personal risk, and on occasion at the cost of death, by great numbers of Italian peasants,' which was 'above all praise.' Any readers who do not know Derry's *The Rome Escape Line* are urged to consult it for a splendid picture of how ordinary people behave under extraordinary pressures.

Derry himself, who had been interrogated before and recognised the signs, was sharply taken aback when at his second meeting with Osborne he found himself being subtly cross-questioned about where he had played on the rugger field, and what place his father took in Newark society at his Nottinghamshire Inline; his father in fact was an alderman, and he eventually held that thousand-year-old office himself. He soon took in that it was sensible of Osborne to make sure that he was who he said he was before trusting him, and that there must have been a rapid exchange of telegrams between Rome, London and Newark. What he did not discover till long after-wards – it was no direct business of his, and he had early picked up the secret activists' rule, Do not ask a question to which you do not need to know the answer – was that in mid-September 1943 Osborne's direct wireless link with London stopped: presumably because the minister had had his ciphers burned, in the anticipation that the Germans were about to hike the legation over. This drastic step did now and again look likely; and O'Flaherty, who cared nothing for the rules of security, was lucky that they never raided the German College.

One final difficulty beset Derry's path. Osborne's communi-cations, such as they were, ran north-westward to London, not southeastward towards Eisenhower and Alexander, the succes-sive Allied commanders-in-chief, still less towards Simonds in Taranto or Cairo. Co-ordination between what Derry was able to arrange or avert in Rome, and what Simonds in N section wanted him to do or to arrange elsewhere in Italy, was therefore likely to be a cumbrous, tricky and time-consuming business. N section sent in an agent, an Italian called Peter Tumiati, to make touch with whoever was to be found in Rome. He made straight for O'Flaherty, who arranged a meeting with Derry in Bernini's colonnade in St Peter's Square. 'My difficulty', said Derry, 'was that one can scarcely ask an MI 9 man for his credentials. The monsignor, in whatever way my questions were phrased, simply said, "Why, me boy, I know him well," and changed the subject.' Derry sent back to Bari by Tumiati's hand a list – already running in November 1943 to nearly 2,000 names – of 'all the ex-prisoners known to be at large'. John May, Osborne's butler, microfilmed the list and hid it in a roll of bread.

Through another Italian working in the British interest, a former parachutist major called Umberto Losena whom Derry described as 'one of my most valuable contacts', Derry was able to arrange for three successful evacuations of escapers from Adriatic beaches, shepherded by the ubiquitous 'Popski's' Private Army. It was unfortunate, yet in the circumstances unavoidable, that so many schemes on which high hopes had been based should founder on troubles of communication and control.

Derry's impromptu and quasi-official organisation amply proved its worth, and he may be left to summarise its achievements in his own words. 'By the time of the liberation, the Rome Organization had on its books the names of 3,925 escapers and evaders, of whom 1,695 were British, 896 South African, 429 Russian, 425 Greek, 185 American, and the rest from no fewer than twenty different countries. Fewer than 200 were billeted actually in Rome, but of the thousands in the "country branch" most, by far, were in the rural areas immediately surrounding the city, scattered in groups varying in size from three to more than a hundred.'

The care taken of the Russians produced the unusual courtesy of a letter of thanks from the Russian embassy in London to the Foreign Office. Not much courtesy was eventually extended to those of this party who did not wish to return to the USSR.

# Intelligence Tasks

Though it was infuriating for MI 9's staff to discover that so many thousand prisoners had been moved away across the Brenner Pass from Italy into the Reich, there was one crumb of comfort that Crockatt was able to extract from this setback. It much enlarged the number of trained observers that he had in Germany.

Readers will recall how easily and how constantly Beaconsfield was able to communicate with prisoner of war camps when arrangements were being made for escapes. The system of code interchange was repeatedly proved perfectly secure; its only disadvantages were that it was rather slow and that preparing messages in it had to be done in the camps behind some sort of look-out screen. Crockatt was fully aware that his sections had not been placed in the military intelligence directorate by accident; obviously enough, much of his time and all of MI 9's attention went on extracting intelligence from captured members of the Axis forces. That MI 9 also had a significant role as a source of intelligence has hitherto been overlooked.

Historical angels will fear to tread at all in the pool of British intelligence performance in the last world war before they have read F. H. Hinsley's still unfinished official history of the subject. No doubt Professor Hinsley, to whose far greater knowledge and capacity we defer, has access to much once highly secret material from which we have quite properly been barred. Yet it may not be altogether foolish to rush into print on this subject. A little can be perceived from the files, and more can safely be conjectured.

It was the task of Rawlinson's staff at MI 19 to get all that they could out of enemy captives; they certainly got a good deal.

How and how much are separate questions, awaiting somebody's book when the papers are available. We need pause no more than a moment to recall that Rait once saw a manuscript minute at the top of a paper of Crockatt's, produced for one of the early interdepartmental meetings about the impending threat from Hitler's revenge weapons, the V1 pilotless aircraft and the V2 rocket. The minute was strongly favourable and initialled 'WSC'. It had in fact been from an MI 19 report, on the indiscretions of two captured German generals, that it had first become known that Peenemünde was the experimental station where the Germans were preparing the V2: hence the RAF's devastating raid of 17/18 August 1943. That Peenemünde was an experimental rocket station had long been known, from the subsequently famous Oslo report; it was also used for the V1.

The American interrogation staffs that worked in MIS-Y in parallel with MI 19 found out a certain amount from their prisoners about how Allied prisoners behaved under interrogation, a subject of lively and perpetual interest to Crockatt and Catesby Jones alike; one or two fragments may be quotable. On 3 April 1944 for example a captured German interrogator remarked that he had found some German-Americans fairly amenable, especially when he could soften them up by letting them visit relatives. He had found the English 'better disciplined and more steady, above all better informed. They knew exactly how to behave themselves in German captivity, while the Americans tended to trust to their own judgement.' According to a captured German IO, over four months later, 'more than 85 per cent of the American P/Ws would give only their name, rank, and serial number. About 10 per cent were responsive to the extent of giving orally their unit, and about 5 per cent carried documents – mostly letters, notes and diaries – which gave valuable information.' (American soldiers will keep letters with them in the line, one of them explained, because 'they cannot get toilet paper and dislike the use of grass'; a straightforward account, if not a polite one. It gets added poignancy from a complaint by an American prisoner in Austria: on arrival at his Stalag, 'Each man was given one roll of toilet paper and this has to last him for a year.')

On the other hand, 'One German officer informed our men that any information received from a German prisoner of war could be relied upon, because no German would give false information', a staggering instance of how far rational self-delusion could progress in the age of Goebbels.

Reports from repatriated Allied prisoners were of enormous value, if the people concerned had been well enough briefed before they left enemy territory and were well enough inter-rogated when they got back; both for understanding the condi-tions in which they had been imprisoned, and for whatever of direct military interest might have caught their eyes on the way out, or have been impressed on them by the SAO or SBO before ever they left camp. One day all these reports should surface, and will need to be sifted through, first by military and then by social historians. The last-named group will hardly find an odder tale than that of the two American prisoners of war 'who struck a deep friendship after discovering from pictures over their respective bunks that they had the same wife.'

Anyone interested in unravelling 'Amy', the RAF's first code, will find among MI 9's papers the little pocket English-German dictionary on which it was based. Book codes were safe enough to be used by the Russian secret service well on into the war; and it was perhaps part of the cover for 'Amy' to use so very common and insignificant-looking a volume – its pages meas-ure less than 2 1/2" x 4"'. Winterbottom pressed on nevertheless with devising more codes. By the late summer of 1942 he had six distributed, one at least of them to MIS-X, and a seventh which Hooker had helped him to prepare which was ready for use; three more were in reserve by the autumn. The Americans after their early fiasco were content to use British codes, and did not devise any of their own. Simonds took the seventh out to the

Middle East on his way back from America. Traffic was brisk; in April and May 1943 two successive records were set, of 367 and 413 messages successfully received in code at Beaconsfield. Forty-seven of the May ones acknowledged receipt of escape kit parcels.

A condition of the efficient working of the code system in the camps was rigorous security. An elaborate watch system was sometimes needed to protect the coders while they were at work, and they had to take particular trouble about burning all their working papers when they had finished. In Oflags, and officers' camps in Italy, this was difficult but not impossible. In other ranks' camps there was much less privacy and there-fore much less security; consequently, fewer opportunities for code users to operate. Goodness knows there was little enough privacy in many Oflags, but the law of the jungle did not work so naturally in them; they were comparatively well disciplined, and rank counted for something.

At first the bulk of the messages exchanged with camps dealt with the minutiae of escaping and the passage of escape equipment, and in some camps the coding system was used for little if anything else. The decision about this lay partly in MI 9's and MIS-X's hands, partly in those of the SBO or SAO. Given that the senior officer was ready to play, the fact was that the British and later the Americans had several thousand highly accomplished watchers, young, lively-minded, observant and well-informed, scattered all over enemy-occupied territory in Europe and all over the enemy's homeland as well. Everyone brought up in the traditions of the old officer class knew – whether himself an officer or not – that it was a standing part of his duty to keep his eyes open for anything he could see about the enemy's behaviour, and to report it to his superior; whether his superior was his section corporal, or the pilot of his crew, or a distant commander-in-chief. The only aspects of this duty that changed when a man became a prisoner were that there might not be much of service interest for him to see, and that his reports did not travel as fast. Such a concept of duty spread rapidly from the regulars, in whom it was ingrained, all through the volunteers and conscripts who manned all three fighting services, British and American alike. Prisoners of war were thoroughly imbued with it. They had slow but sure means of communication; the slowness of it was its major disadvantage. A minor difficulty was that the volume of traffic the means could handle was limited; they could only write a few short letters each a month.

The data so far available on the subject of exchanges with camps are limited. In the USA it was the one point on which inquiries were met with a polite but total refusal of information.[29] In London, only three files of actual messages exchanged have so far been released, those to Marlag-Milag Nord near Hamburg and those from Oflags VIIC and XIIB. It may be conjectured that there are plenty more to come, unless the weeders have had an unusually large bonfire. There is base enough already on which to build some account of what could be done.

On 4 March 1941 for example Oflag VIIC at Laufen reported 'DOUBLED GLIDING SEEN DAILY' – the report was in England by 22 March – and added a week later 'TRIPLE GLIDING SEEN. UNDERSTAND ALL LONG LEAVE STOPPING FROM MID-APRIL'. It is easy in retrospect to associate these messages with General Student's airborne attack on Crete in May 1941. At the time they were more probably taken to presage some airborne blow at a Red Army target – Hitler was known to be preparing to attack Stalin, as he did on 22 June – and this can serve as yet another example of the difference between knowledge and understanding.

The British parachute party that raided the Tragino viaduct in south-central Italy in February 1941 included an unusually

---

29   Neither Pape, *Boldness be my friend*, nor J. M. Green, *From Colditz in code*, nor J. Borrie, *Despite captivity* appeared to have been read in the Pentagon by mid-February 1978. Things may have eased up since.

large number of code users, and by June 1941 – observe the comparative sloth of the Italian posts – the war diary was able to record that 'important information' had been received from them. In the autumn the British chiefs of staff sent friendly secret messages to every camp with which MI 9 was in contact, wishing them luck; so did George VI; so did Churchill; and the Queen of the Netherlands exchanged lengthy messages with her subjects in Colditz.

These were formalities; heartening, not necessarily essential. There was plenty of real work to be done as well. Allied intelligence officers in the large fixed camps in Germany realised quite early on that to secure 'Escaping information was only a subsidiary duty', and that their most useful task was to exploit their position as observers on enemy soil. From the middle of 1941, when the Germans' attack on Russia transformed the face of the war, and the attack's failure to secure another prompt knock-out blow made an ultimate Nazi victory less likely, SBOs in air force camps at least had got control over all the code users under their command, and directed the traffic in information.

The key personalities here were the camp IOs, who conducted the quasi-formal and very searching interrogations of all new arrivals and of returned unsuccessful escapers. More than one German attempt to plant a stool-pigeon in an Oflag was detected at this initial stage. An Egyptian officer for instance who was smuggled into Colditz was placed under close arrest within a few hours of his arrival, thanks to the IO's vigilance; the SBO told the commandant that he would answer for the Egyptian's life by day, but not after dark, and the man was removed. Support for the IOs' work was provided by what Crockatt once called in a moment of pardonable euphoria 'the marvellous security prevailing in all P/W camps'. Behind a tough screen of lookouts, or during an innocent and apparently friendly trudge round the compound, they inquired rigidly into how, where, and why each new arrival had been made a prisoner. Vitally important data were provided for the Air Ministry in this way, both about defects in Allied aircraft and about enemy fighter and anti-aircraft tactics. Cundall's reports from Sagan had an appreciable impact on bomber command's conduct of night raids, for Cundall was able to infer and describe German developments in airborne radar.[30] There were no doubt important points about enemy anti-submarine tactics to be discovered also, though the nearest that the accessible papers get to describing this is a telegram of congratulation to Donald Cameron, VC, from the submarine service, sent clandestinely after his gallant attack on *Tirpitz* had led him into Marlag-Milag Nord. And a whole host of points of interest about land fighting must have been available also.

The principal value of prisoners of war as an intelligence source lay all the same in the brute fact that they were present in the enemy's heartland and were bound to have some notion of what was going on there. Camp IOs reckoned that returned escapers – people who had got out, and were then caught and brought back – were their best sources of all, provided that they had briefed them before their escape on what to observe. If the escape succeeded, then a cornucopia of information could be poured out into the ears of the first service attaché the escaper met on neutral ground. Cartwright in Berne did much more of this work than his opposite numbers in Madrid and Stockholm; they were more concerned with passing ex-prisoners on promptly home, he as a rule had time on his hands before he could find them a route. And if the escape failed, expert cross-questioning after the would-be escaper had done his turn in solitary could extract the main tidbits, and they would reach Beaconsfield as

---

30    Oddly enough Cundall's name does not figure on the long list of those who communicated in code from Sagan (WO 208/3283, 67–70). Jones'] certainly saw his reports (conversation with Jones, 1977); he may have had a code arranged privately with Dansey behind Jones's back, or he may have been left off the Sagan list by mistake.

soon as a letter could get there. MI 9 had adequate arrangements with the postal censorship for the prompt interception and copying of prisoners' mail; Winterbottom found the families concerned were uniformly helpful in bearing with this brief and necessary drill.

If MI 6 had useful agents of its own in Germany during the war, apart from the author of the Oslo report, the secret has been remarkably well kept; this is a point on which Hinsley will be read with particular interest. MI 9 did what it could to fill any gap.

Several camps maintained train-watches – how many trains, loaded with what, in which directions – for years on end. Dobrilugk, Weinsberg, Thorn and Heydekrug, each beside a main railway line, were well placed to do this; Dobrilugk was at the crossing of two. Some maintained airfield watches, though unhappily there is no trace of an organisation fit to mount an airfield watch at Steglitz, the large Stalag in the south-western suburbs of Berlin: a chance to watch the comings and goings at Tempelhof was clearly missed. At Sagan the prisoners watched the local airfield – pine trees hid direct sight of it from the camp, but they were close enough to get a view of most aircraft circling in to land – and from this watch reported German progress with a jet fighter, one of the technical aspects of warfare in which the Germans were well in front of the Allies. A rare fragment of the American correspondence section's information has surfaced here, and is in point: 'Hun engineers claim jet propulsion problem licked. Ready for mass production' on 30 July 1944. Can it be that WO 208/3284, the camp history of the Belaria compound at Sagan which was close to the airfield, has been withheld because it is full of technical information that is still thought to be sensitive?

One important kind of reporting that prisoners could engage in was the identification of German dummies and other camouflage: not only those mile-long strips of netting that were used in vain to baffle radar-equipped bombers about the real shape of German ports, but the presence of simulated aircraft on disused airfields of which the nature might have been impossible to unravel by air photography. Extensive and frequent reports were also provided about bomb damage and the lack of it: 'OPEL WORKS NEAR MAINZ STATION AND SALZBACH OIL REFINERY INTACT EARLY AUGUST' 1944, for instance, or 'BIG OIL PLANT AT HOCHST UNDISTURBED' two months later.

Davies-Scourfield has an anecdote which illustrates vividly how much this sort of reporting was a matter of routine, and what sudden perils could lurk in it. One day in Colditz he and a friend were sitting preparing a bomb damage report, drawn from the observation of a newly arrived inmate. They had papers spread over the table in front of them, in full confidence that the cry of 'Goons up!' from the duty pilot would give them all the time they needed to clear away, before a goon could get up the stairs. For once the duty pilot failed: glancing across the room, Davies-Scourfield saw a German corporal he knew walking up to him. He and his friend both leaned well forward on their elbows, covering up as much of the table surface as they could. 'Come on', said the corporal, tugging at a corner of paper that stuck out from beneath Davies-Scourfield's sleeve, 'I know that's a map – give it me.' 'It's not a map.' 'You promise me it's not a map? Nothing to do with escape?' 'I promise.' 'On your word of honour as an officer!' '*Yes.*' 'Very well, then' – and the corporal walked out.

Besides indicating bomb damage, prisoners could perform another important agent's task: they could indicate targets. The Hadamar camp put up several, including 'BIG HUN HQ IN WHITE HOTEL ABOUT 9 KM N.E. OF PISTOIA ON NORTH SIDE RLY PISTOIA TO BOLOGNA WHERE IT EMERGES FROM TUNNEL', and 'WETZLAR CEMENT WORKS ADJOINING WEST SIDE RAILWAY STATION NOW BECOME STEEL PLANT'. This pair of messages must stand in here for a great many more, which must have been valuable to the British and American staffs whose task it was to hunt for bomber targets.

Much more far-ranging information could be got from

a camp that took its intelligence duties seriously. The air force camps at Heydekrug and Sagan certainly came in this category. At both, trading with the enemy was developed to such a degree that many Germans became more or less willing accomplices of their prisoners and could be persuaded by a sort of benevolent blackmail to part with masses of information. Roger Bushell, who was mentioned as an early escaper from Oberursel, was in charge of trading at Sagan from June 1942, as well as a great many other things; and secured data on a variety of points, which Sagan continued to report home until the camp was moved west on the Russians' approach early in 1945.

The Sagan camp sought and found reports on troop movements; locations, strengths, sometimes even identifications of units; on locations of airfields, with numbers and types of aircraft on them; on details of ground and anti-aircraft defences; on experiments with new weapons – what, where, and how defended; on local railway traffic in troops and raw materials; on German reactions to various types of warfare; on German morale in general; on bomb damage; and on how things stood economically – prices, surpluses, shortages. As the camp staff came from all over the Reich, Sagan's range of information though far from all-embracing was extensive. This sort of report cannot be claimed to have been of overwhelming importance, but it was certainly useful, valuable even, to the Intelligence community in London and in Washington. It provided a series of cross-checks on 'Ultra' interceptions of the most secret cipher traffic the Germans deluded themselves was indecipherable; and on several other sources of information, such as newspapers. These checks were indispensable in assessing other sources' reliability and for probing the veracity of those who proffered data: a perpetual intelligence problem.

If ever 'Ultra' vanished, as – any day – it might, prisoners of war provided much the strongest alternative as a source for whatever of military interest was going on in Germany. The traditionary caution must again be inserted here, to the effect

that the British secret intelligence service may have had numerous and highly qualified agents scattered all round the Third
Reich. Certainly no trace of them was perceptible to the agents
who were parachuted into Germany by the Americans during
the last winter of the war.

One neat minor example can be given of how the escape
services at one moment knew more about Germany than the
Germans themselves. An undated American manual on prisoners' security and escape mentioned that the branch line bridge
over the Rhine a mile south of Remagen, upstream of Bonn,
was unlikely to be guarded. This was the bridge the Americans
found still intact (though no longer unguarded) when all the
others had been blown up, on 7 March 1945.

An odd example of where MI 9 and MIS-X stood among the
other bodies dealing with more or less secret subjects, and
of how they got on with each other, may be taken from the
American files. About 1 August 1943 – uncharacteristically,
he left the date off his letter – Crockatt wrote by air mail to
Catesby Jones, to pass on a captured German corporal's indis-
cretion. Several months earlier this man had been on a fighting
patrol in Tunisia that 'found the Americans asleep in their slit
trenches, without sentry or outpost and were able to take about
fifty of them prisoners before the rest awoke'. Crockatt added
in his own hand: 'We are not making any distribution of this
information other than to you in this letter'. Jones replied with
equal tact and courtesy. He thought on 9 August that it might
be useful to the British in general and Crockatt in particular to
know that the Germans' operations on the currency market in
Lisbon were enabling them to trace the numbers on the notes
passed to Allied agents in France.

A great many prisoners worked as hard as they could to lower
German morale, and by so doing helped to raise their own. The
tone displayed in such books as Sam Kydd's *For You the War is
Over,* a tone of Cockney assurance and invincible ignorance,

must have been maddening for Germans and Italians alike, but it was a tone that most British and some American working-class prisoners adopted: the attitude of men who have been personally unlucky, but remain perfectly sure that their own side is the right one and is bound to win. British captives – even Texan, even Australian captives – were not so cocky towards the Japanese, for reasons that a moment's reflection on the history of the war will make clear there was hardly anything in Asia for the Allies to be cocky about for quite a time.

Nothing is said in this chapter about intelligence provided from camps in Asia, because there the extreme sloth of prisoner of war mail made communications all but impossible. Once – just once – Bevan, the head of the deception service, was able to use a letter sent in to a naval petty officer who was a prisoner in Germany, to mislead the Japanese about the completion date of a new British battlecruiser, but the incident was exceptional.

In one or two camps in Germany the business of lowering enemy morale was taken up in a big way, as soon as the course of the war provided opportunities for German-speaking prisoners. Rhodes's Highgate course always stressed the importance of making as much of an unmitigated nuisance of oneself as possible, as the keynote of a prisoner's attitude to the enemy; provided that the nuisance did not obstruct escape. Hence the value of goon-baiting. Roger Bushell in Sagan added to his other responsibilities the task, codenamed 'Plug', of adapting the Chinese water-on-a-stone torture technique to the minds of the Germans with whom he was in contact. He was a barris-ter by profession, and used a lawyer's subtlety to confuse and dismay them, which over many months' relentless application achieved some notable results. It is not known whether the Gestapo had taken in his importance in Sagan's secret anti-Nazi schemes; but it is certain that he was one of those who went through the notorious Sagan tunnel, and never reached home.

Crockatt was particularly delighted by a captured SS secret report on internal security in Germany, dated 12 August 1943.

Its provenance is unstated in the only accessible copies. Just possibly it was captured in Sicily, in the closing stages of the Axis retreat there; it would be like the SS to send a secret document on to a battlefield everybody else could see was already doomed. In it, the unknown author commented on the self-possessed bearing of British prisoners of war. The hangdog look that had accompanied the victims of the great German drives of 1940 had disappeared.[31] These men always looked well dressed and well fed. Their uniforms, seen from close to, were of far better quality than those of the Wehrmacht. They bore themselves in challenging and aggressive, almost arrogant attitudes, full of confidence in victory. The impact of their distribution of chocolate and cigarettes on the morale of chance-met German civilians was deplorable.

This was precisely one of the effects that Crockatt believed his department had been set up to create. In their small way, prisoners who behaved like this were helping to win the war. Those of them who joined in the provision of intelligence were helping in a much more formidable way. Needless to say this intelligence work had to be kept a deadly secret at the time and for long after; though the inquisitive Philby can hardly have failed to know of it, or to report it to his masters in Moscow.

One of the sharper agonies of imprisonment was provided by letters from home announcing to prisoners that their girl-friends, or even their wives, had thrown them over for someone else. Many were fortunate; many others were not. Inconstant women often said that they had taken up with someone who was still active in the war; how could they know that their

---

31   There was an unforgettable shot in the film *Sieg im Westen* of a disconsolate party of Tommies in battledress, looking thoroughly down in the mouth, accompanied by 'We'll hang our washing on the Siegfried Line' played at half speed on a solo oboe. A Paris audience in October 1940 was less impressed: someone called out contemptuously 'Was that all they took?' (Personal knowledge).

rejected men folk might still be playing an extremely perilous part? How perilous it was, Crockatt well knew, and so did the participants at the sharp end. It might be a nice question for an international lawyer to determine whether a uniformed prisoner of war was legally entitled to amass military information about his enemy, and to try by subterfuge to transmit it back to his own side's staff. No one at the time had much doubt which way such a question would have been decided by a Nazi court. That it never arose is a tribute to the collective, cohesive security of prisoners of war, as well as a tribute to the care that Crockatt and Johnston took to make sure that prisoners never took unjustifiable risks.

# Line upon Line:
## Evasions in Europe 1943–45

*Staff*

To make clear what follows, various boundaries and responsibilities they affected MI 9 and MIS-X must first be set out.
During Crockatt's visit to America early in 1943 he discussed with
Strong, Catesby Jones and Johnston the problem of where each
department had best concentrate its energies. Both sides agreed
that it would be a sensible division of labour if each took the
lead in some areas, and acted consciously as second rather than
as leader in others. On his return to London Crockatt talked this
over with Davidson, the director of military intelligence, and
with his concurrence proposed by cipher telegram on 23 March
the following 'spheres for all purposes (A) War Office EUROPE
AFRICA ASIA MAINLAND and SUMATRA (B) War Dept. america
japan australia and all other Islands East of Sumatra.'

Washington did not reply immediately, but on 26 May
Simonds, in the course of his highly successful American sortie,
was able to telegraph 'have complete approval from General
Strong for "spheres of influence".' On 1 June Strong and
Davidson finally agreed that the British sphere was to contain
Europe, North Africa, the Middle East, India and Burma; the
American, North and South America, the Pacific and China.
Whether Crockatt took in at this stage that by agreeing to this
revised version, he had sawn off the branch on which Leslie
Ride was sitting to perform his extraordinary work in south
China is not clear. Ride was so far away, and communications
with him were so scanty, that it is probable that Crockatt knew

not what he did, and simply bowed to the Americans' insistence that China must be in their sphere: an insistence motivated by domestic politics, rather than by any knowledge of Ride's achievement or even of his existence.

Dudley Clarke was also concerned in the problem of spheres of interest. While Crockatt was in America, on 17 February 1943 – well before the worldwide argument was settled, and even before the fate of North Africa was quite sealed – Clarke proposed to him that A Force, including N section, should work over the whole of Eisenhower's command as well as the entire Middle East. Crockatt gave a rather grudging consent; indeed he had already eleven days earlier sent to Jones via Johnston an organigram to explain the layout:

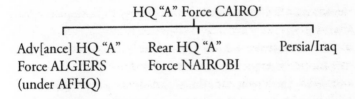

HQ "A" Force CAIRO[1]

| Adv[ance] HQ "A" Force ALGIERS (under AFHQ) | Rear HQ "A" Force NAIROBI | Persia/Iraq |

Tac[tical] HQ "A" Force Tunisia

1    United States National Archives, research group 332, MIS-X box 6, Crockatt file, 6 February 1943

For a time even this extended empire was not too much for Dudley Clarke's phenomenal capacities to control nor for the untiring Maskelyne to tour. They had a particularly valuable American to help them at the AFHQ end, Major Philip V. Holder. He had fought through the 1914–18 war, first in a Canadian infantry battalion and then in the RAF, and had served in south Russia in 1919. Mobilised into the USAAF, he had spent the late summer of 1942 at Holt's elbow in London, and Crockatt thought highly of him: so highly that he drafted a letter to Strong for Davidson to sign on 29 October that year. The letter pointed out that Clarke was very anxious to get his organisation onto an inter-Allied basis and requested that Holder, who was particularly suitable for this suggested assignment, be posted to join A Force. The posting was made, to the great benefit of the alliance and of aircrew serving in the Mediterranean; his imperturbable presence was totally reassuring.

Many months of effort finally convinced even Dudley Clarke that he had extended himself too far, and on 20 August 1944 he handed over the central Mediterranean organisation, by now called IS 9(CMF), to Commander Rodd, RN. Rodd was no more easy to rattle than was Holder, who was still at his elbow, and the handing over made no difference to the support that MI 9 and MIS-X were able to give to those who needed their help.

Simonds' responsibilities, henceforward named IS 9(ME), were confined to the Balkans, the Aegean and anything that might crop up elsewhere in the Middle East; and for reasons of nearness and convenience Yugoslavia and Albania were taken away from him, and handed over to IS 9(CMF). AFHQ at Caserta, near Naples, was generally thought to be a better main headquarters from which to supervise them than Cairo; in fact IS 9(CMF) kept most of its operational headquarters in and near Bari, by the heel of Italy, conveniently close to the main airfields available for clandestine work.

On Hitler's map of Europe Yugoslavia had vanished, partitioned among and into several states, but the Allies continued to treat and write of it as a continuing entity. Its ministers in London, Moscow and Washington were promoted ambassador, and its exiled young king did his best to continue to reign. Allied historians can here safely follow Allied wartime practice.

It is now time to review IS 9's work in more detail; it will be taken section by section, starting at the eastern end.

*IS 9(ME)*

Tony Simonds' excursion into the heel of Italy with Simcol gave him an interlude in a long spell of intricate and intensely difficult work. From Cairo, with a forward base under Wolfson's eye in Istanbul, he had been trying since the autumn of 1941 to build reliable escape lines to run south-eastward out of central Europe. He got sympathy and encouragement from his opposite numbers in the secret service and in SOE, the subversive organisation (known in Cairo as MO4, to add to the acronymic confusion of general headquarters), but – wireless links apart – they could provide him with no actual help outside Yugoslavia and Greece. Such agents as they had in the Danube basin had other fish to fry.

However, Simonds's work with Wingate in Palestine before the war now bore unexpected fruit. He had kept in touch with several friends he had made among the Zionist leaders, when he had been operating with their special night squads in the late 1930s.[32] They had now become senior men in their movement, and he drove a bargain with them. They would provide him with contacts, operators, safe houses in Czechoslovakia, Hungary and all over the Balkans, on the understanding that they could bring out a Jew along the channels thus set up for every Ally they rescued. The risks the Jews ran were even heavier than the risks normally run by helpers in escape lines, for the Nazi regime had never made any secret of its anti-Semitism, and extra severe penalties ending in an extra nasty death awaited anybody who added to the grave offence in Nazi eyes of helping an evader or escaper the unbearable affront of being a Jew. The Jewish Agency was nevertheless prepared to make the offer, which was cleared through Dudley Clarke with Whitehall and at once approved.

---

32   Conversations with Simonds, 1977–8. Much of the next seven paragraphs is gratefully derived from the same source.

The idea was splendid, but the results did not live up to it. There were some scintillating additions to the world's gallery of secretly heroic figures, but no enormous number of escapers and evaders were handled by them. Moreover in Eastern Europe, in Slav territories in particular, the Nazi security forces acted with a dispatch, ferocity, and an efficiency quite unknown in north-western Europe, and still not fully appreciated there or in America.

One example, long celebrated in Israel but little known outside it, may help to make this clear, that of the young poet Hannah Szenes. Her name comes at the head of a list of twenty-five agents, all by their names Jewish (unless we should except a pair only codenamed Dickens and Jones), sent in by Simonds between June 1943 and August 1944 to organise new channels down which evaders could move home. All the women had been recruited into the Women's Auxiliary Air Force before they left, and all the men into the Buffs or the Pioneer Corps. She was dropped into Yugoslavia on 14 June 1943, as 'Minnie' of operation 'Chicken I'. 'Micky', who followed her five days later, was Sergeant Nussbacher of the Buffs. They both reached Budapest, and made touch with the Jewish colony there. For excellent reasons, these Jews were in a considerable state of turmoil, and there were too many informers lodged among them. One of these promptly delated her, as a newcomer and therefore a suspect, to the police. Nussbacher also was soon arrested. Accident once put them in adjacent cells, and she was able to tap out a good deal of information for him before she was taken away for further interrogation, torture, and death.[33]

The fact that Nussbacher knew her well and was on the same mission eluded their captors, and he managed to pass himself off as an 'ordinary' Jew. As such he was first sent to a labour camp near Vienna, and then bundled into a railway cattle truck

---

33    WO 208/3418, letter 66, 4 March 1945, reported her shot in
      Budapest on 6 November 1944.

with several score others and sent on his way to an extermination camp. That particular truck arrived empty; Nussbacher had not been trained by Maskelyne for nothing. He had still got an escape file secreted about his clothing. With it he cut a panel out of his truck after dark and bolted, as did everybody else. He returned to Budapest shortly before Christmas 1944, dug up the transmitter he had buried on arrival, passed on the news he had from Hannah Szenes and much else, and provided for a few weeks the only means of communication between those people in Budapest who wanted Hungary to change sides and the Allies.

Communications at that time and place, long before teleprinters had spread far in the Levant, were often exceedingly tricky. Simonds had an agent called 'Interval' in Sofia, who could send morse on an SOE set to Istanbul. His messages then had to pass through four further signals junctions, Ankara, Aleppo, Damascus and Jerusalem, before they reached Cairo: a system that might have been calculated to maximise clerical error and the chances of garbling. No wonder that Simonds did not want to know when the earliest stages of Eichmann's astonishing offer to swap Jews in quantity, at the rate of 100,000 Jews for 1,000 lorries and some soap and coffee, first reached the Allies through an N section channel.[34] The proposal was immediately passed over to the diplomatic and strategic authorities whose task it was to reject it. No one – or no one but an anti-Semite or a secret policeman, so often the same thing – could fail to be appalled by the impending fate of Hungary's Jews, over a quarter of a million of whom were shortly to be exterminated. But none of Russia's allies could dream of supplying lorries to the Germans, expressly for use on the eastern front against the now usually victorious Red Army.

Sergeant Nussbacher's fate provided a small but significant instance of how much gratitude the Russians felt for this refusal

---

34  See Weissberg, *Advocate for the Dead*, for the details; and Eichmann's sensational trial in Israel in 1961.

to work against their interests. When they drew near Budapest he hid; survived their capture and sack of the city in the second week of February 1945; and reported to one of their headquarters as a friendly Allied agent, who wanted to know what he could do to help. He was at once arrested, severely tortured in an attempt to extract some British codes from him, and sent to a penal camp in Russia.

Months afterwards, a ragged wraith presented himself to the MI 9 repatriation mission in Odessa, and identified himself as Sergeant Nussbacher of the Buffs; having escaped the clutches of the SS, he had brought off the still more difficult feat of an escape from the NKVD. The award of a Distinguished Conduct Medal did not overrate his devotion to freedom.

There will be more to say about Hungary in the following chapter, on escapes; but the 'Chicken' mission – some chickens, as Churchill might have put it – needed mention here, because their task was to have been the setting up of an evasion line.

Simonds had early appreciated the possibility of getting ratlines, as N section called evasion lines – Crockatt detested the comparison with rats – working out of Silesia into Slovakia, which would of course aid escapers as well as evaders; it was not till the late summer of 1944 that his 'Amsterdam' mission was able to get into the field. Sergeant Grünhut and Martha Martinovic ('Uncle' and 'Auntie') composed it. Grünhut may have got in by parachute in August. She certainly arrived by one of the war's odder semi-clandestine operations, a landing by two B-17 Flying Fortresses at Tri Duby, a small grass airfield between Banska Bystrica and Zvolen in central Slovakia on 18 September. Forty-one P-51 Mustang fighters were in attendance as escort, and flew to and fro for the twenty-five minutes the big aircraft were on the ground.

Half a dozen Russian staff officers, previously put in by the Soviet air force, were in attendance on the airfield, and showed keen interest in every detail of the B-17s; for 'Amsterdam' opened up, accidentally, at the crisis of the Slovak national rising, which had broken out on 29 August, when it looked as if the Red Army was about to storm southward through the Dukla pass in the Carpathians and the Germans attempted to occupy the whole of their satellite state. The two aircraft, on one of which Martha Martinovic travelled, brought in four and a half tons of military stores and an OSS mission, and flew out to Bari a delighted party of twelve Americans and three British airmen, and a Czech.[35] Those sixteen men cannot have gathered at Tri Duby by accident. One pair were guided in by Russian officers they met with the partisans. Grünhut may have collected some of them beforehand. His wireless set soon fell into German hands and so did Miss Martinovic's – with two OSS companions to whom she had lent it; and they lost most of their money. They sent out nevertheless by air on 7 October another large party of twenty-eight Americans – evaders and escapers, again mixed – and a couple of New Zealand privates who had found their own way to central Slovakia from Silesia. But the Russians were still stuck on the northern side of the Dukla pass, and the German grip on the Slovak rising was tightening.

---

35   WO 208/3377, 'Amsterdam' report by Colonel G. Kraigher to commander, Mediterranean Allied Air Forces (MAFF), 18 September 1944; information from H. M. Threfall, who like Kraigher took part in the operation. A few of the Americans are identifiable: 2/Lieut. Gerald K. Rothermel and S/Sgt. Robert J. Fleharty of the 736th Bombardment Squadron, shot down over Slovakia on 7 July, who had escaped in a party of thirty from a prison near Bratislava on 2 September and marched eastwards; 2/Lieut. Walter Leach and S/Sgt. Delos Miller, 759th Squadron, shot down 130 miles away on 22 August, and guided by locals; and Corporal P. C. P. Reinhart, 429th Squadron, who had bailed out only four days earlier, on 13 September, and walked. (Simpsons Historical Research Center file 670–614–1, Fifteenth Air Force escapers and evaders. Reports in this large file are kept by the date on which their subject returned to Allied territory; there is also a names index.)

'Amsterdam', reinforced by two more Jewish sergeants called Berdichev and Reisz (the 'Anticlimax' mission) who had marched in from the Yugoslav-Hungarian border – in itself a feat – threw in their lot with John Sehmer's SOE mission called 'Windproof'. They all hid in the Tatra ranges east-north-east of Banska Bystrica, on the northern side of the Hron valley, and hung on. The OSS mission joined up with them; so did a party of nineteen American and two British evaders, who were to have been flown out to the Russians, a plan that came to nothing. (No evaders' names survive.) This was too large a group to stay together as winter drew in, and the Germans held all the towns and large villages; they split into smaller parties. 'Had to remain with P[arti]s[a]ns in very bad conditions,' Berdichev complained on Guy Fawkes' day, 'living in improvised huts in woods where weather is worst possible.' He needed sleeping bags, whisky, and anti-louse powder. 'Where is rest of A Force party? No contact with them.' Sehmer and Berdichev tried to rescue Viest and Golian, the captured Czechoslovak senior officers who had commanded the rising, when the puppet government put them on trial in Bratislava, but both were shot.

Eventually, on 26 December, Sehmer and seventeen British and American companions were surprised in the early morning by the Germans and taken prisoner. Sehmer met his death in Mauthausen, and Reisz Grünhut and Berdichev were no more fortunate, though Martha Martinovic survived. As R. S. Taylor, on MI 9's staff at Bari, put it, long before their fate could even be guessed at 'When the whole story can be told it will undoubtedly be an epic of endurance in the face of extreme difficulties', but the epic has yet to be written.

## Relations with partisans

An incessant difficulty for N section, for its agents forward in the field, and for evaders or escapers who wanted to cross partisan territory lay in the attitude towards all of them of the partisan's leaders. No fine distinctions were made, outside Great Britain and the USA, between intelligence and other secret services. Any Communist suspected any member of the officer class automatically, and the suspicion became intense if the officer belonged to any sort of secret organisation, for it was axiomatic in the Communist world that all such organisations outside it were necessarily devoted to the overthrow of Communism. Months, years of explanation that MI 9's and MIS-X's agents were only seeking to hasten the overthrow of Axis imperialism did nothing as a rule but create deeper suspicion, mixed with some admiration for the elaboration of the cover story that was surely being spun.

It was not merely a matter of getting leave to operate in partisan territory, though that could be difficult enough. For instance, leave for the 'Amsterdam' party to pass through Yugoslavia on their way via Hungary to Slovakia, sought on 21 June 1944, was not granted till 19 July; the matter had to be referred to Tito personally. (In fact as will have been noted these two agents went direct by air.) He can be forgiven for taking his time over it, for he had much else of more importance on his mind. Similar delays were common. Various approaches to the Soviet authorities, through the military attachés in Kuybyshev, for leave to operate MI 9 or MIS-X agents with partisan forces in western Russia met a peremptory refusal. On the other hand, as early as 17 May 1944 the Soviet general staff had put out a message 'warning all Russian troops on fronts where Brit[ish] or American aviators may bale out or crash land that they must be prepared for Allied aviators and help them.'

A worse difficulty was met at a less exalted level. It was simply inconceivable to most partisans that young healthy unwounded men who shared their dislike of Nazism and Fascism, whom fate had cast into their neighbourhood, should want to leave it instead of staying to fight. They were amazed to discover that military airmen had had no infantry training, and were devoid of those elementary skills of tactics and field craft that are ingrained in Balkan children. When what they had at first supposed to be heaven-sent reinforcements turned out to be useless mouths to feed, and a security liability as well, they could not be relied on to remain friendly. We know of no definitely established cases of airmen intent on an evasion that were quietly disposed of by partisans to whom they can have been nothing but a nuisance; but it is only too probable that such a fate did befall some.

There are several cases on record of airmen who bailed out over Polish, Bulgar, Ukrainian or Russian-occupied territory who were roughly handled, fired on from the ground while still descending by parachute, robbed, beaten up, and kicked when they were down, before they had had any chance to establish their nationality or their good will. To help them clear themselves quickly, MIS-X and MI9 distributed a great many 'blood chits': printed cards, bearing prominently Stars and Stripes or a Union Jack or both, with a short clear statement that there would be a reward for treating the bearer well. These were first devised in Arabic for use in the western desert, and were then recast, and translated into several languages of south-east Europe and of south-east Asia. Aircrew often forgot to take them, or had them fall out of their pockets while parachuting. Devising new formulae for them was a staff officers' game; their value could hardly be great among populations not much used to reading, and not in the least interested in foreign flags.

On the other hand, not all country folk were suspicious of strangers. Bread and salt were brought out by the nearest Montenegrin cottager for at least one party of arriving SOE agents; accompanied by a dash of slivovits, as they had turned up by parachute in the middle of a battle. And there were quite a lot of country-bred aircrew who were capable of becoming adepts at mountain warfare. A few of these had the foresight to bring machine guns and ammunition along with them, if they crash-landed instead of parachuting. These weapons might make a formidable difference to the local tactical balance, and would in any case be rapturously received by partisan bands, sure to include a village blacksmith who could improvise gun-mountings. Jules Dominique's band of freebooters in Luxembourg, which specialised in attacking German police, had a heavy machine gun from a crashed American aircraft as its main armament. Lieutenant Charles F. Kingsman whose Liberator was shot down over northern Italy on 25 April 1944, injured himself when he landed by parachute, and lay up for months with an Italian family. While hiding, he held secret classes' for visiting partisans in the use and care of the .50 machine gun, several of which they had been able to secure from crashed aircraft and provided a mass of tactical intelligence for the brigadier of the 7th Indian Infantry Brigade when a Gurkha unit overran the house he was in on 25 September. There were a great many other cases of aircrew who ought according to all their training to have pressed on with the business of rejoining their units, but who preferred – or were pressured into – fighting for a while with more or less irregular bands as infantry.

Few airmen, American or British, knew much about the political complications of the areas over which they had to operate. An entire Flying Fortress crew shot down on 24 May 1944, when trailing behind their formation on the way back from a raid on Vienna, found themselves over Zagreb (Agram), the capital of Croatia. 'The navigator had had a very good briefing on the safe areas in Yugoslavia the morning of the mission. None of them had ever heard of the Ustachi', the Croat terrorists in the centre of whose stamping ground they were, and they were exceptionally lucky to run straight into an OSS mission and thus get flown out fast. The crew of another B-17 which crash-landed about forty miles further east, on 16 July 1944, had had very little briefing on escape; the only advice they could recall was to 'contact the partisans'. This they did to such effect that they were flown back to Italy only four days later.

For by this time OSS's Strategic Balkan Service[36] had got several missions lodged in Yugoslavia, some with Mihailovic's

---

36   Distinguish sharply of course from the British Special Boat Section
     which shared the same acronym, SBS (cp. pp. 92–3, 200–1)

Chetniks and some with Tito's partisans, and the United States
air forces produced a Balkan Air Terminal Service (yes, BATS)
which Operated mainly with C-47 Dakotas, to as many as
thirty-six improvised landing strips. As Mihailovic's standing
with the Allies worsened, the number of these strips in his territory declined, but even after all military aid to him by the British
and Americans, and all propaganda aid to him by his original
trumpeters the Russians, had been withdrawn he continued to
order his men to succour Allied evaders and escapers – most of
them evading aircrew – whenever he could.

Aircrew, like politicians, were of several minds about the
Chetniks. We could instance 2/Lieut. William H. Vean, who had
to bail out north of Sarajevo on 28 August 1944 owing to engine
trouble on his way back from an attack on Budapest. (There is
a study waiting to be written, or at least to be published, about
the proportion of aircraft lost over enemy territory through
faults that developed in flight, rather than through enemy
action.) He reported that 'the Chetniks in the regions where
he travelled with the Partisans, are actively aiding the enemy
against the Partisans.' Three survivors from an aircraft damaged
in odd circumstances during the raid on Ploesti on 28 July 1944
– the aircraft in front of them blew up when a bomb from
another one hit it – found themselves in the hands of a not very
friendly body of Chetniks, who moved them round for weeks
from one safe house to another while they made no attempt
to evacuate them. They 'seemed to be allied directly with the
Germans', who supplied them. The three airmen 'strayed away
from the Chetnik camp on 15 September and ran into some
Partisans who took charge and started them off for evacuation
next day.' On the other hand, Lloyd C. Hargrave, an Idaho
farmer shot down on a ground strafing task a few miles south
of Belgrade on 3 September 1944, was feasted by the Chetniks,
even had his shoes shined, and was offered a commission in
their air force; but he met a United States mission – what sort
of mission, his report is too discreet to specify – and was back

at duty a fortnight after he had been shot down. And a crew from the 830th Bombardment Squadron, who bailed out on 22nd August 1944 in the course of a flight against Vienna, remarked that the Chetniks who looked after them 'fought the Germans'.

Others again were enthusiastic in their support for the Chetniks' local opponents, Tito's partisans; none more so than Staff Sergeant Edward C. Legro of 414th Bombardment Squadron. He had to parachute on 24 March 1944 when his B-17 collided with another in cloud about sixty miles south of Zagreb. When he got back to base, late in the summer, 'he would like to shout from the house tops the kindness and co-operation from Partisans, and the fine job they are doing.'

He must have spent some months in the mountains on the Croat-Serb border before he made touch with an American mission. OSS seems to have taken on directly the business of aircrew rescue in Yugoslavia, which was certainly one of those parts of Europe where Hitler's writ did not run everywhere and where extensive mountain areas could be found in which evaders were more or less safe. Numerous special parties, American-manned, were put into Yugoslavia to work near BATS airstrips, collect evaders, and pass them promptly back to duty. Equally numerous arguments and misunderstandings followed, with Chetniks and Partisans alike; neither body could comprehend why people with a call on aircraft, and constant wireless touch with the Allied high command, staying in their midst, were yet unavailable as a source of ammunition, heavy weapons, medicines, food and clothes. Of the last three items each party tried to keep a small stock for the benefit of wounded, famished or tattered evaders, a stock that was in constant danger of being pilfered or requisitioned by their Yugoslav hosts who felt – intelligibly enough – that after three years or so on the run they had earned the right to any good things that were going.

Lynn Farish, a cheerful and companionable American major known as 'Slim', was attached to Fitzroy Maclean's mission to

Tito, as liaison both with OSS for the Strategic Balkan Service's work and with the American air force for aircrew rescue. In October 1943, at the ruined village of Glamoc on the eastern side of the Dinaric Alps, south of Zagreb and west of Belgrade, he sustained morale by bathing daily in the open air, still wearing his flat air force cap. There was a BATS airstrip close by, from which he hoped to fly out any evaders he could collect. It was the unhappy scene of the young partisan hero Lola Ribar's death in a German air raid a few weeks afterwards; and Farish himself was killed later still on an air operation into Greece.

### Albania

From these tragedies, which still depress the dead men's surviving friends, let us move to a more comical incident which illustrates the extent to which command of the air and inter-secret-service co-operation could develop.

A baker's dozen of nurses, young second lieutenants in the United States 507th Medical Air Evacuation Unit, who had only been overseas for a few weeks, set off on the cloudy afternoon of 1 November 1943 on a routine flight from Catania in Sicily to collect patients from Bari. Their Dakota got lost in the cloud, and the fuel ran low. The pilot landed at the first airfield he found, but took off again at once when one of his crew pointed out they had just taxied past some aircraft bearing German markings. He soon crash-landed in pastureland; they found they were in Albania.

'Right away', one of the girls wrote later, 'we began wondering who had Albania and trying to think where it was on the map.' The crew burned the aircraft, and the party of twenty-five Americans – four crew, thirteen nurses, and eight stretcher-bearers – set off with a self-appointed local guide to hike into the mountains. After two nights in peasant cottages, where they all acquired body-lice, they reached the fortified town of Berat, which was large enough for the whole party to hide in, here and there. Conditions in it were normal, there was plenty to eat, the bars were open; but as women in Albania never in those days wore trousers, as the nurses all did, half the party had to stay hidden.

An Allied mission – from SOE, not MI 9 – was soon in touch with them, sent out word of their plight, and shepherded them on a further set of mountain marches, a day or two, sometimes only an hour or two ahead of the Germans. On 29 December they were all huddled together in ditches at the side of a disused airfield at Argyrokastron, some forty miles south of Berat, when a Wellington and two Dakotas, escorted by thirty-six Lightning fighters, flew over to pick them up. The Wellington was to land first, to provide ground covering fire from its power turrets for the unarmed Dakotas. By an unhappy chance, a German armoured unit had chosen that moment to halt on the road on the opposite side of the airfield from the wanderers, so the Wellington was not given the signal to land. It 'gave the entire party the biggest thrill of their life'. 'If I live to be 100 years old', one of the nurses wrote later, 'I shall never forget nor be able to express my feelings when I saw that swarm of planes sent out by the 15th Air Force just to rescue us.' 'The girls cried and the boys all had lumps in their throats'. An SOE subaltern, Gavin Duffy of Leeds, saw most of them safely onto a motor gunboat near Valona on the night of 8/9 January, and the party stepped ashore at Bari next morning in high spirits.

Three girls had got left behind in Berat. At the moment when the party had to leave, the messenger did not reach the compara-tively remote house in which they were staying, with the brother of a girl who had spent some years in the middle west, in time for them to catch the rest of the group. A couple of Germans called, were satisfied that they were nurses, and let them be.

By February they had got tired of staying indoors and made themselves skirts out of old blankets. After endless delays Captain Smith, an OSS agent, secured them German and Albanian passes and drove them safely through a mass of controls. A final twelve hours' march through the mountains brought them to a secret Strategic Balkan Service base on the coast, where they were picked up by an Italian torpedo boat with its original crew under a British naval officer; they too reached Bari safely on 23 March.

### Balkans in general

One name, still more than Slim Farish's, deserves to be attached to the business of getting downed airmen back from the Balkans: that of Colonel George Kraigher, the commander of the Air Crew Rescue Unit of 15th Air Force. BATS may be regarded as primarily an airfield construction unit, of which the main task once its airstrips had been built was to supply whatever irregular or paramilitary forces lay in its area, and to reinforce or withdraw them as Allied policy from time to time dictated. The job of an ACRU, smaller and more closely defined, was to bring back evading or escaping American aircrew who had reached the strips, or could be found at others such as Banska Bystrica, but as this Slovak example showed just now, Kraigher's ACRU was not going to stand on ceremony and refuse to take off British aircrew also, or Commonwealth escapers, if they presented themselves at a happy moment.

Kraigher's own indifferent opinion of the national armies of liberation with which he had to deal is set out in a paper he wrote at the end of the European war about irregular forces, which the interested inquirer will find at the Simpson Historical Research Center at Maxwell base; it is beside our present purpose. More to the point is a single exchange, illustrative of the colonel's character and method, between him and a young air force historian:

Q, 'Is your work cleared through MAAF?'
A. 'I report to MAAF. I do the thing first and then tell them.'

A general summary prepared by MAAF in the autumn of 1944 showed that by 20 October 3,870 army air force aircrew had it I ready been recovered – nearly a third of them ex-prisoners from Romania. The summary defined an ACRU team – a senior officer, a doctor, 'a radio operator with portable equipment', and an OSS officer: this explains the American Strategic Balkan Service's interest in MIS-X's work. Teams were not of course always available just when they were needed; improvisation, at which so many British and Americans excel, could then take over. Lieutenant T. K. Oliver found himself and all nine of his crew stranded in central Yugoslavia (presumably in the summer of 1944: maddeningly, the same summary gives no date), met and made friends with one of Mihailovic's wireless operators, improvised a code to headquarters 15th Air Force, and had his party grow from ten to 225 airmen, not all of them American, before the air force could collect them.

The problem of whom to bring out was endemic in such organisations. It long exercised Crockatt's, Johnston's and Dudley Clarke's minds, and was a perpetual source of trouble to Simonds. Clarke ordered him on 13 June 1943 to 'Organize operations only in respect of British, Americans, Greeks, and Poles.' Both knew that 'British' was here shorthand for subjects of the British Crown, and included Canadians, Indians, South Africans and so on. In addition, he could accept at his discretion 'isolated individuals, French, Dutch, Belgian, Norwegian, Czech, Yugoslav, Chinese or Russian' who joined parties of the accepted nationalities. The order went on: 'Refuse to handle any personnel NOT in either category as being outside our charter even given most liberal interpretation.'

Just a year later, on 15 June 1944, writing to Simonds to remind him that he was not to go behind his superior's back direct to the War Office, Dudley Clarke added: 'If you are asked to do anything which is outside your existing instructions your proper answer is that you will refer the matter to me for a ruling.' Simonds must take care not to get involved with 'waifs and strays' but to stick to Imperial and American passengers. 'Johnny Bevan is arriving here in a couple of days' time and

I have asked him to come briefed with Norman Crockatt's
views on these problems.' Meanwhile, Greek and Poles may be
carried on sufferance as special cases; the rest, not. The particular waifs and strays Clarke had in mind may be guessed from his
next remark: 'there is no justification for 'N' section handling
Hungarian diplomats or Abwehr deserters.'

### Greece

In the two months of December 1943 and January 1944 Simonds'
parties brought out of the Aegean area as many as 714 people,
121 British, thirty-nine American, 425 Greek, thirteen Cypriot,
seventy-five from the Dodecanese and forty-one Jews. Besides,
they evacuated 'large numbers of Imp[erial] service personnel' from Leros, where a British battalion had gone ashore in
September and had been roundly defeated – for lack of local air
support – a few weeks later.

Simonds made a great deal of play with codes, and the files
of these operations are full of references to jackals, frogs, toads,
scum, lice, birds, bugs and fleas; luckily he jotted down what
they all meant – various secret services and nationalities – and
the jotting survives. A parallel series of more wholesome codes
covered places. Hungary was Ohio, Romania Skye, Bulgaria
Essex and Turkey Kelso. A journey by film from Looe to York
would necessarily pass Bude, but might leave Eton away to port
– that is, a caïque travelling from the Peloponnese to Çeşme
had to go through the Aegean islands, but would not necessarily
call at Athens. Through this light coding haze, some remarkable
activities in the Aegean and in the Ionian islands emerge.

A combined effort was made to rescue the garrisons of Cos,
Leros and Samos after these islands' recapture by the Germans.
The British naval and military attachés in Ankara took charge
of it; Wolfson, Rees and Simonds all threw themselves whole-
heartedly into the effort; and MI 9's fleet of caïques played a
predominant part in the result. As the senior (naval) intelligence officer in Istanbul put it in a telegram on 14 December,

'please bear in mind large part played by MI 9 organisation in general work getting back MIDEAST evacuees wounded and shipwrecked from all services. These number several hundred but discrimination?[37] as between channels handled is? impossible.' After a momentary initial flurry, there were some weeks of model interservice co-operation. No one stood on ceremony and everyone got on with the job.

The old alliance between MI 9 and the Long Range Desert Group was reforged in the Dodecanese, this time with a reversal of mini: it was MI 9 that commanded the transport, the LRDG that provided the passengers. Several LRDG patrols had been on Cos and Leros, and their seniors were particularly anxious to get the survivors back: MI 9 was delighted to be able to help. One day, preferably while witnesses are still alive to tell tales, there is a fascinating book to be written about this minor and dispersed Dunkirk, and one of its main sources will be the Cairo file simply called 'Operations. Islands.' It is full of such telling details as the mention that Midshipman Rankin of HMS *Belvoir* and Private add-on of the medical corps 'arrived on their own' near Çeşme; that the report of this crossed a terse message from Simonds, 'please take immediate action' to recover nine other ranks in mufti on the north-west corner of Leros; that an Australian pilot was rescued from Cos by a Greek in a craft 'made out of a trough lying on the beach and pieces of wood,' which took eighteen hours to cover the few miles to Turkey; that among the many caïque captains, 'Milton' was at once the most daring and the most successful.

'Milton', a Greek whose identity remains hidden behind his codename, made 'countless passages through enemy waters, entering enemy ports, without ever losing a "passenger" or a member of his crew.' Before the war was over, he had an honorary

---

37    [Readers of this sort of deciphered message in the original will recall the cipher clerks' routine of putting '?' after a word that had to be conjectured in a slightly corrupt text.]

civil OBE to put beside his DSO; though characteristically he remarked to a friend that he would rather have had a thousand pounds.

In the course of 1944 the number of caïques in MI 9's pay grew to thirty-two, with a main repair base in Cyprus, and the speed of their reactions improved also. The swiftest rescue perhaps came in July 1944; not by caïque. Warrant Officer Sykes and Flight-Sergeant Foxley of 603 Squadron RAF crashed between Mykonos and Delos in a Beaufighter on the 23 July. Their ditching drill went well, and they rowed in their dinghy to Delos, as the smaller and therefore presumably the safer island. An MI 9 agent who had seen the crash took care of them and sent a message to Çeşme; a high speed launch picked them up thirty-two hours after they ditched.

A few weeks later, the extent to which MI 9 had become a dominant force in the Aegean got a startling if minor illustration in the Dodecanese, of which the outline – unfortunately, only the outline – is known. Two Gestapo agents visited one of the islands in search of an MI 9 agent whom they believed to be there. His information service was better than theirs; he arrested them.

By the spring of 1945, while German garrisons still held on to the Dodecanese after their comrades had withdrawn from mainland Greece; MI 9 had an agent on each of the twelve islands on whom a caïque called fortnightly as regularly as a remote country bus service. Deserters from Rhodes could be bought for a few shillings a head. London in this case approved.

Minor naval and evasion operations were not confined to the Aegean. In March 1944, for example, HM submarine *Sibyl* launched operation 'Clerk'. Captain E. J. A. Lunn and Sergeant Gilmore of the Special Boat Section rowed ashore in Loortha bay on the south coast of Cephallonia, opposite the north-west corner of the Peloponnese, on the night of 23/24 March 1944. A heavy swell swamped their folboat, a collapsible canoe, as they tried to re-launch it; they broke it up at the water's edge, moved inland gave a German sentry a bad fright, buried their wireless set and took to the hills. A French-speaking woman put them in touch with a dentist with an English wife; hence they made touch with the left-wing resistance movement, ELAS, and were 'cordially received … Many vague and optimistic promises' ill concealed a marked reluctance to run any risk at all, but Lunn and Gilmore got away to the neighbouring island, Odysseus' Ithaca, where the German garrison only numbered eight; thence an SOE caïque rescued them. Another SBS pair, Captain Kennard and Sergeant Preece, reconnoitred Ortholitha bay on the western side of Cephallonia, from *Sibyl*, by folboat and on foot on the night of 25/26 March, and reported it 'an excellent bay for landing agents.' Dudley Clarke described the operation as 'a thorough success'; whether anyone for MI 9 was in fact later landed on Cephallonia remains unclear.

An American aircraft had to make a crash landing on a rice field in southern Corfu on 18 November 1943. The ten survivors hid nearby, mainly in Lefkimme village, for over six weeks, spending one night with an unexpected character, 'an EAM clergyman' – evidently, an Orthodox priest of left-wing tendencies. The local EAM, the political wing of ELAS, were in touch with their opposite numbers the Albanian partisans across the subsequently ill-fitted Corfu channel that still keeps Britain and Albania apart. The new were ferried across that narrow strip of sea on 3 January 1944, and hid in Epirus for ten weeks more; a ship rescued them eventually on 15 March.

T/Sergeant D. M. Bennett of the 342nd Bombardment Squadron, whose aircraft broke up in the air on 11 January 1944, had nearly two months' wanderings in the Peloponnese, passing through lateral villages, one of which – Garditsa – was half burned down by the Germans a few hours after he and his guides had left. The burning was no doubt done, as Voltaire said Admiral Byng was shot, *pour encourager les autres.* Bennett was brought out by a caïque from near Nestor's palace at Pylos on 3 April. One of the people on the spot who was handling this sort of task in detail, the future Professor P. M. Fraser, had to point out to Simonds who was raising security difficulties from Cairo that once there was to be an operation the whole village knew the fact in minutes: the vital security precaution therefore was not to set an operation up – which took anything up to twelve hours, assembling mules, donkeys, food, blankets and so on – except in cases when the Germans were at least twenty-four hours' march away. It was easy to forget in the bustle of Cairo (outside the sacred afternoon siesta), or the motorised hum of London or Washington, that in the remoter parts of eastern Europe much of the war still moved at a walking pace.

Yet simultaneously with the friendly feeling shown to the British SBS on Cephallonia, and to an individual American airman in the hills near Olympia, Simonds was having to complain at the hostility shown by ELAS and its political master, EAM, towards evasion operations. All movement in the Peloponnese, he told Clarke on 29 March, was blocked by EAM order, and the same organisation had brought to a temporary standstill his ratlines across Euboea, the long island to the north of Athens. (He did not hear of Sergeant Bennett till later.) Once EAM seized a caïque; but soon returned it.

As may be imagined, fearsome political complications attended the task that was set MI 9 by a request that originated with the Greek government in exile. The 'special charter' mentioned in Appendix 1 has not yet surfaced, but the end result has: '2,089 Greeks (service personnel, Government officials etc.) rescued.' A glimpse or two appears in the files about how this was done. In late August 1944 for instance there was a special MI 9 mission in Athens under 'an outstandingly brave Greek volunteer' who had recently escaped, and then gone back in again at his cabinet's request. This was operation 'Cooking', run single-handed by an agent called Kryonis ('John'), 'a most self-reliant and responsible person' in his case officer's view; he took into Athens with him fifty-four gold sovereigns, fifty million drachmae, and a memorised list of thirty names of men to bring away. Two of these, forming a subsidiary task, were the son and nephew of the Greek Minister of Marine. He reappeared at Çeşme on 6 September with thirteen but of his thirty targets, plus fourteen others, 'mostly compromised MI 6 personnel from Tinos'. 'Others named on list did not wish to come out'. MI 6's local office remarked bluntly that 'We have no record of individuals working for us in Tinos', so it looks as if even 'John' could be imposed on. Still, Simonds telegraphed at once 'Heartiest congratulations to JOHN and all concerned. The highest in the land have been informed and are delighted.'

As one of EAM's objects was to controvert at every opportunity the exiled king, George II, whom presumably Simonds meant by 'The highest in the land' – he could hardly have meant either Farouk or his own commander-in-chief – some of EAM's hostility to N section has a perceptible basis. Simonds was naturally well aware already of the intense politicisation of every aspect of Greek resistance, as indeed of most of Greek life. Already in May 1944, before 'Cooking' had been set up, the Greek navy in search of fully-trained Greek-speaking crews had had to drive a bargain with EAM: two Greek naval officers were allowed to go to Greece to hunt up such men, and bring them out through MI 9 channels, on condition that each carried a written guarantee from his commander-in-chief 'that neither officer will indulge in politics.' Such a document was a highly perilous thing to have on one's person during a clandestine mission; conceivably that was why EAM insisted on it, to endanger their opponents, though they may simply have been careless of the ground rules of urban underground warfare.

Still grosser carelessness could be displayed by EAM's opponents. The work in Athens in April 1944 of an N section agent known only by the Buchanite codename of 'Greenmantle' was obstructed by a ghastly series of confusions and intrigues. He was sent into Greece to make touch with several politicians, including the subsequently well-known Papandreou, and to get them all to a conference in the Lebanon in May. Some were under threat of assassination by nominal colleagues. Others indicated that they would not mind leaving Greece, provided they did so in circumstances that would make horrible trouble for rivals left behind. A Greek diplomat, outside the Nazi orbit, telegraphed the name of One of the people 'Greenmantle' was to collect, as that of someone about to leave Greece, to his colleague at Berne; and telegraphed it in clear. No wonder the agent went off the air suddenly, half way through a message, on 25 April: and vanished entirely. By June, a fresh agent from Cairo called Kodros had replaced him, but the wranglings went on.

What proportion of N section's effort this large Greek undertaking consumed is not easy to judge. A rough guess, on the brute statistics in Appendix 1, would suggest about two-fifths: 2,089 Greeks brought out in the eastern Mediterranean, as against 2,811 Imperial and American service people. Yet who can measure the nervous strain of attending to 'Anticlimax's' plea for whisky and delousing powder against that of trying to pacify an enraged Greek diplomat, or a furious SAS major? All the historian can note is that the requirements of the Greek government in exile laid a noticeable burden on the staff and the field agents of N section, which was gallantly and uncom-plainingly borne.

## IS 9 (CMF): Italy

Over the wild and at first wholly unfamiliar country of central and northern Italy, Austria and Yugoslavia – the main working field of the Fifteenth US Air Force – navigators were encour-aged as part of their escape and evasion training to check their position constantly, and to keep their crews informed about it, so that any sudden emergency would find everybody with a rough knowledge at least of his whereabouts. Numerous evasions endorsed the soundness of this advice.

For example T/Sergeant Frank J. Knoble of the 429th Bombardment Squadron, shot down on 11 March 1944, after bombing Padua, was received on the ground by partisans, one of whom, 'NICK SINKICH, former Chicago gangster, accompanied party all the way and made all the arrangements.' S/ Sergeant Paul B. Miller, of the 348th Bombardment Squadron, bailed out over north Italy when his aircraft's engines failed on 24 July 1944, hurt his ankle when he landed, was looked after by peasant family, walked south when he was better, and fell in with a partisan unit commanded by a British major. He fought with them for some weeks, and then decided he had better go back to the sort of fighting he was trained to do. He had a puzzling time picking his way through the fighting line on 19 October because he stumbled on a Brazilian unit; Brazil had taken up active participation at the front after he had been shot down. He 'had thought they were Jerries but couldn't figure it out because they seemed to be going in the wrong direction': a Brazilian division fought with distinction in the Allied armies in Italy from September 1944.

One of MI 9's field escape sections, whose members might have known better, also had a brush with some Brazilians who 'spoke in guttural accents' and thus attracted suspicion, in September 1944. By that time Italy was well covered with a network of agents dense enough to collect shot-down aircrew without too much trouble, and to connect them up with one or other of the frequent journeys south-eastward – usually by sea – that the service arranged for the many thousand escapers who were still at large in northern Italy.

Air operations became more complex in the last winter of the war. A few weeks before the end, one of MI 9's 'Vermouth' parties in north Italy under a South African sergeant called Fick got the local partisans to prepare a small landing strip. A Fieseler Storch captured from the Luftwaffe, flown by an Italian pilot, landed on this strip and lifted off a few minutes later a wounded Rhodesian pilot, collected by 'Vermouth' from the wreck of his aircraft; British and American fighters providing overhead cover meanwhile. By this time the average daily loss in men in the Mediterranean air forces was ten, reckoned as two dead, two captured, and six evading: a tribute to the effectiveness of MI 9's and MIS-X's training. As was to be expected from any staff under Crockatt's command, IS 9(CMF) as well as IS 9(MEF) was anxious to set up lines for escapers and evaders who were on their way out of the enemy heartland, but from Italy this was quite as tricky as from Egypt. Geography and tactics alike put the north-eastern frontier out of the question: high barren mountains, the few valleys swarming with SS. A way round was imperative: it would have to run through Slovenia and Carinthia.

In Carinthia, on the disputed borderland between the Third Reich and Croatia/Yugoslavia, there was for a time an SOE mission called 'Clowder', which Simonds described as 'working very well with us being most useful' in June 1944. But 'Clowder' was not immortal. Its leader, Hesketh Pritchard, was killed in action (long afterwards, the local Communists annexed his achievements as their own), and the main concern of (Sir) Peter Wilkinson who took over from him was to extricate what remained of the mission safely: which he accomplished. The fact that 'Clowder' was operated and controlled from London, not from either Cairo or Caserta or Bari, provided yet another staff hurdle; by now Simonds, Rodd and Wilkinson were all consummate hurdlers, and no one tripped over it.

This only left Slovenia, and here a special variant on the partisans' frequent general obstructiveness produced a block. As one anonymous officer in Special Forces – whether in OSS or SOE is unclear – put it early in 1945, it was a case of 'the utter hopelessness of ever getting into AUSTRIA overland from SLOVENIA without Partisan assistance. This has been consistently refused, not so much by direct methods as by deliberate obstruction and procrastination.' To safeguard the Communists' fellow travellers from 'infiltrating propaganda and ideas not in sympathy with their own', the partisan leadership barred all travellers out, particularly those from an American or British secret service: a preview of the policy that led eventually to the walling in of East Berlin, lest those inside should wish to flee the Communist paradise. A mission called 'Cuckold' operated for MI 9 in Slovenia for most of the autumn of 1944, till silenced by a big German attack on 23 December, but was not able to do much to help evaders.

### Scandinavia

On the opposite, northern flank of the grand Anglo-American assault on north-west Europe, operation 'Overlord', there was not a great deal that MI 9 either could do, or needed to do, to assist evasion. In Norway, ground was paramount: the terrain was too severe and communications were too sparse for potential evaders to get any counsel but one – move eastwards into Sweden if you can. A few could, and after a brief grilling from the Swedish police took their chance of a ride back to Scotland in the bomb bay of a Mosquito. More were caught, and became prisoners.

In Denmark both ground and tactics were entirely different, Flat farming country with excellent communications provide plenty of opportunities both for evasion lines and for enemy counter-action. Danish resistance organised itself much more slowly than did, say, Polish or Greek; with slight Communist assistance, and not a great deal of help from the West either. MI 6 seems to have left the bulk of the running in Denmark to be made by SOE, and MI 9 followed MI 6's example. The Danes in any case, an independent-minded lot, preferred to run things their own way. Hardly any MI9 or MIS-X files on Danish work have yet surfaced, and there was probably not much that either of these services needed to do beyond briefing aircrew on how to behave if forced down over Denmark.

Jørgen Haestrup, the principal authority on Danish resistance history, states baldly that as late as the summer of 1943 'Regular escape routes were not yet established'; but from that autumn they developed. He cites the case of a Canadian pilot called Donald Smith, the only survivor of a crew of eight returning

from a raid on Stettin, who kept going across Zealand for a day
and a night on his escape pack ration, slept in a stable, met a
friendly farmer who gave him a little food and money – by a too
frequent mistake, he had the wrong purse, full of French francs
– and bumped by chance into some Danish resisters who took
him across the Sound to Sweden in a rubber boat stolen from
the Germans. By the end of 1943 there was a quite frequent
secret boat service across the Sound from Frederikshavn, near
the northern tip of Jutland.

Haestrup quotes another example, late but telling. The
American Major McFarlane bailed out over Lolland, the large
island midway between Copenhagen and Lübeck, on 12 March
1945 – flak had damaged his aircraft over Swinemünde. The
moment he landed he was given a raincoat and a hat, and hidden
in a wood, by a boy who fobbed off a German search party. He
spent several nights in various private houses; watched the fire
Embry's Mosquitoes had started in the Gestapo headquarters
in Copenhagen on 21 March; was smuggled on board a dredger
at Tuborg, and hidden with several companions in the ship's
bottom; and was received by the British consul at Helsingborg
in Sweden two days later.

As Haestrup remarks, 'Every study of the "headquarters
activity" is justified and necessary. But it is never adequate,
McFarlane's path may well seem unplanned, but behind it
there is an organisation, constantly arranging, hooking link to
link. When McFarlane reached Sweden and made his report,
he was not initiated into the mysteries of the organisation,
but he must have felt its existence throughout … The Resistance
is not formed primarily according to directions and orders from
above, but has grown up organically from the constant activity
in its depths.'

### France, Belgium and Holland

Something similar happened in Holland, Belgium and France
in the second half of the war, but with a multiplicity of

organisations at work instead of a single body. As was shown above, the 'Pat' lines faded out after Guérisse's arrest; only the indomitable François Dissart and the equally unbreakable, but more somnolent Mifouf were left to take up again the private struggle to get people away under the noses of their Gestapo neighbours on which they had been engaged before ever they met Guérisse or Groome. 'Comet' survived a large number of betrayals and counter-attacks and continued to send airmen across the Pyrenees, almost at Andrée de Jongh's rate, even after her arrest, even after her father's execution. Madame de Greef, who kept careful accounts, kept also a nominal roll of every passenger. The last one to leave, Flight-Sergeant Emeny of the RAF, was booked out into Spain on 4 June 1944. Thereafter the line, most sensibly, gave up passing people through to Spain, but its members were still on the alert to shelter any evaders or escapers who came their way.

By early 1943 indeed this had become a normal attitude over wide areas of Western Europe. Evaders from casualties in the RAF's night raids over Germany who could get outside the Reich readily found help, and the great day raids by the USAAF over German-occupied territories were often followed with passionate interest by crowds of spectators on the ground, who stood by to help at the fall of a parachute. The raid on Dieppe on 19 August 1942 had given a lot of amateur helpers some early practice, yet it soon became clear that it had only been a raid; it was not the start of liberation. The German surrender at Stalingrad on 2 February 1943, a world-shaking event too big to hide, clearly marked something more substantial. Though the Wehrmacht was still unbeaten it no longer looked unbeatable, and millions of occupied civilians took heart.

A fortnight later, on 16 February, Lieutenant T. P. Mayo of the American 422nd Bombardment Squadron was shot down on his way back from a raid on St Nazaire; several Frenchwomen came up to him as he landed, some of them already carrying plain clothes for him. On 17 May a crew from

338th Bombardment Squadron had to bail out near Lorient; 'An excited crowd of Frenchmen came running across the fields to us and took our equipment'; food and clothing were both ready to start them off on their southward journey. By 29 May, when Lieutenant T. M. Peterson and T/Sergeant J. M. Scott bailed out over western France, each was met and given plain clothes; a woman in Scott's impromptu reception committee had had the forethought to bring a shovel, so that any compromising kit could at once be buried, and they were soon back in England.

When on 24 August 1943 S/Sergeant Claude Sharpless was shot down near Toulouse, a crowd of at least thirty French surrounded him. 'A man had brought civilian clothes with him. In four minutes I looked like any one of the Frenchmen and my [flying] suit and flying equipment had disappeared.'

Most of this help was purely spontaneous; people rushed out to look after the airmen who were fighting their war for them, out of sheer enthusiasm and humanity mixed. By this time they all knew what occupation was like, and what penalties attached to helping fugitives; the penalties only deterred the timid. Some of the help, far from being provided off the cuff, had been foreseen from afar; an ideal instance is provided by T/Sergeant Samuel E. Potrin of 331st Bombardment Squadron. His aircraft was shot down in a raid on Le Bourget airfield near Paris on France's national day, 14 July 1943. His parachute opened; he 'landed in a wheatfield and was rolling up my chute when a Frenchman rode up on a bicycle' – and this Frenchman, already, was his MI 9 contact. 'From here my journey was arranged', that familiar phrase inserted for security's sake to preserve the helpers' anonymity in so many thousands of reports, here came very early on, and he was back at his English base in a matter of weeks.

MI 9's lines were perhaps the most efficient, but they had no monopoly. There were many small private lines, some of them already lost to history; others traceable only through such references as Donald Darling could give them from memory. We might instance the Balfe line, run as he recalled in the neighbourhood of Amiens by 'a former Irish guardsman, his French wife and their two teenage sons … The father was a no-nonsense man of notable physique, as were his two sons, who looked so Irish they might have been born on the "Ould Sod", except for the fact that they were also very French.' In that area, they could find plenty of friends among the Britons and half-Britons who tended the colossal graveyards of the previous world war; in a shed in one of which at least evaders were frequently hidden.

A bigger affair was the Dutch-Paris line, run entirely off his own hut by John Weidner, a Dutch Seventh-day Adventist who had all the splendid stubborn righteousness of that creed. He passed people, Jew and Gentile, from the Netherlands into Switzerland, or on to Spain. Through Dr Visser't Hooft, then in Geneva as the secretary of the World Council of Churches, he had some powerful connections in the free world. An interest was necessarily taken in him in London both by the Dutch government in exile and by the secret services. It was his line that picked up Dourlein and Ubbink, the two victims of SOE's notorious 'North Pole' disaster in Holland who escaped, that guided them into Switzerland, and that later saw them through from Switzerland into Spain. The line saved over a thousand Jews, but at the cost of some 150 arrested members of it, forty of whom – Weidner's sister Gabrielle included – did not survive. Its head was eventually brought over to England by an air pick-up operation, which must have had Dansey's sanction.

Another, smaller Dutch line with which the Dutch-Paris group worked for a time was run by a huge young man called Christiaan Lindemans ('King Kong'). Darling suspected that the worst troubles of Dutch-Paris might have stemmed from 'King Kong', and claimed to have warned London against him in March 1944. Herbert Ford, Weidner's post-war friend and neighbour in California, working on evidence unavailable to Darling, concludes rather that a girl courier broke down under torture by the Gestapo in Paris.

The sketch on the following page, based on the working layout of the 'Burgundy' line in the spring of 1944 (of which more in a moment), shows how the tentacles of this sort of network reached out into a large number of villages, and covered a surprisingly dense proportion of the soil of occupied Europe. 'Comet' worked in much the same kind of way, in areas away to the north-east of those shown on this sketch.[38] It will be noticed that by this time the Balfes have become incorporated in a larger network. Can this have been one of the reasons why the Home Office found it impossible to grant them British citizenship when the war was over?

MI 9 had had its own troubles with 'North Pole'. Neave obtained Dansey's grudging leave to start up an organisation in Holland, and sent in to run it a Dutch air hostess called Beatrix (Trix) Terwindt, who had already proved her self-assurance and capacity for keeping her head by escaping from Holland through Belgium, France and Switzerland to London. Greindl ('Nemo') of the 'Comet' line in Brussels 'was anxious to have a link on which lie could rely for a system of guides from The Hague and Amsterdam.' Trix Terwindt ('Felix') seemed cut out for the task.

No channel was available for sending her except SOE's Dutch section, which landed her on the night of 13/14 February 1943 – well before Dourlein's and Ubbink's escape – slap into the arms of the German secret police. Her level-headedness did not desert her. Fortunately for her, she knew little about SOE, so she could make few damaging admissions; in fact she hardly said anything, and her enemies did not discover that she was working on a quite separate task for a different service. She survived over two years' concentration camps and is alive today. As she put it in a letter to Neave after the war, 'I was an amateur but in war risks have to be taken. I played a game of cat and mouse with the Gestapo with the only difference that I was caged and the cat was free.'

---

38    Information gratefully received from M. Leslie Atkinson.

# ACCOMMODATION FOR EVADERS IN PARIS AREA

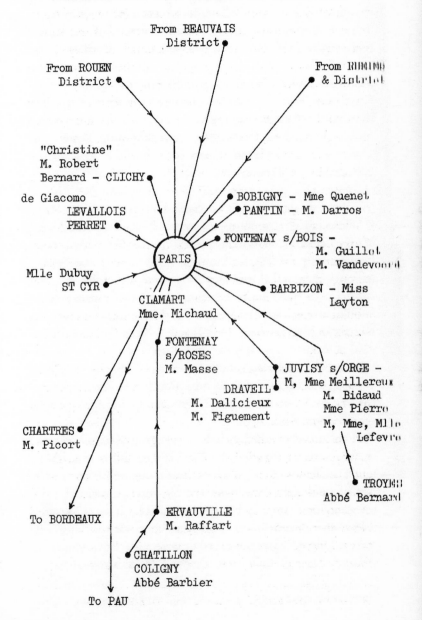

From BEAUVAIS District

From ROUEN District

From RHIMING & District

"Christine"
M. Robert
Bernard - CLICHY

de Giacomo
LEVALLOIS
PERRET

PARIS

BOBIGNY - Mme Quenet
PANTIN - M. Darros

FONTENAY s/BOIS -
M. Guillot
M. Vandevoord

Mlle Dubuy
ST CYR

CLAMART
Mme. Michaud

BARBIZON - Miss Layton

FONTENAY s/ROSES
M. Masse

JUVISY s/ORGE -
M, Mme Meillereux
M. Bidaud
Mme Pierre
M, Mme, Mlle Lefevre

DRAVEIL
M. Dalicieux
M. Figuement

CHARTRES
M. Picort

TROYES
Abbé Bernard

To BORDEAUX

ERVAUVILLE
M. Raffart

CHATILLON
COLIGNY
Abbé Barbier

To PAU

In June of 1943 Neave did what SOE might well have done: dropped an agent into Holland blind – that is, with no reception committee. This was Dick Kragt ('Frans Hals'), a British subject with a Dutch father, who was dropped not far from Deventer. As it turned out, he was dropped in a smart suburban area instead of the open country, and most of his kit – including his transmitter – was handed straight over to the Germans by the Dutch collaborator into whose garden it fell. However, he retained money, wit and initiative enough to keep himself out of enemy hands, made courier contact with 'Comet', got a wireless operator in the end, and did sterling work in the autumn of 1944.

One area remained to be opened up if possible: northwestern France. Two efforts to develop Brittany with the help of Free French naval officers failed. A third one was attempted; In the spring of 1943. 138 Squadron, one of the two special duty squadrons that operated from Tempsford just off the Great North Road out of London never had so much trouble finding anyone else's dropping areas. At the tenth attempt, it succeeded. Two agents were dropped: Vladimir Bouryschkine ('Val Williams'), who had had earlier experience as a helper in the 'Pat' line; and Ray Labrosse, a French Canadian who had escaped across France after Dieppe. Bouryschkine was a White Russian, born in Moscow in 1913, brought up in America, energetic and impulsive.

They were dropped close to Paris – industrial haze turned out to have been the trouble that obscured the spot. Bouryschkine found nearly a hundred evaders hanging about in Brittany, thirty-nine of them in the chateau of Comtesse Betty de Mauduit, who was American. His attempts to shift them by sea failed, because Labrosse's wireless had not survived the drop. He tried to take a party out by train southwards; they were all arrested on 4 June at Pau, between Toulouse and Bayonne. He was imprisoned at Rennes. With the help of a fellow-Russian who was a prisons labourer he escaped, breaking his leg in the process, and turned up in Paris, where he met Labrosse, who had meanwhile returned to England and come out again to France.

Labrosse's journey to England had been arranged by Georges Broussine ('Burgundy'), the most successful of a group of Free French officers who operated in north-western France in 1943–4 under the joint auspices of Colonel 'Passy' of the BCRA and of Room 900, the usual cover for P15. Broussine managed to send out a few parties from the south Breton coast by boat; it was on one of these which was shipwrecked that the heroic Pierre Brossolette was trying to travel when arrested on 3 February 1944. When Broussine could not send people by boat he sent them, as he sent Labrosse, across Spain. He could not save the Comtesse de Mauduit from being sent to a German concentration camp (whence she returned alive), but managed to remain out of German hands himself – just as well, as he was a Jew – and his group brought out a total of 225 men, many of them along a route through Andorra.

Bouryschkine was promptly returned to London by Labrosse's new commander, Lucien Dumais, who had also escaped from Dieppe. Dansey suspected Bouryschkine's story of how he had got out of Rennes prison, and had him locked up for a while as a suspected double agent, a fate visited also by SOE on the 'North Pole' escapers Dourlein and Ubbink. All three were released after the Normandy landings had proved successful.

By that time Dumais and Labrosse had at last got a fully-fledged sea escape line working out of Brittany into Cornwall, called 'Bhelbume'. Dumais' own account of this enterprise, fuller and more detailed than Neave's, is particularly well worth reading, and illustrates exactly the difficulty that Crockatt and the rest of MI 9's staff feared. They were afraid that people of Dumais' superbly combatant aggressiveness would make too much trouble for the enemy, once the invasion had started, and so endanger their passengers. It is true that 'Shelburne' took a great many risks, but they were nicely calculated, and the line not only survived but flourished in secret. This was due partly to its leaders' own capacities, partly to the heroism of their many French assistants of both sexes at the collecting points in Paris and Rennes and near the obscure yet adequate Breton beach at Plouha where the bulk of the passengers were embarked. The bravery of the motor gunboat crews of the Royal Navy who ran the risks of collecting them, not often noticed in escape literature also deserves remark. All told, 'Shelburne' claimed 307 succeesses, no mean score for less than a year's work.

A different sort of bravery, of a more old-fashioned kind than Dumais' commando-style ferocity, was displayed by a senior officer in the RAF, with unexpected consequences. (Sir) Ronald Ivelaw-Chapman came from what in the Habsburg monarchy used to be called a *Kaderfamilie* – that is, he belonged to the old officer class. He had won a Distinguished Flying Cross in France in 1918 at the age of nineteen. He had made his life in the service, and like any other good officer he believed he should never give an order he was not prepared to carry out himself.

Service accident promoted him in February 1944 to the rank of air commodore and to the command of a highly secret air formation, of which it was the task to fly over German radar defences in north-west Europe, measure wavelengths, pinpoint stations, and so provide data for the radar counter-measures which formed an important part of the invasion plan. Ivelaw-Chapman was uneasy at sending younger men out on so dangerous and delicate a task, and thought he ought to go on one operation at least. He did, in mid-May, and the aircraft carrying him was shot down over Britanny.

Another aircraft in the same squadron counted the para-chutes and reported that everyone's had opened. This report slumbered in a group captain's in-tray at the Air Ministry over the weekend; Whitehall then leapt into activity. Langley was informed by Desmond Morton, the Prime Minister's private secretary for secret matters, that Ivelaw-Chapman was to be recovered *coute que coil*, or if he could not be recovered he was to be eliminated. This was because the unhappy air commodore knew a great deal about the time, place, scale and method of the imminent invasion, and had overlooked the rule that no one half as fully informed as himself was to venture anywhere near enemy territory, until it had begun.

Broussine recovered him within forty-eight hours; reported the fact, to Langley's and everybody else's intense relief; and held him in a safe house, pending a sure chance of returning him to England. The safe house was not safe enough; Ivelaw-Chapman fell into German hands in mid-June. By then his special knowledge had ceased to be especially secret. He had the common sense to pass himself off as an evading squadron-leader from bomber command and saw the war out in a prisoner of war camp in Germany.

Two other air force evaders are worth a mention, whom Langley has long quoted as examples of the shortest and the longest evasions of which he knows. The story of the shortest was that of a young fighter pilot in the RAF. One Saturday in the summer of 1943 he got engaged to a stunning girl at a dance at the Savoy, and promised to meet her there again in a week's time for a party to celebrate. On the following Monday he was shot down in a dawn sweep over northern France. It was his first parachute drop; he did not manage it neatly, and landed on the roof of the greenhouse of a chateau. The gardener, who was a secret resister, hid him in a potting shed, and was trying to clear away the parachute and the mess when his master, a count, unexpectedly strolled by. The count insisted on being introduced to the pilot, whom he entertained for two nights in the chateau. In the middle of the second night the pilot was suddenly woken up, taken out of doors, and bundled into a Lysander in the park: the count also was a secret resister, and kept a safe house for SOE. The pilot kept his date at the Savoy, and later married the girl; though SOE insisted he spend six months cooling his heels in the Scottish Highlands, lest he talk too much.

The longer evasion can be more briefly told. A squadron leader shot down over France in 1941 got as far as Paris, went to a race meeting, won some money, and settled down to win more. He was twice visited by emissaries from MI 9 and consistently maintained that a journey farther than Longchamps would be dangerous for anyone as senior as himself. By the summer of 1944 – he had a good eye – he had a racehorse of his own, as well as a charming companion, and MI 9's second emissary found him ensconced in a flat near the Bois de Boulogne. After the liberation of Paris he consented to return to duty. To Crockatt's great annoyance, no charge under King's regulations could be drawn up against him that was certain to stick at a court martial, and he got off scot free.

### Help for 'Overlord'

Much thought was devoted by Crockatt, Holt and their staffs to the best way in which the escape services could help in 'Overlord', the impending invasion of north-west Europe, commonly called the Second Front. (Why on earth that phrase was never applied to the campaign in the central Mediterranean, that knocked Italy out of the Axis in September 1943, is an odd question in history and propaganda, asked but not answered here.) IS 9(CMF)'s experiences gave some indications of the sort of problems that would arise, and the sort of forces that would be required. Plenty of transport, massive communications, and warm and close relations with special forces of all kinds as well as the air force authorities, seemed to be the main things needed. The Americans were content to leave the lead with the British; as Catesby Jones put it in a minute to Strong of 30 August 1943, 'The British have a functioning underground in France. It is efficient enough to chart the progress of all evaders. I believe it unlikely that we could set up as successful an organisation.'

Who was to take command? In September 1943 Langley had handed P15 over to Neave, and taken de Bruyne's place at Beaconsfield in charge of MI 9b. Crockatt soon let him know that he had been chosen as joint commander of a new unit,

Intelligence School 9 (Western European Area), or IS 9(WEA).
He was to be promoted lieutenant-colonel and to share the
command with Lieutenant-Colonel Richard R. Nelson, an
insurance magnate from Kansas City, Missouri. Fortunately, he
and Dick Nelson got on very well together, and had not the
slightest trouble working in double harness.

A War Office file survives to explain the British content
of this body, formed at Camp 20 – notionally on 14 January
1944 – and stationed at Fulmer Hall near by from 1 May. It
was to have fourteen British officers and twenty-six other
ranks, a vehicle for each officer, 'one box, stationery, field,
large,' '1 pr, handcuffs,' two felling axes, a normal quantity
of small arms and small stores, and three no. 22 wireless sets.
The Americans matched the British, rank for rank and jeep
for jeep.

What was IS 9(WEA) for? Langley and Nelson went to
Crockat and Holt to ask; and the brigadier, with his usual gift
of clarity and desire to make his intentions crystal clear to his
subordinates, explained. Langley does not claim after thirty-
four years to repeat Crockatt's statement word for word, but
it was so clear and concise that no further directive was ever
necessary. It went like this:

'The ill-conceived "stand fast" order in Italy resulted in a
fiasco which did much harm to the concepts of escaping. The
situation is unlikely to be repeated in enemy occupied Western
Europe or Germany, but none the less Colonel Holt and I are
determined that MI 9 and MIS-X shall have representatives
in close touch with the commanders of the fighting forces.
IS 9 (WEA) will be attached to Supreme Headquarters Allied
Expeditionary Force (SHAEF) and will therefore be ultimately
responsible to General Eisenhower. You will maintain close
contact with all departments in his headquarters of which the
actions might affect escapers, evaders or POWs in Germany.
These contacts will be extended to cover Army Groups, Corps,
Divisions, etc. You will therefore be in a position to keep

Colonel Holt and myself informed as to what is happening or likely to happen in the field and to transmit our requests and views to the relevant commanders.

'You will be responsible, in conjunction with P15 and the organisations in France, Belgium and Holland, for the continual tion of escape and evasion until the war in the west is over. You will set up reception and interrogation centres for all escapers and evaders and arrange for the dissemination of all intelligence information and the onward transmission of the men to the United Kingdom.

'No one knows when or how the POW camps in Germany will (216) be liberated and the participation of IS 9(WEA) will depend on initiation at the time. You will receive orders and instructions III due course.

'Finally, a word of warning. Commanders of regular units, for the most part, dislike and mistrust private armies and frankly they have my sympathy. You will ensure that under no circumstances does IS 9(WEA) ever become classed as another "Popski's" Private Army. Should I learn that IS 9 is being so regarded and treated, your command will be immediately terminated. Any Questions?'

Langley had only one. 'What exactly will be the relationship between the Americans and ourselves within the unit?'

Crockatt explained: 'You will be completely integrated and will live and work as one unit regardless of nationality. In the absence of Dick [Nelson] you will have the right to award punishment to American officers and other ranks and vice versa. In the event of a difference of opinion which you cannot settle yourselves the matter will be referred to Colonel Holt and myself. However, I don't expect this situation to arise.' Nor did it; the integration was an entire success. It was not quite unique – one signals section at SHAEF was as completely integrated, and on Eisenhower's as on Alexander's staff there was plenty of warm Anglo-American co-operation – but the blend was certainly of interest.

The main weaknesses of IS 9(WEA) were three. One was its small size. 'Small is efficient' was always Crockatt's motto, as has been said before, but a group only eighty strong in all ranks combined might be overwhelmed by a sudden flood of work, as indeed happened in the spring of 1945. However, in the winter of 1943–4 eighty men were all that could be spared. The second difficulty followed from the first: not all the people posted to the unit were up to their job. None of the Americans had had any experience of clandestine work and few had been shot over, but they were intelligent and quick to learn. With the British element the case was different. MI 9 produced some excellent officers but of those that came in from outside at least one was suffering from battle fatigue, and others were under the illusion – which was difficult to dispel – that IS 9(WEA) was a private army, with all the privileges and loose discipline associated as they thought with such unofficial units. Some of the other ranks were excellent. Two had served prison sentences and few had clean sheets in their army records. Britain was of course by this time scraping the manpower barrel, with the best long since consumed.

The third and worst trouble was that of inadequate communications. Half a dozen twenty-two sets of short range and uncertain performance hardly sufficed to keep jeep patrols in touch with the nearest army headquarters. For long range discussions, particularly for contact with Beaconsfield or with P15, IS 9(WEA) was dependent on the hospitality of the signals staffs of various formations on the Continent: not a satisfactory arrangement. Langley has grateful memories of the help and courtesy extended to him by the MI 6 signals unit that was working, under a suitable cover, at 21st Army Group's advance headquarters, but so *ad hoc* an arrangement should not have been the best that could be done.

Within the unit, friction between the British, the Americans, and the occasional attached French, Belgian or Dutch advisers – whose cover was that they were interpreters – was minimal;

hardly any serious tiffs are remembered. The worst was when the British other ranks, who had voted to a man to draw American rations instead of British, got bored after a few weeks and demanded to change back.

Ian Garrow was the unit's original operations officer, but was incapacitated by a bad accident just before D-Day. Major P. S. McCallum from MI 9 replaced him till Neave could finish handing over P15 to Darling; Crockatt, seeing how busy IS 9(WEA) was going to be, let both Neave and McCallum serve with it. The two adjutants, the British 'Johnny' Johnson from the Eighth Army and the American Fred Blakeman, who like Holt had fought with the American expeditionary force in 1918, were both experts at calming down the high command when some enthusiast in one or other of the operational teams seemed indiscreet. Blakeman was well over the age limit the Americans sought to impose on their staffs, but Holt persuaded Eisenhower that the adjutant's presence was an operational necessity.

Four officers in IS 9(WEA) served in the House of Commons after the war, three of them – Airey Neave, Hugh Fraser and Maurice Macmillan – with distinction; the fourth, Peter Baker, had a less happy career. He was convicted of fraud, was sent to prison, and died soon after his release.

Three other officers brought individuality to the unit. One was Captain Peter Murray of the 4/7 Royal Dragoon Guards, who behind the impeccable cover concealed the real identity of Prince Pierre Murat, a direct descendant of the greatest of Napoleon's cavalry commanders by the emperor's sister, Caroline Bonaparte; and his mother was a descendant of the equally famous Marshal Ney. As he was perfectly bilingual, he had picked up some odd anecdotes about the British and American view of the French. He was one of the unit's chief interpreters. Another was Rolfe Elwes, who had been wounded and captured while commanding a platoon of the Coldstream Guards in 1918, and thus knew at first hand what a prisoner of war's life was like.

The third officer, 'Johnny' Evans, was attached to IS 9(WEA) as air liaison officer, but was not to any noticeable extent under its control. He had a motor caravan, and came and went as and when had chose. Liaison back to the Air Ministry, sideways to the Second Tactical Air Force (2nd TAF), and forwards to its squadrons and to any RAF escapers or evaders he could find, was his task; founded on the theory that no soldier could be expected to understand the technicalities of current air warfare. Langley and Nelson could never find him when they wanted him, and had no idea how he spent his time, but at least his presence in Normandy and Belgium ensured that IS 9(WEA) never had any difficulties with the Air Ministry at all. A fairly full file of his activities during 'Overlord' in fact shows that he spent most of his time lecturing to the Second Tactical Air Force, and exchanged numerous notes with Langley about likely safe or safeish areas for airmen to lie up and wait for the battle to catch up with them.

This was the general advice given to evaders in the first few weeks of the Normandy battle. Early on, Langley thought that passage through the fighting line there would be easy for men used to risk and danger. He based this view on some early SAS forays near Caen; but it was soon seen to be a mistake. IS 9(WEA) found itself in everybody's way in a crowded beach-head, and was able for the moment to do little good. Some of the more restive of the 'retrievers', as the operational parties were known, had to be sent back to England for the time being.

The efficiency of the schemes that had already been put to work, and that Langley and Nelson were about to operate, can be judged from a single telling statistic. During 'Overlord' it was reckoned that an airman shot down unwounded over German-occupied territory had an even chance of evading successfully, instead of becoming a prisoner of war. The odds remained tilted against people shot down over Germany, indeed as the weight of the air war rested more and more heavily on the Germans aircrew were more likely to be lynched than ever; but west of the Third Reich, and in Denmark and Luxembourg as well, the efforts of MI 9 and MIS-X had brought the betting down to evens.

Flying Officer H. Furniss-Roe of 66 Squadron, RAF, had crash-landed near Evreux in Normandy on 22 August 1943, and was back in England via Spain by November. When on 25 January 1944 he force-landed his Spitfire in France again, 300 yards from a German anti-aircraft battery, he had the high spirits to send a last message before he unstrapped himself from his cockpit – 'back in two months'; nipped into a passing peasant's cart; met an MI 9 helper within twenty-four hours, and was back on British soil on 10 April, only three weeks late. This can be dismissed as a piece of exuberance, ordinary fighter command high morale; but quite a number of journeys as prompt as Furniss-Roe's were to be provided with the help of the escape services during the following summer.

When at the end of July 1944 the Americans broke through on the right flank as planned, and a phase of more open warfare began, IS 9(WEA) showed its worth; it became clear also how effective its preliminary planning had been. Crockatt and Holt had taken a lot of care over a suggestion, first put up by Neave that was code-named 'Marathon'. This was a scheme to concentrate evaders in areas likely to be out of the way both of the Germans and of the eventual Allied advance, in woodland camps: there was to be one near Rennes in eastern Britanny; one near Châteaudun west of Orléans, and one in the Ardennes astride the Franco-Belgian border. Everyone concerned in MI 9 and MIS-X was sure that by setting up these camps they would improve the evaders' chances of safety. Still more important, they would lessen the risk to the families of helpers who would otherwise have to shelter them, probably in large and police-filled cities such as Brussels and Paris. It was foreseen that retreating Germans might have ragged nerves; Oradour-sur-Glane provided tragic evidence that this foresight was correct. Crockatt was haunted by the spectre of a general massacre of

Allied troops or airmen caught at large in occupied territory, and resolved to prevent one if he could.

Several Belgian agents of high quality, notably Baron Jean de Blommaert ('Rutland'), had been sent forward by parachute as far back as the autumn of 1943 to ensure 'Marathon's' success. They had the usual difficulties with the Germans. Conrad Lafleur, another Dieppe escaper and one of their wireless operators, was caught in the act of transmission at Reims, but shot his way out of the ambuscade and was rescued by 'Comet'. De Blommaert had the traitor Desoubrie on his back for a time; escaped by 'Comet' also in March 1944; and parachuted back into France in April to set up 'Sherwood', the camp near Châteaudun. Thirty men were I here by D-Day, and over a hundred by the end of July, almost all Of them airmen; sustained partly by parachute drops of food and Mores, partly by what could be bought locally. In the end, 152 were rescued by Neave himself and the American Captain Coletta, under guard of a big SAS patrol, by a bus convoy from Le Mans in mid-August.

Neave entered Paris on 25 August, on the heels of Leclerc's leading troops. One of the first people he met there was Donald Caskie of the Seamen's Mission at Marseilles, 'thin and pale after years in the hands of the Gestapo,' but alive.

'Comet' had not approved of 'Marathon'. Neave searched the Ardennes in early September for his expected camp; it was not there. Instead, he found a fair number of evaders living it up in Brussels; where the resident IS 9(WEA) field section set up house in what its newsletter tactfully described as 'two hotels of a type not met with in the U.K.' – that is, former brothels. Elwes, its commander, was too good a Roman Catholic to sleep sound in a madam's bed, and soon moved his unit out to the famous monastery at Montaigu near Louvain.

During the war of rapid movement in late August and the first half of September 1944, many evaders were overrun in odd places, besides de Blommaert's and other organised parties, and many of them got lifts back to England or even to America from friendly transport pilots, without passing through any of the solicitously prepared IS 9 interrogation teams. On the other hand, all IS 9 (WEA) staff found themselves bombarded with requests, denunciations, counter-denunciations, information, misinformation, and disinformation; for everybody in France and Belgium who met them leapt wrongly and immediately to the conclusion that they were a sub-unit of the all-powerful Intelligence Service. Their unit sign – three witches on a broomstick, in distant tribute to E. H. Jones's *Road to En-Dor* – did little to counteract the myth.

### Arnhem

More mythmaking lay immediately ahead. As Eisenhower's armies began to run out of petrol, the vast airborne operation called 'Market Garden' sought to break through the German right flank by seizing a series of river and canal crossings at Eindhoven, Nijmegen and Arnhem.

Four days before 'Market Garden' was launched, a Dutch agent who had made touch with an IS 9 team in Antwerp was sent back into Holland near Eindhoven, at his own request, 'to collect evaders he was sure would be hiding with his resistance friends in that area,' The man 'was a boastful extrovert whom I disliked,' Langley wrote long afterwards, but he had been given full security clearance by 21st Army Group. Colonel Pinto, the security chief at Dutch advance headquarters, sent a word of warning to Langley, but added that he had no proof; it never crossed Langley's mind that 21st Army Group had not been warned also. As soon as Eindhoven was liberated the man – Christiaan Lindemans, the notorious 'King Kong' – was denounced as a traitor, broke down quickly under interrogation, and later committed suicide.

Newspaper rumour had it that 'King Kong' betrayed 'Market Garden'; but as Colonel Boeree long ago pointed out, the dates really do not fit. General Brereton, the operation's commander, did not make even an outline plan till the evening of 10 September, by which time two SS armoured divisions were already in process of re-forming in and near Arnhem. The essential details of the drop on Arnhem were not fixed till after 'King Kong' had crossed the lines. General Student, who is supposed to have inferred the attack on Arnhem from remarks made to him by Lindemans about an impending attack on Eindhoven and beyond, flatly denies it; never met Lindemans; and adds, 'The truth is, nobody in the German command knew anything about the attack until it happened.' This does not stop speculation that Lindemans was really a good Dutch patriot who was unlucky; but the weight of available evidence tells the other way.

Once the attack had happened, and had gloriously failed – First Airborne Division, expected to hold out for two days, held out for eight – several hundred evaders from it were left hiding in what was left of Arnhem, in the villages to the west of it, and in Ede, the next town of any size in the same direction. The most resolute and the badly wounded of them came out at once – Captain Eric Mackay, for example, the engineer commander at the fatal bridge, who had taken his escape training to heart. With three companions, he escaped on the way into Germany; they stole a boat, and paddled clandestinely down the Rhine to Nijmegen. But many more remained.

Dick Kragt, 'Fabian' of the Belgian SAS, and an MI 9 operator called 'Ham' provided some chances of contact with these men. Much more directly, there was a private telephone circuit, still open and untapped by the enemy, between the power station at Nijmegen which was in Allied hands and the power station at Ede, which was in occupied territory but manned by sound Dutchmen. Neave, having clandestine antennae, spotted this link, which Dutch resisters were already using. In the teeth of stick-in-the-mud staff opposition outside MI 9, he determined to make use of it.

South-west of Ede, opposite the town of Tiel, Dutchmen started slipping across the river at dead of night, sometimes bringing an evader or two with them. Neave has given a powerful account of how he mounted operation 'Windmill', to put an agent called 'Harrier' and an American parachutist into Tiel who would get these evasions onto a more settled basis. Langley approved the operation, from Brussels, on the written order that 'Harrier' and his companion remained in uniform and did not leave their safe house in daylight. They crossed the river on the night of 10/11 October, and went to stay with the Ebbens family in Tiel, an address provided by Kragt. A leading Dutch official, Dr J. H. van Roijen – later Netherlands ambassador in London – crossed by the same skiff in the opposite direction, bearing important news for his government about the state of the starving Dutch.

'Harrier', a jumpy young Englishman who fancied himself as a secret agent but had had no relevant training, disobeyed his orders, and was seen by day in a street in Tiel in plain clothes, recognised as a stranger by a Dutch quisling, and shopped to the Gestapo. He managed to establish a false identity as an evading airborne officer who had lost touch with his unit, was sent to an Oflag, and survived the war (he is now dead; there is no point in giving his name). But his American companion vanished altogether; and both his Ebbens hosts were shot. There was great and just indignation about this case in Holland, then and later. Evans, by a gross breach of security, told 'Harrier's' parents what had happened to their son, and Crockatt was only able with extreme difficulty to avert questions in the House of Commons.

'Pegasus', the unit's other operation across a river – over the Rhine at Randwijk, some six miles south of Ede and eight west of Arnhem – made a better start. A company of Royal Canadian Engineers at Nijmegen had some assault boats, with which they had already rescued many First Airborne Division survivors at the close of the main Arnhem battle. After 'Harrier's' arrest on 17/18 October, the Germans stepped up river bank patrols and searches, but telephone messages from Ede still indicated that there were not too many Germans about. A party of as many as 138 evaders were ferried across on the night of 22/23 October, headed by (Sir) Gerald Lathbury, one of the Arnhem briga-diers. Neave and Fraser acted as beachmasters on the southern bank. Neave was astounded to welcome two Dutch naval officers who had been in Colditz with him, who had seized this oppor-tunity to complete their escape. He also recognised 'The Voice', that had been reading lists of casualties to him for weeks over the telephone from Ede; it belonged to Major Digby Tatham-Warter, whose 'calm and ingenuity' Neave praised for their impact on 'Pegasus I'; it had been Tatham-Warter's company that reached the critical bridge, object of the divisional drop. The beachmasters on the north bank had been Colonel Dobie, a parachute battalion commander who had already made a daring solo evasion, and a young Canadian officer called Leo Heaps who volunteered for the task, and was at once taken on the strength of IS 9(WEA).

The operation was of great value, both for establishing what had happened in the actual battle of Arnhem, and for discov-ering a mass of targets and other valuable fragments of intel-ligence. It was also clear that Hugh Maguire, the divisional IO who had remained behind, had still got several score men with him, for whom a rescue would need to be mounted.

While 'Pegasus I' was a great success,' 'Pegasus II' was a shambles. It was mounted a month later, on 23/24 November, a few miles closer to Arnhem. Storm boats were used; an artil-lery bombardment again covered the boat engines' noise; 40mm Bofors firing tracer again gave some clues to the crossing point. Only seven men were rescued; the rest fell into an ambush, and were scattered, recaptured or killed. (Maguire was recaptured.)

The blame for this can reasonably be laid on the London journalist interviewed some of the evaders on Pegasus I, under the pretence that he was an officer of IS 9, and still more on the censor who passed his piece for publication. The Germans can hardly have failed to read it and to profit by it. Crockatt was fully aware when he approved the plan for 'Pegasus II' that the odds were very heavy against its success, but no further risks for the Dutch families who sheltered the evaders were acceptable.

Neave went back to London to begin work for the Dutch wards bureau, but Fraser remained on the spot, still in touch with Dutch resistance – rather slowly, because Kragt and 'Fabian' both communicated through London ('Ham' had fallen into enemy hands). He was able to raise some S-phones, extra secure radiotelephones, from SOE, and this improved working conditions for him a lot; they were quite as useful for passing intelligence as for arranging evasions. A quiet, steady, secure traffic by canoes through the marshes of the Biesbos, farther down stream, was developed through the winter. One of its most distinguished passengers, then Brigadier Hackett, has written an unusually vivid book about what it was like to be wounded at Arnhem, to hobble out of a prison hospital, to spend months in a devout private house in Ede which backed onto a Feldgendarmerie billet, and then to be brought out suddenly into the company of old friends, and away by canoe.

When he and Warrack, the divisional medical officer – also the author of a notable book – emerged, the IS 9(WEA) group at First Canadian Army noted: 'never an interrogation had given us so much pleasure.'

All through the last winter and spring occasional evasions went on across Holland and Denmark, Germany and northern Italy; Evans went on lecturing; Maskelyne went on lecturing; Germans went on fighting, to the very bitter end. Liberated Frenchmen, Belgians, Brabanters found life much more pleasant without the Gestapo but were still woefully short of food and fuel, and found their lives quite often disrupted by denunciations, by Hitler's revenge weapons, or by the December panic of the Ardennes offensive. This chapter need not end on quite so dour a note; let us turn for a moment to farce.

A British heavy bomber crew got into difficulties during a night raid on Germany. All their direction-finding equipment, including their wireless and their main compass, was shot away, and their altimeter damaged. They ran into thick cloud. Their engines and petrol tanks were intact; steering by guess and by God, they waited for daylight. In the mirk of dawn, as petrol ran low, they caught sight of some level pasture, and landed. A peasant walked by, remembering their escape lecturer's advice to make friends with labouring people in occupied countries, they sent the most proletarian member of the crew across to talk to him. 'Where are we, mate? Oo somm noo?' 'Olland,' the peasant grunted, and walked on. The crew ran back to their aircraft, set it on fire, broke out their Dutch escape purses, and were trying to plot a course on one of their escape maps when a man in dark blue uniform bicycled up and asked them, in perfect English, if they needed an ambulance? They turned out to have landed in south-east Lincolnshire, in fact in Parts of Holland. The Air Ministry was furious; Crockatt was vastly entertained.

# Over, Under or Through:
## Escapes in Europe 1943–45

The great turn of the war's tide at Stalingrad affected escapes as well as evasions. Once the size of the disaster had sunk into ordinary Germans' minds, they realised that the Wehrmacht was no more invincible than the Führer was infallible. They did not in 1943 think that they had lost the war, but they knew that they had not – or not yet – won it. By the autumn of 1944, after the loss of western Russia, of Rome and of Paris, secret weapons provided the only serious hope left alive, and that too failed. These shifts in German morale affected prisoners' guards as much as anybody else, and made the business of more or less genteel blackmail, that was so helpful in getting escape kit that could not be sent in from outside, considerably more easy. The same point about morale applied with greater force to Germany's satellites than to the Third Reich itself.

In Poland there was no satellite government, a fact of which all Poles are justly proud. Professor Bartoszewski's books show how harsh the German occupying regime was to the surviving natives; most Commonwealth and American prisoners of war could count themselves lucky they were not Slavs. MI 9's advice, to MIS-X and everybody else, was to avoid the risks and dangers of an east-about escape; though in fact this route was managed by one in seven of all the successful escapers from Germany, it was thought in London to call for exceptional courage and luck. Some general interest attaches to de Bruyne's comment on a particular escaper, a Czech sergeant called Volka who turned up in the west by way of the USSR: 'Individual instances of successful escapes by this route do not invalidate th[e] general instruction' not to attempt it, for one is likely either to be shot out of hand – either by the Germans or by the Russians – or to be imprisoned indefinitely, 'as has been the fate of many British escapers who up-to-date can still not be traced.' It is only fair to add that the original source for this advice lay in the Polish government in exile in London, a body that by the winter of 1943–4 was unhinged by the disastrous news from Katyn, but there is evidence enough to suggest that it was sound. The Russian attitude was even in a wry way defensible: the Red Army was too busy fighting off the Germans to have time to bother about feeding or housing a few strange foreign escapers whose presence could only be unsettling to morale and who from a Marxist staff officer's standpoint were least nuisances dead? Beyond warning people not to get entangled in it, with this range of atrocity MI 9 and MIS-X had hardly anything to do.

## Hungary

Nor were they able to achieve a great deal in Hungary. Early in the war, Budapest – still then a neutral capital – had been an important staging-post for escapers coming out of Poland, and a centre from which some of the more eager Polish exiles tried to work back into their homeland. But step by step the regime of Admiral Horthy, regent for the notional Habsburg king in exile, had been driven into closer and closer co-operation with Hitler, in spite of the admiral's eventual clandestine approaches to OSS and SOE (he tried SIS, who did not want to know).

Great Britain, at Stalin's insistence, declared war on Hungary in December 1941, but a lot of pro-British sentiment remained among Hungary's aristocratic ruling classes. The Regent gave an affectionate personal farewell to the retiring British and American ministers, and both Szombathelyi, his chief of staff, and Kallay, his Prime Minister, were anxious to get out of the war. An OSS mission that was parachuted into Hungary in mid-March 1944 arrived just in time for its leader Florimond

Duke – formerly *Time* magazine's advertising manager – to be arrested and sent to Colditz, where he passed the rest of the war helping to sustain his fellow prisoners' spirits. What dished Duke's mission was the complete German occupation of the country on 19 March; followed on 15 October by a *coup d'état* by the Arrow Cross, the Hungarian Fascist movement, which pre-empted Horthy's attempt to surrender.

What meanwhile was happening to escapers from German prisoner of war camps who got as far as Hungary? In principle they were interned, but more as guests than as prisoners, in Count Andrassy's castle at Szigetvar, well to the south near the Yugoslav border. Their senior officer, Colonel Charles Telfer Howie, had been captured in Tobruk in 1942 – he was a South African AA artilleryman – and had already brought off a remarkable feat enough, an escape from a camp in Silesia and a march to the middle Dunube. On this march he was accompanied by Sergeant Tibor Weinstein, a Jew who was spending the war in British uniform. Weinstein turned out to be a trained wireless operator; there is not a word in the files to confirm or to deny what the Hungarians suspected, that he and indeed Howie as well were British secret agents of some kind. Weinstein had lived in Budapest as recently as 1937, and spoke fluent Hungarian and German.

There is no need to suppose that Howie was anything but what he said he was, a senior escaper. He was treated with marked consideration by the regime when he and Weinstein reached Budapest in mid-September 1943. The Unitarian bishop Sandor Szent-Ivanyi looked after him, and through the bishop Howie was able to meet the Regent's son Nicholas, a diplomat, and various other members of a group of well-placed young resisters.[39] Ostensibly Howie had a stomach ulcer, treatment for which necessitated his staying in the city.

---

39  By courtesy of Dr Leslie Veresa, who translated it for us, we have
    been able to read the bishop's article on the Howie episode in

Six months' talk brought no serious advance; parallel negoti-ations were going on meanwhile with the British through SOE's office in Istanbul. When the Germans invaded on 19 March 1944, Howie was hidden in a flat close to the Gestapo head-quarters, and spent a week in the Regent's own apartments. He was flown out of Hungary on 22 September with a Hungarian general, Naday, in a Hungarian aircraft that crash-landed near Termoli; Naday was entrusted with one more attempt to get Hungary out of the war, which failed.

The escapers in Szigetvar dispersed as soon as they heard of the German invasion. Some were recaptured, some made their way through Yugoslavia to safety; Simonds had an agent in Yugoslavia, near the Hungarian border, who reported at Bari on 15 June 1944 that if people pretended to be French, movement in Hungary was comparatively easy: 'present officials in Hungary are easy to bribe.'[40] Details are only available in a single case, that of a quiet, well-spoken RAF warrant officer called Reginald Barratt, who was using at the time the name of G. S. Godden. He made his way to Budapest, where he was succoured by an English girl called Evelyn Gore-Symes whom nobody had bothered to intern and by a young Hungarian lawyer called Dr Raphael Rupert. Rupert introduced him to Kristof Kallay, son of the Prime Minister, though it is no longer clear when.

Barratt stayed for some time in Rupert's flat, and was clearly engaged in some sort of intelligence activity. In the late autumn of 1944 he had access to a clandestine transmitter, possibly Nussbacher's, which was repaired for him by another helpful Hungarian called L. Csuros, now a senior official in the British electricity industry. Rupert remembers taking Barratt for a

---

*Magyar Hirado* (Vienna 1 October 1974). The bishop now lives in the USA. See also Weissberg, *Advocate for the Dead*, 51–4, for the story of a quarrel.

40   'Albert's' report in WO 208/3381. He had taken a month to come through from Budapest himself, and is not further identifiable.

pillion ride on a motor bicycle to investigate the results of RAF mining of the Danube, and of German efforts to demagnetise the mines by flying JU-52 trimotor transports over them equipped with anti-magnetic coils.

This was getting out to the edge of MI 9's brief. Barratt met Weinstein and sent him through to the Russian lines early in December 1944 with some target information, of which the Russians made use. On 8 December Rupert, Barratt and a Dutch officer, Lieutenant van der Vails, were overrun by the Russians; all disappeared. Barratt is known to have been held prisoner by the Russians in Bratislava at midsummer 1945; for many years there was no later news of him at all. Rupert, who was eventually released, now lives in Ireland. Van der Vails' family were officially informed from Moscow in the middle 1950s that, by a regrettable breach of Socialist legality, he had been imprisoned in the Lubyanka and had died there of pneumonia. Barratt's widow discovered at about the same time that her husband had been shot by Communist police in Bratislava, 'while trying to escape', an all too familiar cover for the disposal of troublesome prisoners.

### *Romania*

In Romania there was a good deal more conventional escape activity, among American aircrew shot down in the various great day raids on the Ploeşti oilfield. For example, there were numerous reports of tunnelling at a camp at Timisol de Jos, from which two men got as far as the Bulgarian border, and there was some contact with people from the Jewish Agency; but there seem to have been no completely successful escapes till the second half of August 1944, when King Michael engineered a *coup d'état* against his own government and Romania changed sides.

Maskelyne's and other lectures bore useful fruit. In Camp 13 in Bucarest, the capital, for instance, most of the prisoners of war had retained discipline and organisation enough for them to be prepared to react *en masse* if the Germans tried to take over their camp from the local guards. Captain George W. Call, a journalist from Waco, Texas, shot down in an aircraft of 414th Bombardment Squadron on 22 July 1944, was among the leading spirits who were arranging a march out into the hills to link up with partisan groups that were at work there already.

If American discipline remained good, Romanian did not. There are various odd tales of the ease with which agents of British and American subversive and escape services could communicate fairly freely with the outside world, even at one remove with Wolfson or others in Istanbul, from inside prisoner of war camps or even prisons in Bucharest. Simonds sent in several pairs of his Jewish agents by parachute, starting as early as 1 October 1943 with operation 'Mantilla'. These two, sergeants Liova and Fichman, were arrested on arrival, and held at Timisol, but could communicate with their colleagues from prison, and were let out to live under surveillance in Bucharest. 'Goulash', sergeants Macarescu and Levy who dropped on 2/3 May 1944, were also soon arrested. Three other parties, 'Schnitzel', 'Ravioli', and 'Doiner' were dropped in during the summer. So, at the second attempt – at the first, she burst into tears on nearing the dropping zone and declared she couldn't bear to go[41] – was a good-looking young blonde called Sarah Braverman. She was to have worked with Berdichev, but fortunately for her he left her behind when he moved away to Slovakia. All of the agents left in Romania were safely recovered in the last few days of August, after the *coup d'état* of the 23/24th and the subsequent Russian occupation.

It then emerged that Macarescu had done particularly creditably, having survived ninety-six days' solitary confinement enlivened by 'constant interrogation and threats', and having kept his morale high enough to organise his fellow-prisoners for escape work once he had been released into a camp. 'Great

---

41    Simonds' recollection, 1978.

tribute has been paid by senior American Officers to the work done by our agents,' by him especially. Two British soldiers and twenty-seven members of the RAF were among those rescued, as well as two Dutch naval officers and a French soldier; the great bulk of the recovered prisoners were from the American air force. In the first rescue flights 474 officers and 652 enlisted men were brought out; five of Simonds' agents remained behind in Bucarest, hunting up about a hundred prisoners who were believed to have gone astray in the late August confusion. It may be presumed that as soon as they had completed this task, Romania's new and pro-Russian authorities were glad to see their backs, but on this point the files are silent.

The USAAF had reacted very promptly when Romania became an ally; transport aircraft were flying into Bucarest airfield to collect ex-prisoners of war within a matter of hours – 1,274 men had been extracted from Romania by 20 October. This was a magnificently prompt administrative effort, but can hardly be classified as escape.

### Bulgaria

In Bulgaria life was a lot rougher and tougher: so rough that Private R. W. Richardson, shot down on 22 July 1944 on his first mission, to Ploesti, had more to complain of when he returned than ubiquitous rats and lice in a filthy camp at Shumen, and a severe shortage of food. He happened to parachute down near a German radar crew, who beat him up before handing him over to the Bulgars. He was fed on soup, a little mouldy bread, and promises. In the camp hospital there were no medical stores, gangrene in wounds was common, and he saw a Bulgar surgeon who was about to amputate a leg have his patient anaesthetised by a blow on the head with a rifle butt.

The 303 Americans brought out of Bulgaria in September 1944, by contrast with their well-treated colleagues in Romania, had had a thoroughly disagreeable time. MI 9 counted 305 – 135 officers and 170 enlisted men – when they reached Aleppo by train; 'a virtual clearance' of Bulgaria. Eleven officers and eighteen NCOs from the RAF, two Dutch officers, one Polish officer and five Italians completed the party; a Syrian autumn made a welcome change after a Bulgar summer. Holder visited Bulgaria for a few days, to see what could be done about tracing helpers and hindrances, but found in fact there was hardly anything he could do.

Some of these people must have escaped into Bulgaria (how else can the Dutch for instance have got there?), but no escapes out of Bulgaria seem to be on record. This was not for lack of attempts by Simonds to engineer some.

On 20 October 1943, Wolfson told him, he had on his desk an offer to release the crews of four American heavy bombers held in Bulgaria, 'with connivance senior members German I[ntelligence] S[ervice],' for a hundred thousand gold dollars. 'This figure fantastic,' Wolfson's telegram added justly enough. Simonds replied on the twelfth, offering £5,000. The War Office, six days later, inquired 'is not cost exorbitant and will it not be bad precedent?' The whole negotiation petered out; the Germans' cupidity outran their discretion, and their greed exceeded what any Allied authority was prepared to think of paying.

One pair of agents, both called Yusef ('Chair' and 'Carpet' of operation 'Interval'), were sent to the Turkish-Bulgarian border in July 1944; with no results so far reported.

### Greece and Albania

The Russians rapidly conquered Bulgaria and moved on northwestwards. The Germans pulled out of mainland Greece, though they left well-stocked garrisons behind in the Dodecanese and in Crete. Follow-up parties from MI 9, among other bodies, trod quite closely on their heels as they moved away. In Salonika in mid-November as many as 113 people turned up and asked for MI 9's aid, as escapers or evaders: a note that happens to have survived divides them by nationality, and shows how important it had remained to remember Dudley Clarke's rules about who could, and who could not benefit from such services as MI 9 could offer. Two of them were British, one was Australian, six were Cypriots, twenty-four were French, twenty-five Belgian, fifty Polish, and the remaining five Czech.

Albania was the scene of a simple, elegant escape by someone who had heard and pondered a lecture on what to do if he found himself in enemy hands. An American lieutenant, John D. Murray, bailed out over the coast when engine failure made his aircraft unmanageable on 26 August 1944. He and most of his crew were at once captured, and were piled into a lorry with Germans to guard them. With one of his crew, he managed to fall off the back of the lorry, unnoticed for the moment. By the time a search party came back to look for them they had vanished. They joined up with a British mission, and were flown out to Italy on 21 October.

### *Italy*

A previous chapter has described in some detail the mess that was made in Italy at the time of the Italian surrender. It did not attempt to quantify the number of escapers who made themselves scarce after the Italians had dropped their guard, and before the Germans imposed their own, and estimates vary widely. Christopher Soames noticed that the German broadcasts claimed 50,000 taken away to Germany; over 70,000 had been notified by the Red Cross as in Italian camps; only about 4,000 had been recovered by the time of his inquiry, half in Italy and half in Switzerland. Where were the rest? Had there been a massacre, or were they all evading? After the war, it was clear there had been no major catastrophe, only the colossal misunderstanding discussed above. The then British ambassador in Italy Sir Noel Charles once put the figure of those who had gone spare from the camps, and were hiding up in the countryside, as high as 30,000. This last estimate seems to us a good deal too high, but we have not found data on which to found an exact figure.

N section was busy, needless to say, probing for information about ex-prisoners' whereabouts, and came up late in February 1944 with the following rough locations:

> over 2,000 in the Gran Sasso, a mountain range ENE of Rome
> 5,000 near Venice
> 2,000 near Padua, to the west of Venice
> 1,000 near Belluno, in the Dolomite foothills north of Venice
> 1,000 near Treviso, midway between Belluno and Venice
> 100 in Florence
> and 60 in Slovenia, moving south. (Slovenia was the north-easternmost province of wartime Italy.)

In any case, before the troubles began Philip Holder had been quite right to remark to Ed Johnston that 'It is not difficult to break out of any prison camp in Italy. It is, however, extremely difficult to get out of Italy itself.' A very few exceptionally brave and capable people managed to do so. Lieutenant (later Admiral Sir) Ian McGeoch was captured, wounded in the eye, when HMS *Splendid*, his submarine was sunk off Capri on 21 April 1943; lost the sight of the eye; but retained vigour and initiative enough to get out of his hospital at Bergamo, thirty miles north-east of Milan, on 10 September 1943, an hour before the Germans arrived. Three days later, sustained by his MI 9 training, he walked into Switzerland 'at a part where there were neither patrols nor wire.' Later he found his own way to Spain. Towards the other end of the social and military spectrum, Lance-Corporal H. G. Challenor of 2 SAS, who parachuted into central Italy on a special operation on 7 September 1943, fell so ill with malaria that he did not hear of the armistice for a fortnight; made himself useful to partisans in his Apennine neighbourhood till he was taken prisoner on 20 January 1944; escaped from prison at L'Aquila, fifty miles north-east of Rome, disguised as a charwoman; and headed for the battle line. In the danger zone as he approached it he was again captured on

5 April. His captors removed his boots, pending a more secure hold on him; he ran off in his stockinged feet, and was back with the British army on 7 April.

After the Italian surrender in September 1943 a marked shift in opinion took place. Fascism had long ceased to be popular; and now, in Sir Noel Charles's words, 'the majority of the Italian people formed a strange alliance with the prisoners, and they worked together against the Germans and the Republican Fascists.' One domestic example of this, a trifle absurd, is characteristic both of English and of Italian feeling. A naval chief petty officer, H. W. Cantle, captured on 15 June 1942 from HMS *Bedouin*, escaped from a big camp at Chiavari on the coast some twenty miles east of Genoa on 13 September 1943 by using his wits and exploiting local feeling. Prisoners had had a few days' comparative freedom while standing fast as ordered, and the main gate was momentarily not strongly held. He slipped out, mingled with a crowd of local people, got into a bus, and – having previously bothered to learn some Italian – threw himself on the mercy of his fellow passengers. He stayed in a hill village called Isolona: 'All the village knew of my presence, and were so keen to feed me that I sometimes had as many as three dinners a day.'

There were many thousands of escapers who like Cantle were cherished by the peasantry among whom they found themselves. There is a striking example in Newby's book of peasants who looked after him, in the hope that somebody else would look after their sons in Russia. Some of them settled down to make themselves useful as woodcutters, farmers, shepherds.

In mid-July 1944, N section's emissaries remarked how difficult it sometimes was to winkle ex-prisoners out of village communities in which they had become comfortable and accepted members. Quite a few of these people merged quietly into the local population, were missed by N section and everybody else, and have never bothered to surface. Others declared their identity when eventually the battle caught up with them, in 1944 or 1945, returned to Britain or America or New Zealand or wherever, and ceased to try to pass as Italians. Others again were more uneasy, lacked the language skill or the manners to get on with the locals, feared the onset of winter, and roamed the countryside in irresolute bands, wondering where they would find their next meal.

There was a steady south-eastward flow of ex-prisoners who tried to walk back, and N section gradually developed ratlines to help them as they got close to the battle area. Interrogators at the Bari base got used to hearing praise of their agents' helpfulness, without letting on to the escapers that much of the help had been prearranged. Yet ratlines close to the battle did not suffice to meet either the needs of the escapers, or the combative instincts of Rodd and Holder at AFHQ or of Fillingham and 'Squad' Dennis who were in charge of the Bari base. Fuller and closer contact needed to be made with the indigenous resistance movement.

At the working escapers' level, this was not difficult. For example, the American Sergeant Warren H. Cook ditched off Salerno on 25 August 1943 and was picked up by an Italian seaplane. He thrice escaped, and was thrice recaptured; 'Had been briefed very well on escape procedure and said it aided him immensely'; escaped for a fourth time, got right away into the Apennines, and fought for some weeks with a unit of Montenegrin guerrillas (and how on earth, one cannot help wondering, did they turn up there? No doubt by some freak of Italian conscription policy in conquered Albania). On 22 June 1944 he is recorded as having 'returned to duty': not the happiest of phrases for someone who could hardly be described as having been off duty for the previous ten months.

Fillingham and Dennis believed that they could arrange more escapes by sending agents in by boat or parachute to establish lines deep in German-occupied north Italy. A number of these people had some startlingly odd cover jobs, redolent of operetta as much as war: Dick Lewis for example, during a spell of six weeks in enemy-held territory, found himself acting as billeting officer for a Luftwaffe squadron. Two of their agents were outstanding: Kunieri and Losco. Lieutenant Ugo Ranieri ('Hugh') ran for seven months a highly successful ratline on the Adriatic coast north-east of Rome, from December 1943 to June 1944. In spite of arrests and murders, he saw through over 400 men. He was then overrun, and after a short rest briefed for a further mission, to make contact with the north Italian Committee of National Liberation (CNL) which had its head-quarters in Milan.

His main object was to help escapers in Piedmont and Lombardy to find their way into Switzerland. If he could reach the liberation committee, he was to say that 'We cannot praise too highly the generosity and self-sacrifice of all classes of the Italian people who have so readily helped Allied escap-ers and evaders … We receive continual reports of the excel-lent work being done by the CNL in this connection. The Allied command attaches great importance to the rescue of Allied personnel at large in enemy territory (for reasons of morale, man-power and humanity). Therefore it is requested that the CNL continue to do all in its power to assist P/W and route them to safety in neutral or Allied territory.'

It is worth pursuing this contact with the CNL for a moment. Several months later, on 16 November 1944, Dennis held a meeting at Bari at which four leading members of the CNL were able to be present: Longhi, Parri, Franchi and Mari. Parri (subsequently Socialist Prime Minister) inquired what priorities Dennis would lay down for rescuing Allied servicemen. Dennis replied, first, those conducting any sort of special operation in the neighbourhood; second, aircrew; third, those who had taken part in the current campaign in Italy; and fourth, escaped or released prisoners of war from earlier battles. Parri estimated that 'some hundreds' of escapers were living with families in the Po valley, and 'agreed to notify and instruct all Partisan bands' in touch with his committee to give 'every help' to IS 9, as N section had now come to be called. Parri was less affected

than were some of his colleagues in national liberation movements farther east by a tendency that one of Simonds' agents in
Yugoslavia described thus a couple of month earlier: 'the closer
the Russian forces get, the more indifferent the Partisans are
becoming to the Anglo-Americans.' Parri shortly returned to
Milan; where he soon fell into enemy police hands.

Milan had, before 'Ugo's' visit, been the beat of the other
star agent, Captain Andrew Losco ('John'), but at the moment
of Ranieri ('Hugh's') second mission Losco was recovering after
one of several spells in an Axis prison. This time he got out in late
May 1944 with a South African corporal called Vivier who was
on his fifth escape and a partisan lieutenant called Penna. They
had been held in the town jail of Macerata, about fifteen miles
north-west of the Tenna valley where many escapers congre-
gated. There were five warders in the jail; Losco's party over-
powered them all, and walked out.[42] They moved back towards
the Tenna, and had the good fortune to meet one of the most
forceful of N section's forward operatives, Jock McKee. Losco
was back in action in September, when he rescued – presumably
with BATS' help – about a hundred prisoners from Maribor,
north of Zagreb near the Austrian border, before being caught
yet again.

McKee had shown courage and energy at Sulmona in
the earliest days of the Italian crisis. He had now gone over
to a longer-term, still more demanding task: working, mainly
behind the more-or-less-fixed battle front, to mobilise parties
of escapers, marshal them down to a suitable secluded beach,
and see them onto one boat or other of N section's private fleet
that was stationed sometimes at Termoli and sometimes at
Manfredonia.

One of these sea operations, 'Darlington II' on 24/25 May
1944, is claimed by Fillingham as undoubtedly the most successful

---

42   WO 208/3416, newsletter 27, 3 June 1944; sent by Crockatt to
     Davidson, who minuted 'Good show'.

pickup conducted by any service anywhere on the peninsula; this was thanks to a sublime stroke of luck. The two craft which took part, an American patrol boat and a British infantry landing-craft (LCI), got separated on the outward journey from Termoli. The American craft, the P-402 (Lieutenant Gene P. Moritz, of the 22nd Army Air Force Emergency Boat Crew), reached the mouth of the Tenna. 'Underwood was sent ashore with two dinghys. He never showed up again. We were 100 yards from shore. The sea was flat calm. There were lights ashore [to guide him in]. The man had four oars, two well inflated dinghys and a lifebelt on. God knows what happened to him; we don't... Another night like that one,' Moritz remarked, 'and I am going to apply for old age pension.' He had to beach his craft – no light matter, for she was 63 feet long – collect the twenty-six escaped prisoners of war who were waiting for him, and kedge off again. He made it.

The LCI, having failed to find anyone at what its crew believed to be the mouth of the Tenna, was also returning to base when, several miles to the southward, the correct signals were spotted from an unknown beach. The correct reply was given; a commando covering party went ashore; and in just over half an hour had been re-embarked, with 127 escapers and evaders.

N section ran its own craft, mainly with Italian crews: how the craft were found, who paid for them, who fuelled them are questions we are in no position to answer, but which need one day to be cleared up. Gene Moritz's work in 1944 in P-402 was described as 'outstanding' when his health at last broke down at the end of the year. Sub-Lieutenant Ian MacPherson RN, who had joined the section in November 1943, 'looked after the practical side of all our boating operations... extremely well and personally participated in all landings and evacuations', on both sides of the Adriatic; he too was withdrawn, a few weeks after Moritz left, to rejoin a combined operations beach command. The little fleet remained in being. Service in such a unit was not the professional's dream of a pathway leading straight to high command and high responsibility. Yet it called for seamanship of high quality, for strong nerves, and for versatility; and the men who served in this forgotten corner of the war could read the good they were doing easily enough in the faces of the men they brought out from Axis Europe.

Covering parties for such excursions, when they were judged desirable, had to be found from outside N section. Commandos, SAS, and 'Popski's' Private Army all from time to time took part. They seldom had to fire a shot, but welcomed the training, the risk and the adventure. 'Popski' did not think highly of the first partisans he met, when there was a brief spell of open warfare in midsummer 1944: 'all seen so far just playing Red Indians bristling with weapons much odio[u]s red scarves no guts no intelligence no military sense no nothing should be suppressed. Hope found them less scared further north.' He did; within a fortnight he had found ones with whom he could gladly work.

The quantities of ex-prisoners rescued by these parties – most of them on the Adriatic coast, but some also on the western shore – are much harder to establish than the fact that such operations were going on. A count in November 1944 reckoned that in the previous fourteen months 2,156 people at least had been recovered by IS 9 parties at work on Italian soil: rather larger than the total strength at that moment of the SAS brigade operating into northwest Europe, and some indication of the amount of work the parties run from Bari had been achieving. Among those who came out safely was de Bruyne's brother; who bothered, as few did, to write a letter of thanks. When the personal files emerge, it will be possible to sort out more details on some passengers of quality. Two highly distinguished generals, Neame and O'Connor, and Air Vice Marshal Boyd, arrived at Termoli in a fishing-boat just before Christmas 1943, after a series of escapades described in Neame's book in lavish detail. A party of five brigadiers arrived with eleven other escapers at Termoli by boat in mid-May 1944; bringing with them a warning that 'the enemy is fully aware of many of the activities occurring behind his front line and reacts every now and again in sheer desperation.' They had been collected, transported through numerous hitches, and finally seen onto their boat by Losco and several other agents. A few days later came one of many reports of German agents disguised as British troops, touting for help from peasants, and then arresting them when it was given. A small reward, 5,000 lire, was offered by the Gestapo for anybody who denounced a *passeur*. It would be interesting to know how often it was claimed. Five or six renegade Allied prisoners were working with the *Dienststelle Schistler*, hunting mainly for tactical intelligence and trying to recruit MI 9 guides; again, one day, it will be interesting to know what became of the renegades.

An even more distinguished character than O'Connor or Neame, General Carton de Wiart, VC, got home before either of them. He was recaptured not long after his escape from Florence by the Italians, who treated him with the respect that a man of his standing and bravery commanded; and the Italian government used him, during the protracted armistice negotiations between Mussolini's arrest on 25 July and the official surrender on 8 September 1943, as a semi-secret envoy to Lisbon and London to discuss (he thought) the precise conditions on which they were to surrender unconditionally. The initial proposal to use him was made through the captured transmitter of an SOE operator who was in prison in Rome.[43] His mission was not an unqualified success, because the Italians' real object was to discover how much help the Allies could give them against the Germans: not quite the inline proposition. But while he was in England, he stayed quietly with Crockatt

---

43   See Dorothy Barlow, 'From Enemy to Co-Belligerent: Italy mid-July to mid-October 1943', unpublished Manchester MA thesis (1972), 126.

at Beaconsfield, and so was able to give the head of MI 9 some direct impressions, even if at a rarefied level, of what life in an Italian prisoner of war camp was like. What impressed Crockatt even more was Carton de Wiart's account of the difficulties that had been brought on unintendedly by the 'stand fast' order.

There was a good deal of air as well as sea activity aimed at helping the thousands of escapers who were roaming around Italy. Ships were better for getting them out of occupied territory than aircraft were – the Termoli LCI could carry over 250 men with ease. Aircraft on the other hand were better than ships for distributing food, clothing and blankets to parties in mountain areas. In the first nine months of 1944, for example, eighty-three tons of stores and nineteen agents were parachuted for escape purposes into northern Italy. Aircraft were not available for special duties of this kind in vast numbers, and they had many commitments to partisans in the Balkans – not to speak of Poland: during the Warsaw rising the Polish special duties squadron lost all but one of its aircraft[44] – but they could usually meet Fillingham's requests for drops. A minimum of discipline and common sense on the dropping zone, and some sort of organisation for moving the stores away from it, were all that were needed, at the escapers' end; once an N section agent had made touch.

Unhappily, a prolonged spell in a prisoner of war camp does not always sharpen the military character: on the contrary. One 'stupid, ill-organised and ill-timed' result is on record; there may well have been others. In March 1944, near the front of 2 Parachute Brigade, a batch of more than forty escapers – including a major and three captains – with as many as 150 Italian refugee hangers-on attempted a mass unarmed break through the front lines. They had an N section guide with them, 'Domenico', who was keen but over-enthusiastic and under-informed. The movement of a crowd of nearly 200 could not

---

44   Conversation with the surviving pilot, Warsaw 1978.

be kept a secret. The party was shattered by a storm of rain and fell into a German ambush; the officers failed to take command; and three-quarters of the whole mob were shot.

Another entry on the debit side of the Allied account, though this time no sort of fault of IS 9's or of any escaper's or evader's had to be made at the beginning of December 1944. A Lysander, that invaluable aircraft originally designed for front-line army co-operation – for which it was all but useless – was on its way with an IS 9 agent on board to a prearranged daylight reception not very far from Venice, when it was bounced out of the sun and shot down by a passing P-51 Mustang fighter, which mistook it for something hostile. Agent and pilot were both killed.

A strong combative spirit remained active in IS 9(CMF)'s agents. Lieutenant McArthur for example, who reached Bari just after Christmas 1943 with a party of seventy-three other escapers – three of them officers – from Croatia, was put ashore at the northernmost tip of the Adriatic in early April 1945, just before the German front collapsed altogether; was recaptured; was very severely tortured; and was still quite cheerful when, like Losco, he was released by the final Allied advance.

Though the Adriatic coast naturally enough preoccupied the IS 9 staff at Bari who lived close to it, the section had some parties at work on the western coast also. Peter Fowler distinguished himself here, particularly on a mission to Gordon Lett, a Royal Indian Army Service Corps officer who ran a partisan force at first about 300 strong in the mountains west of Genoa. He was armed by SOE, and could pick and choose among the escapers who tried to join him. He settled on six: two Australians, one an infantry sergeant and one an anti-tank gunner; an ordinary seaman, RN; and three English privates from regular battalions. His force got smaller – he and casualties between them had reduced it to about forty by November 1944 – but he kept his six escapers, and did sterling work with them.

Fowler tried to visit him in a ship of a rival private navy, run for SOE in Corsica under the codename 'Balaclava' by that formidable character Andrew Croft. Of the fifty-two operations Croft attempted, either from his main base at Bastia or from the subsidiary one at Calvi, twenty-four succeeded; five of these operations were on Fowler's behalf, of which two succeeded – two organisers were landed in Italy on 18 February and four on 28 April 1944. All three IS 9 failures were due to the absence of a reception committee on the beach. These committees could be delayed or distracted for a myriad of reasons; still, Croft did note that only four of his operations ever failed for lack of reception, and three of these were Fowler's.

Croft would have approved the action of an SOE party in Italy who were approached in January 1945 by a man who claimed to be an A Force courier, but could give no password, nor either the real name nor the code name of anyone in A Force: they shot him. He was as sad as everybody in IS 9(CMF) when Fowler, joining like Croft in the general exodus of staff officers to the Continent in August 1944, was killed in action in the south of France.

On 10/11 August, the night before he was killed, there were some agonising decisions to be made. A C-47 transport landed in Provence at a nominally deserted grass airfield to collect some assembled aircrew, but there turned out to be as many as twenty- six of them: too great a weight. Eight deplaned; eighteen men were safely flown out; by the next night the Germans had reoccupied the field. At that point the file falls silent, but operation 'Dragoon' was about to liberate Provence in any case, and it can be hoped that the eight disappointed men were not disappointed for long.

## Switzerland

A minor useful side effect of 'Dragoon' was that the frontiers of Switzerland were no longer sealed. Brigadier General B. R. Legge, the American military attaché in Berne, personally saw a party of sixty-six aircrew over the Savoyard border when the

Swiss opened it again in September. These were some of the successful escapers from Swiss internment, from among several hundred aircrew who had necessarily suffered that fate. For they had made forced landings at Dubendorf airfield by Zürich, on finding that their aircraft had been too badly damaged by flak or fighters to stand the journey back to base; and in those circumstances it was no good trying to follow the MIS-X lecturer's advice, and pretend that one had been a prisoner and had made a bona fide escape. This last resort, often used by the USAF by day, was not taken up by the RAF at night.

In November 1944 the Swiss government suggested to the British that the remaining ninety British military interned in Switzerland might be released, in return for releasing an equal number of military Germans to Germany, and a few weeks until they proposed to the United States to release 1,503 Amerlom internees against the return to Germany of 1,503 soldiers, custom officers and border guards. Airmen in the American party were not to operate again in Europe. The British did not think this worth pursuing, and the Americans' first reaction was that in the Germans' current manpower crisis anything that presented the enemy with two fresh battalions was to be deplored. General Legge however pitched in a telegram on 10 December in which he remarked on the high value for the Pacific war of the 790 American airmen still stuck on Swiss territory, General Arnold backed him up, and the exchange finally went through.

### France

France in 1943–4 presented hardly any escapers' problems save one, but that one was serious. Under Hitler's 'Commando order' of October 1942, 'all terror and sabotage troops of the British and their accomplices, who do not act like soldiers but rather like bandits, will be treated as such': the protection of the Geneva Convention was refused to the Special Air Service brigade.

This was an international brigade, mainly British and French, but including also a Belgian independent company, some Yugoslavs, a Pole, a few Spaniards and a few concealed Austrians. It operated by parachute, fairly close behind the main fighting front, in uniform. An SOE spectator reported that SAS 'supplied the trained military direction' which the French *maquisards* inevitably lacked, and 'formed the hard core of French resistance in the field'. About a hundred SAS were taken prisoner; six survived. Four escaped, one (the Pole) was overrun too badly wounded to stand, one was exchanged in a similar state for an unwounded and much-decorated German, and the rest were either shot in cold blood after capture, or taken to a concentration camp and executed there. In particular, a party some thirty strong, surprised and captured near Poitiers, were executed on the spot.

As early as 24 August 1944, about seven weeks after these particular killings, Cordell Hull, the American Secretary of State, proposed a strong but secret protest. Diplomatic argument lasted through the winter. By the spring of 1945, Eisenhower's chief of staff, Bedell Smith, was much exercised about this, and wrote to the American chiefs of staff on 3 March to urge both an official protest and a propaganda campaign against this treatment of men 'carrying out legitimate military tasks'. On 24 March 1945 a broadcast in Eisenhower's name was made to the Wehrmacht, stressing the illegality of executing parachutists and threatening legal reprisals: 'The excuse of having carried out orders received from above will not be considered as valid.' The process of interdepartmental, let alone international consultation was far too slow for anybody to get to the point of decision before the war was over, and the atrocity, bad as it was, looked comparatively minor by the time Belsen and Dachau had been discovered.

At a much lower but not in this case a less effective level, rough justice had been meted out months before. Several quite junior army and air force officers were appalled at the massacre near Poitiers, the largest illegal killing of SAS in the field. A signals sergeant had evaded the disaster, and had still got his set,

his codes, and good local friends. SAS signals were provided for
them by a squadron of the 'Phantom' regiment which specialised in long-range wireless telegraphy, commanded by (Sir)
J. J. Astor. Information from the sergeant was slipped, demi-
officially, through an SAS staff channel to the TAF Mosquito
squadron that had been attacking targets the SAS party
had signalled. Some Mosquito pilots pursued the SS unit
that had done the killing, burned up several barracks in which it
tried to shelter, and reduced its strength by four-fifths: an ample
revenge.[45] The SS officer responsible in Paris, Josef Kieffer,
was tracked down and hanged after the war; to the annoyance
of SOE, SAS had him arraigned, condemned and strung up
before SOE had had a proper chance to interrogate him.

### Germany

To conclude this chapter we must consider Germany, still the
main field for escape endeavour. One tremor of a change was
perceptible: 'guidance and help' from isolated south German
and Austrian peasants was reported for two recent British officer
escapers, in battledress, in the very early spring of 1944. The
same report added an ever-necessary warning: all escapers had
to be vigilant against the 'helper' who was too smartly turned
out, who moved about too cavalierly in daylight, and who kept
pressing for service information; because such a one would very
probably be a Gestapo nark working in a bogus line.

Crockatt continued as always 'to discourage violent mass
break' outs because of the danger of mass reprisals'. One
mass escape of 1,500 Canadians from Stalag IID at Stargard
in Pomerania in November 1944, 'involved a considerable
number of deaths', and seems to have borne him out. There
were three successful escapes from Stargard, one by a pair of
NCOs, Sergeant MacMillen and Corporal Nelson, who cut
the wire and got away on 9 June 1944, hid with French prisoners

---

45   Personal knowledge.

at Swinemünde for three days, and spent a fortnight on an involuntary Baltic cruise before they reached Sweden on 1 July. The Canadian J. H. Kimberley, Royal Hamilton Light Infantry, left a week earlier, but was fool enough to have forgotten his cigarettes, and sensible enough to go back for them; he was spotted and rearrested. On 3 August he skipped from a working party in Stargard town. This time he had plenty of cigarettes on him, and with 250 of them he bought from a French driver a lift to Stettin. Here he visited the foreign sailors' brothel, which was out of bounds to Germans – one of MI 9's most ingenious rendezvous – and found help. By an unlucky accident, it was demolished in an air raid a few days after Kimberley called at it. A ship took him across to Sweden, where he swam ashore on 11 August. He always preferred to do things his own way.

One well prepared mass escape was made from Oflag VIIB at Eichstätt in Bavaria on 3 June 1943. A strong escape committee, plentifully aided by MI 9, had long been at work on several schemes; a tunnel enabled sixty-five officers to get out at once. All were recaptured and brought back in a fortnight, but during that fortnight they had absorbed the attention of 50,000 Germans: police, troops, home guard, and *Hitlerjugend*. This in principle was a useful diversion of enemy effort, on just the lines foreseen by Holland before the war. In practice it did not turn out quite so well, for it gave the Bavarian authorities plenty of opportunities of learning how to look out for strangers and round them up. This made Bavaria much more dangerous for evaders from the RAF's disastrous raid on Nuremberg in March 1944.

In January 1944 Crockatt was able to review the achievements of his department over the previous four years at a secret press conference which was designed to explain to London newspaper correspondents both what MI 9 was and did, and why in wartime no reference to its existence or activities could be made in any published paper. In his survey of what had already been done, he mentioned that he reckoned one officer in four among all the British prisoners in Germany 'has been at large' already. After the war, when he had a chance to review the German field at more leisure, he drew up an interesting if perhaps over-precise table of percentages:

|  Successful Escapes from Germany [46] | |
| --- | --- |
| *Via* | *Per cent* |
| Sweden | 29.79 |
| Western Europe | 24.49 |
| Switzerland | 18.50 |
| Russia | 14.29 |
| Balkans | 12.93 |

People often write of life under Nazism as if it had been drearily uniform, with that sameness which is one of the many vices of dictatorships and of prisons. But the Third Reich was large, its regime was new, dullness had not yet set in universally; and a survey of the surviving camp histories suggests eccentricity quite as much as conformity. A few examples of the oddities may help to establish the point.

There was an Oflag – IX A/Z – at Rotenburg, south-west of Cassel, in the premises of a former girls' boarding school, with the ex-headmaster as commandant. There was among its overcrowded prisoners – there were as many as 566 in April 1943, including 154 Americans captured in North Africa – an unusually large number of elderly officers. A result of this was, or seemed at any rate to the Dominion prisoners in the camp to be, a degree of over-organisation by the escape committee. Plans were too grandiose; too much attention got paid to details by outsiders; too many men were involved in each project for safety. Only two people ever got clean away from the camp, two Indian officers who managed the journey of some 250 miles

---

46    WO 208/3242, 79.

into Switzerland. This was a considerable feat, more startling still for Asians than for Europeans; unfortunately, there is no available record of their names.

There was one fort at the vast Stalag XX at Thorn, Fort XVII, from which escape seemed much more easy than from anywhere else in the camp: a visit to that beautiful city showed why. On the left, unbeautiful bank of the Vistula, Fort XVII is slap opposite the railway station, a point nobody had bothered to mention in the camp history. It was from here that Paddon, Hawtin and several others got away, but one needed luck as well as judgement; the sentries were trigger happy, and the prisoners' count of those shot arbitrarily by them rose as high as twenty-two. Still, there; were thirty-one former inmates of Thorn back in the United Kingdom before the end of the war. They did not include Private J. Gilliland, a Cameron Highlander who escaped eight or nine times and was 'finally shot by the Germans' whose patience had run out, according to Lance-Corporal A. Coulthard of field security, who also made nine unsuccessful escapes, but survived to say so.

Other camps had a steady run of parcels – Thorn had none at all until 1943. 'Opinions were mixed' here about the success of a scheme of Langley's, the dispatch of boxes of Christmas crackers by the Lancashire Penny Fund intended to reach camps by mid-December 1943, accompanied in each case by an open letter to the commandant inviting him to share in this harmless good cheer, and preceded by a code letter warning the camps which colour of box they should secure for the prisoners, not for the commandant. Half the crackers were as innocent as they seemed the other half contained maps, money, dockyard passes, compasses and other escapers' goodies. In some camps this worked like a charm; in others suspicious commandants discovered what Langley was up to, and uttered unseasonable thoughts. The Germans even complained to the Red Cross Society, as there had been red crosses on some of the labels.

At Stalag XVII A at Kaisersteinbruch bei Bruch, south-east of Vienna and conveniently near the Hungarian border, the

French prisoners had a wireless set; but they could never resist the temptation to gossip about the news they heard on it, and so the French quarters were constantly being raided. The British prisoners bought a wireless for 3,000 Reichsmarks from a local sympathiser, observed rigid security, and were never searched at all. About thirty people escaped from this camp, but they were all recaptured and brought back. At Stalag XIII C, at Hammelburg-am-Saale east of Frankfurt-am-Main, there were two home-made crystal sets, a fact kept a deadly secret. Work here was so hard that even the Australians found themselves 'completely exhausted by the evening', and no escaper got clean away. On the other hand at Stalag IV A at Hohnstein in Saxony the guards were so thoroughly bribable that a prisoner could borrow a wireless for five cigarettes an evening. And at Steglitz in the suburbs of Berlin, at Stalag II D, there was never any trouble with parcels: one man got eighteen running from the Licensed Victuallers' Association, none of them censored, all of them loaded with escape equipment.

The Russians here were exceptionally badly treated, dying like flies from typhus. Yet one of the sub-camps, at Genshagen, was used by the Germans as a sort of holiday camp, with decent food, sheets on the beds, a little alcohol, an atmosphere of comfort: intended to weaken non-Slav prisoners' morale by softening them up.

An alternative dubious way in which prisoners could raise their morale was by gambling. Bridge or poker certainly provided a method of taking one's mind off one's predicament, and several camps had serious card-playing clubs; one SBO complained that gambling was so heavy in a small group of officers, British and Sikh, that it endangered the discipline of his camp at Querum.

Dangerous though that small group was, another group in the same camp managed to be dangerous in a different way: they built a home-made generator, so that they could still hear the news on their secret wireless when the Germans cut off the power. At Colditz the two forms of danger were combined. A large treadmill was built, disguised when not in use as a ward-robe, to power the motor stolen from the organ in the disused chapel; power from the motor enabled the prisoners never to pass a day without hearing a news bulletin; and in the last few months of the war large sums of money changed hands in sweepstakes on the dates at which towns fell to the Allies.[47]

The prize for sheer eccentric brilliance must go where an Englishman would expect it to go: to the Royal Navy. Lieutenant D. P. James was captured from his sunken motor gun-boat off the Dutch coast on 28 February 1943. 'Owing to the large number of uniforms to be seen in Germany I resolved to attempt to escape in full British naval uniform, carrying a card purporting to be a Bulgarian naval identity card in the name of I. Bagerov, a trade name that will be remembered long after my own is forgotten.' He slipped away from a bathing parade at Marlag-Milag Nord on 9 December – his fellow prisoners fudged the count for him, with the help of a portable dummy; changed in a lavatory into his smartest kit, which his family had sent out to him; and got as far as the dock gates at Lübeck via Stettin before a pettifogging sentry unmasked him. Quite undaunted, he did the bathroom trick again soon after he had served his spell in solitary, and this time adopting the quieter disguise of a Swedish sailor hid – with a Communist stoker's help – in a Finnish ship at Danzig. This took him, via an uncomfortable call at Lübeck, to Stockholm. He could never have attempted either escape without the detailed information about dockyards sent in by IS 9.[48]

Morale at Colditz as elsewhere varied with the war news, the composition of the camp, and with occasional local triumph or disaster. As Neave had been there himself, he could provide

---

47  Reid, *Colditz*, 461–3, with evocative drawing of the treadmill in use.

48  WO 208/3242, 157–65; and his own *A Prisoner's Progress*. He is now a back-bench Conservative Member of Parliament for Dorset.

detailed knowledge – if it was ever needed – on points of tactics and on personalities. The basic position remained the same there as it does in any camp, in any prison: how to get over, under, or through the barriers round it. As Colditz was the spot where the fine flower of unsuccessful escapers from several nations was concentrated, there were many ingenious attempts, but the second half of the war was less fertile in successful expedients than the first.

The news of the Sagan tragedy was an extra depressant at Colditz, for several of the dead men had friends there, and Colditz was one of the places where the rhythm of escape work was noticeably slowed down by the atrocity. One man there, though, would slow down for nobody: Michael Sinclair.

Michael Sinclair was one of those men who felt that they have been given a second chance at life. On the fourth anniversary of his country's entry into the war, 3 September 1943, an attempt of his to escape from Colditz misfired. He had disguised himself with real brilliance as the camp sergeant-major, beady eye, bristling moustache, highly polished uniform, tricks of speech and intonation, way of walking, everything. At a suitable moment after nightfall, he marched two nondescript 'German' soldiers – also perfectly accoutred, to the eye – up to the main gate, as if relieving the guard. He could not know that, when crossing a little bridge out of sight of the prisoners' quarters, the real sergeant-major always glanced right and left into the ditch it spanned. The omission caught the eye of Corporal (*Gefreiter*) Pilz, who was on the main gate, looked at the newcomer narrowly, and challenged him. After a moment's bluster had proved ineffective, Sinclair was standing with his hands above his head when the over-excited Pilz shot him, at point blank range, through the chest. The bullet passed clean through him, two inches from his heart; and he came out of hospital more determined to escape than ever.

On 19 January 1944 he made another attempt, with one of Colditz's 'ghosts', Jack Best. By a complicated system of ropes, bar cutters, wire cutters, comradely help, and split-second timing, they got clean out of the castle in seventy seconds flat; accidentally pressing an alarm bell on the way, without alerting the guard to what was going on. They were recaptured two days later just short of the Dutch frontier. Best did his solitary under a false name; the camp police had mis-identified him.

Sinclair was obsessed with the idea that he had to escape; the nearer the war seemed to finishing, the keener the obsession became. On 25 September 1944, when those prisoners who cared to do so – he usually did not – were taking an hour's heavily guarded walk in the park below the castle, he suddenly ran for the wire surround, and was shot as he tried to climb it. He died a few minutes later, leaving an unforgettable impression of bravery and strength of character behind him. 'The Red Fox', as the Germans called him, had gone out in what the next visiting Red Cross team described as 'an act of despair [which] throws a light to the adverse conditions under which in particular some of the young officers suffer.' His heroic and pathetic end may have been brought on as much by a death-wish as by a sense of honour affronted by captivity.

There are many NCOs' escapes fit to be mentioned in the topmost class for enterprise and bravery, just as much as those of the better-known officer escape stars.

Consider for example the enterprise of Sergeant Clayton who had a short spell in Oflag XII B at Hadamar. He was sent on a working party to Trier, wangled a job as storeman, secured and secreted some civilian clothes in the store, and on 31 July 1940 when nobody was looking changed into them, and walked away III the railway. He jumped a train into Luxembourg and walked away again, this time with a stolen scythe over his shoulder, into France. He went to his home near Lille to look after his family, an officially reprehensible step but not one for which, forty years on, any but an officious moralist would want to blame him; otherwise, he might have beaten Private Coe by several months.

Driver Thomas Speed, from a field battery in the 51st Highland Division, crawled out of a work camp near Erfurt on 23/24 May 1943 with a party of friends, who separated. He rode south on a series of stolen bicycles – one of them a policeman's – till he came to the Rhine, north-west of Zürich. Quite simply, 'I tied my clothing on my back and swam to the opposite bank. I do not know how long I was in the river, but I was exhausted when I reached the other side.

'A Swiss peasant found me on the river bank and gave me shelter until the police arrived.'

Fusilier Purvis, a miner from Ashington, Northumberland, was in another work commando in the same camp. He took part in the thirty-five man escape which was as much a protest against the lice as a serious attempt to get away; and met a serious punishment. On 29 April 1943 he could bear work in a salt factory no longer, and walked away into the forest. He came back next night to raid the kitchen for food, and then went to look over the labels in the railway goods yard. He got into a railcar full of salt bound for Italy, spent six 'disagreeably thirsty' days in it till he heard French being spoken at a halt, got out safely onto Swiss soil, and was fighting with a maquis in south-west France in August 1944.

John Dominy's book on *The Sergeant Escapers* has done much to bring out the devotion and courage of a group of RAF warrant and non-commissioned officers, many of them regulars, who worked whole-heartedly in Sagan and Heydekrug to confound the King's enemies and make them fall. Warrant Officer J. A. G. Deans, their elected camp leader, is one of his heroes; a greater is Warrant Officer George Grimson, a Putney boy shot down early from a Wellington. All the people who knew him well 'refer to Grimson as the greatest man who ever lived'.

Grimson got out of Sagan disguised as an electrical repair worker, who dropped his pliers on the outside of the topmost barbed wire fence while checking the insulation, slipped past the sentry on the gate to fetch them, and then had the sentry distracted: simple, but a stroke of genius. He was recaptured and sent Heydekrug, out of which he walked dressed as a ferret, with a well forged pass. His object was to set up a ratline – though he did not use that phrase – from Heydekrug to Danzig, or any other suitable port he could find, and thence to Sweden. In the course of this work, he vanished suddenly in April 1944, and it has never been quite clear whether he was shot then or later – Heydekrug is now deep in the USSR. So, conceivably, is Grimson, but it is not easy to think that so marvellously independent-minded a man would endure such a system for long.

At Heydekrug the professional detectives of the Gestapo had met their match. There were frequent and intensive searches, ferrets sneaking about at almost all hours and in almost all places; quite in vain. The duty pilot system – there called 'Tally Ho!' – worked faultlessly. Forgery and tailoring went on pretty well continuously, thanks to a deft piece of carpentry. Late one night, the Heydekrug prisoners built themselves an extra room, about fifteen feet by six, between the camp library and the camp office; its doors were always kept locked unless someone was passing through them. The cover story was that it was for watch repair, and indeed there was always somebody in it repairing a watch, whenever there was a ferret near by. When the Germans tumbled on it, they 'made no comments and appeared to be quite unsuspicious.'

Maps, money and compasses were received from IS 9 without any trouble at all, and in the secret room a wealth of papers could be forged: identity cards for *Volksdeutsch* – *Gummideutsch* the prisoners preferred to call them, that is, citizens of the supposedly defunct Polish republic with Germanic ancestry; or for French volunteer workers, or temporary workers on airfields; passes for Danzig harbour; passes, Luftwaffe or civilian, for the gate of their own camp; Luftwaffe paybooks; civilian travel permits and letters of introduction. A camera, provided by IS 9, was a weighty tool in the blackmail business; a German would be photographed with it arm in arm with a prisoner, be shown his own photograph, and then be told that it would be passed to the commandant – clear evidence of complicity with the prisoners – unless he did what they wanted.

There was a naval camp at Heydekrug, in a quite separate compound with which there was no liaison; but there was close and constant touch between the RAF and USAAF compounds, which were side by side. The extent to which the prisoners ran the camp can be judged by the remark in its history that the Germans never normally knew that a man was missing 'until the Escape Organisation had decided that it was no longer necessary to conceal the fact.' All this tremendous display of solidarity and energy only produced two 'home run' escapes: Warrant Officer Flockhart, whose name had long been familiar in IS 9 because he had taken a leading part in so many attempts, and Aircraftsman Gewelber, an English Jew who prudently enough gave his name to the Germans as Gilbert when he was captured in Crete. Each followed Grimson out through the Heydekrug gate in January 1944 and he saw each onto a boat for Sweden. Townsend-Coles, the next man to go, fell into Gestapo hands and was shot, and thereafter the incipient line seems to have been snuffed out.

The other main airmen's camp, the smaller Stalag Luft III at Dobrilugk, had extra high morale under Warrant Officer R. J. Alexander, RAF, its elected leader. 'The whole Camp was united in any scheme designed to damage the German morale, or to further escape plans.' But like Haina Kloster, it was so small that; there was no privacy for forgery or tailoring; food was short; and so not much escaping could be done.

Airmen were not of course the only users of the Baltic ports. There was, for instance, Signalman P. J. Harkin, who had had a cushy job at general headquarters of the 1939–40 expeditionary force. He had been captured in Calais on 26 May 1940 and after nearly four years as a prisoner decided it was time to go. He listened to such advice as he could get in a working party in Silesia, and chose a companion from his own regiment, J. B. O'Neill. They slipped away from work, with no trouble, on 24 April 1944, and lay up in a deerstalker's hut near Karlsbrunn, living mainly on chocolate. They got some help from French workers, and their camp escape committee had given them money enough to take trains. They tried the Stettin brothel, made friends with some Swedish sailors, walked onto their ship, were hidden by the crew when the Germans searched it, and were in Stockholm on 29 May. The actual process of boarding a ship and hiding on it could be extremely tricky. Philpot's book gives a terrifying immediate account of how perilous it could be, yet Eric Williams, who had got out of Sagan through the same wooden horse, simply strolled up a gangway – following, it is true, a new-made friend in the crew – and got away with it.

For once, there is a slight variant in what an escaper reported at the time and what he published long afterwards. Eric Williams said in his original report that, in a hotel in Stettin, 'On Wednesday, 3 Nov. we had breakfast with a Colonel and two Captains of the German Army, all three producing bread from their pockets to eat with their coffee. We produced American ration biscuits, feeling quite in order.' In his book they all ate bread.

Having got to Sagan, we must now deal with the disaster.

This particular camp's history is unusually full, and can be supplemented further from associated files compiled by its former inmates. It was a camp so large and so well run by its prisoners that the escape set-up in it needs an organigram to explain it. This smells a little of the lamp, but officer prisoners of war have a great deal of time on their hands, and some of them liked to put everything hard and fast. The tunnel committee was larger and more powerful than usual – observe that the diagram overleaf gives it joint control, with the security staff, over a wide range of supplies, as well as the normal sub-sections for engineering and disposal. The wooden horse tunnel was a speciality, and only involved a couple of dozen people intimately. Incidentally,

Wing Commander R. H. Maw built the actual vaulting horse round which the whole scheme turned, and Flight Lieutenant A. W. McKay had the awkward and delicate task of sealing up and hiding the inner end of the tunnel after Williams, Conder and Philpot had disappeared down it. Its success was followed by 'Chattergun Friday', 29 October 1943, when the camp was full of nervous Germans loosing off their machine pistols; fortunately no one was hurt, and they found little. Between sixty and seventy tunnels were begun at one time or another. Three flight lieutenants dug one in the summer of 1942, soon after the camp was opened, went through it to Sagan airfield, 'could not see any promising aircraft', and were caught at Stettin; this was how Jack Best earned his sojourn in Colditz. Three teams each of seventeen men dug a three-hundred-footer, plus a hundred-footer for sand storage; the Germans found both in October 1942.

Eventually the escape committee decided to concentrate on three big tunnels, called 'Tom, Dick and Harry'; and 'Harry', 120 yards long and twenty-five feet deep, was finished in the spring of 1944. There was an enormous tailoring and forging operation to match the tunnelling; it was aided by the dumbness of the guards. The *Feldwebel* in charge of the clothing store for instance removed all the buttons from all the Red Cross overcoats that reached the camp, in the belief that this would render the coats unusable in escapes. Squadron Leader R. Abrahams, responsible to the escape committee for clothing, simply abstracted all the buttons from the shelf on which the *Feldwebel* had put them down.

The escape committee decided to allow a mass break-out through 'Harry'.[49] There has been long debate among prisoners and staff officers about whether mass break-outs are worthwhile. The case against them was that if only ten or a dozen men got out, they could have the best of everything, fine

---

49   Excellent diagram of 'Harry' in P. Brickhill and C. Norton, *Escape to Danger*.

# OVER, UNDER OR THROUGH

## Ideal Camp Organisation

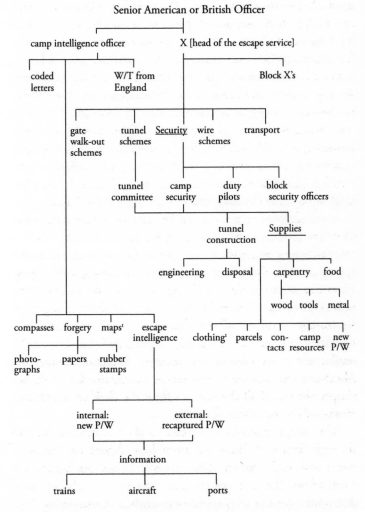

Senior American or British Officer

camp intelligence officer — X [head of the escape service]

coded letters — W/T from England — Block X's

gate walk-out schemes — tunnel schemes — Security — wire schemes — transport

tunnel committee — camp security — duty pilots — block security officers

tunnel construction — Supplies

engineering — disposal — carpentry — food

wood — tools — metal

compasses — forgery — maps[1] — escape intelligence — clothing[1] — parcels — contacts — camp resources — new P/W

photographs — papers — rubber stamps

internal: new P/W — external: recaptured P/W

information

trains — aircraft — ports

[1]   In the original – WO 208/3244, 6 – these two were counterchanged, either by an error of memory, or to suit a peculiar set of camp conditions and personalities.

clothes, good maps, plenty of money, practically perfect papers; whereas a large party was bound to overstrain the resources of the camp's forgery and tailoring departments. It was generally held that proper civilian clothes were twice as much use at least as camp-made coats, and the quantity of them was bound to be limited. On the other hand, was it reasonable to ask or to order several hundred people to toil for months on an escape scheme, and then not allow them to participate? MI 9 and MIS-X had been pouring in dyes, maps, money, patterned blankets and so on for years; searches by the Germans seldom found much of importance. The committee, having weighed all this up, came down in favour of a mass escape, provided that those who had done the hardest parts of the work went first. The rest drew lots.

Paul Brickhill has given an excellent account both of the digging, and of the final difficulty – marshalling 200 people into a single hut. At 22:15 on 24 March 1944 Flight Lieutenant L. C. Bull, RAF, opened the exit shaft, got out, and saw the next twenty men through the exit. Many of the escapers had not been down a tunnel before; many had bundles with them too fat to fit. By 2 a.m. it was clear that only one hundred at best, not two, were going to get through; at 04.50 hours it was decided that the eighty-seventh escaper was to be the last.

'Just as this man was disappearing down the entrance shaft, a shot was heard. The escapers still in the tunnel were called back, men were put to watch from every window, and the remainder of the two hundred started burning all their forged papers, getting out of their civilian clothes and hiding all their compasses and food.'

Seventy-nine people passed through the tunnel. Three were arrested close to the exit. Three – all in the first batch to leave, and all Continentals by birth – got right through to the United Kingdom: Flight Lieutenant van der Stok, who came through Holland and France, and two Norwegian Spitfire pilots, Sergeant Pel Bergsland and Second Lieutenant J. E. Miller. They went together straight to Stettin, and were in Sweden within ten days. All the remaining seventy-three were recaptured in various parts of the Reich – Roger Bushell got as far as Saarbrücken, with a friend; several others got into Austria. Fifty of them were shot dead, after recapture, without trial, on orders from the top.

Each of the dead men was said to have been shot while trying to escape. Contrary to the otherwise unvaried practice of burial,[50] all their bodies were cremated. Detailed study of where each urn full of ashes returned to Sagan came from made it possible to establish the place of death in every case. The prisoners' clothing was also all returned to Sagan; none of it bore any bloodstains or bullet holes. And there were no wounded. For once, it is pretty clear who decided what. In the words of Wileden, a fairly senior SS officer in charge of the criminal police at Breslau, 'The shooting took place on the express personal orders of the former Führer Adolf Hitler.'

Two major-generals, one about to hand over to the other the command of the *Kriegsgefangenenwesen*, the office for administering prisoners of war – Graevenitz, who retired in April, and Westhoff – went to see Field-Marshal Keitel, the head of Hitler's military staff, who was 'very excited and nervous and said: "Gentlemen, this is a bad business ... Gentlemen, these escapes must stop. We must set an example. We shall take very severe measures. I can only tell you that the men who have escaped will be shot – probably the majority of them are dead already." Graevenitz said: "But Sir, that's out of the question. Escape isn't a dishonourable offence. That is specially laid down in the convention." Keitel replied, "I don't care a damn; we discussed it in the Führer's presence and it cannot be altered."' Gestapo Müller handed down the order, and declared the subject 'forbidden'. Westhoff complained that 'I didn't sleep a wink for nights

---

50   We are glad to acknowledge our indebtedness to the Imperial War Museum for sight of an unnumbered file of papers on which the next two paragraphs mainly rely. On a macabre detail, see Dominy, *Sergeant Escapers*, n – 13.

on end. Alter all; one does have one's feelings of honour. But we couldn't do anything about it.' The bankruptcy to which the German officer class had reduced itself could hardly be more clearly expressed. Even Kaltenbrunner, the head of German security, not the most fragrant of Nazis, said 'I considered it a dirty affair', when lying to exculpate himself from any part in the Sagan executions.

No principle is discernible by which some were taken, and some were left. Among those who were left was 'Wings' Day, a member of the Sagan escape committee from a very early stage. He, on being arrested, was neither shot nor returned to Sagan: he was put in a place of safety, the *Straflager* at Sachsenhausen concentration camp, while higher authorities were consulted about who would rid them of this turbulent fellow. Day wasted no time in consulting higher authorities than his own common sense. He and a few other recaptured fellow escapers in the same hut began a tunnel within twenty-four hours of arrival, digging as fast as they could and dumping the spoil beneath their hut. Ten days later they were out. They had no papers, no money, no maps; though Day had retained a small MI 9 compass. They moved by night, westward, and hid by day. By bad luck they were reported to the police as suspected looters; the luck turned to their advantage. For they were rearrested and recorded in the books of the ordinary police; it was therefore more awkward for the Gestapo to rub them out as if they had never been outside Sachsenhausen. They were returned to an *innere Straflager* at that grim camp, chained in separate cells; were moved south in April 1945 to be mixed in with the more famous *Prominente* near the Brenner; and were eventually rescued by an American patrol as a result of a stroke of Day's initiative.

# The Asian War: 1941–45

The war in Asia ran more or less in parallel with the war in Europe, but not quite at the same times. It ran from 1937–45 for the Chinese and Japanese governments, 1934–49 for the Chinese Communists, 1941–5 for the Americans, the British and the Dutch, 1940–2 for the French: the dates give a faint initial notion of the complexity of the problems. The reader who wants more detail can still be referred to Renouvin for the historical background, Calvocoressi and Wint for an accurate summary of the campaigns. What made complexity almost infinitely dense for MIS-X and MI 9 was the attitude of the Japanese towards any prisoners they took: this was so hostile, and the distances of Asia and the Pacific are so vast, that in MIS-X it was at first believed that there would hardly be any opportunities for the section to work there.

Time brought opportunity, but not with ease: infinite hardship and suffering were the lot of prisoners in Asia. For the Japanese held a still more honour-ridden concept of warfare than did their opponents of European origin or descent. Japanese soldiers, sailors and airmen alike were brought up to believe surrender to be un-thinkably dishonourable. The rigid rules of their society had come to decree that if anybody nevertheless did surrender, and survived, and returned home, he would not be received back into the community; his own wife, his own children would reject him. So they hardly ever surrendered, unwounded, till very late in the war; and looked with abhorrence on any opponent who had brought himself to commit an act that so disgusted them. Officer prisoners from the Allied forces, even senior ones, were indulged little if at all;

other ranks got still shorter shrift. Their prisoner of war camps were strictly guarded, by sentries who would shoot a prisoner with no more compunction than they would shoot a rat; and run on a system of reprisals, not stopping short of the death penalty for recaptured escapers or for any fellow prisoner who seemed to have helped in preparing an escape.

Moreover, even if someone of European descent did manage to escape from a Japanese camp, he ran into two all but insuperable difficulties. One was the sheer size of Asia – the colossal distances to be covered, on foot, across formidably severe terrain. The other was that it was impossible for a white- or black-skinned escaper to make himself look like the population round him. Unless he had extraordinary luck, short stature, dense wrappings, and darkness, he was bound to stand out in any crowd of people, to be the thing above all that men on the run always seek not to be – conspicuous. That several score people were nevertheless spirited away from occupied Hong Kong is one of the oddest tales this book has to tell. From Singapore, in the closing stages of that disastrous campaign, a few men of enterprise did manage to get away by sea; wholly on their own initiative, and often against orders. From the camps in Malaya, Burma, Thailand, hardly a soul could escape, save for one large group of enterprising Indian soldiers.

It was early clear in Whitehall how bad things were. For instance, a Foreign Office inquiry to Chungking about the accuracy of a *Manchester Guardian* report of killings in Hong Kong after the surrender there on Christmas Day 1941 produced an immediate reply – 'at least three cases of torture and murder of prisoners appear substantiated.' Three weeks later, stiffer reports were to be had: after the public execution of two officer prisoners and three nurses, 'Other British nurses were then raped by Japanese troops. Fifty bodies of British Officers and men seen bayoneted to death in one area their hands and feet first being tied ... Conditions in prisoner's camp deplorable. Housed in wrecked huts without doors windows light or sanitation. No complaints possible. This studied barbarism undoubtedly employed with object of breaking morale.'

None of this was made public at the time, and as late as the autumn of 1945 it was still MI 9's object to minimise tales of atrocity lest they cause needless distress to the relatives of those who had gone into Japanese captivity. This merciful view we are happy to accept, but after so long an interval it is allowable to instance the sort of thing that went on. For relatives' and decency's sake, there is no need to be specific about names.

As the Japanese despised their prisoners, they treated them with unusual savagery; except that they shrank from the final solution of genocide, they were no gentler with Europeans or Americans than the Nazis were with Jews. It was quite common for recaptured escapers to be beheaded or bayoneted to death, in public. The one method of execution the Japanese never used was shooting: in van der Post's phrase, 'held in some profound *oubliette* of their own minds,' they beheaded or stabbed or strangled or buried alive instead. One or two more examples, beyond that of the three Voluntary Aid Detachment uniformed nurses whose Christmas present it was in 1941 to be publicly executed on their hospital forecourt, may set the deplorable tone. Three men who escaped from a camp in Java were stripped naked on recapture, lashed to the barbed wire fence round it, and slowly bayoneted to death in the sight of their paraded fellow prisoners: to discourage the rest from contemplating escape. The same fate, also in Java, awaited three men who had done nothing more offensive to the Japanese than each receive from his own wife's hands a small parcel during a forced march.

Against this degree of sadism, only the other side's victory is ever likely to provide a defence; and a retrospective defence at that. 'A slow worker, that Time, and no anaesthetist', as Stevie Smith remarked. And against that sort of enemy there was not an enormous amount that either MI 9 or MIS-X could do.

Part of the trouble was that terror had its intended effect; it deterred all sorts of people from wanting to run any risk.

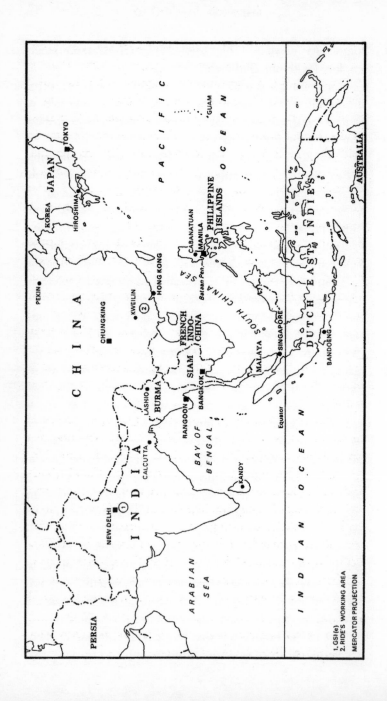

Senior officers captured at Hong Kong were especially sensitive on this point. Either they had not read Army Training Memorandum 34, or they decided to ignore it, for they ruled that conditions in Hong Kong were such that no one was to try to get away. As an unhappy subordinate put it, 'The most disappointing feature of the officers' camp was the manner in which the great majority accepted their prison life and appeared to be contented with it, never entertaining any serious thoughts of attempting escape, or in any way wishing to take part in further hostilities. No doubt this was largely, if not in many cases entirely, due to the lead set by the senior officers, who were so strong in their determination that no one should attempt to escape.' Of one officer who did get out, his colonel remarked sourly that the fellow would undoubtedly be court-martialled for desertion if he got through. The state of prisoners' morale in the Hong Kong camps was several times described as bad by those who had managed to leave, and one or two of them dropped hints that the colony had not been defended with the vigour to be expected of a British Imperial garrison: a point that an official or a regimental history can hardly be expected to touch.

It was from Hong Kong nevertheless that there developed the British Army Aid Group (BAAG), MI 9's altogether extraordinary contribution to the Asian war, which worked for three years in Kwangtung, the province in Hong Kong's hinterland, and in Kwangsi, the next province to the west of it, on a combined task of rescue and intelligence. BAAG was set up by the local initiative of a single man, Lieutenant-Colonel (Sir) Leslie Ride, quite independently of MI 9's advance base in New Delhi. This base, called GS 1(e) – later 'E' Group – was set up in October 1941 by Lieutenant-Colonel Robin Ridgway, in peacetime a modern languages master at Winchester.[51] But Ridgway's

---

51    We are particularly grateful to his widow, now Mrs Anne Grantham, JP, for access to his papers.

existence was at first unknown to Brigadier Grimsdale, the military attaché in Chungking, to whom Ride originally reported. Though the omission was cleared up before long, it illustrates the kind of complication with which Ride had to deal.

China was not for British official purposes a theatre of war; that was why the War Office had omitted Grimsdale from the list of those informed of GS I(e)'s existence. What indeed was China in 1942? It was an enormous, amorphous mess, nominally ruled by Generalissimo Chiang Kai-shek from Chungking, where the apparatus of a central government – including a diplomatic corps – was maintained. In fact Chiang's authority did not often extend far. Several war-lords competed with each other, with the Japanese, and with the Chinese Communist party for control of south China; most of north-east China was securely – for the time being – in Japanese hands; an embryo Communist state existed in north central China already. Grimsdale and his successor Hayes, as military attachés at Chungking and therefore part of an established British embassy, had to go through the form of getting Chiang's regime's approval for all they did. Ride as a British officer working in an allied country had to subordinate himself to the British military attaché, and therefore to Chiang. Hence some of the worst of his troubles.

For, unknown to him, a personage of much weight at Chungking – General Tai Li, the chief of Chiang's secret services – was passionately anti-British, and particularly hostile to the government of Hong Kong. Tai Li had visited Hong Kong in the summer of 1941, had been found by the local security authorities to be setting up what they described as a private Gestapo among the colony's Chinese inhabitants, had been abruptly hustled out of the territory, and had sworn revenge. He therefore seized every opportunity that came his way to obstruct any initiative that seemed to stem from Hong Kong. Ride thought this was simply oriental bureaucratic delay; it is reasonable to assume malice as well.

Ride, born in Australia in 1898, had twice been wounded

in the Australian army in 1917–18, had distinguished himself at Melbourne University and at New College, Oxford, and had become professor of physiology at Hong Kong at the age of thirty. He held his army rank as commander of the field ambulance unit of the Hong Kong Volunteer Corps, and surrendered with everybody else. It was at once clear to him that the prisoners of war in Hong Kong – including about 600 officers and nearly 9,000 other ranks – were in grave need of medical services; and that neither the Japanese, nor their own seniors, were going to lift a finger to provide them. He therefore saw his own duty clear: to get out fast, and get something set up from outside.

He managed to get smuggled into captivity five decent civilian suits. Choosing his moment and his sentry carefully on the evening of 9 January 1942, he and four friends dressed up in them; they looked utterly unlike their fellow prisoners, who were wearing scraps and tatters of uniform, and walked out of camp unchallenged.[52] They benefited from one of MI 9's soundest rules: if you escape, escape quickly. Overnight he found friends, and was outside British territory early on the 10 January. He found that 'safety lay almost at the gates of the camps', for the Communist guerillas who held the immediate hinterland were intensely anti-Japanese. He progressed through the territory they controlled, and through a belt run by pro-Chiang guerrillas, into an area run by more or less orderly Chungking government forces, and was in the capital by mid-February, to provide Grimsdale with some authentic tales of atrocity quoted just now. Grimsdale sent him back to Kwangtung province late in February, to organise further escapes and do what he could for those still in Japanese hands. For over three years Ride's British Army Aid Group worked on, usually with its main base at Kweilin. As soon as he got back to his working area in early March, he found a few more service

---

52    Alan Birch in *South China Daily News*, 12 October 1973, the first of two useful articles (the other came out next day) on BAAG.

escapers, whom he recruited; he collected also a number of
Chinese refugees from Hong Kong, who stayed with him. His
eventual strength, counting in the families of these Chinese,
rose in September 1944 – when he had to pull out westwards –
to 248. How far this was above his establishment we shall not
know till 2010, when the relevant file is to be opened; why on
earth, one wonders, is it still closed? He was formally appointed
MI 9 representative on 16 May 1942, with a right to call on up
to £3,000 a quarter from the military attaché's funds. By then
he was already hard at work, fortified by a visit from Grimsdale
and from John Keswick of Jardine, Matheson's and SOE, who
brought with them the news that Madame Chiang herself was
interested in what he was doing. This was cheering, but as Ride
remarked later, 'Is it any wonder that a BAAG chit was more
valuable in these forward areas than an official chungking pass?'
For his mission was soon handling about 30,000 patients a year,
providing medical aid on a scale undreamed of for centuries in
an area where the Chinese army 'had no medical service at all',
and at a moment of famine in 1943 fed 6,000 people a day.

Yet he was in charge of something much more than a local
honestly run welfare organisation. During the second half of
1942 he built up a ring of forward posts round both Hong
Kong and Canton, the great port eighty miles up-river from
it. Each post's orders ran: '(i) Absolute frankness with the
Chinese officials concerning our work; (ii) Nothing to be left
undone which would raise British prestige; nothing to be done
which would lower it; (iii) Maximum medical attention to all
guerrillas, soldiers and officials in the area; (iv) Distribution of
authentic war news to all official Chinese bodies and foreigners in the area; (v) Maximum help within our limited means
to the Chinese Forces and their full access to our intelligence
reports concerning the enemy.' Absolute frankness was a rarity
in China, and reaped large local rewards. It helped Ride to get
on well with Marshal Li Tsai-sum, Chiang Kai-shek's rival and
nominal subordinate at Kweilin. He put out a weekly Kweilin

Intelligence Summary (KWIZ), which was eagerly read by the limited circles it reached.[53] It was based partly on what he learned from refugees and escapers, partly from what his agents told him. The twice-daily weather reports which his forward posts made as a matter of routine were of essential interest to Chennault's 'Flying Tigers' and to all other Allied air forces in China; as important as the twice-daily weather reports from the Polish Home Army were to bomber forces in Britain.

These immediacies apart, Ride's reports had to be issued from Kweilin by runner – it took them a fortnight to get to Chungking. Tai Li's hand was heavy enough to ensure that Ride never had adequate wireless facilities; indeed Ride had to get Chungking's permission for any of his officers to change his permanent post at all. This permission never took less than four weeks, might take as long as four months to be granted. The main trouble here, apart from Tai Li's jealousy, was political. For BAAG found that 'the most active, reliable, efficient and anti-Japanese of all the Chinese organisations' was the Communist party, which controlled the hinterland of Hong Kong; while 'As far as the Central Government was concerned, the reds were public enemy No. 1; the Japanese came a poor second.' A couple of British other-rank escapers from the Argyle Street main camp in Hong Kong, Privates Daniel Hodges and Joseph Gallagher of the Royal Scots, gave their hosts some small arms instruction, as a return for the hospitality they received while crossing Communist territory. Both privates got Distinguished Conduct Medals, but for years afterwards BAAG was accused by officialdom of 'training the Reds'. In Ride's words, 'Security as we know it did not exist in S[outh] China,' in spite of six competing secret police forces; it was a daily wonder to Ride that he and his colleagues did not suffer much more than they

---

53    Unhappily only the concluding number is on file (WO 208/3492); it deals with the engineering operations Ride conducted when he left Kweilin. The rest are either withheld, destroyed, or mislaid.

did from betrayals. They managed to get a surprising amount done, on their proper front of escape and evasion as well as in providing intelligence and welfare.

Ride claimed that only two air force evaders in his territory were not picked up and brought out to safety by his rescue teams; and these two were too badly wounded to leave the wreck of their aircraft, where the Japanese found them. Thirty-eight American airmen were saved, including one who landed actually within sight of the Argyle Street camp, but was nevertheless at once spirited away. Vast local publicity attended every American evasion; the British were moved more discreetly. The 'almost complete lack of escape-mindedness among the prisoners' in Hong Kong itself militated against much success. Camp morale was improved by messages Ride managed to smuggle in, written in invisible ink, carried by Chinese drivers of Japanese vehicles, but the Japanese were so intensely suspicious and watchful that even this channel did not flow smoothly. It was used nevertheless for 'very valuable' supplies of medical drugs. In July 1943 there was a disaster. One driver was arrested; what emerged under torture implicated two more; and several officer prisoners were hauled in as well. One of these Captain Douglas Ford of the Royal Scots, underwent protracted torture for several weeks on end without breathing a word of what his enemies wanted to hear. This stoicism earned him even his torturers' respect – they placed him on the right of two men senior to himself when all three were at last executed – and a posthumous George Cross.

Ride made a plan to seize Kai-tak airfield and carry out a sudden mass evacuation by air – 'the unexpected always confuses and irritates the Japanese' – but to envisage this was to build castles in the air: where was he going to get no Dakotas and a three-battalion covering party? Thirty-three actual escapes from the Japanese in Hong Kong were recorded up to the end of May 1943, including, besides Ride, two naval and two army officers and the Chinese Private Lee, of Ride's field ambulance, who got out with him on 9 January 1942; and three subalterns from 5 Light Anti-Aircraft Regiment, White, Clague and Pearce. (Sir) Douglas Clague stayed with Ride for many months, and stayed on with MI 9 after he left China, rising to be a lieutenant-colonel before the war's end and doing much valuable work.

Having repeatedly failed to get prisoners of war away in any quantity, Ride decided to use his developing contacts in Hong Kong to harm the Japanese in other ways. Two important British bankers were smuggled out 'in broad daylight and from the heart of the city'. Some hundreds of other people whose services were likely to be useful to the Crown, of British, of Indian and of Chinese origin, were persuaded to leave Hong Kong, with their families; they were routed westward, through the Portugese territory at Macao, thus leaving Ride's military ratlines which ran north-westward uncluttered by civilian traffic. A hundred and twenty-seven of them formed themselves into a Hong Kong Volunteer Company, and fought in Burma; others helped the war effort in other ways.

The most ingeniously devised of these parties, brought out piecemeal – some scores at a time – through a Chinese agent of BAAG, consisted of the dockyard artificers, 'matey s' as they were locally called: most of them British, many of them with Chinese wives. Wives and children came too. The brilliance of this stroke lay in the fact that without the mateys – and almost all of them left – the value of Hong Kong dockyard to the Japanese slumped; it became in fact a liability, as skilled workmen had to be imported from Japan to keep it going. They were valuable also for intelligence they brought with them, both about the dockyard area and about the state of the Japanese warships they had handled.

Yet for intelligence purposes they were eclipsed by Ride's Post Y, so placed in the New Territories that it could keep Kowloon, Hong Kong harbour, Kai-tak airfield, and the main POW camps at Argyle Street and Sham Shui-po 'under constant observation' for some months from the autumn of 1942. As Post Y had to work through Communist logistic support, and Tai Li got to know of the fact, the post had to be closed down early in 1943: a worse example of secret service short-sightedness it would be hard to find.

Ride's own work was beyond price. At the moment he began, the British were regarded with greater contempt by the Chinese than had been the case for a century. His mission's devotion, straightforwardness, and steadfastness made a strong impression, and in September 1944 when the Japanese broke through locally and advanced on Kweilin the favourable impression became stronger still. Ride had already remarked the readiness of the Chinese to run away at the first sign of an attack; he was also fully aware of the perilous nature of the province's roads. He found that the Americans were abandoning on the local airfield a large stock of 500-lb bombs. He packed off all his staff and their families westward, got hold of some elementary engineers' stores, and with a few friends set out to demolish every bridge, every gorge along the visible Japanese axis of advance. He gave a magnificent example of how to conduct a fighting retreat. In reward, he was summoned to Chungking to receive a rocket from Grimsdale for using demolition stores without authority.

This petty conclusion symbolised what was happening to BAAG. Its relations with SOE were, as they had been from the start, excellent. Colin Mackenzie, SOE's head in south-east Asia – one of the most influential figures in the war there, unmentioned in any published work of history till July 1978 – knew and admired Ride, and supported BAAG's work in every way he could. MI 6 was a good deal less favourable. Ride was given to understand that he had the monopoly for the provision of intelligence from the area where he worked; and then found MI 6 busy counteracting him. OSS offered him full co-operation; and then tried to bribe his runners behind his back, so that OSS could see what news he had from Hong Kong before it appeared in his intelligence summaries. Fourteenth US Air Force expressed itself highly satisfied with all the information he provided; and then set up an intelligence service of its own. MIS-X sent Lieutenant Schoyer on a voyage of reconnaissance to Kweilin in September 1943; and then instituted an elaborate Air Ground Aid Service (AGAS) to take over the whole of Ride's work of helping evaders.

Ride had been operating, with great gallantry, skill and flair, on a shoestring. As all these various professional bodies moved in, he found himself elbowed out of the way: defeated by a mixture of malice, ignorance, jealousy, empire-building and anti-imperialism. The *coup de grâce*, or what would have been a *coup de grâce* to any less resilient unit, was applied by a newly-formed administrative headquarters called British Troops in China. Just as Tai Li's almost interminable objections had been overborne, and BAAG had got some efficient wireless and telephone equipment – manned by Ride's Chinese assistants, who were excellent clerks – British Troops in China laid down that all communications equipment was in all circumstances to be handled by members of the Royal Corps of Signals. At this degree of over-centralisation Ride protested in vain.

Before we leave the prisoners in Hong Kong for other Asian theatres of war, one more character commands mention: a young New Zealand naval volunteer lieutenant, R. B. Goodwin. He was wounded on 21 December 1941 and in hospital when he became a captive. As soon as he was able to stand, he started planning to escape; it took him nearly three years. Food was a main difficulty; so far as British doctors could tell, 'on a calorie basis, PWs were all being slowly starved to death', and when in the spring of 1944 Red Cross food at last started to arrive in bulk, the first the prisoners knew of it was when the pile of empty tins outside their guards' quarters overtopped the fence. Petty annoyances were legion: when the prisoners levelled a sports field, the Japanese took it over; when they grew some tomatoes, the Japanese dug the crop in when it started to turn ripe; 'it was some months before everyone had a bed', and the bed-bugs were so bad that some still preferred the concrete of the floor.

Goodwin's intention to leave did not waver. At last, on the blustery night of 16/17 July 1944, he tiptoed out of his hut at Sham Shui-po and clambered over the main wire barrier. He made a dreadful noise, but no sentry came. He got to the sea wall, swam across the bay, and for some days hid in bamboo thickets by day and moved on a little each night. Once a woman came and cut at his thicket till she saw him, but did not give him away. Once he walked slap into two sentries, but 'just walked silently backwards until completely out of sight again' – an advantage of being barefoot, however badly his feet were lacerated. Another time, 'he felt that something was wrong and stopped to listen. Suddenly a sentry grounded his rifle with a crash a few feet in front of him and he retired rapidly.' At last on 27 July he met some friendly Chinese and was wafted through to one of Ride's British officers whom he met on 3 August. By then, from strain and malnutrition, he was nearly blind; his sight took three months to recover. His was a tremendous feat of initiative and endurance, and an epitome of the spirit Crockatt tried to inculcate throughout the armed forces.

The nearest we have found to an official history of AGAS makes interesting reading. Fragments in USAF formation histories are useful also, such as a mention of Lieutenant Hogon of the 311th Fighter Group who was shot down in November 1943, presumably somewhere in Japanese-occupied China, spent eighteen months in prison, lost three close friends who died in agony, endured lice, filth, disease, thirst and hunger, and on rejoining his group in June 1945, 'courteous, considerate and gracious as always', made it his first business to seek out the man who had packed his parachute and thank him for having done his job properly. Unluckily the report does not explain how or whence AGAS recovered him.

In the last year of the war, several units of B-29 Superfortresses were operating over China, and there are a number of extraordinary tales of how crews managed to walk out from the edge of Japanese-controlled territory into Allied hands; usually with help from AGAS, sometimes with help from BAAG. These evasions succeeded because above all, in the words of a late MIS-X circular, ninety-nine per cent of the Chinese were ready to help. 'Throughout North China, the farmers have been instructed to take care of evaders and lead them at once to the guerrillas', whose help was to be relied on. These Communist troops 'know what they are fighting for and the Japanese have behaved so savagely that they also know against whom they are fighting.' Of course there were perils in the way; in Fukien province, for example, 'In the mountainous region, tigers prowl during the hours of darkness. Be alert, and do not walk the mountain paths at night.' By day life is safer, for 'All Fukien has been organised to render assistance to downed airmen'; the helpers included all the magistrates and the telephone operators. (Fukien is the coastal province north-east of Hong Kong.)

An AGAS explorer who went up-country into the Lolos' area of western China in the summer of 1944 passed successively a solitary and rather overbearing British Pentecostal missionary, a village where no white man had been for thirty years, and a few days later a place where 'No white man has ever been in this part of the world before and the writer was like a freak in a sideshow.' He established that 'A crew which bails out, one hour by air from its base needs a month's time in which to return by foot and horseback.' One crew had fallen among some opium-eating Lolos who first robbed them – taking them for Japanese – and then got to like them, gave them a tremendous party, and in the end let them find their own way home, bearing with them to pay their way a frying-pan from one of their escape kits filled with opium. Contrast the American bomber crew, who bailed out in Burma in December 1944, were feasted by the Japanese, and then all executed next day: the Japanese thought this a great joke.

Clayton Hutton's pocket escape kits had never run even to a Tommy cooker, let alone anything as big as a frying pan. Much more elaborate equipment had been worked out for the fresh requirements of the Far East. E Group and MIS-X pooled some ideas, and disposed – they hoped – of a continual trouble in Europe: people would leave their kit behind, or carry it loose in a pocket so that it fell out during a parachute drop. MI 9 found a good formula to cover this, and prefixed it to the most secret bulletin which was the intelligence officers' Bible on escape:

> He dropped into the garden and crept into some bushes. To his horror he realised he had left his food tablets, maps and compass on the wrong side of the wall, as a result of which he later suffered considerably.

This prisoner, who escaped in the Boer War, is now the
BRITISH PRIME MINISTER
BUT
THE MORAL IS STILL THE SAME.
*ALWAYS CARRY YOUR ESCAPE AIDS WITH
YOU.*

The RAF designed a garment called the Beadon suit, which included maps, hacksaw, compass, machete, anti-malarial tablets, and escape kit, all in buttoned pockets to avoid Churchill's disaster. The suit was made in a material light enough to be worn over a minimum of clothing in the tropics without bringing its wearer to the boil. The Americans added a mess tin, a frying pan and a smokeless field cooker, all done up in a package called an E-kit which was attached to parachute harness. Later they devised their own suit, called an E-vest, to do the carrying.

After all, the Japanese had proved by their advance through the Malay states that the jungle which the British had thought impenetrable to troops – so impenetrable that all Singapore's permanent defences faced seaward – was no more impenetrable than the Ardennes had been impassable to armour in May 1940. Wingate's Chindit expeditions, aided by the volunteer company

Ride had brought out of Hong Kong, proceeded to overtrump the Japanese in 1943–4 the jungle of north Burma. E Group and MIS-X were ready to overtrump them on a smaller scale anywhere that aircrew or ground troops could be found to rise to the challenge. The headquarter staff of each body regarded themselves simply as vehicles for passing on Crockatt's and Johnston's orders, and for adapting those orders to east Asian and Pacific conditions; they took no personal credit for the rescues secured by individual junior explorers at and beyond the fighting fronts, and by the dogged courage of the evaders.

It will be as well to interject who was in charge of E Group's work. Ridgway started off in October 1941 in GS 1(d), a particularly secret corner of the New Delhi intelligence directorate. He formed GS 1(e) as an independent section in May 1942 – he and Ride got their charters to act at the same time; and he provided Ride's channel of approach, when one was needed, to the rest of the intelligence and general staff world. He paid one valuable visit to Kweilin himself in the summer of 1943. Ride was able to provide him *inter alia* with a set of Japanese printers' type, which was useful in New Delhi. Ridgway had a small efficient staff under him, including notably Major R. C. Jackman his GSO 2, who joined him in September 1942 and served useful attachments at Highgate, Beaconsfield and Washington in 1943. In June 1944 Ridgway moved on to be personal assistant to Sir Claude Auchinleck, then commander-in-chief, India; and Jackman, promoted lieutenant-colonel, took over the section and ran it for the rest of the war.[54]

GS I(e)'s name was changed to E Group in the autumn of 1943, when Mountbatten took over supreme command in south-east Asia. He ran his war from Kandy in Ceylon (now Sri Lanka), and E Group consonantly had an office there under Lieutenant-Commander Brochie, RN; there was also an operational

---

54  Jackman provides the main source for this paragraph and the next five.

headquarters at Calcutta under Clague, who by this time was a major. This dispersal of headquarter effort, imposed by the scale of Asia, was not without its hardships. A staff officer ordered to mount an operation into Indo-China complained that it was like trying to operate into the Caucasus from a headquarters divided between London, Vienna, and Sfax in Tunisia.

As there was virtually no communication with the prison camps, E Group could not hope to emulate the achievements of MI 9 and MIS-X in Europe. There was no local amalgamation with MIS-X. China apart, the American involvement in the war as viewed from New Delhi or Kandy was virtually restricted to air operations northward over 'the Hump' in northern Burma, and the occasional ground incursion southward into the same area by the forces of General Stilwell. And in any case MIS-X's incursions into Asia were belated. Ridgway's New Delhi office made up and distributed evasion kits, silk maps and blood chits; its only direct attempt at an active operation, made early, was a disaster. When Singapore and the Dutch East Indies fell in the spring of 1942, it was at once clear that the huge island of Sumatra, some 1,100 miles long, had on it a great number of prisoners of war and of civilians who had been interned, and Ridgway determined to send a small party on reconnaissance to try to get some definite news. The party was safely put ashore from a submarine; not a word was ever heard from or of it again.

Thereafter, E Group concentrated on building up by more orthodox means, such as air reconnaissance, an adequate body of information about where prisoners of war were being kept; eventually with striking success. Any data that it got were promptly distributed to the RAF and USAF, in an attempt to preserve prisoners from avoidable bombing attacks. The Japanese, not being bound by the Geneva Convention they had never ratified, quite often put prisoners' camps alongside ammunition dumps.

The other great preoccupation was with jungle training. E Group ran two schools for this, one in Ceylon under Squadron

Leader Puckridge who had been a Malayan planter, the other in Assam (north-east of Calcutta) under Squadron Leader D. Vint, who had long worked in Siam (Thailand). Their lectures, based on first-hand knowledge, encouraged people cast adrift in the depths of south-east Asia not to feel lost or even discouraged.

As an MIS-X note put it of a couple of light aircraft pilots who had walked out after a crash in central Burma, 'with gun, machete, compass, canteen, halozone tablets and matches, enough clothing and plenty of good old common sense, the Burma jungle need not be a nightmare to anyone. Hang on to that chute – it's the roof over your head and the bed under your back.' Westerners needed to be told a few simple facts of jungle life: what to eat, what not to think of eating; how to use bamboo, as spear, staff, water-carrier, mug, fuel, raft or house;[55] how to scare off snakes and animals, always much more alarmed than a confident man; how to dispose of leeches; how and when to hide and to show oneself. People who enjoy as a treat the *coeurs de palmier* that sometimes appear as *hors d'oeuvres* in expensive restaurants may like to reflect that evaders were encouraged to shin up palm trees and cut these delicious, tender shoots raw from their tops.

In principle, once the novelty of Japanese occupation had worn off, most of the populations of Japanese-held territories were inclined to help rather than to hinder Allied escapers and evaders. Japanese promises of independence proved hollow, and Tokyo turned out no more agreeable a remote imperial capital than London, Paris or The Hague. There were a few exceptions: Indians in Malaya were to be avoided at all costs, as were Arabs in the Celebes. The Menadonese in the Celebes, on the other hand, being Christians, were always likely to help. The Americans moreover were everywhere more welcome than the British. For in the only part of the combat area where they had

---

55   E Group produced an excellent illustrated pamphlet on this, attached to WO 208/3252, 'E' Group Bulletin.

any political past of their own, the Philippine Islands, they had been seen as some improvement on their Spanish predecessors, and were already known to envisage Filipino independence. Henry L. Stimson, called out of retirement to be Roosevelt's Secretary for War, had been a popular governor at Manila in the late 1920s, not least because his wife was polite enough to wear Filipina dress at an official reception.

Yet formal activity by MIS-X came late. Johnston and Holt were eager to press on with the European war, and neither at first believed in any Asian possibilities. De Bruyne heard something of Ride's work from Crockatt, and urged Johnston to reconsider. A joint Australo-Americo-British MIS-X headquarters for the south-west Pacific was set up at Brisbane late in 1943 under Wing Commander Lamb, RAAF, and Major Kraus, USAF, and was soon able to provide safe area maps, detailed escape briefings on local attitudes, and other useful intelligence. Kraus had had 6,171 combat aircrew briefed by the middle of March 1944. Some of its bulletins have been quoted already. It was not until 8 November 1944 that Lieutenant-Colonel Robley E. Winfrey could report to Johnston that an MIS-X staff had been set up in the Pacific Ocean Area.

This and the other Far Eastern branches of MIS-X had wider responsibilities than this book is able to encompass. For, beyond training fighting men in how to behave if by mischance they fell into enemy hands, and in how to survive if a different mischance cast them on their own resources in the jungle, MIS-X there tackled all the problems of air-sea rescue. These involved a myriad of difficulties about timing, signalling, wavelengths, maps, charts, availability of air and sea rescue craft and crews to man them, worth one day the detailed study this book cannot hope to provide.

A word or two is needed about how to behave in Japanese hands, even though one American escaper went so far as to say that any other fate was preferable, short of suicide. Several versions of the standard MIS-X lecture on the subject have survived. They boil down to this: be patient, courteous and respectful in quite firmly declining to give any information beyond your name, rank and number; when pressed, as you certainly will be, explain that your military code forbids you to say more. In no circumstances try to deceive your enemy, and do not dream of appearing superior to him; on the contrary, flatter him and his service. E Group added a warning not to cringe, and suggested that it was best to play dumb, and not mind that the interrogator was probably in fact dumber. The golden rules were simple: '*Your duty on capture is to avoid being a source of information and to escape if the opportunity arises.*' RAF aircrew were eventually allowed to say a little beyond name, rank and number, provided they gave away nothing on order of battle, cipher, signals, tactics or secret equipment. An appeal to the instinct of loyalty might impress a Japanese brought up himself to be intensely loyal. A further useful tip: avoid badges of rank senior to lieutenant.

All this sort of sound advice will read oddly to survivors of the Japanese conquest of Malaya and Singapore. Wavell – by then commander-in-chief of the ill-fated Anglo-Americo-Australo-Dutch combined forces in south-east Asia – sent on 15 February 1942 an order to the local commander on Singapore island, General Percival, that gave him discretion to surrender. He added at once: 'Before doing so all arms, equipment, and transport of value to the enemy must of course be rendered useless. Also just before final cessation of fighting opportunity should be given to any determined bodies of men or individuals to try and effect escape by any means possible. They must be armed.' Desire outran capacity, as it usually does: the great bulk of Percival's surviving forces became prisoners of war, and no desperate armed parties clawed their way out. Lieutenant-General Gordon Bennett, the senior Australian officer on the spot, who had commanded an Australian brigade in France at the age of twenty-eight in the previous war, broke through the Japanese lines with a party of staff officers, and got away in a

junk from the western coast of Johore ; an inquiry after the war
held he had not been justified in relinquishing his command
at the moment of surrender, but that 'he acted from a sense of
high patriotism and according to what he conceived to be his
duty to his country'. He brought out much valuable information about Japanese methods of jungle warfare, but never held
another operational command. His government evidently felt
he should have shared the tribulations of his men.

For several days previously, ships filled with a mixture of
civilians and of service troops and airmen who had no more
local work to do had been escaping from Singapore as best they
could, through seas infested by hostile aircraft and warships.
To the meticulous list of them compiled by Captain David
Nelson of the Singapore Volunteer Corps on the information
available in Changi prisoner of war camp – as he says, 'absolute
accuracy cannot be expected' – a little further information can
be added. On 13 February small detachments from some units
then engaged in the fighting were sent to the docks and told
that they were to be shipped out so that they could contribute
some experience of Malaya to a reconquering expedition when
it was mounted – just Bennett's aim. But the ship assigned to
take them was sunk. They were then told to get away if they
could, and some of them succeeded in doing so. About twenty
of these evaded on the small tug *Siong Aik*; two gunner sergeants
coaxed its broken-down engine into enough spasmodic life to
bring it, a week later, to Sumatra. By a stroke of luck, 'we were
always' – one of the evaders recalls – 'either motionless or drifting back towards Singapore when Japanese aircraft came and
took a look at us; presumably they thought we were not worth
wasting any ammo on, for they never fired a shot'. They joined
up on Sumatra with a few other small parties who had been as
lucky, and were taken away in a destroyer the day before the
Japanese arrived.

Nelson, too obedient to think of breaking away when the
whole system round which his life as a municipal civil servant had

been built collapsed at Great Britain's imperial nadir, remained orderly even in captivity. He helped to organise among his fellow prisoners at Changi, on the eastern tip of Singapore Island, a Bureau of Record and Enquiry which established and maintained as complete a record as was possible of everybody who passed through that enormous camp. At first he was one of ninety people allotted to a solitary married officer's bungalow: an example of the degree of overcrowding. In defence of the Japanese, it is fair to mention that – like the Germans in France twenty months before – they were surprised by the large number of prisoners they had on their hands. This can explain some of the prisoners' sufferings, which stemmed in part at least from maladministration rather than from sadism.

People who like to cast up account-books of atrocity must reserve space for one item here: the Burma-Siam railway, hurriedly built by the Japanese with captive labour at a cost of some fifteen thousand lives of prisoners of war. This rate of casualty almost stands comparison with Hitler's or Stalin's concentration camps, or with what the Nazis did to Red Army prisoners of war, and makes the Sagan killings look more like a peccadillo than a crime. Conditions on the Burma-Siam line have been conclusively treated in two fiercely direct books of personal reminiscence, quite unforgettable: A. G. Allbury's *Bamboo and Bushido* and Ray Parkin's *Into the Smother*. Parkin, the last man off HMAS *Perth* when she was sunk with the USS *Houston* on 1 March 1942, was an imperturbable sailor whom not even the Japanese could terrify.

By sheer incompetence rather than design his captors stumbled on a device that was a deliberate feature of SS state policy in concentration camps in Germany, where it was designed to lower prisoners' morale. Up-country in Siam there were never enough latrines, so that it was only possible to relieve oneself after wading through one's comrades' excreta, and one could never be rid of the smell. Cholera followed; the outbreaks were usually fatal till the devotion of Colonel Harvey, RAMC, took them in hand. With a warm recommendation to Allbury and to Parkin's two books, there we must leave this melancholy subject; for there was virtually nothing MI 9 could do to help and MIS-X was not involved.

Early in 1944 Captain Bairnsfather of the Chinese maritime customs organised operation 'Vancouver', which with the help of Chinese army and guerrillas rescued 500 Indian troops from camps in Yunnan; but alas no more than that bare astonishing fact has so far surfaced in the records.

During the war the Japanese made spasmodic efforts at least to assert that they would stand by the general tenor of the Geneva Convention; not with much effect visible to the average prisoner. Nelson ends his book with a tribute to the humanity and courtesy of some of the enemies with whom he had to deal; this is another way of saying that the Japanese are as much human beings as the rest of us.

At least they had the collective straightforwardness at the time to behave consistently themselves. There were two large and fatal riots by Japanese prisoners of war who attempted mass break-outs and were shot down. They tried, honourably by their own standards, to sell their lives in suicidal combat, as their Kamikaze pilots did in the last year of the war. One riot, in the spring of 1943 at an internment camp at Featherston, east of Wellington, New Zealand, left forty-six dead and sixty-six wounded. The other, in the small hours of 5 August 1944 at Cowrah, west of Sydney, New South Wales, was messier still: 231 Japanese were killed or died of wounds and seventy-eight were wounded; four of their Australian guards were killed and four wounded. In neither case did anyone who, having failed to die, found himself outside the wire remain unrecaptured for more than a few hours. That one astounding party of Indians and the mateys apart, no Allied attempts at mass breakaways are on record in Asia.

What E Group could and did do after the tide of war turned in the Allies' favour, and the reconquest of Burma was begun, was to develop search and rescue parties who were sited well forward, who had a call on light aircraft, and who were occasionally able to help in the recovery of aircrew who had escaped from aircraft that crashed in the jungle.[56] Plenty of trouble was taken to educate the friendlier tribes, such as the Karens and the Nagas, in the value of helping airmen to return. A few almost random examples may show some of the oddities of these minor operations.

Pilot Officer Z. A. Shah, of 9 Squadron, Indian Air Force, bailed out from his damaged Hurricane at 9:20 on the morning of 2 August 1944, over the Chin Hills in north-west Burma. By four o'clock that afternoon E Group was in touch with him, and in spite of some bungled map references he was back with his squadron within seventy hours. Warrant Officer R. A. G. King of 42 Squadron RAF belly-landed his Hurricane fighter-bomber on 27 August 1944, after attacking a bridge in central Burma. He burned the aircraft, and marched out NNW in his Beadon suit, with perfect drill and discipline, exactly as briefed. He was met on 1 September by an E Group patrol that had gone out to look for him, and was operating with his squadron again by the 7 September. On that day Warrant Officer A. C. Farrell's Hurricane force-landed slap in the middle of a Japanese unit; by daring and resource, and luck, he managed to get away. He survived for five days on nuts, raisins and vitamin tablets, and then met some locals who befriended him till E Group could collect him. All such successes depended on pilots who took the trouble to report promptly when and where other aircraft were seen to crash. Every such report was investigated, not always with useful result; but the results that were useful enormously encouraged the RAF.

One American, Lieutenant H. Erikson of the 490th Bombardment Squadron, fell down seventy feet of precipice

---

56   An incomplete map in WO 208/3251 shows ten active operational areas, six in Burma, two in Malaya, one in Sumatra and one in Indo-China.

after landing by parachute on 11 August 1944, and lost all his kit except his compass. Still clutching that and his parachute, he struggled through pouring rain for several days, till he collapsed. Some Nagas brought him round, and guided him to the British after they had persuaded him to leave his parachute with them; twenty-four panels of silk would clothe the whole village.

Nagas were not universally helpful. A Spitfire pilot, Flight Sergeant J. C. McCormick of 155 Squadron, met a fortnight later (5 September 1944) a couple of them, each armed with a formidable Thompson sub-machine-gun. He greeted them as his evasion lecturer had recommended with a smile, but they 'only grunted and went on up the hill very fast.' He was able to look after himself, and was back in the British lines next day.

Two Cameronian riflemen, separated from their unit on 6 March 1942, wandered round for nineteen months from one Karen village to another, trying to be useful and unobtrusive at once; they were shopped in the end by a Burmese pedlar, and taken prisoner on 10 October 1943. A British NCO – unfortunately also anonymous – who got out of Singapore 'in the general disorganisation' on 18 February 1942, and got across to Sumatra, was recaptured there three weeks later, sent to work on the Burma-Siam railway, escaped even thence in September 1942, but after six months' work with a local guerrilla unit was quietly handed over to the Japanese by some Burmans in March 1943.

The Americans ran some Air Jungle Rescue Detachments which did lively work in Burma in the last winter of the war. The Kalagwe incident, as it was called – Kalagwe is a village ninety miles WSW of Lashio – took place in January and February 1945 and illustrates the form. A B-25 Mitchell light bomber was shot down on 5 January. The navigator bailed out separately from the rest, and took six weeks to pick his own way back to safety through friendly villages where he was hidden from the Japanese. The other four of the crew were collected, again by friendly villagers; and an air jungle rescue team caught up with them several days later. The team cleared a small airstrip.

Three successive L-I light aircraft summoned by wireless flew into the strip; all crashed, on landing or take-off, though without casualties. E Group thereupon lent Captain Sein Tun, one of its most promising and experienced Burmese members. He parachuted in to join the party, now numbering seven besides himself. He had a cheerful and commanding presence, and at once took charge. They all set out on a westward march through the hills to the Irrawaddy, nearly forty miles away. He organised the making of bamboo rafts for the river crossing, in which one of the airmen was drowned. Just before the rest finally got through to safety, they stumbled on a hidden Japanese machine gun team. The airmen ran for it; Sein Tun took on the enemy single-handed, and was killed in action. As one of the L-I pilots put it, 'He had more guts than any man I have ever seen.'

The coda to escape and evasion in Burma was provided in Rangoon. The town jail had been converted into a prisoner of war camp, and a highly disagreeable one: the usual complaints of little food, getting less, and no medical care applied with unusual strength. 'In the early days PW were beaten up upon arrival as a matter of policy.' The technical difficulties of getting out of the jail were severe, and no one had any confidence that, once out, he could get away; townspeople were much more pro-Japanese as a rule than country people. 'Several escapes by Indian PW are reported but no details are available.' When one British prisoner did escape, twenty were executed in reprisal. As in Hong Kong, pellagra and beri-beri were common. The annual death rate ran at over one in five, much the same as the rate on the more notorious railway.

Early on 2 May 1945 a Mosquito flew over Rangoon, high up, to make a final photographic check of the state of the defences; 'Dracula', a large combined operation, was about to engulf the city. There was no anti-aircraft fire, so the pilot made a second run from a much lower level. Something out of the usual caught his observer's eye; they flew lower still. They read in large letters on the roof of the jail the clear if inelegant message

EXTRACT DIGIT JAPS GONE. Emboldened, they landed
on the deserted airfield and went into town, to find several prisoners just capable of walking who told them that the garrison
had pulled out a few days earlier, taking all the fit prisoners with
it. 'Dracula's' covering fire plan was thereupon cancelled, and
the survivors in the jail could at least feel that they had saved
their countries a large expenditure in ammunition.

It turned out that on 25 April nearly 400 prisoners had been
marched out eastwards for four days, at the end of which time
they were told they were free and could go where they chose;
between thirty and forty had already escaped during the journey. The SBO, Brigadier Hobson, and several others had the
extreme bad luck to be killed in an Allied air strafing attack at
this very last moment before liberation; because they were still
wearing khaki, like the Japanese, and not the jungle green in
which Slim's army was by this time fighting. In spite of this, the
morale of the rest was reported 'extremely high'; so was that of
their 120 ill companions, who were recovered in Rangoon.

We must pass to a more gloomy subject, the fate that befell
American prisoners in the Philippines. The heroic defence
of the Bataan peninsula needs no repetition from an English
pen, and the death march thence to the prison compounds
at Cabanatuan is almost as familiar to American readers as
Pickett's charge at Gettysburg. As at Singapore and Hong Kong,
the trouble lay partly in weak administration, as well as – even
in some cases instead of – deliberate bloody-mindedness. Yet
it was as true in Luzon as in Java or Hong Kong or Singapore
or Rangoon, whence the phrase is drawn, that 'all PW, whatever their rank, are regarded by the Japanese as inferior to their
lowest ranking soldier.' As Allbury remarked, 'All Japanese officers N.C.O.s and O.R.s had to be saluted at all times, and didn't
they enjoy it!' The Japanese drivers on the road to Cabanatuan
who wanted to see what a human body looked like after their
truck had driven over it, and who left many specimens on

their way to encourage their victims' comrades, were expressing their view about the nation that had dragged Japan out of its medieval seclusion into the modern world only eighty-eight years before.

Every prisoner of the Japanese had to ask himself, far more searchingly than prisoners of war needed to do in Europe, 'What will be the effect on my companions who stay behind if I escape?' The Japanese often threatened executions in reprisal; the sharp example of Rangoon was quoted a moment ago. There are too many public beheadings with ceremonial swords on record to prove that – unlike some of the Germans – they meant their threats.

In the Philippines they usually organised their prisoners in groups, and gave each group to understand that all the rest of them would be beheaded if any one of them vanished: an effective stopper on activity among people who had already developed comradely feelings for their companions in arms or in suffering. Ironically enough they named this scheme 'collective security', the name used in the west for the League of Nations system that had failed to check their imperial advance. A group of prisoners in Camp O'Donnell on Mindanao found a way round this problem. It was under the command of Major William E. Dyess of the 21st Pursuit Squadron, who reported that during the original 'death march', 'One Japanese soldier took my canteen, gave the water to a horse and threw the canteen away.' He got his next drink, after twelve hours' marching, 'from a nearby caribou wallow', and next day and night marched for twenty-one hours on end; he then sat for twelve hours more in a dense crowd in the tropical sun. He also saw an officer beheaded for possessing a Japanese coin. So he was not much attracted to his captors. He made careful inquiries among the rest of his party, seven other officers, a sergeant, a private, and two Filipino murderers thrown in by the Japanese to keep the others company. They all agreed with him that the unknown horrors of the jungle were less than the known horrors of their camp. The whole group escaped *en bloc* and there were no reprisals.

Dyess was lucky in his companions. He joined the local guerrillas – he had already had some experience of infantry fighting before being captured on Bataan – and became chief of operations for a guerrilla division which had about 150 Americans in it, some of them women. It was a self-sustaining and optimistic organisation, which built a number of disguised airfields; work with it was refreshing after life in Camp O'Donnell, where the prisoners had only a little rice to eat, and could see oranges and lemons rotting on the ground outside the wire.

This paradox of dire poverty in the midst of plenty, even in a farming area so rich that five crops could be harvested with little effort every two years, much depressed Laurens van der Post at Bandoeng in Java. 'There was not a person', he declared, 'in my own prisoner-of-war camp in 1945 who was not suffering from deficiency diseases of some kind; beri-beri and pellagra were, as far as we were concerned, the least of them. The ones most feared were the many and painful forms of malnutritional neuritis, which made men's nerves burn so much with pain that they could not sleep, and in many cases deprived them of their sight.' Only with the help of the local Chinese community, whose members smuggled in to him at enormous risk money which he could use to bribe Japanese and still fiercer Korean guards to buy food, was his camp able to survive at all.

In the autumn of 1943 Roosevelt tried to put a brake on atrocity propaganda in the American press, and Marshall supported him strongly; word had by then spread quite far along the service grapevine around the British and United States armed forces. In the spring of 1944 the Spaniards, who looked after Japan's interests at Washington, passed on a note of 3 May which said that the Japanese government 'cannot but express utter astonishment' at American accusations of atrocities, made in a note to Madrid of 5 February that year; the Japanese went on to complain that their prisoners in the United States had had to clean latrines. Conceivably the Japanese service departments kept the Ministry of Foreign Affairs in sublime ignorance of what was really being done to American prisoners of war; there is no other honourable explanation.

There was nothing at all MIS-X could do for prisoners in the Japanese homeland, beyond having trained them in how to behave and what to look out for, as there was virtually no mail through which escape aids could be sent in or information be sent out. According to the Red Cross, 'There is no way to send personal parcels to our POW in Japan' as late as 21 October 1944. However, as the war reapproached the Philippines in the second half of 1944, a very little could be done, and the best American servicemen continued to behave in astoundingly brave ways under stress.

Sergeant Howard G. R. Moore, namesake of the famous Sergeant Moore in the Long Range Desert Group, was taken prisoner on Bataan at the age of twenty-seven. He came from Houston, Texas, and had a quiet military task as a headquarters staff draughtsman. This did not, he felt, exempt him from combat. He soon escaped by boat, but was recaptured at sea. He escaped for a second time, killing a sentry in hand-to-hand combat during which he was bayoneted near the eye. Next he organised guerrillas in the Zambales Mountains north of Bataan, to such effect that he claimed that he attracted a force of about 10,000 Japanese to mop up his own unit. He found spy fever so rife among the guerrillas that bands often fought each other instead of the enemy, and the Japanese caught him again. They beat him up repeatedly, through a month of questioning; he kept smiling, because he found they disliked hitting a man who put on a brave front. A court martial sentenced him to four years' prison. By now he found the Japanese so frightful that he would take any risk to get away, and managed to break prison; for after a few days' intensity his captors, as usual, lowered their guard, and he was able to escape from an outside working party. He went back to the hills, and in September 1944 was brought out to Australia.

MIS-X's advice already, on 7 September, was that 'Chances are, airmen downed on Luzon will find it best to remain in the hills with friendly peoples until Allied troops take over.' Winfrey was not quite happy with this, and managed to get fast enough communications with the Philippines for him to rescue, for example, some US Marine Corps survivors from the massacre in north Palawan on 14 December 1944. By the end of January 1945 he could claim in a monthly report that his people had rescued ninety-two navy and nineteen army escapers from the Philippines, and that a further sixty-eight sailors and eighty soldiers were in the category 'rescued and remaining' – that is, had got away into the hills and were being looked after till the islands were freed, or at least till the next boat or Catalina amphibious aircraft called.

One pilot in the 41st Squadron of the USAF, Second Lieutenant Robert C. Lightfoot, bailed out over Mindanao – the southernmost large island of the group – on 1 November 1944; remembered, as was the universal advice in all the MIS-X bulletins, not to pull his rip-cord till he was down to about 3,000 feet, to lessen the chance of being spotted by the wrong people; and hid in the hills for two days, living on his escape ration, till he was sure no hunt for him was going on. He then met four Filipino boys who were out canoeing; they took him to a house where he fed and lay up for a couple of days more. A guerrilla sergeant then took him over, and led him to a headquarters whence his safety was reported by wireless. He lay up for some weeks with an American officer who was engaged in the deadly efficient business of coast watching, and was unobtrusively picked up by a Catalina. In the whole of his report on the incident, he made no reference to the Japanese at all after the first day.

# Mopping up: 1945 and After

In August 1944 much of Langley's and Nelson's time at IS 9(WEA) was absorbed by a plan called 'En-Dor', which envisaged the imminent German collapse that most Allied staffs then took for granted. The plan's object was to process released ex-prisoners as fast as possible, and in its revised version it stated that 'No interrogations by IS 9(WEA) officers shall be allowed to hold up the return to U.K. of any British or American prisoner of war.' The extent to which administrative detail had been foreseen may be gauged by a note of McCallum's to SHAEF: each interrogator would have sixty pounds of personal baggage plus 100 pounds of stationery, and a further nine tons of stationery were held in forward reserve.

On to what targets was this paper barrage to be fired? An IS 9 estimate of 5 September 1944 supposed that there were about 160,000 British Commonwealth prisoners in German hands, over 100,000 of them east of the Elbe, and over 30,000 Americans, three-quarters of them in the same area.

A few days later Crockatt summoned Nelson and Langley to confer with himself and Holt at Beaconsfield about the conduct of 'En-Dor' and the future of IS 9(WEA). At this conference there was a general feeling of cautious optimism that Germany would be overrun in a matter of a few weeks, that the war in Europe would end by Christmas and that the rescue of the few evaders and escapers in Holland would be merely a matter of collecting them from their hiding places and ensuring that they were interrogated. When this had been done, the unit would be available for any final tasks in connection with prisoners from the Oflags and Stalags, and perhaps to search for the men and women of the escape organisations who had been sent to concentration camps. As usual Crockatt's orders were clear and concise and left little room for discussion.[57]

'The liberated POWs will first be sent to SHAEF staging camps in France and Belgium where you will be responsible for ensuring that every individual completes a short form which Colonel Holt and I have prepared, before he is flown to England. These forms will supply all the information that we require for a possible more detailed re-interrogation later in England or the States. No ex-POW will be permitted to board the aircraft until he has filled in one of these forms. Any questions before I outline your other minor duties?'

Nelson and Langley looked at one another, the same picture forming in each of their minds: row upon row of released prisoners, many of them prisoners since May 1940 and some embittered by the fiasco that had followed the 'stand fast' order in Italy, sitting like schoolboys at an examination to answer questions which the majority would feel were a waste of time and utterly pointless now the war was over. 'I don't think,' said Nelson, 'that they will take kindly to such treatment. They will regard it as one more maddening obstacle delaying their return home. I think we will have a lot of trouble on our hands.'

Crockatt smiled as he replied, 'I don't for a moment think they will take kindly to such interrogation and I expect their reactions will be vociferous and occasionally violent, but those are your orders and you will carry them out. Now for my second point. The staff at the staging camps will prepare nominal rolls and I wish you to go through these and pick out anyone who is on the list we have prepared; they are men who were inveterate, if unsuccessful, escapers, members of the escape committees and so on, who have performed outstanding work on escaping. You will tell them that Colonel Holt and I look forward

---

57   As on pp. 216–7 above, what follows is not claimed as an absolutely verbatim record, but it gives the gist of what was said.

to meeting them after they have been on leave and to learning more of their activities.

'Further, we have also drawn up a black list of names of those POWs who are suspected of having collaborated with the enemy. You will be on the look-out for these men, inform us of any you identify and hold them pending further instructions.[58] Any questions?' Nelson and Langley exchanged glances again, and Langley asked, 'Do we put these men under close or open arrest?' It was the turn of Crockatt and Holt to glance at each other.

'It is a question we both hoped you would not raise,' Crockatt replied. 'The whole matter is fraught with difficulties as in some cases the evidence is insufficient to justify such action and in most is largely unsupported and consists of vague accusations which may well be prompted by personal antagonism. No arrest until you receive an order and don't start asking how you are going to hold any suspects back without arousing their suspicions. That's your problem. Finally I wish to make it absolutely clear that Colonel Holt and I are not having the teams or interrogation sections swanning all over Germany. You may authorise specific missions to locate and help our people such as Pat or Dédée in the concentration camps, but no general unauthorised roving around.'

As Nelson and Langley drove to Northolt to fly back to Paris and Brussels respectively the sky was filled with the throbbing of aircraft engines as an armada of troop carriers and gliders passed overhead. Operation 'Market Garden' was under way and 'En-Dor' went into storage for another six months. All through that time IS 9(WEA) was busy with routine briefing work, with rescuing 'Market Garden' survivors, and with providing reports codenamed 'Mercury' on whatever turned up of value for evaders. Twenty-three of these reports were issued between 13 July 1944 and 31 March 1945.

---

58 The black list and all relevant files are at present withheld from research. (Dame) Rebecca West, *The Meaning of Treason*, remains by far the best study.

Most fighting forces would have given in by the stage of all-round defeat the Germans were at in early September 1944. Yet their leadership, including wide swathes of the educated classes, recalled how Frederick the Great of Prussia had snatched victory from the jaws of defeat in the Seven Years' War nearly two centuries before, and hoped against hope that the miracle would be repeated. The last serious spasm was the Ardennes offensive of 16 December 1944, which petered out on Christmas Day before it had got even half-way to its objective, Antwerp. United States prisoners played an unwitting part in such success as it had: 2,300 complete American uniforms were forcibly removed by the Germans from the Red Cross clothing store in a camp in Pomerania on 1 November 1944, and the same number of US army paybooks were confiscated. This provided Skorzeny's Panzerbrigade 150 with 2,300 opportunities to confuse the Allies next month.

Meanwhile, as the German mood hardened, from almost all the camps came coded presages of the fate that SAOs and SBOs feared was about to overwhelm them: massacre. With our subsequent knowledge that massacre was only a mirage – 166,560 British Commonwealth prisoners had in fact been recovered by 4 June 1945 – are these worried senior officers to be written off as alarmists? By no means. When the Army Council instructed the military mission in Russia to do what it could to secure the prompt release of Commonwealth prisoners overrun by the Red Army, it stated that 'Few questions arouse stronger feeling throughout the British Commonwealth than the treatment and welfare of our prisoners of war in German hands', and it is possible that the German government was aware of this: by midwinter 1944–5 its leading members were past caring.

Goebbels indeed put up to Hitler in February the proposal that the Germans should repudiate the Geneva Convention and shoot every pilot they held. As Trevor-Roper puts it, 'This, he said, would both stop the Allied bombing and deter German soldiers from surrendering in the West, lest they be treated likewise. Those already captured, apparently, could be written off.' Rumours of this conceivably leaked out, perhaps down some Luftwaffe grapevine; in any case, given the Nazis' known views on men and methods, and the more and more desperate straits into which the course of the war was driving them, some sudden and savage blow was only to be expected. Nor was there any reason to believe that pilots alone would suffer.

Crockatt and Johnston had to consult higher authority on a point of so much weight. It was not a mere intelligence technicality, such as the decisions that there were code-users enough already in the camps, which Crockatt had made as far back as the end of 1943 (the American rate of change of pilots was so high that Johnston was still encouraging the teaching of fresh code users as late as the summer of 1945). After the Sagan executions had become known in England in early May 1944, and after the war had taken a decisive turn for the better when the Germans were bundled out of France and Belgium in September, the problem of whether it remained a captured fighting man's duty to escape was referred as high as the British chiefs of staff. Crockatt meanwhile sent a direct order to Colditz: there were to be no more escapes from there. The chiefs of staff considered the point at the turn of the year, and ruled that while escape was still praiseworthy, it need no longer be considered a duty. This was passed on to Marlag-Milag Nord early in January 1945 in these words:

'IN VIEW INCREASING GERMAN RUTHLESSNESS AND LACK OF REGARD TO GENEVA CONVENTION CHIEFS OF STAFF RULE THAT UNDER PRESENT CIRCUMSTANCES IT NEED NO LONGER BE CONSIDERED DUTY OF P/W TO ESCAPE BUT IT IS NOT FORBIDDEN TO DO SO DO NOT LET GERMANS KNOW.' The Americans agreed that their orders and training should conform.

A further, difficult problem now arose: ought prisoners of war in Germany, faced with the possibility of massacre, to be armed? Some camps had already taken the bit between their teeth. Private Edward J. Zayd, captured unconscious near Salerno in mid-September 1943 and repatriated a year later, reported that Stalag IIIB had bought pistols, light sub-machine-guns and ammunition in exchange for coffee, cigarettes and chocolate: an enterprising piece of trading with the enemy. Even at Colditz, supposedly the strictest though not as has been shown the securest of camps, the prisoners built and hid in an attic a glider in which a couple of them could escape into the countryside in a dire emergency, and David Stirling of SAS had them organised to attempt to overpower their guards below by unarmed combat.

Crockatt and Holt attended a conference at SHAEF's main headquarters at Versailles in February 1945. Colonel (Sir) Robin Brook, SOE's liaison officer at SHAEF, attended: so did Langley and Nelson. Evidence that Hitler would order the mass extermination of prisoners of war was reviewed. It was agreed that the SS would carry out such an order with alacrity, even with relish. It was as well that no one present was aware that a reorganisation at the highest level in Germany had already handed over to Himmler, the Reichsführer SS, from October 1944 command *inter alia* of the *Kriegsgefangenenwesen,* the main administration of prisoner of war camps: luckily for these prisoners Himmler had too much else on his mind – such as the final solution of the Jewish problem, which he believed to be in sight – to bother about prisoners of war at all. Whether Wehrmacht units guarding prisoners would obey orders to mow them down was more doubtful; but was hope in the Wehrmacht's mercy to be the only resource? Numerous camps had requested pistols at least. Ought not a much more massive armament to be provided?

Pistols could be dispatched easily enough by parcel, but with all the changes and chances of the parcel system was this a risk worth running? If a snap Gestapo raid on a parcel office found even a single round of pistol ammunition, would that not provide the Nazis with excuse enough to denounce the Convention and open fire? Crockatt at any rate thought so, and the rest agreed.

Only air supply remained. To drop containers direct into camp compounds, then in itself a difficult feat of airmanship, would only be to invite a fusillade from the watchtowers by which almost every camp was surrounded. The only troops who might be available to accompany an arms drop, and had the rare and necessary qualifications of bravery, agility, skill at arms, initiative, parachute training and combat experience, seemed to be the survivors of the 'Jedburgh' teams who under Brook's direction had reinforced the French maquis with so much success during 'Overlord's' opening stages; but they numbered less than 300 men in all. Survivors of the SAS brigade and of the OSS operational groups also involved in 'Overlord' and 'Dragoon', might have been considered as well, had the committee not gone on to consider what was to happen after a camp had been armed. All the difficulties that had been apparent in Italy about converting prisoners of war into efficient infantry at the fall of a parachute were still painfully in point; by 1945 there was no prospect of infantry holding ground for more than a few minutes against armour and artillery, of which the Germans still had plenty, and no prospect that wandering bodies of armed prisoners in a strange land could maintain themselves for more than a few hours.

To throw more good men away in order to give their prisoners a chance to make a series of heroic Custer's last stands seemed to Crockatt and Holt a feckless, indeed an infantile plan. The SHAEF conference unanimously agreed that 'Jedburgh' teams should stand by to fly in to the aid of directly threatened camps, as a very last resort, if an emergency appeal by wireless was received and immediate armed intervention provided the only hope of saving the inmates' lives; but that there should be no general attempt to arm the camps. This decision was so obviously the only practical one that both Nelson and Langley wondered why it had been thought necessary to have a conference at all. The answer was that the ghost of the Italian 'stand fast' order haunted the high command. Crockatt was not alone in his determination that in any subsequent inquiry there would be ample evidence that the future of POWs in Germany had been given the fullest possible consideration; further, that the decisions had been unanimous at all levels, so that there was no question of order, counter-order, disorder.

The business of clearing the camps was made much more intricate by a run of more or less panic German decisions, as Germany disintegrated under invasion from east, south and west at once. The theory seemed to be that no camp was to be overrun with prisoners still in it. Even from Auschwitz and Birkenau, the great killing-grounds west of Cracow, the concentration camp inmates who happened still to be alive were marched out, or packed into westbound cattle trucks, as the Russians drew near. Prisoners of war got the same treatment with less brutality. Thousands of them around Thorn for example were moved away by train to Falling-bostel south of Hamburg, where the indispensable Warrant Officer Deans quietly exerted his authority. Not even he could persuade some of the army prisoners not to trade independently with the thoroughly demoralised guards, but he bought enough pistols, ammunition and grenades to overpower the gatehouse if the worst came to the worst. Numbers had swollen to 12,000 by 18 April 1945, when the whole party were marched off towards Lübeck; those who stayed with it were liberated on 2 May.

Most of the sailors in Marlag-Milag Nord were marched towards Lübeck also, in the fortnight 10–23 April, in company with a large RAF-USAF contingent who had made a much longer march already, from Sagan. By a stroke of bad luck, their column was shot up by a pair of P-47 Thunderbolts on the second day, 11 April; three prisoners were killed at this distressingly late moment, and two wounded (an example of the weakness of the air weapon against alert troops). Twelve officers and nine ratings escaped during the first two days. Captain E. H. B. Baker, RN, the SBO, then banned further escapes; he had noticed that the Germans were sweeping the surrounding woods for their own deserters, to whom they gave short shrift, and reckoned potential escapers were safest in the main party. This was sensible, but earned him few immediate thanks. Other SBOs and SAOs were more flustered. Small wonder that some senior officers, who had had no opportunity to exercise a wholly independent judgement for years, made some mistaken decisions at the crisis of liberation. When finally the Third and Last Reich foundered in a cloud of putrid dust, some 250,000 British, Commonwealth and American prisoners marched briskly out of the ruins.

Immediately after the Armistice in May, IS 9(WEA) set about its final task. Everyone not otherwise engaged – teams in Holland were busy with famine relief – was sent to reinforce the interrogation sections which, as had been anticipated, were not having an easy time. Most liberated prisoners accepted, though often sullenly, the reimposition of service discipline, and filled in the prepared 'En-Dor' forms, though the replies ranged from an uninformative 'yes' or 'no' to obscenities. The major exceptions were two. First came those who utterly refused to co-operate and promptly went absent without leave, usually to visit friends in Belgium or France made during an earlier abortive attempt to evade or escape, and then hitchhiked back to England, there rejoining the stream destined for home.

Secondly were those who regarded the MI 9 forms as a totally unexpected but none the less heaven-sent chance to pour out all their grievances from capture onwards, and to give vent to all their frustrations. These people gave IS 9(WEA) most trouble. Their outpourings were usually vicious accusations of collaboration with the Germans by fellow-prisoners, or self-justifications of their own activities, in the form of long rambling accounts of their unsuccessful attempts to escape. The staff could do no more than keep them supplied with paper and pencils. These essentials, notably pencils, often ran short, for the staff failed to take into account the habit acquired in prison camps of pocketing any small object that might serve some useful purpose in the future. There was much silent sympathy for those in MI 9 or MIS-X whose task it would be to evaluate these statements.

None of these forms have yet been released. They may all merci-
fully have been pulped. A few disgruntled members of escape
committees worked up a series of grudges against MI 9, for
being too slow and for failing to provide the earth and a quarter,
when they came to write camp histories. There was also a small
minority who could not write or whose English was insufficient
for understanding or answering the questions.

The hope that SHAEF's administrative staff would be able to
supply accurate nominal rolls in the three main ex-POW transit
camps, at Antwerp, Brussels and Rheims, proved unfounded.

Groups of liberated prisoners would arrive, frequently without warning, at all hours of the day or night, hungry, dirty,
often in rags. Dealing with their immediate requirements was
given priority, and on many occasions men had left on the next
stage of their journey home before the interrogators saw any
nominal roll or had time to read over anything that had been
written down on the 'En-Dor' forms. As a result only one man
on the black list was picked up at Brussels: a British corporal
who had been captured wounded at Dunkirk and had since
accumulated some serious black marks.

Crockatt refused to allow this man to be put under arrest or
handed over to the military police, and ordered that he be kept
at IS 9(WEA) headquarters until such time as an MI 9 officer
could be sent over from Beaconsfield to conduct him back to
England for further questioning. He was put in the charge of
a senior NCO but slipped away during the night, and as far
as Elwes and Langley were concerned he was never seen again.
There were reputed to be more than five hundred British and
American deserters hiding in Belgium and northern France,
mainly near such ports as Antwerp. It was not difficult to slip
aboard a ship returning to England and thence into the oblivion
of civilian life. Even this chance was missed by one pathetic character, an Ordnance Corps private taken prisoner with all his unit
by a single German officer in a tank on 13 June 1940. He had
the enterprise to slip away five days later, and walked westwards,

hoping for a boat to the Channel Islands; could not find one; got work as a farm labourer; had a brush with the police about a stolen bicycle; and ended up, pretending to be a Fleming, building pillboxes on the Atlantic wall: Ichabod, Ichabod.

The available figures indicate that out of the 166, 000 odd Commonwealth prisoners alive in Germany at the end of the war, about 54,000 filled in the 'En-Dor' forms. Not unnaturally the IS 9(WEA) staffs became depressed at what they felt to be failure to carry out their duties. However, Crockatt and Holt made it clear that they were more than satisfied with what was being achieved, and this encouragement kept the staffs going till the transit camps were closed down. IS 9(WEA) was formally disbanded in August.

Its supreme advantage had been that it operated in countries with strong pro-British and pro-American sentiments dating back to 1914–18 and beyond, and with a section of the population prepared from 1940 onwards to help evaders and escapers without regard to the risks involved or the fearsome penalties inflicted by the Germans if they were caught. To this was added the backing of the lines arranged through P15, and strong support from the governments in exile of France, Belgium and Holland (the French were not recognised by the Americans or the British till October 1944).

'Pat' Guérisse was safely recovered, shaken but not crushed by Natzweiler – where he caught sight of his former courier Andrée Borrel on her way to the furnace – and by Dachau. And one of the anonymous grey wraiths who were left upright in Ravensbrück turned out to be Andrée de Jongh. She had managed to swap identities with a girl who looked quite like her, and thus to evade a Gestapo search made particularly for her; she got lost in the ruck, looked after her sick companions, and held on. None of the forty-odd SAS in Belsen survived. They were too well known to their captors, and there was no crowd in which they could hide. None had the luck and courage combined to imitate John Godwin, and take one with him when their time came to be shot.

Among the debris to be cleared away in the ruins of Germany there emerged again Harold Cole, the scourge of the 'Pat' line's early days. He surfaced in the American zone, again called himself an English captain, and indicated he was engaged on some unspecified intelligence task. When the British heard of this he was arrested and taken to Paris, still in American custody. He was not closely watched, and had no trouble in slipping on an American sergeant's tunic and strolling away. He hid up in the flat of a woman he knew; a neighbour caught sight of the tunic, and reported him as a suspected deserter. Two gendarmes came to question him. He opened fire, wounding one of them; the other shot him dead.

IS 9(CMF)'s experiences were less paper-laden – there were fewer prisoner of war camps to be overrun in Austria than in Germany – and can be more summarily treated. Jock McKee, whose adventure at Sulmona may be recalled, had another and a more effective chance to assert his personality when a sizeable body of quite senior SS officers tried to refuse their own *Oberbefehlshaber*'s order to surrender: McKee had personality enough, in a captain's battledress, to overawe these figures in immaculate black leather, several of whom were shortly on trial for war crimes. (Skorzeny had laid on a ratline by which the wilier SS high command could slip away to Argentina, but that is not an MI 9 story.)

The oddest business on the southern front was the apparition of those two revered figures from the stresses of the late 1930s, Leon Blum the French Socialist and Kurt Schuschnigg the Austrian Catholic, accompanied by Giles Romilly, Michael Alexander and Lord Hopetoun, *Prominente* from Colditz castle. They had all been spirited away in mid-April 1945, at a moment when it looked as if the Nazi redoubt in Bavaria might after all be going to mean something: their lives were to be used as bargaining counters. Romilly and Alexander's account of how the entire hostage project fizzled out is too good to miss.

Routine problems continued to dog the section to the bitter

end, above all the old one about whom to move. On 11 April Derry had to remind 'Squad' Dennis that 'your charter covers Polish troops captured by the enemy while fighting for us and NOT deserters from the German army'; above all, Dennis simply needed to use his common sense to see what was reasonable to do, and do it.

A. F. Tuke, a future chairman of Barclay's Bank, was overrun in Padua with about fifty fellow-guardsmen captured south of the Po; they had disengaged themselves from their retreating captors and were behaving with the Brigade's usual imperturbability. Fillingham, who had acquired a captured Mercedes to help him sort out evaders and encourage helpers, remarked that 'We have never worked so hard in all our lives.'

A word is needed in conclusion on the war in Europe about those who tried to escape eastabout from Germany – or westabout from Japan – through the USSR: attempts that led sometimes to success, usually to imprisonment, sometimes to disappearance, often to disillusion.

As early as 18 April 1942, one of General Doolittle's crews who had taken part in his famous raid on Tokyo had landed at Vladivostok instead of trying to regain their carrier. They were all interned for several months in a village near the Urals. With the connivance of a local magnate, they escaped over the Persian border on 11/12 May 1943, met the nearest British consul, and were escorted by him to Quetta on the western confines of India.

They had by then formed an 'exceedingly poor opinion of the Russians', and gathered it was reciprocated.

Not long before this crew was interned in Russia, the British mission in Kuybyshev (the Soviet government's rear headquarters) at last got a positive answer to a long series of inquiries made of the Russians, about whether they had any news of escapers who were known in London, through coded letters, to have moved eastward, usually from Thorn. Their first object would have been to make contact with the Polish underground, in the hope of a passage to Sweden or a move into the Balkans. Failing that they might try the USSR in hope of repatriation.

Littledale, Sinclair and Davies-Scourfield had had promising friends in Warsaw, and there were other cases; but those who pressed on into Russian-occupied Poland for the most part simply disappeared. In fact when arrested they were treated as political prisoners and confined in appropriate jails. After the German invasion of Russia in June 1941 fresh inquiries were set on foot, with the same negative results. Yet a few months later the Russians informed the British military mission that they had 'discovered' some ten British prisoners, and arrangements were made to fly them to Archangel; there they could take an aircraft for home.

Their story was an odd one. In June 1941 they were in a train en route, so they understood, for a slave labour camp in Siberia. Suddenly they were transferred to a train going in the opposite direction, and ended up in a luxury hotel in the Crimea where for some weeks they lived off such fat as there was in the land, until physically at least they showed little sign of the privations they had undergone. They got back to Great Britain eventually, after a rough journey; it was not an incident that anyone concerned in it remembered gladly.

Several later British escapers, including Cyril Rofe the travel agent, did succeed in picking their way through the vast and confused eastern combat zone to safety in the Russian lines and eventual return home. Several more set off, and never arrived: presumably disposed of by one or another of the several combatant sides. For the war in south-west Russia was a more intricate affair than the straight Nazi-Soviet head-on collision that figures in all the textbooks. There were at least five combatant groups, German, Jewish, Polish, Russian and Ukrainian, with roots on the spot, not to speak of the Spaniards, Hungarians, Romanians and others dragged along in the Germans' wake. Any one of the five main groups might, under sufficient pressure,

fight any of the other four, and there were fearsome complications that need to be unravelled one day; though not while
the area bears its present political complexion. No fate was
more likely than a prompt journey to oblivion for an escaper
born an English-speaker who tried to cross the Ukraine in the
early 1940s.

There was never any direct liaison between MI 9 or MIS-X
and any Soviet staff; all relations were conducted through
the service attachés in London, Washington, and Moscow/
Kuybyshev. It was even supposed in MI 9 that there was no
equivalent Soviet department. On the other hand, there are a
few traces in the American archives of exactly what on *a priori*
grounds one would have expected: 'a highly developed Russian
intelligence organisation' for infiltrating prisoner of war camps
in which Red Army and air force prisoners were held, collecting
information from them, and organising escapes. One document
is dated on All Fools' Day; and we have found no trace at all
of any Soviet organisation to help evaders from the Russian air
force, who must have been many. Their orders may be presumed
to have been to get in touch with the nearest reliable partisan
gang and await instructions.

Several Russian escapers have been mentioned already,
who turned up in the west and were helped along IS 9's
lines. It is just worth mentioning the two youngest, boys of
sixteen and seventeen who deserted to the Allies from a unit
of Vlassov's Russian collaborationist army in Normandy. They,
like the rest, were interrogated by John Buist, who spoke good
Russian, and handed over to the Soviet embassy in London;
after which nothing more of their fate is known. They may be
presumed to have encountered at least the minimum sentence,
of five months in a penal battalion, which the Soviet regime
visited even on successful escapers if they had ever put on a
German uniform.

On German soil there were awkwardnesses: the worst when
the Red Army overran Stalag IIIB and opened fire on the

American prisoners, killing some fifty and wounding several hundred; they said they took them for Hungarians.

By a decision made at Yalta, MI 9 was able to send a small delegation to Russia to look after Commonwealth prisoners of war overrun by the Red Army on the eastern front. MIS-X sent a similar team to look after Americans. After a short visit to Moscow, the two teams settled side by side on the waterfront in Odessa, the port to which those seeking to leave the USSR were all directed; and to which those being returned to that stern regime were shipped from the west. A shipborne interpreter has indicated the contrast between the glumness of those going back into Russia and the cheeriness of those coming out.

Quite a crowd in fact turned up in the end, over 2,500 each of British Commonwealth and of American citizens – thus bearing out Crockatt's calculation that as many as one in seven of all the successful escapers from Germany came this way, for all the horrors, difficulties and dangers attendant on the journey. This is no contemptible figure, and is a tribute both to the escapers' courage, and to the courage of the thousands of unrecorded Polish and Soviet citizens who helped them on the earlier stages of their journey.

Averell Harriman, then American ambassador in Moscow, 'expects some severe criticism of the Russians from the American prisoners now on their way home', according to his British colleague; and indeed some Americans – like some Englishmen – were vociferous about the dirt, the harshness, and the plain theft they had encountered near the front. Many Soviet citizens helped themselves to any capitalist wrist watches, fountain pens, or other nice-looking portable objects they met, remarking airily '*You* can get another when you get home.' But a moment's reflection made it clear that the main problem was lack of organisation and resources, not negligence or even ill-will. Colonel Frederick W. Drury, overrun in a camp in Poland in late January 1945, reported that he had had an uncomfortable, underfed, overcrowded journey; still, 'the Russian officer who was with us lived in exactly the same conditions in which we did ... I feel the Russians gave us everything they had and that their attitude was friendly and as helpful as conditions permitted.'

In Odessa, Buist's opposite number was Major Paul S. Hall; each had a doctor and a small clerical staff. There was plenty of volunteer clerical help from prisoners who were glad to have something constructive to do again, beyond shoring up tunnels or fabricating *Ausweise*. Conditions were rough, but the best that the ruined city could afford, and as well as the constant ineffectual pumping by Tass correspondents there were superlative opera and concert performances, and a splendid circus.

The Asian war did not slacken at Hitler's death: on the contrary, Mountbatten and MacArthur, the two principal supreme commanders, were each preparing combined operations of great complexity, subtlety and strength. In a remote American desert an international team of scientists – eminent among them Niels Bohr, who had been spirited away from Copenhagen in 1943 – was preparing in deadly secrecy a bomb that would make any previous bomb look like a fire-cracker. The Japanese, wholly ignorant about the bomb, were feeling the pinch of war very tightly indeed, and some of their diplomats were beginning to wonder how to get out of it, but their dominant military caste seemed to grow less and not more flexible as things got worse: like the English at the battle of Maldon long ago. Prisoners were still treated as less than the dust beneath their captors' feet. Only wild chance or wild heroism made escapes possible, and the implacable terrain, the huge expanses of ocean, militated as ever against evaders.

Crockatt had been out to Asia in the middle of winter, seizing a moment in passing to see his son Dick who was a subaltern in the Royal Scots in Burma. He could not fail to notice while he was in India the utter lack of MI 9/MIS-X integration there, and on 28 January 1945 sounded off about it in a private and manuscript letter to Johnston: 'I wish to God people would forget about themselves and their nationalities and get on with this bloody war, so that you and I could get our boys back', a *cri de coeur* that Johnston certainly echoed. MIS-X had another new set of superiors under whom to work: he had returned to Washington from a highly successful visit to London in mid-June 1944 to find 'all of G-2 being upheaved'. Catesby Jones had gone across to a policy desk, and Colonel Russell H. Sweet had become head of Captured Personnel and Materiel; at least Sweet, being new to the job, gave Johnston no trouble. But the incessant jostling for jobs that is common in all capitals did not leave MIS-X in perfect peace, when the whole of the American war machine was being re-geared to cope simply with a trans-Pacific instead of a trans-Atlantic and a trans-Pacific war. Many British commentators have remarked how the tendency of Americans to do things their own way, always marked, became more marked than ever after July 1944, when for the first time they had more troops in contact with the Axis enemy than the British did. Even the warm friendship that had grown up between Johnston and Crockatt came under strain – marked by de Bruyne's somewhat abrupt return to England in the spring of 1945 after a storm in a teacup. Crockatt and Holt remained firm allies, but Holt's office in London lost its *raison d'être* with Germany's defeat, and he went home.

To the Americans and Europeans who knew the Japanese best, the eastern sky seemed overcast with portents, especially where the fate of prisoners of war was concerned. Nothing seemed more probable than that they would be swept away in massacres, by guards who would follow their ceremonial killing with mass ceremonial suicide.

Laurens van der Post has explained, with force and grace, how even the fiercest and proudest of the Japanese were released from the shame and dishonour of defeat by the new kind of catastrophe that overwhelmed Hiroshima and

Nagasaki: bombs that rightly appalled good Christians, and yet provided for a devout Buddhist warrior an ample excuse to bow his head.[59]

> But this was something miraculously new, something not foreseen in their or our own philosophy. It was something on so gigantic and undeniable a scale, such a manifestation of new power at work in life, that even they would know, as we who had been its terrible instrument of delivery would have to learn to know, that all the old ways, laws, rules, conventions and creeds which had brought us to this terrible impasse, had been judged invalid by life and something else would have to take their place.[60]

The work of rescue of the emaciated waifs who survived in the Japanese camps – about 140,000 from the British Commonwealth and 20,000 Americans, plus nearly 60,000 Dutch, both military and civilian – does not fall within our scope: this was medicine and administration, rather than organising evasion or escape. Douglas Clague, more or less single-handed, overawed the Japanese in Siam and secured the surviving prisoners' prompt release. And when Mountbatten was negotiating the details of surrender in Burma and Malaya, E Group provided him with a map of the locations and strengths of the prisoner of war camps in his command that astounded the Japanese by its completeness, its accuracy, and its superiority to their own scrappy information.

Up to the last moment, which came when the Japanese at MacArthur's instance signed an act of surrender on an American warship in Tokyo Bay on 2 September 1945, there was much

---

59    Contrast G. E. M. Anscombe, *Mr Truman's Degree* with van der Post, *The Night of the New Moon,* two utterly sincere works that arrive at opposite conclusions.

60    Ibid. 124.

unease and some flurry about how their armed forces were going to react to total defeat. MacArthur put out an order, which Mountbatten's staff copied and passed on, that the honourable susceptibilities of Japanese generals were to be observed: they were to be allowed to keep their swords. Slim, having discovered what the Japanese had done to prisoners from his Fourteenth Army, and having satisfied himself that this was not just a local whim, but a matter over which their commanding generals had had control, decided that these were not men of anything he could recognise as honour. He disobeyed MacArthur's order, insisted on holding a ceremonial parade to receive the sword of the principal Japanese he had defeated, and kept it on his own chimneypiece thereafter.

As the fighting drew to its spectacular close, with the fall of Berlin to the Russians at the end of April 1945 and the collapse of Japan under the impact of two atomic bombs in August, a rather more acrid note than hitherto crept into some of the prisoner of war files in Washington and London. Staff officers could be found to argue that, now that Germany had vanished from the world map – as happened, temporarily, at the Potsdam conference – prisoners from the Wehrmacht were no longer covered by the Geneva Convention, and could be used as slave labour. This indeed was the fate of a large number of those captured on the eastern front, where there was more repair work to be done, where the Convention did not apply, and where consciences were less tender than in the west.

A different sort of scare, a minor one, raised by administrators in the Pentagon may serve to bring the military narrative to an end. On 20 April 1945 G-1 there wrote to G-2 to propose that lepers, of whom fifteen had been discerned already among Japanese prisoners of war, should be segregated into the leper colony at Molokai in the Hawaiian Islands. Now Molokai had made a small mark already in history: it had been there that Father Damien, the Belgian peasant boy turned missionary, had gone to work among the sick and had died of leprosy himself. Andrée de Jongh the inspirer of 'Comet', rescued from Ravensbrück, looked first after what was left of her family, and then remembered how much her dead father had admired Father Damien as well as Nurse Cavell. She worked for many years in a leper colony in Ethiopia and now does so in Senegal.

Though the military narrative is over, the administrative burden was not one lightly to be laid down. Crockatt handed MI 9 over to Sam Derry, the organiser of the Rome escape line, and retired to private life; not over-burdened with honours with a CBE, to which the Americans added a Legion of Merit and the French the Legion d'honneur and a Croix de Guerre. The playing of the fountain of honour is notoriously a shade erratic; nobody however would dream of grudging 'Pat' Guérisse his George Cross or Andrée de Jongh her George Medal. As she was technically a civilian, while he was technically a serving officer in the Royal Navy, their more or less equal services were unequally rewarded: an instance of the intricacies of the British system, which not even the British altogether understand. Johnston and Holt retired early also, leaving it to younger men and women to run the awards bureaux that were set up in liberated Europe (where not banned by liberators of Marxist leanings) to trace helpers and to offer them at least a token of a reward.

There were endless difficulties, not least in fending off self-interested collaborators with the enemy who were looking for a quick cover to protect themselves against irate neighbours, or in establishing just what had been done, and for whom, by undoubted secret helpers who could give no traceable details of the people with or for whom they had been working. There were political troubles as well. De Gaulle's government, for example, officially warned Peter Murray (Prince Murat) that as he had committed the enormity of accepting a commission in a foreign army,' if he re-entered France he would be liable for a court martial on a charge carrying death, or life imprisonment and forfeiture of all his property, as probable penalties. SHAEF took this up, equally officially, and the threat was withdrawn, hardly before time.

One further incident, this time all-British, tarnished the work of the bureaux. When the format and wording of certificates of thanks had been agreed, the question arose of who should sign them. For a number of reasons it was thought inappropriate to ask the Monarch, and the obvious second choice was Churchill, once himself an escaper. He accepted with alacrity, promising to sign each one personally rather than use a rubber stamp. Then the Air Ministry, perhaps disgruntled at the War Office's control of MI 9, protested that as a high proportion of evaders had been airmen, signing should be the duty of a senior officer in the RAF. The outcome was that the certificates were rubber-stamped with the signature of (Lord) Tedder, Eisenhower's second-in-command. The Americans were less riddled with interservice jealousies in Western Europe; Eisenhower signed the American equivalent, though again with a rubber stamp.

In Italy nearly 90,000 claims that help had been given were received, assessed and sorted. Certificates were signed either by Field-Marshal Alexander or by the American General McNarney. Many Italians seemed pathetically grateful, after a generation under Fascism, to find that any government would honour its word for anything.

The Air Ministry did something important to atone for its unfortunate intervention over the certificate signatures: it sponsored and financed the RAF Escaping Society, which took over where the awards bureaux left off and flourishes down to the present day. That the Air Ministry gave this venture such strong support was entirely due to the determination of some RAF officers who had themselves evaded or escaped, Embry at their head, that the men and women who had risked and sacrificed so much to help them should not be forgotten. Some of these helpers did not wish to remember; it was an interlude in their lives so tragic and sorrowful that they had no desire to have it recalled by services or reunions.

Crockatt founded a 919 dining club, which had an annual dinner at which former members of the staffs of MI 9 and MI 19 could meet each other and various eminent former escapers, evaders, organisers or helpers; it was wound up a few years after his own death in October 1956. His regiment, at least, had recognised him for what he was, and he was for ten years its Colonel.

Of the various friendly commemorative groups, *amicales* that were set up in Western Europe among groups of helpers after the war, only 'Comet' has survived intact: that seems, like the line, to be indestructible. Every year there is a reunion in Brussels and a requiem mass for those who died in the line's service. P15, the British and American air attachés, a strong contingent from the Escaping Society and representatives of the vigorous USAF Escaping Society are always present. And when Andrée de Jongh's mother was on her deathbed, Air Transport Command found it convenient to route a training flight from Aden to Wiltshire via Addis Ababa and Brussels; and sent one back on the reciprocal course after the funeral; carrying the line's inspirer each way. Both the American and the RAF Escaping Societies have done a great deal of valuable work in looking after helpers' families; an interesting and refreshing contrast with what some other comparable bodies have had to leave undone.

An agreeable Easter present awaited all the American prisoners who got home in 1945: a circular by Stimson and Forrestal, Secretaries of War and Navy, on 31 March informed them that they were all to be promoted one rank at least, to make up for the promotions they would have earned had they not been prisoners. The poorer and more Treasury-ridden British reverted to their war substantive rank after three months in prison, and with the outbreak of peace lost that. By 30 November 1945 a minute by Russell Sweet recorded that 'MIS-X has been entirely liquidated', an unhappy phrase to a European; he only meant it had been disbanded.

There is hardly need to do more than refer the reader again to Appendix 1, if he wants to review the scope of MI 9's and MIS-X's work: about three divisions' worth of active men recovered from captivity, or the risk of it, for the war. Crockatt's gloss on the apparent total of 26,190 Commonwealth escapers and evaders was: 'It can be fairly claimed that of these 90 per cent of evaders and 33 per cent of escapers were brought out as a result of MI 9 organisation and activities.' The American proportions were certainly no lower.

After the world war, the subject has not been left to slumber as it did in the 1920s. MI 9 has been succeeded in Britain by an interservice unit comprising intelligence and rescue teams; the Intelligence Corps and the Special Air Service both keep a keen eye on the subject. Various people were active in the Korean war of 1950–3, at which Guérisse was present as the chief Belgian medical staff officer, an appointment that did not keep him from being decorated yet again, this time for rescuing wounded under fire.

That the Americans also keep the subject under constant review is shown by an odd incident in the Vietnamese war, on 21 November 1970. In operation 'Kingpin', United States airmen and rangers tried – much as Charles Lamb had advocated at Laghouat – a rescue a party of their imprisoned colleagues by an airborne landing at a camp at Son Tay, not far west of Hanoi. A technically brilliant *coup* was spoiled by the brute fact that the camp had been empty for some weeks.

The dark glass of the future is as impenetrable as the jungle leaves round Son Tay. Bombs today make the Hiroshima bomb in turn look like a fire-cracker, and governments today talk and write in apparently good faith of using them. In that sort of war there will not be much scope for the comparatively archaic devices we have discussed; nor is any future combatant likely to allow prisoners of war – if he takes any – to communicate with their homeland at all. The world is getting back to the state Jacky Fisher threatened at the first Hague conference, when he remarked that the way to get peace was to let it be known that any prisoners you took, you would promptly boil in oil.

It remains true that free men cannot be cooped up indefinitely, no matter how well-intentioned or how dialectically correct the system that seeks to coop them. Equally, men on the run will always find helpers. Even in the iciest wastes of Siberia, the most torrid central or southern African or American jails, prisoners go on escaping, as Day escaped from Sachsenhausen, as Dyess escaped from Camp O'Donnell. Anyone who has to embark on such an adventure will be lucky if he has a staff to back him in secret that is in hands a tenth as capable as Norman Crockatt's.

# Appendix 1

# Statistical Summary

*Commentary*

This is an interesting table, but like any other body of statistics it cannot be claimed as perfect.

Its left-hand column, meant to show the areas or theatres of war it deals with, calls for a gloss. 'Western Europe' covers escapes and evasions through Denmark, Holland, Luxembourg, Belgium, and France; the 'operational rescues after "D" Day' in Normandy, 6 June 1944, mean such operations as 'Marathon' or 'Pegasus'- Those included under 'Switzerland' are not counted again under 'Western Europe'. The dividing line between 'Mediterranean West' and 'Mediterranean East' appears to put Italy and Tunis on the western side, the Balkan Peninsula and the Libyan Desert on the eastern; this was not quite the line of division between IS 9(CMF) and IS 9(ME).

The table contains minor slips – no mention of the Dutch and French officers who escaped from Colditz, a miscount of the nurses who evaded from Albania – ten instead of thirteen, no mention of the European Allies who were recovered in the Mediterranean; and a number of major eccentricities.

The Pacific is ignored entirely, presumably because there were no British Commonwealth escapers or evaders there, or at any rate none of whom London had heard. Whoever the 2,690 Indian Army other rank escapers in Asia were, few of them appear in E Group's history of its own activities. Might they not have been better categorised as stragglers, who had eventually rejoined their units – perhaps with some cover story of having spent a few hours in Japanese hands? Is it really credible that hardly a single US army escaper got into Switzerland, while

## Return of Escapers and Evaders up to 30 June 1945

| Area of Theatre | Nationality | NAVY | | | | ARMY | | | | AIR FORCE | | | | TOTALS | | | |
|---|---|---|---|---|---|---|---|---|---|---|---|---|---|---|---|---|---|
| | | ESCAPERS | | EVADERS | | ESCAPERS | | EVADERS | | ESCAPERS | | EVADERS | | ESCAPERS | | EVADERS | |
| | | Offrs | ORs | Offrs | ORs | Offrs | ORs | Offrs | ORs | Offrs | ORs | Offrs | ORs | Offrs | ORs | Offrs | ORs |
| WESTERN EUROPE (a) | British | 10 | 13 | 6 | 8 | 106 | 711 | 36 | 344 | 46 | 63 | 401 | 946 | 162 | 787 | 443 | 1298 |
| | Dominions | — | 1 | — | — | 13 | 109 | 3 | 10 | 26 | 18 | 291 | 328 | 39 | 128 | 294 | 338 |
| | Colonial | 1 | — | — | — | — | — | — | — | — | — | 1 | — | 1 | — | 1 | — |
| | Indians | — | — | — | — | 1 | 68 | — | — | — | — | — | — | 1 | 68 | — | — |
| | Polish French Dutch Czechs | — | — | — | — | — | 31 | — | 1 | 2 | 1 | 2 | 6 | 2 | 32 | 2 | 7 |
| | Russians | — | — | — | — | — | — | — | — | — | — | — | 1 | — | — | — | 1 |
| | Americans | — | — | — | — | 37 | 463 | 3 | 7 | 105 | 108 | 1380 | 1312 | 142 | 571 | 1383 | 1319 |
| INDIA S.E.A.C. and B.A.A.G. | British | 4 | 6 | 13 | 38 | 14 | 21 | 16 | 46 | 3 | 1 | 34 | 19 | 21 | 28 | 63 | 103 |
| | Dominions | — | — | — | — | — | 1 | — | — | — | — | — | — | — | 1 | — | — |
| | Indians | — | — | — | — | 55 | 2690 | 9 | 376 | — | — | — | — | 55 | 2690 | 9 | 376 |
| | Americans | — | — | — | — | 1 | — | — | — | 5 | — | 10 | 23 | 6 | — | 10 | 23 |
| SWITZERLAND | British | 5 | 7 | — | — | 184 | 2276 | — | — | 24 | 17 | 17 | 35 | 213 | 2300 | 17 | 35 |
| | Dominions | — | — | — | — | 40 | 1392 | — | — | 20 | 15 | 1 | 11 | 60 | 1407 | 1 | 11 |
| | Colonials | — | — | — | — | — | 312 | — | — | — | — | — | — | — | 312 | — | — |
| | Indians | — | — | — | — | 23 | 537 | — | — | — | — | — | — | 23 | 537 | — | — |
| | Americans | — | — | — | — | — | — | 2 | — | 12 | 12 | 95 | 106 | 12 | 12 | 97 | 106 |
| MEDITERRANEAN WEST | British | 12 | 119 | — | — | 393 | 6355 | — | — | 36 | 109 | 15 | 86 | 441 | 6583 | 15 | 86 |
| | Dominions | — | — | — | — | 97b | 3221b | 5 | 1 | 4 | 1 | 20 | 9 | 101 | 3222 | 23 | 10 |
| | Colonials | — | — | — | — | — | 262 | — | — | — | — | — | — | — | 262 | — | — |
| | Indians | — | — | — | — | 38 | 1129 | — | — | — | — | — | — | 38 | 1129 | — | — |
| | Americans | — | — | — | — | 31 | 786 | — | 12 | 103 | 142 | 1039 | 1363 | 134 | 918 | 1039 | 1375 |

| MEDITER-RANEAN EAST (h) | | | | | | | | | | | | | | | |
|---|---|---|---|---|---|---|---|---|---|---|---|---|---|---|---|
| British | 1 | 3 | 1 | 17 | 38 | 163 | 47 | 121 | 8 | 23 | 46c | 130c | 47 | 189 | 94 | 268 |
| Dominions | — | — | — | 16 | 351 | 36 | — | 982d | 2 | 8 | 16e | 12e | 18 | 359 | 52 | 994 |
| Colonials | — | — | — | — | 245 | 2 | — | 116 | 4 | — | 1 | — | 4 | 245 | 3 | 116 |
| Indians | — | — | — | 3 | 58 | 5 | — | — | — | — | — | — | 3 | 58 | 5 | 2 |
| Americans | — | — | — | — | — | 10f | 6 | 11 | — | — | 137g | 187g | 6 | 11 | 147 | 187 |

| | | | |
|---|---|---|---|
| Total British, Dominions etc. | 1236 | 20357 | 1022 | 3645 |
| Total Americans | 300 | 1512 | 2676 | 3010 |
| Grand Total (h) | 1536 | 21869 | 3698 | 6655 |

NOTES:

(a) Includes escapes from P/W Camps, clandestine operations in EUROPE before 'D' Day and operational rescues after 'D' Day.

(b) Includes 85 Offrs. and 1454 O.R.s of whom no breakdown by services available but majority are Army.

(c) Includes 11 Offrs. and 19 O.R.s internees ex TURKEY.

(d) Includes 786 recovered from GREECE and CRETE in Summer of 1941; no nominal rolls were available. 'A' Force considered they should be regarded as Army evaders, the majority of whom belonged to NEW ZEALAND and AUSTRALIAN forces.

(e) Includes 5 Offrs. and 5 O.R.s internees ex TURKEY.

(f) Nurses.

(g) Includes 25 Offrs. and 44 O.R.s internees ex TURKEY.

(h) 2,089 Greeks (Service personnel, Govt. Officials, etc.) rescued by I.S. 9 (M.E.) under a special charter, are *not* included.

| Summary by Areas | British | Americans | Summary by Services (British, Dominions, Colonial and Indian only) | | | Summary by Nationalities | |
|---|---|---|---|---|---|---|---|
| | | | Offrs | ORs | Total | | |
| Western Europe (includes 70 Allied Personnel) | 3631 | 3415 | | | | British | 13193 |
| India & S.E.A.C. | 3346 | 39 | Navy | 53 | 212 | 265 | Dominions | 7058 |
| Switzerland | 4916 | 227 | Army | 1178 | 21900 | 23078 | Colonials | 1012 |
| Mediterranean (West) | 11910 | 3466 | Air Force | 1016 | 1831 | 2847 | Indians | 4927 |
| Mediterranean (East) (Includes 2089 Greeks rescued by I.S. 9(M.E.) under special charter) | 4546 | 351 | | | | 26190 | Greeks, Polish, French, Dutch, Czechs, Russians } 2159 |
| | 28349 | 7498 | | | | | Americans | 7498 |
| Grand Total to 31st August 45 | 35847 | | | | | | |

Source: WO 208/3242,65.

nearly 5,000 British ones did so? The figures of American air force escapers and evaders do not tie up at all with the American figures of those interned in Switzerland, as negotiated with the Swiss government in the winter of 1944–5. Many swiftly escaped prisoners, who only spent a few hours in enemy hands, rejoined their units without ever figuring in MI 9's statistics at all. And who on earth, one cannot help wondering, was the solitary Russian sailor who is classified as an evader, not an escaper, through Western Europe?

Another aspect of these figures that might mislead an unwary reader lies in the division between officers and other ranks: a real division in the armed forces of those days, as at present, however closely the two groups might intermingle in the stress of battle. The proportion of officers to other ranks among escapers and evaders shown here – one to six-and-a-half – is by no means the same as it was in the armed forces as a whole, where it was about one to eleven; on the other hand, in air forces a much higher proportion of officers were at risk of capture, and this explains why the air force proportion of officer to other rank escapers and evaders is that of five to nine for the British, and for the Americans (who commissioned a still higher proportion of their aircrew) as high as seven to eight. There are no data, either way, in this table to support or to confute any suggestion that the officer class was defter or less deft at escape and evasion than any other stratum of society. One day, if an historian can be found with the patience, the statistics, and the computer to work out a more sensitive set of figures, there may be more to be known.

It is reasonable to conjecture that Crockatt, preparing his final report, asked his chief clerk to compile him a return; his admirable personal assistant, Susan Broomhall – cousin of Colonel W. M. Broomhall, RE, once SBO in Colditz – was away on a visit to MIS-X in Washington at the close of the war. Crockatt himself was too busy writing his report, writing citations, and looking after the handover to Derry and the disbanding of MI 9 to give more than a glance to the return, see that it looked workmanlike and plausible, and extract the essential figures from it.

If MIS-X drew up a table similar to Crockatt's, the present writers have missed it. There is however a note on file in Washington, prepared by Russell Sweet for Catesby Jones at the war's end, which gives the following figures for American escapers and evaders – not distinguished from each other – as 'reported by theaters' up to 25 August 1945.

| | |
|---|---:|
| Occupied France, Belgium, Germany | 3,096 |
| Occupied Holland and Denmark | 47 |
| Italian prisoner of war camps and German-occupied Italy | 6,335 |
| North Africa | 18 |
| Occupied Greece | 100 |
| Balkans including Albania and Yugoslavia | 1,333 |
| Japanese occupied territory<br>  including 83 from prison ships sunk | 218 |
| From China through AGAS | 853 |
| TOTAL | 12,000 |

The final figures are, of course, suspiciously round. Some of them are near enough to Crockatt's to suggest a common source – MI 9 for instance reckoned 3,462, compared to the Americans' 3,143, for the top two figures in Sweet's table. Others are far astray; MI 9 only had 3,466 Americans collected in the western Mediterranean, against over 6,000 in Sweet's table; and the Far Eastern figures do not begin to marry up. Sweet was certainly much better placed than Crockatt to estimate the number of Americans who had evaded and escaped in Asia; the reverse may be true of Italy.

Deliberate exaggeration can be ruled out; transmission or copyists' errors can not. A fair conclusion would seem to be that Crockatt's grand total of Americans – 7,498 – was below the true figure, but that Sweet's might be somewhat above it.

Conjecturally, 2,000 might be taken off Sweet's figure of escapers and evaders in Italy. This would leave a grand total of British, Commonwealth and United States escapers and evaders, for the whole war, of 35,190: about three divisions, and no mean feat.

# Appendix 2

# Specimen Lecture

The following notes, in typescript in WO 208/3449, Advanced A Force HQ in North Africa, bear neither date nor signature. They are clearly intended for RAF operational aircrew new to the North African desert, and were probably prepared about November 1942.

*MOST SECRET*[61]

My talk to you today is on the subject of your own safety and wellbeing, not whilst you are actually flying, but in the event of your being unlucky enough to have to bale out or forced land behind the enemy's lines.

### PART I

Now I had better explain that there is an Inter-Service Branch in the M[iddle] E[ast] whose job it is to try and drill Air Crews, and indeed personnel of all three services, in their conduct as P/W, and to try to do everything possible to help evaders and escapers if they are unfortunate enough to find themselves P/Ws.

In order to do this, certain 'Aids and Devices', as they are called, are issued to all Air Crew, and to a limited scale in the Army and Royal Navy, and the experiences of many escapers and evaders are collected and passed on to Air Crews via the Branch representatives.

Of course the actual rescue or help given to evaders is the side of the Inter-Service Branch which naturally appeals to Air

---

61 [This category was later replaced by 'TOP SECRET', to suit American staff custom.]

Crews, rather than the other side of its work, but never-the-less the work devoted to drilling personnel of all three Services in their conduct as a P/W is of prime importance to our War effort, and in this talk we will take that side first.

1. It is everybody's duty to evade capture or to escape and to rejoin their Units.[62]
2. If for any reason you are unable to evade capture, then you still have a duty to your country. That is to deny to the other side information which he badly needs.
3. There is no doubt that an enormous amount of information is obtained from P/Ws and much trouble and time is spent by the enemy in obtaining this.
4. As members of the R.A.F. you are particularly prized as sources of information, although in the past the R.A.F. have been extremely security-minded: and direct Interrogation has more often than not failed to produce any useful information to the other side.

Do not imagine, however, that direct questioning is the only method the other side employs to obtain the information he wants.

You all probably know what happens if a German or Italian Air Crew bales out or forced lands anywhere near a R.A.F. Unit. They are promptly, but quite wrongly, from the official Interrogation Branch point of view, invited to the Mess where they are given food and drink and an air of friendliness prevails.

Similarly with yourselves, and you will find that the amount of drink consumed will loosen your tongue. A few indirect questions put by the German or Italian Interrogation Officer, or other officer if he is not present, leads you to say things you would much prefer to keep quiet about.

---

62 [Here, and at the dots following, brief references to vanished notes are omitted.]

Again after three years of war both sides have been able to build up records and personnel of Units, and it is a shaking experience to find that the Interrogation Officer asks you how so-and-so is of your own particular Squadron, or says that last week so-and-so was taken P/W.

The natural reaction to all this is 'Well, if he knows all about us, why should I worry to be careful'.

But you must realise that it is only because others have talked, or have carried documents with them against orders, that such records can be built up.

Quite apart from direct questioning there are many other methods employed in order to obtain information – stool pigeon etc...

Another means still used successfully is the phoney Red Cross Form.

Therefore be always on your guard and give nothing but RANK, NAME and NUMBER.

The film on the subject which a number of you have seen in U.K. is very true to life and should be remembered...

## PART II
### Escaping in Europe

Now when one looks at the map of Europe and the countries occupied by the enemy one might be forgiven for thinking 'What the Hell? We haven't a chance.' That is wrong, for although difficult, the task is not impossible as has been proved by so many. There is still a trickle of escapers coming back to M.E. and to U.K.

It is impossible to set out how this is done but you will find in all P/W Camps in Europe an Escape Committee who will give you all the necessary help and advice.

What we can do now is to give you one or two hints and possible routes.

Initiative and luck play a great part in any escape work, but remember that the task is not impossible.

Of course hundreds of P/Ws make an escape from P/W Camps and the average time 'out' for those recaptured is about five days. Even if recaptured they have had a good deal of fun and excitement, their punishment is maximum thirty days in the Jug; (actually, from letters received, this is twenty-one days).

All those having a crack are doing a good job of work, for more guards have to be used and these might otherwise be used as active fighting soldiers.

A few hints …

*ROUTES.*

*SICILY.*

The chances of getting away from Sicily are slim, but the inhabitants are likely to be anti-Fascists and some may be found to give help. The less closely guarded coastline is between PALERMO and MESSINA and there may be a chance of stealing a boat along that coast. Make for TUNISIA West of BONE.

*ITALY.*

The east coastline along the ADRIATIC is more open and less populated than the rest of ITALY. The FOGGIA area is likely to be more friendly and anti-Fascist and it may be possible to stow away or to steal a boat. Make for the YUGOSLAV border in the SPLIT Area. Where the YUGOSLAV guerrillas are operating.

Another possible outlet is in the heel of ITALY where it might be possible to get a boat across to GREECE in the vicinity of CORFU . This area is mainly inhabited by ALBANIANS and GREEKS and will certainly give aid to British personnel but remember there is an Italian Seaplane base at CORFU. Once in GREECE the areas to make for are the:

YANNINA (or JANINA) AREA

LARISSA AND VOLOS AREAS

ATHENS AREA MIDDLE PENINSULAR S.E. OF SALONIKA

SOUTH PELOPONESE

EAST COAST LINE OF GREECE

EUBOEA AND MT. OLYMPUS

The general rule is to head for the Eastern Coastline of GREECE.

In the Mount OLYMPUS area there are Greek Guerilla Bands operating.

If an escaper can make for the TRIESTE/FIUME area it is likely that help would be given by the inhabitants who are very anti-Fascist.

To cross the Italian-Switzerland border it is suggested that COMO area is likely to be possible.

*CRETE.*

The Western end of the Island and among the hills affords the greatest chance of evasion and help will be found there.

*GREECE.*

The inhabitants of GREECE are extremely anti-enemy and have given and are giving every possible help to our troops. If help is given, give a chit to the helper stating what was done and sign it giving your rank, name and number.[63] This chit will be honoured and a good reward paid when we are in occupation again or possibly before.

*GERMANY & FRANCE.*

Possible routes through to SWEDEN, FRANCE and SPAIN. Help[64] is likely in these countries and help in particular might be found at TOULOUSE and MARSEILLES. In both these towns escapers should hang around cafes in the lower quarter. The Pyrenees should be crossed 15/20 miles inland from GERONA which is just N.E. of BARCELONA near Cape S. SEBASTIAN.

*NEUTRAL COUNTRIES.*

If you manage to get to a neutral country demand to see the nearest British Consul and state you are an escaper even though you may not have been actually captured.

*Now for Evasion in N. AFRICA and LIBYA.*

This Inter-Service Branch has for some months passed organised rendezvous in the Western Desert and TRIPOLITANIA

---

63    [A wartime reader noted in the margin of this copy: 'dangerous'.]

64    [The same hand added here 'trained'.]

behind enemy lines. At these rendezvous are British Officers and local Arabs, and they are there for one purpose only, to get any person cut off or forced landed back to our lines.

In this work they are assisted by local tribes of Arabs under our influence (and cash).

This rescue work has had a good deal of success in spite of the dangers and during the past few months over eighty personnel of the three Services have been assisted back to their units by means of this organisation, the Arabs, and by means of the Aids and Devices.

(Now to explain the Aids and Devices)

These should not be considered as toys for they have proved their worth time and time again. But they must be carried sensibly. It does not require a great deal of thought or trouble to see that they are hidden away, especially in battle dress. So do please see that you have them with you.

It may be that Jerry knows all about them, but this should only mean a greater incentive really to hide them.

The blood chits should also always be carried whenever you take off on an operation, and have been the means of saving a number of our boys in the Western Desert.

When approaching Arabs in TRIPOLITANIA do so if possible when they are alone, in case they have recently been beaten up by the enemy and are scared. If in doubt as to their feelings always push off after having accepted a meal.

If you manage to make them understand that you are heading for a certain direction and require to know the way, always ask for two or three different directions, just in case.

The Arabs of TRIPOLITANIA and TUNIS are not on the whole so friendly as were the Arabs of CYRENAICA, but the more successful our Armies the more friendly the Arabs become.

From time to time check up with your I.O. and your map the latest information and rendezvous sent out by the Inter-Service Branch.

Do remember that if you bale out or forced land out in

the blue, rest and compose yourself and make a plan of action before starting off. It is essential that you should be feeling as good as possible before starting out on what may be a longish journey.

If you are forced to land by day remain with your aircraft until dark unless you have cause to think the enemy has spotted you. Your aircraft may be seen by one of our own aircraft.

In principle travel by night. In summer you must find shade by daytime and in the winter walking at night will keep you warm.

Before starting out on operation see that you have your Aids and Devices, also your water bottle and your Aid Box.

*Now for the final word, and that is SECURITY.*

Although the enemy may know of the Aids and Devices he does not know of the existence of an organisation to help evaders and escapers.

We must rely on *YOU,* who have listened to all this, NOT to talk about the Aids and Devices and the help given by the Arabs, nor the existence of rescue parties operating behind the enemy lines.

You will not only spoil your own chances of rescue, but you will also imperil the lives of our chaps in the organisation who are working on your behalf.

Do not discuss these matters between yourselves *or with anyone* but your Intelligence Officer.

Remember that the lives of our own boys and the lives of officers and others in TRIPOLITANIA, TUNISIA and EUROPE will be in greater peril, if you, through carelessness, spill the beans.

# Appendix 3

# Specimen Code

With grateful acknowledgements to J. M. Green and Messrs Robert Hale we summarise from pp. 161–71 of his *From Colditz in Code* the code that he used, and give the following specimen to show how it worked.

6/12/42.

Dear Dad,

Where is the pile of cig parcels I should be getting? I suppose the day'll dawn when I'll find literally dozens at my disposal. Got a line from Alec yesterday. I can't fathom him – aged about a hundred years and behaves like a cross between Lothario and Laurel. To reach his age and be ordered about like him by the merest chit of anything in skirts is pretty revolting. My finger's perfectly OK – it's now healed absolutely splendidly – my only grief is my parting increases in extent weekly and at this rate I'll have no more hair than you in less than a year!

I suppose Grandma is returning to Ayr for Xmas. She'll stop at Westfield as usual I suppose. I wonder if the same old crowd still gathers there. How did the old lady enjoy her stay in Dunfermline? Alec writes she skinned him at cards.

I received two copies of the Dental Journal last week and was very interested. I see from them that my old friend Forbes Finlayson is a casualty he was at hospital with me. Did you get my letter asking for my uniform and cap? Please send them out with my next parcel.

Fondest love to you all,<br>Your affectionate son, <u>Julie</u>

The form of the date on this letter – 6/12/42 instead of, say, 6 Dec. 1942 or 6-12-42 – and the underlined signature showed that it contained a message in a prearranged code.

The length of the message was found by multiplying together the number of letters in the first two words after the invocation: in this case, 'Where is' = 5 x 2 = 10 words in all.

Everyone's code might vary. Green's was called 56–O. This meant that, starting in the second line after the invocation, one read straight through the text, and picked out the fifth and the sixth word alternately. If this process settled on the word 'the', it meant: ignore the rest of the sentence – or the paragraph: trial and error soon showed which – and start the spelling code.

Green's spelling code table began with the letter O. That is, it set out the alphabet in three columns, starting with O and with a full stop after Z. Each letter was allotted a three-figure number, consisting of one of the twenty-seven patterns, in which the digits 1, 2 and 3 can be arranged, in this form:

| (1) | O | 111 | (2) | P | 211 | (3) | Q | 311 |
|---|---|---|---|---|---|---|---|---|
| | R | 112 | | S | 212 | | T | 312 |
| | U | 113 | | V | 213 | | W | 313 |
| | X | 121 | | Y | 221 | | Z | 321 |
| | . | 122 | | A | 222 | | B | 322 |
| | C | 123 | | D | 223 | | E | 323 |
| | F | 131 | | G | 231 | | H | 331 |
| | I | 132 | | J | 232 | | K | 332 |
| | L | 133 | | M | 233 | | N | 333 |

In the letter above, a spelling code warning 'the' occurred in the fifth sentence ('by the merest chit'). The decoder took the first letter of each of the first three words of the next sentence, My finger's perfectly = M f p, and put down the number of the column in the table that each fell in: 2 for M, 1 for f, 2 for p. 212 in the table stands for S. Next came OK it's now = O i n =

113 = U; then h a s = 322 = B; then m o g  = 212, S again; then i m p = 122, a full stop.

This full stop meant: go back to counting every fifth and sixth word from the start of the next sentence in the letter. SUBS of course meant submarines, in a time when people bothered much more about submarines than about substitutes or subscriptions; there was in this case no need to try the next paragraph (in which the spelling code gave an unpromising '.UPAZXN' for a start).

The end of the message was usually indicated by a 'but' in a coded spot in the letter text. The example given uses 'stop' instead.

There was really no need for either, as the length of the hidden message had been given at the start of the open letter, in the first two words.

The decoder made a grid to fit the lengths of these first two words, and wrote in it what the code extracted:

| dawn    | at        |
|---------|-----------|
| line    | fathom    |
| hundred | cross     |
| to      | ordered   |
| SUBS    | returning |

He then started in the bottom right hand corner of the grid, and read backwards and upwards, giving RETURNING SUB[MARINES ORDERED TO CROSS HUNDRED FATHOM LINE AT DAWN, a small but useful nugget of naval intelligence for the Admiralty and Coastal Command.

# Appendix 4

# What Was Said at the Time

The passage that follows explains itself. It describes an English escape.[65]

MOST SECRET
*MI9/S/PG(G)676*

The information contained in this report is to be treated as
MOST SECRET
Interim account of escape of
Lt. NEAVE, AMS 1 SEARCHLIGHT REGT. RA
Captured: 26 May 40
Escaped: 6 Jan 42
Arrived: Switzerland, 9 Jan 42

1 CAPTURE

I was Troop Commander in 2 Bty. 1 Searchlight Regt. RA. We retired from ARRAS and took up position 2 kms. south of CALAIS on 19 May 40. On 24 May I was wounded while defending a forward position and was taken to a French hospital, which was shelled and bombed during the

---

65    From WO 208/3242, 173–5. The first page ends: 'Distribution of this Report:–

IS9

MI 9(d)

(MI9(d) Lecturers (7 copies)

MIs(D) [War office liaison]

Chief Instructor, SIC, Harrow [MI 19]'.

next two days. On 26 May I contacted the last line of defence of the British forces, but it was impossible to evacuate the wounded. I was captured on a stretcher on the shore at about 1730 hrs on 26 May.

Being wounded, I did not reach Germany till August and from then I was in three camps altogether.

Aug 40–Mar 41
OFLAG IXA.
SPANGENBERG

(1) *OFLAG IXA, SPANGENBERG, SPANGENBERG, nr. KASSEL, Hesse. Aug 40–Mar 41.* This was a well guarded Schloss, considerably overcrowded by 250 P/W. Medical stores were scanty, and health was bad as a result. No Red Cross parcels had as yet arrived and food was poor. There were several cases of brutality.

Mar–May 41
STALAG XXA
THORN

(2) *STALAG XXA, THORN, Poland. Mar–May 41.* This was a reprisal camp for Fort KINGSTON, Canada.[1] The following conditions obtained:

Underground rooms with no daylight. (Windows were boarded up if necessary);

Guards with rubber truncheons;

Three appels a day;

Revolting sanitary conditions;

Officers were locked in their rooms at 2000 hrs till 0700 hrs.

The effect on morale was negligible, and the Germans seemed rather ashamed of the whole affair. After a month most of the restrictions were withdrawn. The food was the same as elsewhere.

---

1   [German complaints of maltreatment.]

1st ESCAPE

On 16 Apr I attempted to escape to Russia, but was captured near WARSAW and handed over to the Gestapo. During my escape I observed:–

i)    All crucifixes and many religious monuments have been deliberately destroyed in occupied Poland.

ii)    In LESLAU I saw a young member of the *Hitlerjugend* beat an old Pole about the head and stamp on his hat in the street amid roars of applause.

iii)    I was told that the Ghetto in WARSAW is in a bombed quarter of the city and that leaving the boundaries of it was punishable by death.

iv)    I was in the Strafgefängnis in the town of PLOCK. It is run by the Gestapo and political prisoners of both sexes were mixed with thieves and other criminals. I saw people being kicked and heard sounds of beating.

v)    Members of the Gestapo admitted to me that hundreds of Germans were being murdered by the Poles.

vi)    The morale of the Poles is remarkable and they are always ready to help escaped prisoners.

May 41–Jan 42
OFLAG IVC
COLDITZ

(3)    *OFLAG IVC, COLDITZ, Sachsen. May 41–Jan 42.* This is a camp for "Ausbrecher", or escapers. There were also Jews and political prisoners there. The total number was over 550 and it is very strongly guarded by a complete battalion. General morale was very high and everything was done by escapes, demonstrations, etc.,

to keep guards occupied. The result was a series of minor incidents and reprisals. There is overcrowding and little opportunity for exercise. Medical attention is poor, but parcels come in well. Censorship of letters and books is very inefficient.

*Account of Escape*

6 Jan 42
ESCAPE

On 6 Jan 1942 I made my escape with a Dutchman, both of us dressed as German officers. By a complicated scheme involving breaking through a ceiling we emerged from the guard house and passed two sentries without arousing suspicion. At 0545 hrs we took a train from LEISNIG

LEIPZIG

to LEIPZIG. There we learned that the best train left at 2052 hrs. We therefore spent the day in the town, visiting the cinema twice. From LEIPZIG to REGENSBERG (where we changed) and then to ULM we travelled without difficulty.

At 1030 hrs on 7 Jan we attempted to take a ticket to ENGEN near SINGEN in the frontier district. We attracted some suspicion here and were handed over to the Reichsarbeitspolizei, to whom we presented our Dutch papers. They seemed satisfied with these, but said they were not valid for travel beyond ULM. A Policeman accompanied us to the Reichsarbeitsdienst where we were supposed to report. Fortunately, he said that, as we spoke such good German, he would wait for us below. We went upstairs and managed to make our exit through a door at the other end of the building.

8 Jan 42
SINGEN

As it was now impossible to travel by express to the frontier, we walked and travelled by local trains until we were 3 kms from SINGEN about 0400 hrs on 8 Jan. There we were questioned by workmen on bicycles who seemed suspicious, and we heard them say they would inform the police. We had hoped to get over the frontier during darkness, but we were now obliged to hide up for a whole day. We hid in a small hut and slept there. Weather conditions were terrible and the temperature very low. At 1800 hrs we left the hut carrying large spades and a couple of long white coats found in the hut. A *Hitlerjugend* patrol stopped us and we satisfied them that we were Westphalian workmen. They told us they were looking for two prisoners of war who were reported in the district. We entered SINGEN and from the station we walked west as far as a signpost to GOTTMADINGEN 4 km. There we travelled north and then round a large wood that fringed the GOTTMADINGENSINGEN road, eventually travelling south over the railway line that runs north of this road to a point where road and frontier meet for about 50 yards. There we threw away the spades and put on the white coats. An open space lay before us with woods all round. Seventy metres away we saw a sentry at a barrier and cars being stopped. This was to our left. At about 0030 hrs, walking and crawling, we crossed the road and this open space which was about 200 yds across and thus passed over the frontier. We saw no Swiss guards and no lights. After accidentally cross back into Germany (which we discovered by observing a sentry to our left – i.e. to the East) we followed a compass line to RAMSEN and were there interned at 0100 hrs.

9 Jan 42
RAMSEN

*Notes*

1) As far as our observations went, no one but the military were asked for passes on trains.

2) It would attract undesirable attention to eat chocolate in public or smoke too much.[2]

3) Station waiting rooms may be dangerous, as I have noticed that railway police ask civilians for passes, particularly on large stations at night. Coffee and beer can be bought without difficulty.

4) Cinemas are good places to rest in.

5) It seems probable that the local civilian population in the frontier areas are instructed to question strangers who may be prisoners of war.

---

2   [Later, Neave was more forthcoming, and admitted his 'terrible blunder' in absent-mindedly munching 'a huge bar of Red Cross chocolate' in the main station tea-room at Leipzig. 'A young woman with fierce hysterical eyes, gazed at the chocolate as if she had seen a ghost'; and Neave and Luteyn got out, before they were lynched.–*They have their exits*, 95.]

6) Since the black-out in Switzerland [starts] at 2200 hrs there will be no lights visible as a guide after that hour.

7) Trains are very stringently controlled in occupied countries, especially Poland, and it was generally thought too dangerous to travel in them.

8) Advantage can be taken from the presence of two sorts of foreigners in Germany:

a) Volksdeutsche (German nationals) who may speak very little German and who have been repatriated from places like Bessarabia, Volkynia,[3] and Lithuania. This is particularly useful for those escaping in Poland where large transplantations of the population have taken place.

b) Workers from occupied countries and Italy, especially Dutch, Walloons, and Flemish. There are many of these in industrial areas of Germany adjoining Holland. All of these speak only a certain amount of German.

---

3   [Volhynia, an old Polish province centred on Zhitomir, between Lvov and Kiev.]

# Note on Sources

$P$rinters' and publishers' costs have lately risen so far that we cannot extend to our readers the traditionary courtesy of a footnote to explain the source of every statement of fact. The footnotes exist, and a copy is held by each of the authors and by the publisher; reference to any of whom will provide the authority for any statement in the text.

## *1 Archives*

The great bulk of our material has come from contemporary archives, mostly British in origin though sometimes American in location. Those of MI 9's papers that have survived to reach the Public Record Office are in WO 208, a collection of miscellaneous intelligence papers. About 500 files in WO 208 appear to have originated with MI 9; we have seen all those that have been released, and Foot holds extensive notes on them. We are given to understand that the files withheld from us – about 250 of them, some of them very large – will not be open to public inspection till 2010, and that the principal reason for keeping them back is that they might reflect on the character or behaviour of people still living, or of their close relatives. In Peter Watson's words in another context, 'Things are kept secret not to preserve national security but so as not to embarrass someone'. There may of course also be genuine operational reasons for keeping some material hidden, such as the bulk of the files of correspondence with camps, or all Clayton Hutton's files on escape devices; there is no point in advertising clandestine methods that might be used to the national advantage another time.

The most important of these files is WO 208/3242, Crockatt's 'Historical Record of MI 9', some 325 pages of foolscap typescript. This consists partly of Crockatt's own commentary on what his department did, and partly of reports from his subordinates or from individual escapers that bear on points he wanted to make. Some subsidiary histories have surfaced also, particularly:

WO 208/3245, Report by Air Force POW in Germany
3246, History of IS 9(WEA)
3250, History of IS 9(CMF)
3251, Summary of MI9 activities in India and SEAC

3253; Simonds' summary of MI 9 activities in the
eastern Mediterranean
and 3260, Ride's particularly valuable report on China.

Camp histories of many POW camps in Germany, compiled in the late summer
of 1945 by SBOs and camp IOs – some of them still in a bad temper – fill WO
208/3269–95. (No such reports have been found for camps in Italy.) Technically,
these are all secondary sources, compiled after the events they describe, but
written soon afterwards by senior participants who had a proper grasp of their
subject-matter and, temper apart, wrote with a fairly balanced judgement.

There are also some real working files on particular operations, such as
WO 208/3376 and 3377 on 'Amsterdam', 3378 on the Aegean islands, 3381 on
the Yugoslav-Hungarian border, 3423 on 2nd TAF, 3432 on 'En-Dor'. Several
large and useful files contain weekly news-letters for 1944–5, encouraged by
Crockatt to stimulate morale among his staff: WO 208/3416 and 3418 for Italy,
3417 for the near east, 3425 for the First Canadian Army, 3426 for the Second
British Army. Files 3485–3500 deal with eastern Asia, but in one of them, 3492,
Kweilin weekly intelligence summaries, which should have been the most
interesting of all, at present only one document is to be found. Such little
interchange of code letter traffic as has so far surfaced is in WO 208/3501–3.

Some parallel papers in the Record Office have also been read, particularly
WO 165/39, MI 9's headquarters war diary, a cardinal source; it began with
almost daily entries, but was soon written up once a month. Another useful
war diary, that of 'Popski's' Private Army, lurks at WO 170/3962B under the
title of 1 Demolition Squadron. A few of the files of Combined Operations
Headquarters in DEFE 2 have been used, particularly DEFE 2/123 and 1126
on John Godwin's operation 'Checkmate'. The Foreign Office's exchanges
with the legation in the Vatican, e.g. FO 371/37576, 44215, 50084, formed a
useful supplement to Derry's *Rome Escape Line*. An entire War Office class,
WO 224, with over 200 files in it, is taken up with Red Cross reports on
German and Italian POW camps and with diplomatic comments.

Some 2,000 British evaders' and escapers' reports, sedulously guarded
from public view in the record office at Kew, can be seen by those who venture
as far as the Albert F. Simpson Historical Research Center at Maxwell Air
Force Base, just outside Montgomery, Alabama. Jackman's interrogation of R.
B. Goodwin, for example, can be found there in file 805–615B.

The vast American archives, both at Maxwell Base and in and near
Washington, D.C., have been more cursorily skimmed; all the same, there is a
great deal more waiting to be quarried out from them. We hope at least that this
book will serve as a pioneer study, and help to show later researchers where they
might usefully look. It may be added that the United States and British authorities adopt similar, but not precisely identical, principles for guarding old intelli-

gence files. The Americans, under the stimulus of their Freedom of Information Act, make escapers' and evaders' reports available in great bulk, but are more reserved about files on intelligence method. No files for example from MIS-X's correspondence section were to be seen in February 1978, except for one headed 'Target Information' of which the provenance had been so well concealed that it took in even the official weeders, who presumably let it through by accident.

The Simpson Historical Research Center deals with the United States Army Air Force, and has abundant holdings of two sorts of file relevant to the subject of this book: intelligence summaries issued by senior headquarters, particularly in east Asia, and escapers' and evaders' reports, such as 670–614–1 on south-east Europe for 1944 or the huge bulk labelled 142–7621 which covers north-western Europe in 1942–5.

The main National Archives building in Pennsylvania Avenue, Washington, D.C., holds the American and Combined Chiefs of Staffs' papers, the (accessible) Joint Intelligence Committee minutes, and all the main General Staff correspondence, including that of the operations and planning department in which much detailed policy was made. At the archive center at Suitland, just over the Maryland border, are kept the papers that remain from MIS-X, in Record Group 332. We have looked cursorily through the first eight boxes (about twenty files to a box), on headquarter problems, and at an almost random box, 121, full of escapers' reports from France in the last two years of the fighting there, 1943–4

There is one obvious gap: enemy archives.

We have not attempted Japanese papers, since neither of us understands Japanese (inquiry moreover revealed that, even if we did, no archives would be accessible for study); nor Italian, since the papers of the OVRA, even if accessible, could tell us little of what we wanted to discover. The Gestapo's documents, equally, are notoriously hard to find; and the papers of the *Kriegsgefangenenwesen*, the German administrative body charged with the care of prisoners of war, seem to have vanished down the gulf of time. They were removed from Germany by the British in the autumn of 1945, and were of some use in preparing the prosecution's case for war crimes trials at Nuremberg and elsewhere. They were neither passed on to America, nor returned whence they came. Neither the Cabinet Office, nor the Foreign and Commonwealth Office, nor the Judge-Advocate-General's Department, nor the Ministry of Defence, nor the Public Record Office, nor the Imperial War Museum admits to possessing them now.

## 2 Interviews

We have talked with a number of former escapers and evaders – who still abound – and as many of the senior surviving staff of MI 9 and MIS-X as we have been able to reach. A few of them have helped us with their private archives. None of these interviews were taped, but in every case we made notes on the points that mattered. Mainland western Europe is honeycombed with *amicales* of various sizes and strengths, composed of former helpers; we have seen most of the 'Comet' one.

### 3 Books

To compile a complete bibliography of escape literature would be a large task, though one worth attempting; it falls outside this book's scope. It may just be worth re-listing the books which are of most use for placing the subject in perspective. All are published in London (as in the longer list that follows), if no other place is specified.

On the war as a whole, the best single-volume treatment remains Peter Calvocoressi and Guy Wint, *Total War*. Details can be pursued in Marcel Baudot and others, *Encyclopédie de la Guerre 1939–1945*. M. R. D. Foot, *Resistance* and Jørgen Hæstrup, *Europe Ablaze* attempt to set the European escape organisations, among other bodies of resisters, in their historical context.

For MI 9, Airey Neave, *Saturday at MI 9* is outstanding. J. M. Langley, *Fight Another Day* describes 'Comet' and other lines from the staff angle; Lucien Dumais, *The Man who went back* tackles 'Shelburn' on the spot. Among hundreds of escape stories, special mention is deserved by Eric Williams, *The Wooden Horse* on three prisoners' departure from Sagan; Sam Derry, *The Rome Escape Line*; and P. R. Reid, *The Colditz Story* and *The Latter Days at Colditz*, the two later combined in one volume as *Colditz*. The flavour of imprisonment in south-east Asia is caught with unusual force in Laurens van der Post, *The Night of the New Moon*.

It will be noticed that none of these eleven books is by an American. This seems a field where the Americans' literary gifts have yet to reach full flower.

A list follows of all the works referred to in the text, or in the original footnotes. Only a few page references are included, for a few long works from which isolated points are extracted.

L. Albertini, The Origins of the War of 1914 *(3 V Oxford* University Press 1952-7), ii.674

Alexander, see Romilly

A. G. Allbury, *Bamboo and Bushido* (Hale 1955)

Louis Allen, *Sittang the last battle* (Macdonald 1973)

G. E. M. Anscombe, *Mr Truman's Degree* (private, Oxford 1956)

Joan Bright Astley, *The Inner Circle* (Hutchinson 1971)

Sir R. H. Bacon, Life of Lord Fisher of Kilverstone (2V Hodder & Stoughton 1929), i.121

Elisabeth Barker, *British Policy in South-East Europe in the Second World War* (Macmillan 1976)

W. Bartoszewski, *Warsaw Death Ring* (Interpress, Warsaw 1968),

——, *The Blood Shed Unites Us* (same, 1970)

M. Baudot and others, *Encyclopédie de la Guerre 1939–1945* (Casterman, Brussels 1977)

C. Bauer and Th. A. Boeree, *The Battle of Arnhem: the betrayal myth refuted* (Hodder & Stoughton 1966)

E. C. G. Beckwith ed, *The Mansel Diaries* (Wildwood House 1977)

P. Beesly, *Very Special Intelligence* (Hamish Hamilton 1977)

Benson, see Warren

Dan Billany and David Dowie, *The Cage* (Longman 1949)

Dan Billany, *The Trap* (Faber 1950)

Alan Birch, article in *South China. Daily News* (Hong Kong, 12–13 October 1973)

Boeree, see Bauer

Bootle-Wilbraham, see Quilter

John Borrie, *Despite Captivity* (Kimber 1975)

Russell Braddon, *Nancy Wake* (Cassell 1956)

R. G. Brickell, note in *Journal of the Institution of Civil Engineers*, xx.108–12 (April 1943)

Paul Brickhill, *The Great Escape* (Faber 1946)

——, *Reach for the Sky* (Collins 1954)

—— and C. Norton, *Escape to Danger* (Faber 1946)

V. Brome, *The Way Back* (Cassell 1957)

Bundy, see Stimson

K. Burt and J. Leasor, *The One that Got Away* (Michael Joseph 1956)

P. Calvocoressi and Guy Wint, *Total War* (Penguin 1972)

Earl of Cardigan, *I Walked Alone* (Routledge 1950)

Sir Carton de Wiart, *Happy Odyssey* (Cape 1950)

Cartwright, see Harrison

D. Caskie, *The Tartan Pimpernel* (Oldbourne 1957, Fontana 1960)

Cate, see Craven

(Sir) Winston S. Churchill, *The Second World War* (6v Cassell 1948–54)

(Sir) G. N. Clark ed *The New Cambridge Modern History* (14v Cambridge University Press 1957–70), xiy,6i

Ronald W. Clark, *The Man who Broke 'Purple'* (Weidenfeld & Nicolson 1977)

Dudley Clarke, *Seven Assignments* (Cape 1948)

William Colby and Peter Forbath, *Honourable Men* (Hutchinson 1978)

W. F. Craven and J. L. Cate, *United States Army Air Force in World War Two* (7V University Press, Chicago 1948-58)

Aidan Crawley, *Escape from Germany* (Collins 1956)

C. G. Cruickshank, *The German Occupation of the Channel Islands* (Oxford University Press 1975)

——, *The Fourth Arm* (Davis-Poynter 1977)

Donald Darling, *Secret Sunday* (Kimber 1975)

——, *Sunday at Large* (same 1977)

A. P. Davies, *When the Moon Rises* (Leo Cooper 1973)

Sir F. W. D. Deakin, *The Embattled Mountain* (Oxford University Press 1971)

Sam Derry, *The Rome Escape Line* (Harrap 1960, Ace 1962)

John Dominy, *The Sergeant Escapers* (Ian Allan 1974)

P. Dourlein, *Inside North Pole* (Kimber 1953)

A. J. Deane Drummond, *Return Ticket* (Collins 1967)

L. Dumais and Hugh Popham, *The Man who went Back* (Leo Cooper 1975)

Michael Duncan, *Underground from Posen* (Kimber 1954)

H. G. Durnford, *The Tunnellers of Holzminden* (Cambridge University Press 1926)

R. Eggers, *Colditz: the German Story* (Hale 1961)

——, ed *Colditz Recaptured* (Hale 1973)

Sir Basil Embry, *Mission Completed* (Methuen 1957)

A. J. Evans, *The Escaping Club* (The Bodley Head 1921)

J. C. Fest, *Hitler* (Pelican 1977)

*Field Service Regulations* (HMSO 1935)

Louis FitzGibbon, *Unpitied and Unknown* (Bachman & Turner 1975)

Peter Fleming, *Invasion 1940* (Hart-Davis 1957)

M. R. D. Foot, *SOE in France* (HMSO 1968, 1976)

——, ed *War and Society* (Elek 1973)

——, *Resistance* (Eyre Methuen 1977, Paladin 1978)

——, *Six Faces of Courage* (Eyre Methuen 1978)

Forbath, see Colby

Herbert Ford, *Flee the Captor* (Southern Publishing Association, Nashville, Tenn., 1966)

M-M. Fourcade, *Noah's Ark* (Allen & Unwin 1973)

John Furman, *Be not Fearful* (Blond 1959)

Geneva Convention, Cmd 3941 (HMSO 1931)

Michael Gilbert, *Death in Captivity* (Hodder & Stoughton 1952)

H. J. Giskes, *London calling North Pole* (Kimber 1953)

Goebbels, see Trevor-Roper

R. B. Goodwin, *Hong Kong Escape* (Barker 1953)

J. M. Green, *From Colditz in Code* (Hale 1971)

N. S. Gulbenkian, *Pantaraxia* (Hutchinson 1965)

Sir John Hackett, *I was a Stranger* (Chatto & Windus 1977)

Jørgen Haestrup, *Secret Alliance* (3V University Press, Odense 1976–7)

——, *Europe Ablaze* (same, 1978)

Hague Conventions, *British and Foreign State Papers* (HMSO), xci.995-7, c.351–3

James Hargest, *Farewell Campo 12* (Michael Joseph 1945)

M. C. C. Harrison and H. A. Cartwright, *Within Four Walls* (Arnold 1930)

Leo Heaps, *Grey Goose at Arnhern* (Weidenfeld & Nicolson 1977)

G. Higginbotham, *Rugby School Register* (1929), iv.299, 361

E. Howell, *Escape to Live* (Longman 1947)

C. Clayton Hutton, *Official Secret* (Max Parrish 1960, Four Square 1962)

Robert Jackson, *A Taste of Freedom* (Barker 1964)

——, *The Fall of France* (Barker 1975)

D. P. James, *A Prisoner's Progress* (Blackwood, Edinburgh 1947)

E. H. Jones, *The Road to En-Dor* (John Lane 1920)

R. V. Jones, *Most Secret War* (Hamish Hamilton 1978)

M. Jullian, *HMS Fidelity* (Futura 1975)

H. Jung, *Die Ardennen-Offensive 1944/45* (Musterschmidt, Gottingen 1971)

H. Koch-Kent, *Sie Boten Trotz* (Hermann, Luxemburg 1974)

H. Krausnick and others, *Anatomy of the SS State* (Collins 1968)

Sam Kydd, *For You the War is Over* (Futura 1974)

Charles Lamb, *War in a Stringbag* (Cassell 1977)

J. M. Langley, *Fight Another Day* (Collins 1974)

Anne Laurens, *L'Affaire King Kong* (Albin Michel, Paris 1969)

Leasor, see Burt

Leigh Fermor, see Psychoundakis

P. Leverkuehn, *German Military Intelligence* (Weidenfeld & Nicolson 1954)

Sir M. Lindsay, 'Escapers All' in *British Army Review*, liv.28 (December 1976)

P. Lorain, *L'Armement Clandestin* (L'Emancipatrice, Paris 1972)

C. A. Macartney, *October Fifteenth* (University Press, Edinburgh 1961)

Mansel, see Beckwith

Jasper Maskelyne, *Magic – Top Secret* (Stanley Paul 1949)

(Sir) J. C. Masterman, *The Double-Cross System* (Yale University Press, New Haven, Conn. 1972)

——, *On the Chariot Wheel* (Oxford University Press 1975)

Henri Michel, *Jean Moulin* (2 ed, Hachette, Paris 1964)

——, *Vichy Année 40* (Laffont, Paris 1966)

——, and others, *European Resistance Movements* (Pergamon 1960)

Martin Middlebrook, *The First Day of the Somme* (Allen Lane 1971) 313

George Millar, *Horned Pigeon* (Heinemann 1946)

——, *The Bruneval Raid* (The Bodley Head 1974)

Ewen Montagu, *The Man who never Was* (Penguin 1956)

——, *Beyond Top Secret U* (Davies 1977)

A. Muir, *The First of Foot* (The Royal Scots, Edinburgh 1961)

David Mure, *Practice to Deceive* (Kimber 1977)

Sir P. Neame, *Playing with Strife* (Harrap 1947)

Airey Neave, *They have their Exits* (Hodder & Stoughton 1953),

——, *Little Cyclone* (same, 1954)

——, *Saturday at MI 9* (same, 1969)

Airey Neave, *Nuremberg* (Hodder & Stoughton 1978) and Hugh Verity, *We Landed by Moonlight* (Ian Allan 1979), both relevant, appeared after this book had gone to press.

D. Nelson, *The Story of Changi Singapore* (Changi, Perth, W.A, 1974)

Eric Newby, *Love and War in the Apennines* (Hodder & Stoughton 1971)

Nuremberg trial, see Trial

P. Paillole, *Services Spéciaux 1935–1945* (Laffont, Paris 1975)

Richard Pape, *Boldness be my Friend* (Elek 1953)

Ray Parkin, *Out of the Smoke* (Hogarth Press 1960)

——, *Into the Smother* (same, 1961)

V. Peniakoff, *Private Army* (Cape 1950)

C. E. Lucas Phillips, *Cockleshell Heroes* (Heinemann 1956)

O. Philpot, *Stolen Journey* (Hodder & Stoughton 1950)

Popham, see Dumais

Laurens van der Post, *The Night of the New Moon* (Hogarth Press 1970)

J. Presser, *Ashes in the Wind* (Souvenir Press 1968)

T. F. Prittie, *Through Irish Eyes* (Bachman & Turner 1977)

G. Psychoundakis tr P. Leigh Fermor, *The Cretan Runner* (Murray 1955)

D. Quilter ed. *No Dishonourable Name* (Clowes 1948)

P. R. Reid, *Colditz* (Hodder & Stoughton 1962)

Robin Reilly, *The Sixth Floor* (Frewin 1969)

'Rémy', *Une Affaire de Trahison* (Solar, Monte Carlo 1947)

——, *Reseau Comete* (Perrin, Paris 1966 ff)

Pierre Renouvin, *La Question d'Extrème-Orient* (Hachette, Paris 1946)

Cyril Rofe, *Against the Wind* (Elmfield Press, Leeds 1975)

G. Romilly and M. Alexander, *The Privileged Nightmare* (Weidenfeld & Nicolson 1954)

R. Rupert, *A Hidden World* (Collins 1963)

A. P. Ryan, *Mutiny at the Curragh* (Macmillan 1956)

Cornelius Ryan, *A Bridge Too Far* (Hamish Hamilton 1974)

Benjamin F. Schemmer, *The Raid* (Macdonald and Jane's 1976)

W. C. Sellar and R. J. Yeatman, *1066 and All That* (Methuen 1930)

W. B. K. Shaw, *Long Range Desert Group* (Collins 1945, Four Square 1959)

R. C. Shay, jr., *British Rearmament in the Thirties* (University Press, Princeton N.J. 1977)

Lord Skelmersdale, see Quilter

Sir William Slim, *Defeat into Victory* (Cassell 1956)

R. Harris Smith, *OSS* (University of California Press 1972)

Stevie Smith, *Novel on Yellow Paper* (Penguin 1951)

H. L. Stimson and McG. Bundy, *On Active Service in Peace and War* (Harper, New York 1947), 138

Bickham Sweet-Escott, *Baker Street Irregular* (Methuen 1965)

Christopher Sykes, *Orde Wingate* (Collins 1959), 127–81

Bishop Sandor Szent-Ivanyi, article in *Magyar Hirado* (Vienna 1 October 1974)

Sandy Thomas, *Dare to be Free* (Wingate 1951)

Christopher Thorne, *Allies of a Kind* (Hamish Hamilton 1978)

Ian Trenowden, *Operations – Most Secret* (Kimber 1978)

*Trial of German Major War Criminals at Nuremberg* (23V HMSO 1946–51), iii.213, xi.279

Leopold Trepper, *The Great Game* (McGraw-Hill, New York 1977)

Raleigh Trevelyan, *The Fortress* (Penguin 1960)

H. R. Trevor-Roper intr *The Goebbels Diaries: the Last Days* (Seeker & Warburg 1978)

Graeme Warrack, *Travel by Dark: after Arnhem* (Harvill Press 1963)

C. E. T. Warren and J. Benson, *The Broken Column* (Harrap 1966), on J. F. Wilde

P. Watson, *War on the Mind* (Hutchinson 1978)

Ritchie Weaver, *True Spy Stories of World War II* (Carousel Books 1975)

A. Weissberg, *Advocate for the Dead* (Deutsch 1956)

Dame Rebecca West, *The Meaning of Treason* (Macmillan 1949, Pan 1956)

Elvet Williams, *Arbeitskommando* (Gollancz 1975)

Eric Williams, *The Wooden Horse* (Collins 1949)

Wint, see Calvocoressi

J. E. R. Wood, *Detour* (Falcon Press 1946)

C. M. Woodhouse, *Apple of Discord* (Hutchinson 1948)

——, *The Struggle for Greece* (Hart-Davis, MacGibbon 1976)

Barry Wynne, *No Drums, No Trumpets* (Barker 1961)

One other comment on escape books in general may be allowed. Those that have appeared about the wars of 1939–45 compare most favourably with books about simultaneous adventures in other fields of clandestine activity and derring-do. Too many authors trying to deal with deception, espionage, sabotage, subversion, have been swept away by the excellent stories they have encountered, and have woven fine-spun prose narratives that grip their readers' attention, and yet do not always stick to the verifiable truth. People who have to undergo the stark life of a prisoner of war camp develop a noticeable attachment to realism.

# Abbreviations

A       Force Deception and escape organisation [Cairo, Algiers]
AFHQ   Allied Force Headquarters [Mediterranean]
A GAS   Air Ground Air Service [China]
AI      Air Intelligence [London], specifically:
AI      9 cover name for MI 9
BAAG   BRITISH Army Aid Group [China]
BATS    Balkan Air Terminal Service
BBC     British Broadcasting Corporation
BEF     British Expeditionary Force [France]
CCS     Combined Chiefs of Staff
CMF     Central Mediterranean Forces
COHQ   Combined Operations Headquarters [London]
COS     Chief(s) of Staff
CPM     Captured Personnel and Materiel [branch of G-2,Washington, D.C.]
CSDIC  Combined Services Detailed Interrogation Centre
DDMI   Deputy Director of Military Intelligence
DMI     Director of Military Intelligence
DNI     Director of Naval Intelligence
Dulag  Durchgangslager (Luft) [transit POW camp (for airmen)]
E Group  Escape organisation [New Delhi]
EAM     Ethnikon apeleftherotikon metopon [Greek national Liberation front]
E & E   Escape and evasion; escapers and evaders [for distinction, see p. 13]
EM      Enlisted men [American = British ORs]
ETO     European Theater of Operations
FAA     Fleet Air Arm
F/O     Flying Officer
G-I, G-2, G-3, G-4   Administrative, intelligence, operations, supply branches
                of American General Staff
Gestapo  Geheime Staatspolizei [German secret state police]
GSO     General Staff Officer
HK      Hooker code
IO      Intelligence Officer
IRCC    International Red Cross Committee
IS 9    Intelligence School 9 [also used as cover for MI 9]

| | |
|---|---|
| JIC | Joint Intelligence Committee |
| LCS | London Controlling Section |
| LRDG | Long Range Desert Group |
| MAAF | Mediterranean Allied Air Forces |
| MEF | Middle Eastern Forces |
| MI | Military Intelligence [British], specifically: |
| | MI 1A organisation |
| | MI 5 security |
| | MI 6 intelligence |
| | MI 9 escape and evasion |
| | MI 14 German army |
| | MI 19 refugees and enemy prisoners |
| MID | Military Intelligence Department [American] |
| MI R | Military Intelligence Research [British] |
| MIS | Military Intelligence Section [American], specifically: |
| | MIS-X escape and evasion |
| | MIS-Y captured enemy personnel and signals |
| MO 4 | Cover name for SOE in Cairo |
| MTO | Mediterranean Theater of Operations |
| N section | Escape and evasion section of A Force [Cairo, Algiers, Balkans, Italy] |
| NCO | Non-commissioned Officer |
| NKVD | Narodny kommissariat vnutrennich dyel [people's commissariat for internal affairs, Russia] |
| OBLI | Oxfordshire and Buckinghamshire Light Infantry |
| Oflag | Offizierslager [officers' POW camp] |
| ORS | Other ranks [British = American EM] |
| OSS | Office of Strategic Services [American] |
| OVRA | Organizzazione di vigilanza e repressione dell'anti-fascismo [organisation of vigilance for repressing anti-Fascism, Italy] |
| PAO | 'Pat' escape and evasion line |
| P/O | Pilot Officer |
| POA | Pacific Ocean Area |
| POW | Prisoner of war |
| PPA | 'Popski's Private Army |
| PRO | Public Record Office [London] |
| P/W, PS/W | Prisoner(s) of war |
| PWE | Political Warfare Executive |
| RAAF | Royal Australian Air Force |
| RAF(VR) | Royal Air Force (Volunteer Reserve) |
| RAN | Royal Australian Navy |
| RCAF | Royal Canadian Air Force |

RN    Royal Navy

RNVR   Royal Naval Volunteer Reserve

R/T    Radio telephony

SAO    Senior American officer [in a POW camp]

SAS    Special Air Service

SBO    Senior British officer [in a POW camp]

SBS    Special Boat Section [British]

SBS    Strategic Balkan Service [American]

SD     Sicherheitsdienst [security service, Germany]

SEAC   South-East Asia Command

SHAEF Supreme Headquarters Allied Expeditionary Force [in ETO]

SIS     Secret Intelligence Service

SOE    Special Operations Executive

SS     Schutzstaffel [protection squad]

Stalag Stammlager [fixed POW camp for ORs]

SWPA   South-West Pacific Area

TAF    Tactical air force

USAAF United States Army Air Force

USAF   United States Air Force

USN    United States Navy

WEA    Western European Area

WO    War Office

W/O    Warrant Officer

W/T    Wireless telegraphy

X      Escape

Y      Wireless interception

# Index